Microsoft®
Visual Studio® 2010
A Beginner's Guide

About the Author

Joe Mayo started his software development career in 1986, working on an RCA Spectrum 70 mainframe computer, programming in assembly language where input was via Hollerith card, output was a line printer, and the debugging experience was a light panel where you had to push buttons to load registers and step through commands. Since then, Joe has worked with various mini-computers, workstations, and PCs. The operating systems he's worked on include proprietary, UNIX-based, MS-DOS, and Windows. Besides assembly and dozens of scripting languages, Joe has worked professionally with C, C++, VBA, Visual C++, Forte Tool, Java, VB.NET, and C#. In addition to software engineering, he has worked in many positions, including team lead, supervisor, manager (even running a 24×7 computer operations center with over 50 people). Today, Joe runs his own company, Mayo Software, providing custom software development services and specializing in Microsoft .NET technology. He is the author of *LINQ Programming* (McGraw-Hill Professional, 2008) and other books. Joe is also the recipient of multiple Microsoft MVP awards. You can follow Joe on Twitter: @JoeMayo.

About the Technical Editor

Roy Ogborn has worn almost every hat one time or another during his interesting and continuing career in the Information Technology field. He was systems manager and developer for Texaco Europe Research, Inc., in Moscow, USSR, during the attempted coup. Back in the United States, he has designed and implemented a GIS system for managing oil and gas wells and leases, and has architected and implemented an enterprise workflow system that managed the business process of taking wells from conception to completion. He architected a system for Forest Oil in Denver that linked disparate accounting, lease management, and production tracking systems for business intelligence for senior executives' daily and strategic decisions. Recently he architected and designed a SharePoint-, Silverlight-, and CSLA-based greenhouse gas emissions evaluation, prediction, and decision tool for a multinational environmental engineering firm using the new Visual Studio 2010 Architecture Edition tools. Roy is an independent software architect consultant in the Denver Metro Area specializing in custom solutions that leverage SharePoint. In January 2010 he presented SharePoint 2010 for Developers at the Denver Visual Studio .NET User Group.

Microsoft®
Visual Studio® 2010
A Beginner's Guide

Joe Mayo

New York Chicago San Francisco
Lisbon London Madrid Mexico City
Milan New Delhi San Juan
Seoul Singapore Sydney Toronto

The McGraw-Hill Companies

Cataloging-in-Publication Data is on file with the Library of Congress

McGraw-Hill books are available at special quantity discounts to use as premiums and sales promotions, or for use in corporate training programs. To contact a representative, please e-mail us at bulksales@mcgraw-hill.com.

Microsoft® Visual Studio® 2010: A Beginner's Guide

234567890   DOC DOC   109876543210

ISBN   978-0-07-166895-8
MHID   0-07-166895-0

Sponsoring Editor   Jane K. Brownlow

Editorial Supervisor   Patty Mon

Project Manager   Madhu Bhardwaj, Glyph International

Acquisitions Coordinator   Joya Anthony

Technical Editor   Roy Ogborn

Copy Editor   Bob Campbell

Proofreader   Lisa McCoy

Indexer   Karin Arrigoni

Production Supervisor   Jean Bodeaux

Composition   Glyph International

Illustration   Glyph International

Art Director, Cover   Jeff Weeks

Cover Designer   Jeff Weeks

To my son, Kamo.

Contents at a Glance

PART I   Understanding Visual Studio 2010 Essentials

  1 Introducing Visual Studio 2010 3

  2 Learning Just Enough C# or VB.NET: Basic Syntax 35

  3 Learning Just Enough C# and VB.NET: Types and Members 67

  4 Learning Just Enough C# and VB.NET: Intermediate Syntax 89

PART II   Learning the VS 2010 Environment

  5 Creating and Building Projects 113

  6 Debugging with Visual Studio 143

  7 Working with Data 181

PART III   Building Programs with VS 2010

  8 Building Desktop Applications with WPF 217

  9 Creating Web Applications with ASP.NET MVC 249

10 Designing Silverlight Applications **285**

11 Deploying Web Services with WCF **299**

PART IV Enhancing the VS 2010 Experience

12 Customizing the Development Environment **341**

13 Extending Visual Studio 2010 .... **371**

PART V Appendixes

A Introduction to XML **403**

B Introduction to XAML **409**

Index **417**

Contents

ACKNOWLEDGMENTS xvii

INTRODUCTION xix

PART I Understanding Visual Studio 2010 Essentials

1 Introducing Visual Studio 2010 .... **3**

What Is Visual Studio 2010 About? 4

    Automatically Generated Code 4

    Rapid Coding Experience 5

    Everything at Your Fingertips 5

    Customizability and Extensibility 5

Installing Visual Studio 2010 6

Navigating the Visual Studio 2010 Environment 13

    The Menu 14

    Toolbar 15

    Work Area 15

    Toolbox 16

    Solution Explorer 16

    Status Bar 16

Managing VS Windows 16

    Expanding and Collapsing Windows 17

    Docking Windows 18

Floating Windows	19
Tabbed Windows	20
Closing and Opening Windows	21
Modifying Environment Settings after Setup	22
Exporting Selected Environment Settings	23
Importing Selected Environment Settings	24
Resetting All Settings	28
Familiarization with Visual Studio Project Types	30
Windows Projects	32
Web Projects	33
Office Projects	34
SharePoint Projects	34
Database Projects	34
Summary	34
2 Learning Just Enough C# or VB.NET: Basic Syntax	**35**
Starting a Bare-Bones Project	36
Examining the Code Skeleton	39
The Main Method	40
The Program Class	41
The FirstProgram Namespace	42
An Overview of the VS Code Editor	43
Class and Member Locators	44
Bookmarks	44
Setting Editor Options	45
Saving Time with Snippets	47
Coding Expressions and Statements	49
Making Intellisense Work for You	49
Running Programs	51
Primitive Types and Expressions	52
Enums	55
Branching Statements	57
Loops	61
Summary	66
3 Learning Just Enough C# and VB.NET: Types and Members	**67**
Creating Classes	68
Class Syntax	68
Class Inheritance	70
The class Snippet	71
Writing Methods	72
Declaring and Using a Method	72
Declaring Parameters and Passing Arguments	75

Returning Data and Using Method Results 78

Method Snippets 80

Coding Fields and Properties 81

Declaring and Using Fields 81

Declaring and Using Properties 83

The Property Snippet 86

Summary 87

4 Learning Just Enough C# and VB.NET: Intermediate Syntax **89**

Understanding Delegates and Events 90

Events 91

Delegates 94

Event, Delegate, and Handler Code Completion 95

Implementing Interfaces 96

Creating an Interface 97

Making Classes Implement the Interface 98

Writing Code That Uses an Interface 101

The interface Snippet 106

Applying Arrays and Generics 107

Coding Arrays 107

Coding Generics 109

Summary 110

PART II   Learning the VS 2010 Environment

5 Creating and Building Projects **113**

Constructing Solutions and Projects 114

Creating a New Project 115

Navigating the Solution Explorer 116

Examining Property Settings 118

Assembly Name 119

Default Namespace 119

Target Framework 119

Output Type 119

Startup Object 120

Icon and Manifest 120

Assembly Information 121

Referencing Assemblies 122

Adding a .NET Assembly Reference 123

Managing Assembly References 124

Referencing Your Own Class Libraries 125

Using Code in Class Libraries 126

Compiling Applications 129
   Building Solutions/Projects 129
   Rebuilding Solutions/Projects 130
   Cleaning Solutions/Projects 130
   Managing Dependencies and Build Order 131
   Managing Compilation Settings 133
Navigating a Project with Class View 136
Using the Class Designer 137
   Class Designer Visualization 137
   Class Designer Code Generation 138
Summary 141

6 Debugging with Visual Studio **143**
Example Code for This Chapter 144
Development-Time Code Tools 148
Configuring Debug Mode 150
Setting Breakpoints 155
   Creating a Breakpoint 156
   Customizing a Breakpoint 157
   Managing Breakpoints 158
Stepping Through Code 158
Inspecting Application State 160
   Locals and Autos Windows 160
   Watch Windows 161
   The Immediate Window 162
   The Call Stack Window 163
   The Quick Watch Window 163
   Watching Variables with Pin To Source 164
   Working with IntelliTrace 165
Solving Problems with VS Debugger 166
   A Program with Bugs 167
   Finding the Bug 171
   Fixing the First Bug 174
   Debugging and Resolving NullReferenceException Problems 175
Summary 180

7 Working with Data **181**
Working with Databases 182
   Introduction to Server Explorer 182
   Creating a Database 183
   Adding Tables 185
   Relating Tables with Foreign Keys 187
   Adding Stored Procedures 192
   Configuring Database Options 193

Learning Language Integrated Query (LINQ) 194
    Querying Object Collections with LINQ 194
    Creating a LINQ Projection with Anonymous Types 198
    Using LINQ to Sort Collection Results 199
Handling Data with LINQ to SQL 200
    Setting Up LINQ to SQL 200
    Working with the LINQ to SQL Designer 201
    Introduction to Querying LINQ to SQL 203
    Performing Queries on Multiple Tables 205
    Inserting Data with LINQ to SQL 210
    Updating Data with LINQ to SQL 211
    Deleting Data with LINQ to SQL 212
Summary 214

PART III   Building Programs with VS 2010

8   Building Desktop Applications with WPF **217**
Starting a WPF Project 218
Understanding Layout 220
    Grid Layout 220
    StackPanel Layout 222
    DockPanel Layout 223
    WrapPanel Layout 224
    Canvas Layout 225
Using WPF Controls 226
    Managing Windows for Controls 226
    Setting Properties 228
    Handling Events 228
    Coding Event Handlers 233
Working with Data in WPF 234
    Setting Up a Data Source 235
    Configuring a ComboBox 241
    Reading and Saving Data 243
    Using the DataGrid 244
Summary 247

9   Creating Web Applications with ASP.NET MVC **249**
Understanding ASP.NET MVC 250
Starting an ASP.NET MVC Project 251
Creating the Models 254
Building Controllers 254
Displaying Views 256
    Looking Inside a View 256
    Organizing View Files 258

Assigning MasterPage Files 258
Partial Views (a.k.a. User Controls) 260
Managing Routing 262
Building a Customer Management Application 264
Creating a Repository 265
Creating a Customer Controller 268
Displaying a Customer List 269
Adding a New Customer 274
Updating Existing Customers 279
Deleting a Customer 281
Summary 284

10 Designing Silverlight Applications **285**
Starting a Silverlight Project 286
Navigating the Silverlight Designer 290
Using Silverlight Controls 290
Running Silverlight Out-of-Browser (OOB) 294
Deploying Silverlight Applications 297
Summary 298

11 Deploying Web Services with WCF **299**
Starting a WCF Project 301
Specifying a Contract with WCF Interfaces 302
Implementing Logic with WCF Classes 308
Hosting a WCF Service 314
Following General Hosting Procedures 315
Installing IIS 7 on Windows 7 315
Creating a Web Site on IIS 7 on Windows 7 317
Deploying the WCF Service to IIS 321
Communicating with a WCF Service 326
Creating a Service Reference 326
Coding Web Service Calls 329
Deploying a Client That Consumes a Web Service 336
Creating a Web Service in a Web Site 337
Summary 338

PART IV Enhancing the VS 2010 Experience

12 Customizing the Development Environment **341**
Implementing Custom Templates 342
Creating New Project Templates 343
Creating New Item Templates 347
Creating Custom Snippets 353
Creating a New Snippet 353
Managing the Snippet Library 358

Writing Macros 360
  Recording a Macro 360
  Saving a Macro 364
  Editing Macros 365
Summary 370

13 Extending Visual Studio 2010 .... **371**
Creating a Visual Studio Add-In 372
  Running the Add-In Project Wizard 372
  Examining an Add-In Wizard Solution 377
  Drilling into the *Connect* Class 378
Adding Functionality to an Add-In 383
  Reviewing the *OnConnection* Method 384
  Implementing the *Exec* Method 391
  Setting Status with *QueryStatus* 395
Deploying an Add-In 397
Where to Go Next 399
Summary 400

PART V Appendixes

A Introduction to XML **403**
VS 2010 XML Editor 404
XML Prefixes 404
XML Elements 405
Attributes 405
Namespaces 406
The XML Menu 407
Configuring XML Options 407
Summary 407

B Introduction to XAML **409**
Starting a WPF Project 410
Elements as Classes 411
Attributes as Properties 411
Executing the XAML Document 411
Property Elements 412
Markup Extensions 414
Summary 416

Index **417**

Acknowledgments

A work of this magnitude is never the ramblings of a single author, but a successful combination of dedication from a team of highly skilled professionals. I would like to personally thank several people who helped make this book possible.

Jane Brownlow, Executive Editor, helped kick off the book and got it started on the right path. Megg Morin, Acquisitions Editor, took the reins from Jane and led the rest of the way. Joya Anthony, Acquisitions Coordinator, helped keep the flow of chapters moving. Madhu Bhardwaj, Project Manager, and Patty Mon, Editorial Supervisor, helped coordinate copy edits and final layout. I would really like to thank you all for your patience and assistance. There are many more people at McGraw-Hill who helped put this book together, and I am appreciative of their contributions and professionalism.

Roy Ogborn was the technical editor for this book. I've known Roy for several years and was delighted when he agreed to tech edit the book. Besides catching many of my errors, Roy provided valuable insight that made a difference in several areas, continuously asking the question of whether a beginner would understand a concept, what is the proper application of the language to accomplish a goal, and perspective on what parts of a technology needed emphasis. Thanks to Roy for outstanding technical editing and advice.

Introduction

Visual Studio has been the primary integrated development environment (IDE) for Microsoft software development for several years. Visual Studio 2010 (VS), the subject of this book, is therefore a mature evolution, building upon the success of its predecessors. This book will show you how to leverage Visual Studio 2010 to your advantage, increasing your skill set, and helping you become more productive in building software. The software you will learn to write will be for .NET (pronounced "Dot Net"), which is a Microsoft platform for writing different types of applications.

As the title suggests, this is a book for beginners. However, there are many opinions about who a beginner is, so let's discuss what beginner means in the context of this book. You should probably have some understanding of what programming is from a general perspective. It would help to have at least written a batch file, macro, or script that instructed the computer to perform some task. A beginner could also be someone who has written software with technology, such as Cobol, Dreamweaver, or Java, but who is unfamiliar with Visual Studio. Whatever your background, this book provides a gradual on-ramp to developing applications with Visual Studio 2010.

This book has 13 chapters and is divided into four parts and a couple of appendixes as reference material. The following provides an overview of each section:

- **Part I: Understanding Visual Studio 2010 Essentials**   Chapter 1 begins with an explanation of what VS is, its benefits to you, and what type of applications VS will help you build. Hands-on guidance starts at the point of installation, giving you tips as to what is being installed and where it goes on your computer. Chapters 2 through 4 are an introduction to C# and VB, two of the most widely used programming languages supported in VS. Notice that the titles of these chapters include "Just Enough," indicating that you will learn the language features you need throughout this book. As you progress through the book, you'll be exposed to all of the language features discussed and see how they are used. Even if you already know how to program, you might want to peruse the programming language chapters anyway because I've sprinkled in dozens of valuable tips that will make your coding experience in VS much more pleasurable.

- **Part II: Learning the VS 2010 Environment**   There are a few universal tasks most developers perform every day, which include working with projects, debugging code, and manipulating data. While Chapter 5 is titled "Creating and Building Projects," there is much involved when working with projects. Pay particular attention to the guidance on assemblies and class libraries, as they tend to become more prominent as your development activities progress beyond simple programs. Regardless of your development philosophy, the need to fix bugs has always existed and will continue to be important in the future. Chapter 6 is designed to help you use the many tools of VS to find and fix bugs. Another common task you'll have is working with data. VS allows you to create databases, add tables, and much more. When the database is ready to use, you'll learn how to write code that works with the database. I chose to cover LINQ to SQL because it's one of the simpler database technologies, yet powerful enough for professional application development.

- **Part III: Building Programs with VS 2010**   With the foundations of programming languages and a feel for the VS environment, you'll be ready to use VS to build applications. The .NET platform supports various technologies, and this book takes a forward-looking approach, choosing technologies that were the most recently introduced. The focus in these chapters is not to teach you everything about these technologies, which can fill entire books themselves, but rather to show you how to leverage VS in building applications. You'll get the foundations that will give you a head start in building your own applications. Both Chapters 8 and 10 use a form of

Extensible Markup Language (XML) called XML Application Markup Language (XAML). Considering that this is a beginner's book, I added a couple of appendixes that cover XML and XAML. I recommend that you read the appendixes before reading Chapters 8 and 10. Additionally, you should read Chapter 8 before reading Chapter 10, because many of the same concepts used to work with Windows Presentation Foundation (WPF), a technology for building desktop applications, are applicable to Silverlight, a technology to build Web applications. The other two chapters in this part will show you how to build Web applications with ASP.NET MVC and how to create Web services with Windows Communications Foundation.

- **Part IV: Enhancing the VS 2010 Experience**   In addition to all of the wizards, tools, and editing help that VS offers, you can extend VS to make it work even better. Chapter 12 shows you how to create your own project and project item wizards, how to create code snippets that automatically generate code, and how to create macros that automate the VS environment. If the macro capability you learn about in VS isn't powerful enough, read Chapter 13, which shows you how to build an Add-In, a program that you can install to add new features to VS.

From installation to customization of the IDE, VS is a helpful and powerful tool. I hope you enjoy this book and that it helps you learn how to make VS work for you.

Part I

Understanding Visual Studio 2010 Essentials

Chapter 1
Introducing Visual Studio 2010

Key Skills & Concepts

- Learn What Visual Studio 2010 Can Do for You

- Install and Choose Among Installation Options

- Understand What Types of Applications You Can Build

Your first experience with Visual Studio (VS) 2010 is often installation. As with most software, VS is rather easy to install; this chapter describes the installation process and gives you tips to help understand available options. Once installation is complete, you'll open VS for the first time and need to know how to navigate the VS environment; this chapter gives you a high-level view of how VS is organized, how to find the features you need, and how to work with windows. Finally, you'll learn how to find the different application types that VS helps you build. At this point, you know that VS will help you build .NET applications, but let's start off with a more detailed explanation of what VS will do for you.

What Is Visual Studio 2010 About?

Visual Studio 2010 (VS) is an integrated development environment (IDE); a set of tools in a single application that helps you write programs. Without VS, you would need to open a text editor, write all of the code, and then run a command-line compiler to create an executable application. The issue with the text editor and command-line compiler is that you would lose a lot of productivity through manual processes. Fortunately, you have VS to automate many of the mundane tasks that are required to develop applications. The following sections explain what VS will do for you and why VS is all about developer productivity.

Automatically Generated Code

VS includes a suite of project types that you can choose from. Whenever you start a new project, VS will automatically generate skeleton code that can compile and run immediately. Each project type has project items that you can add, and project items include skeleton code. In the next chapter, you'll learn how to create projects, add project items, and view automatically generated code. VS offers many premade controls, which include skeleton code, saving you from having to write your own code for repetitive tasks. Many of the more complex controls contain wizards that help you customize the control's behavior, generating code based on wizard options you choose.

Rapid Coding Experience

The VS editor optimizes your coding experience. Much of your code is colorized; you have *Intellisense,* tips that pop up as you type; and keyboard shortcuts for performing a multitude of tasks. There are a few *refactorings,* features that help you quickly improve the organization of your code while you're coding. For example, the Rename refactoring allows you to change an identifier name where it is defined, which also changes every place in the program that references that identifier. VS introduces even more features, such as a call hierarchy, which lets you see the call paths in your code; snippets, which allow you to type an abbreviation that expands to a code template; and action lists for automatically generating new code.

Everything at Your Fingertips

You'll really want to learn how to navigate the VS environment because a plethora of tools are available to aid you in your quest to rapidly create quality software. You have the Toolbox jam-packed with controls, a Server Explorer for working with operating system services and databases, a Solution Explorer for working with your projects, testing utilities, and visual designers. By the way, there are compilers too.

Customizability and Extensibility

You can customize many parts of the VS environment, including colors, editor options, and layout. The options are so extensive that you'll need to know where to look to find them all. If the out-of-the-box VS development environment doesn't offer a feature you need, you can write your own macros to automate a series of tasks you find yourself repeating. For more sophisticated customization, VS exposes an application programming interface (API) for creating add-ins and extensions. Several third-party companies have chosen to integrate their own applications with VS. For example, Embarcadero's Delphi language and development environment is hosted in Visual Studio. The rich and customizable development environment in VS helps you work the way you want to.

As you move through this book, keep these important concepts in mind and look for all of the tips that will help you use VS to your advantage. Your first step in using VS will be installation, which is discussed in the next section.

Installing Visual Studio 2010

Hopefully the preceding discussion whets your appetite on what VS can do for you. If you haven't already installed VS, this section walks you through the setup process. The guidance along the way will explain how to choose among available options to customize the installation to your needs. The following steps explain how to install VS:

System Requirements

As of this writing Microsoft recommends you have a 32-bit x86 or 64-bit (x64) CPU, at least 1GB RAM, a 5400 RPM hard disk drive, 3GB hard disk space, DVD-ROM, DirectX video at 1280 × 1024 resolution, and a 1.6 GHz processor. Recommended operating systems include Windows Vista (all versions except for Starter), Windows XP SP2 or later (all versions except for Starter), Windows 7 (only Ultimate at the time this chapter was written), Windows 2003 (SP1 or R2 or later), and Windows 2008 (SP1 or R2 or later). Be sure to check Microsoft Developer Network (MSDN) online, as system requirements can change over time.

1. When you first place the VS DVD into the drive, you'll see the Microsoft Visual Studio 2010 window, shown in Figure 1-1. Available options are to Install Microsoft Visual Studio 2010 and Check For Service Releases. Click Install Microsoft Visual Studio 2010.

Figure 1-1 Microsoft Visual Studio 2010 Setup window

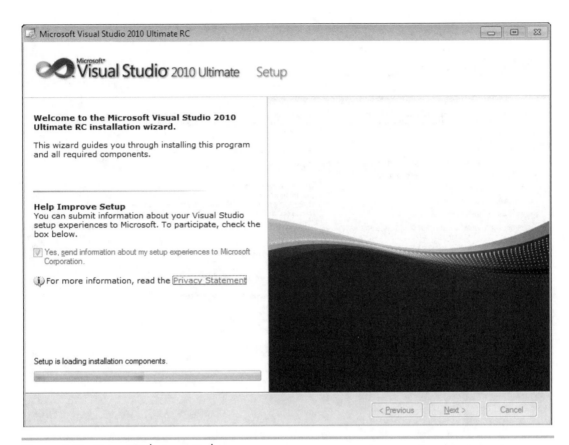

Figure 1-2   Setup Welcome window

2. The next window you'll see, Figure 1-2, is the welcome window, titled Microsoft Visual Studio 2010. Figure 1-2 shows that I'm installing the Ultimate version. Installation for other versions is similar, but the number of features available to install varies.

If you check the box on this page in the Help Improve Setup section, the installer will gather logs produced during the setup process and send them across the Internet to Microsoft after the setup is complete. To help you make an informed choice as to whether to check this box, there is a Privacy Statement link under the check box to click and read if you would like more information about what Microsoft does with setup information. When you're ready, click Next. After setup components are loaded, you'll see the licensing screen in Figure 1-3.

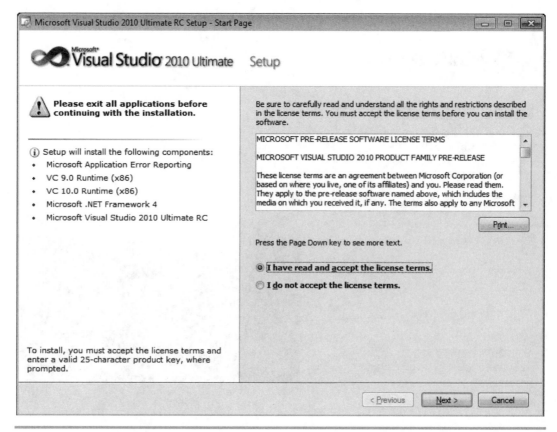

Figure 1-3 Setup Licensing window

3. In Figure 1-3, you'll see what components will be installed. You'll need to read the VS license to ensure you understand what the terms are. The licensing terms can differ, depending on what type of package you acquired and your particular country or region. Once you've read the license, you'll need to check "I have read and accept the license terms" to proceed. Next, enter the license key that comes with your software and enter your name. The installer will automatically fill in the product key if you downloaded VS via Microsoft Developer Network (MSDN). Click Next and you'll see options for customizing product installation.

4. Figure 1-4 lets you choose between full and custom installation. If you click the Custom option, you'll be able to choose precisely which components should be installed. This is a good opportunity to uncheck the items you won't ever use. If this is

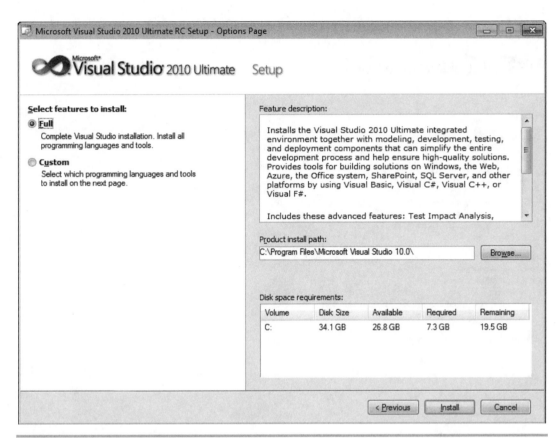

Figure 1-4   Setup Customization window

your first installation and you have plenty of storage, you might want to go through the list and check everything to take a look at what is available. You can always return to this installation later and make adjustments.

The configuration screen in Figure 1-4 shows that you can also change the location of where to install VS. Take note of the installation location because this is where you will go to find sample code, common assemblies, and more items affecting the development environment. Evaluate the disk space requirements to ensure you have enough available storage. You've now completed the configuration options for installation. Click Install to start the installation. You'll see a screen similar to Figure 1-5 during the installation process where the small check marks indicate which VS components have successfully installed.

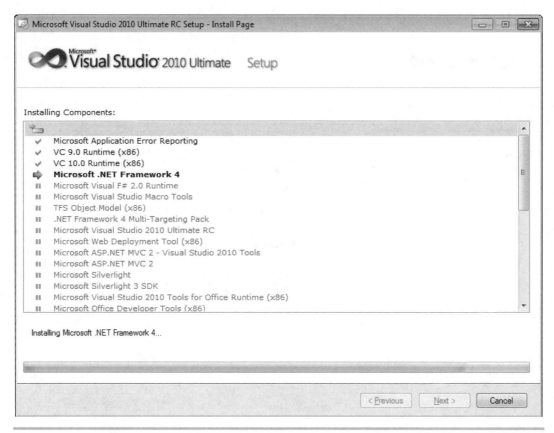

Figure 1-5   Setup Progress window

5. During the installation, the VS installer will need to reboot your computer, showing the restart message in Figure 1-6. Make sure you close any applications you currently have open so that you don't lose your work, and then click Restart Now.

Figure 1-6   Setup Restart window

Figure 1-7 Setup Success window

6. When installation completes without error, you'll see the Success window, shown in Figure 1-7. If you have errors during installation, this window will give you guidance on what to do to solve the problem.

Your installation is now almost complete. You can install product documentation by clicking the Install Documentation button, shown in Figure 1-7. The initial installation screen that appeared when beginning the installation will reappear, as shown in Figure 1-8. You should also check for service releases; not only for the updated functionality to VS, but also because service releases often include important security updates.

You are now ready to run VS for the first time. At that point, you'll need to perform one more easy configuration step, where you will choose your default environment settings, as shown in Figure 1-9.

Figure 1-8 Checking for service releases

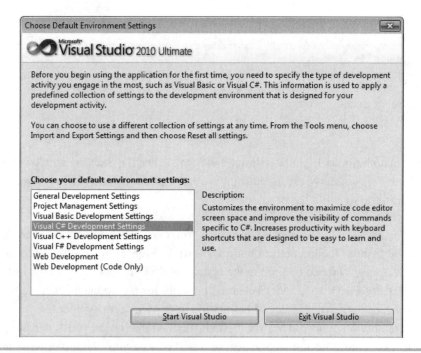

Figure 1-9 Default Environment Settings window

The choice you make for default environment settings depends a lot on what language or environment you'll use to write software in. The environment settings choice isn't locked in stone and can be reset if you decide you don't like the settings. A later section of this chapter, "Modifying Environment Settings after Setup," explains how to change environment settings. This book covers both VB and C#, so you would most likely want to choose the setting specific to the language you will use. The examples in this book will use either VB or C# settings, depending on the topic. The choice of settings determines how VS will lay out the windows and the default options that are set throughout the VS IDE.

NOTE

C# or VB, which Should I Choose? Both C# and VB are first-class languages on the .NET platform. The languages themselves are stripped down to bare syntax, with all additional services moved into the .NET Framework Class Library, which is common to all languages. There are a few small differences between the languages, but in reality, the choice really comes down to personal preference. In practice, knowing both languages is an advantage because much has been written in articles and books showing how to use .NET techniques that doesn't depend on which language was used. You'll not want to miss out on excellent content regardless of the language it is written in.

You should now have a good installation with the configuration and environment settings of your choosing. With VS open for the first time, the next section describes the high-level parts of the Start page.

Navigating the Visual Studio 2010 Environment

This section is a high-level view of VS, describing what is available when you first start Visual Studio 2010, also known as the Visual Studio integrated development environment, commonly known as the IDE, which is pronounced by saying the letters I-D-E. Seeing what is available will help you find features more quickly. Additionally, knowing what is available by default will help you differentiate between default functionality and the context-sensitive features of the software items you're working on.

Figure 1-10 shows how VS appears when first started. It refers to portions of the screen, helping you see how the IDE is organized. The following description will associate each feature with a name so that you can understand where to look when discussing these features in more depth throughout the rest of this book.

The following sections describe portions of the Start screen shown in Figure 1-10.

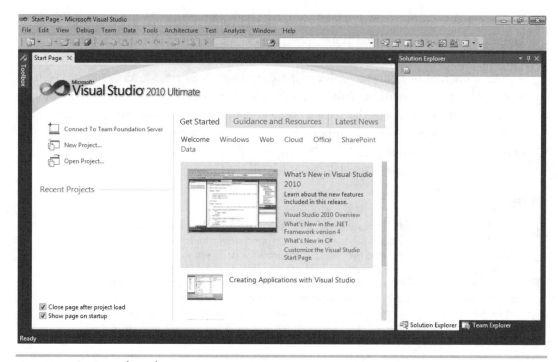

Figure 1-10 Visual Studio 2010 Start screen

The Menu

At the very top left of Figure 1-10, you'll see the menu bar, which includes the words "File," "Edit," "View," "Tools," and so on. The menu bar is a standard part of most windows applications. Besides standard file management functionality, the File menu is where you visit to create new projects. The File menu also gives you access to recently opened files and projects.

The Edit menu has your standard cut, copy, and paste operations. It also gives you access to a bookmark feature for providing easy navigation through source code.

It would be worth your effort to explore the View menu to see what is available, but if you are just learning Visual Studio and how to write software, it's best to not click these different views just yet; we'll explore most of those views and what they're used for later. The View menu gives you access to all of the tool windows in VS. The View menu also has a menu item named Other Windows that includes more application windows that will come in handy as you create new software.

The Tools menu contains a grab-bag of functionality; for instance, you can attach a debugger to see your other programs run, line by line; connect to a database for data; set add-ins, macros, and more. One very important menu item on the Tools menu is Options, which exposes hundreds of settings for customizing your VS environment.

You can use the Test menu to find all of the functionality for performing unit tests to test your new software one part at a time. This is also where other editions of VS include access to other types of testing tools.

The Analyze, Architecture, and Team menus have advanced functionality for improving the performance of an application, working with application architecture, and integrating with Microsoft's Team Foundation Server.

The Windows and Help menus are similar to most other application types, where the Windows menu allows you to manipulate the VS windows and the Help menu is where you visit to find the technical documentation on VS.

TIP

Many menu items contain shortcut keys that perform the same action as selecting the menu item. If you are curious about what shortcut keys are associated with a particular action, you can often find them by opening the menu to see if there are shortcuts associated with that action. For example, to open the Solution Explorer window and visit the View menu, the shortcut keys are CTRL-W, S.

Toolbar

Beneath the menu in Figure 1-10, you'll find a toolbar. The toolbar contains frequently accessed functionality that is a subset of what is available via menus. The toolbars are context-sensitive, showing and hiding depending on what you are doing in VS. You can display any toolbar by selecting View | Toolbars.

You can also customize toolbars by right-clicking the toolbar of your choice, scrolling to the bottom of the list, and selecting Customize. The toolbar customization window allows you to add any feature you would like to the current toolbar.

Work Area

In the center of Figure 1-10, you can see the Start page. This is the same area that you'll use to write code and work with visual designers. The Start page is divided into two sections: project management and information. The project management side of the page, on the left, offers a quick way to start new projects or work with a list of recently opened projects. The information side of the page, on the right, contains resources to help you get started with VS, such as links to the Microsoft Web site, walkthroughs to help you learn new features, and a tab that updates with the latest developer news from Microsoft.

Toolbox

On the far left side of Figure 1-10 is a vertical tab, titled Toolbox, which contains a context-sensitive list of controls that can be dragged and dropped onto the current designer surface. The term "context-sensitive" means that certain items are visible or hidden, depending on where you've clicked last or what context you are working in, such as creating or editing a new Web page. If you're following along, you don't have a designer surface open right now, so the Toolbox is empty.

Solution Explorer

The Solution Explorer window, to the right of the Start page in Figure 1-10, is where your solutions, projects, and project items will appear. This is where you can find and organize all of the files and settings that belong to a project. In Figure 1-10, the Solution Explorer is blank because there isn't an open solution. If you close this window and need to find it again, just remember the View menu discussed earlier.

Status Bar

At the very bottom of Figure 1-10 is the Status bar, which communicates what is happening with VS at the current time. In Figure 1-10, the Status bar displays the word "Ready" to indicate you can begin using VS at any time. As you work with VS, the Status bar changes in a context-sensitive way to give you information specific to the task you are working on. For example, the editor displays line, column, and other information pertaining to the status of the editor.

Managing VS Windows

Looking at the VS screen in Figure 1-10, you can see how the windows in the work area—Toolbox, Start, and Solution Explorer—are decorated with various title bars. Window title bars include a set of three icons: Window Position (down arrow), Maximize/Restore Down (window), and Close (cross). Figure 1-11 shows the Solution Explorer with these three icons on its title bar at the top-right corner.

The Window Position allows you to treat the window as Dock, Float, Dock As Tabbed Document, Auto Hide, and Hide. You can expand a window to fill the entire work area or allow the window to be resized and float freely around the work area with the Maximize/Restore Down icon. In the docked position, the Maximize/Restore Down icon becomes a pin that can be used to pin the window open or allow it to slide shut. The Close icon allows you to close a window. The following sections describe how use these title icons to manipulate these windows through expanding and collapsing, docking, floating, tabbing, and closing and opening.

Figure 1-11   Window title bar icons

Expanding and Collapsing Windows

Hovering over the Toolbox tab will expand the Toolbox and display a set of three icons in the title bar of the Toolbox window: Window Position (down arrow), Hide (pin), and Close (cross). You can see what the Toolbox window looks like when expanded in Figure 1-12; the pin in the Hide icon is sideways and the vertical tab still appears in the left margin.

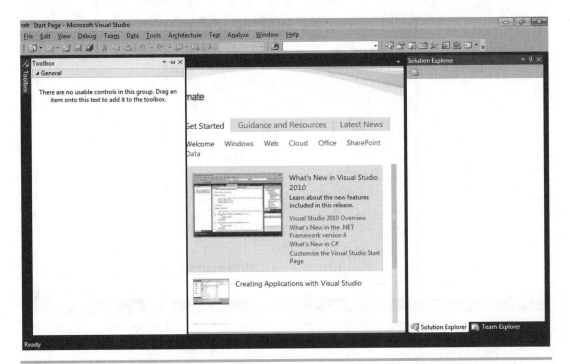

Figure 1-12   Expanded Toolbox

If you move the carat away from the Toolbox, the Toolbox will collapse and turn back into a tab on the left side of the screen.

For any collapsed window, such as the Toolbox, you can expand that collapsed window and click the Hide (pin) icon to pin the window, which will make the window layout similar to the Solution Explorer. Figure 1-13 shows the pinned window; the pin in the Hide icon (above the Auto Hide tooltip) is vertical and you no longer see the Toolbox tab in the left margin.

Clicking the Hide icon on any expanded window will cause the window to collapse and display as a tab, similar to the Toolbox. Another way to collapse a window is by selecting the Auto Hide option on the Window Position (down arrow) menu.

Docking Windows

The Dock option displays the window in an open docked position, similar to the Solution Explorer in Figure 1-10. You can move a docked window to any position in the work area. To move a docked window, select its title bar and drag the window out of its current position. Figure 1-14 shows VS when you're dragging a window.

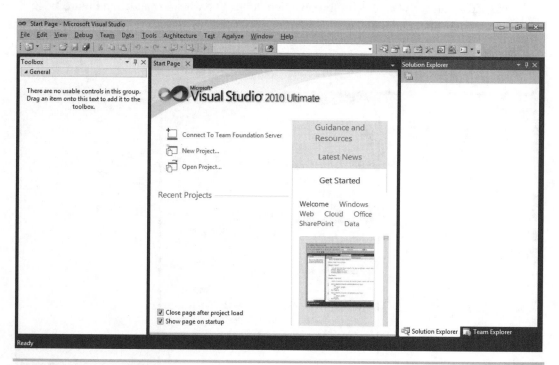

Figure 1-13 Pinned Toolbox

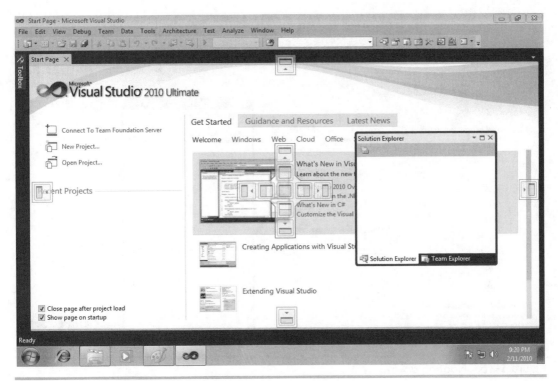

Figure 1-14 Dragging a window for docking

As shown in Figure 1-14, you'll see a visual set of icons appear over the workspace, indicating the docking zones where you can move the window to. The shadow of the window will show what the new location will be whenever you drag a window into a docking zone. Dropping the window into the docking zone will move the window from its old docking zone into the new docking zone.

Floating Windows

The Float option allows windows to appear anywhere in the VS IDE, where you can move them at will. You move a floating window by selecting the floating window's title bar and moving the carat to the new location where you want the window to be. Alternatively, you can double-click on the title bar. Figure 1-15 shows the Toolbox floating over other windows.

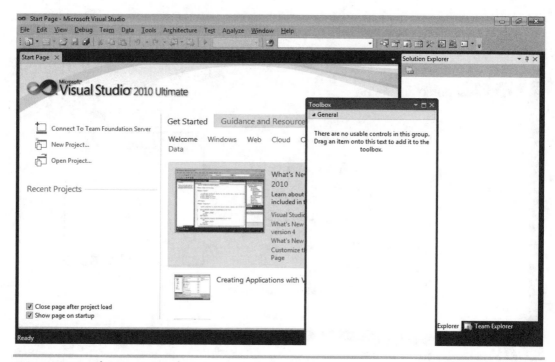

Figure 1-15   Floating a window

Tabbed Windows

An example of using the Dock As Tabbed Document option is the Start page. Any window set as Dock As Tabbed Document will appear as a new tab in the work area, along with all the other windows set as Dock As Tabbed Document. For example, if the Toolbox is set as Dock As Tabbed Document, it will become a tabbed document in the same group as the Start window, as shown in Figure 1-16.

TIP

Position windows in a way that makes you most productive. In practice, you probably don't want your Toolbox to be a tabbed window. You'll see examples in later chapters of this book that drag-and-drop items from the Toolbox to a designer page, which is also laid out as a tabbed document window. So, trying to drag-and-drop between two tabbed document windows can be cumbersome. There are several options for working with Windows in VS, and after working with VS for a while, you'll want to pick the layout that works best for you.

To change a window from a tabbed document, select the tab and drag the window away from the other documents, making it a floating window.

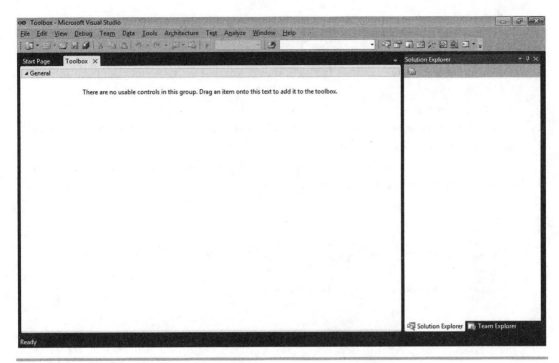

Figure 1-16   Tabbed document windows

Closing and Opening Windows

Clicking the Close icon on a window title bar will close the window. Another way to close the window is by selecting the Hide option from the Window Position icon menu.

Reopening a window depends on what type of window it is: VS or Project Item. If the window is from VS, you can re-visit the View menu and select the window you need to open. Alternatively, you can use a keyboard shortcut key to open a window. These shortcut keys for the windows are displayed on the right side of the menu item in the View menu.

Other windows are for project items in the Solution Explorer. In most cases, you would re-open a project item by locating it in the appropriate project of Solution Explorer and double-clicking it. There are edge cases where you open project items by right-clicking the project item in Solution Explorer and selecting a menu item, but I'll explain those cases when I discuss them specifically in the rest of this book.

You can now manipulate windows, customizing the layout of your VS environment as you need. Sometimes, though, you'll want to reset your layout to the original default, as you'll learn about in the next section.

Modifying Environment Settings after Setup

Reasons for modifying environment settings include wanting to reset everything back to a default, importing shared settings from another developer, or switching between settings for different projects. This section will explain how to modify your settings and achieve each of these goals.

With VS open, select Tools | Import And Export Settings, which will start the Import and Export Settings Wizard shown in Figure 1-17.

From Figure 1-17, you can see the options to Export, Import, and Reset settings. The following sections explain each of these options.

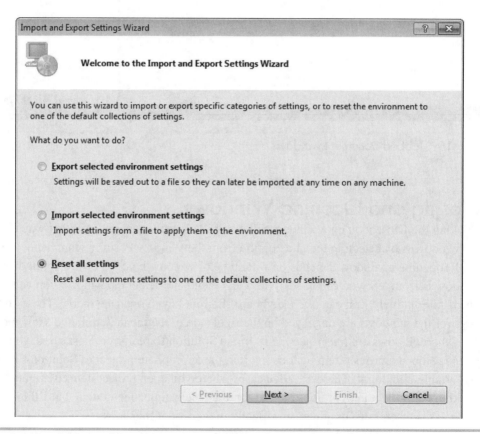

Figure 1-17 Import and Export Settings Wizard

Exporting Selected Environment Settings

We'll start off with export, which you might use to share your settings with another developer. This could also be useful if you planned to make significant changes to your settings and wanted a backup in case you wanted to revert to previous settings. To perform the export, choose the "Export selected environment settings" option from Figure 1-17 and click Next to display the Choose Settings To Export window in Figure 1-18.

There is a tree of options you can choose from to determine what settings to export. The warning sign indicates settings that you might not want to export for personal or security reasons. The warning settings typically have something to do with system file paths or something outside of VS that you wouldn't normally share with other people. After you've selected options, click Next to display the Name Your Settings File window in Figure 1-19.

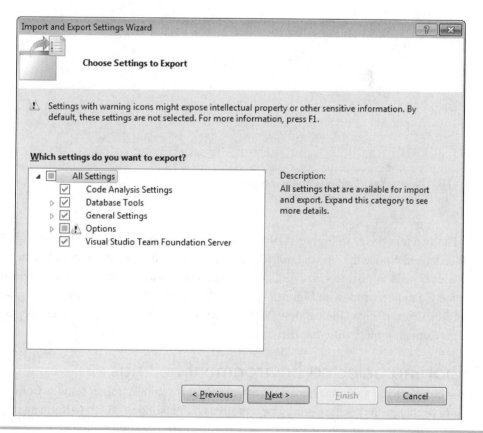

Figure 1-18   Choose Settings To Export window

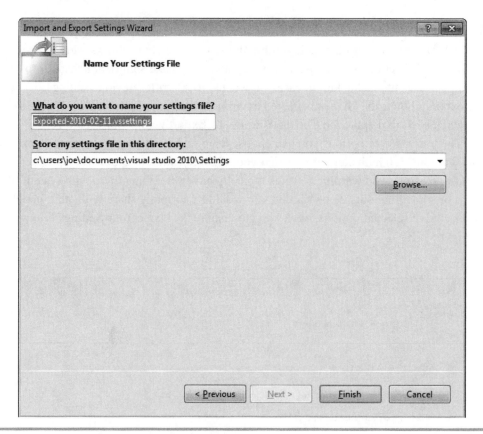

Figure 1-19   Name Your Settings File window

The two text boxes in Figure 1-19 are for a filename and path where the settings file will be saved. Notice that the default filename includes the date, which could be helpful if you ever need to restore settings. Click Finish, which will perform the export and show you the Complete window in Figure 1-20 after the export operation is done.

Click Close to close the window. With an exported settings file, you or another person can perform an import with that file, as described in the next section.

Importing Selected Environment Settings

You would perform a settings import to restore previous settings, import settings from another person, or change to specific settings for a project you're working on. To perform an import,

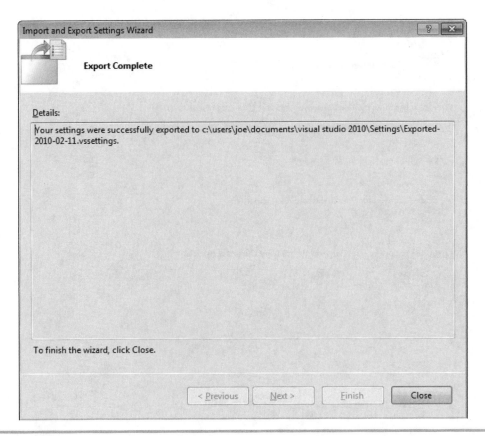

Figure 1-20   Export Complete window

open VS and select Tools | Import and Export Settings, which opens the Import and Export Settings Wizard shown in Figure 1-17. Choose the "Import selected environment settings" option and click Next to view the Save Current Settings window shown in Figure 1-21.

TIP

You can search for various color schemes for Visual Studio on the Internet to download. One site, at the time of this writing, is http://winterdom.com/2007/11/vs2008colorschemes; it offers schemes made for Visual Studio 2008 but that also import into Visual Studio 2010.

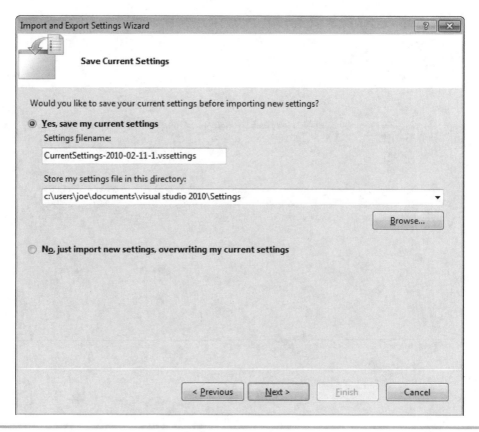

Figure 1-21 Save Current Settings window

The Save Current Settings window allows you to back up your current environment settings before changing them. If you do a backup, you will be able to restore later in case something doesn't work out the way you intended with the import. You can choose not to back up also. Click Next to view the Choose A Collection Of Settings To Import window in Figure 1-22.

As shown in Figure 1-22, you can import some of the predefined settings that are part of VS under the Default Settings branch or import custom settings under the My Settings branch. Custom settings include the current settings and any other settings that you've saved to the default path, shown in Figures 1-19 and 1-21. Optionally, you can

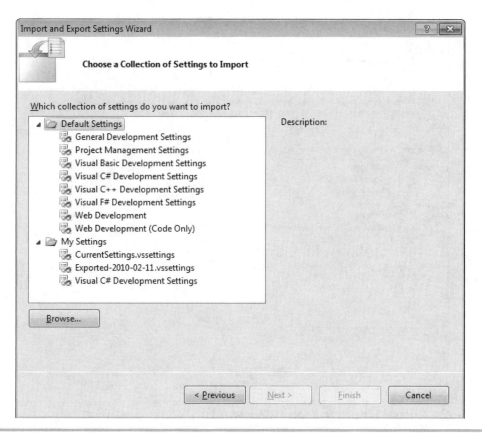

Figure 1-22   Choose A Collection Of Settings To Import window

click Browse and navigate to the location where a settings file is located. After selecting a settings file, click Next, which brings you to the Choose Settings To Import window shown in Figure 1-23.

The Choose Settings To Import window allows you to specify only those settings that you want in your environment. It will only update the settings checked in Figure 1-23. All of your other current settings, those that are unchecked in Figure 1-23, will not be changed. Click Finish to begin the import operation. When import is done, you'll see the Import Complete window, shown in Figure 1-24.

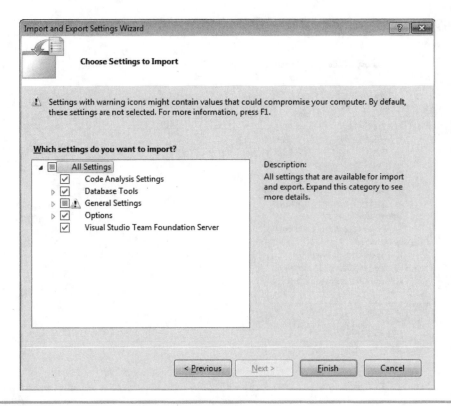

Figure 1-23 Choose Settings To Import window

Your import is now complete, and you can click the Close window. Another settings option is to reset your current settings to one of the VS default options, explained next.

Resetting All Settings

You could reset settings if you wanted to restore the default settings in VS or if you wanted to switch between default VS settings. For this book, I switched between default settings for VB and C# to ensure the environment settings were appropriate for whichever language I was discussing. To perform a reset, open VS and select Tools | Import And Export Settings, which will open the Import and Export Settings Wizard shown earlier in Figure 1-17.

Choose the Reset All Settings option and click Next. You'll see the Save Current Settings window, which is exactly the same as Figure 1-21. Choose your save option and click Next to view the Default Collection Of Settings window shown in Figure 1-25.

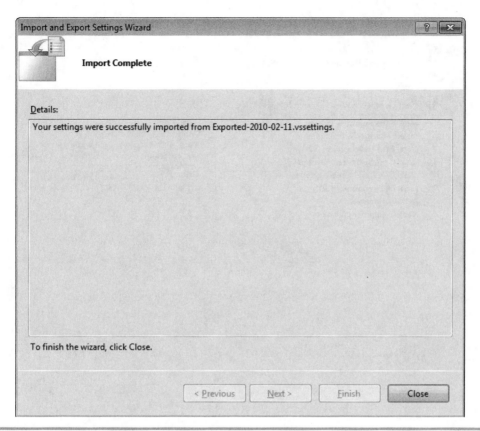

Figure 1-24   Import Complete window

Figure 1-25 shows that you can select among a set of default settings for VS. Each of these default settings are the same as what you selected during installation, previously shown in Figure 1-9 and the Default Settings branch of Figure 1-22. Choose a setting and click Finish, which starts the reset operation. When the reset is done, you'll see the Reset Complete window, shown in Figure 1-26. The reset is now complete, and you can click Close to close the window when you're finished.

Earlier in the chapter, we discussed projects very lightly, but we will gradually dig deeper as this book progresses. The next section takes you a little bit further by describing what project types are available in VS.

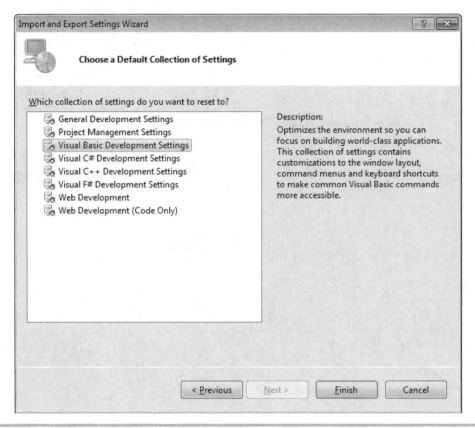

Figure 1-25 Default Collection Of Settings window

Familiarization with Visual Studio Project Types

Visual Studio includes a plethora of project types, making it easy to build applications with premade templates. The following discussion will show how to find what project types are available and describe what those project types are.

To see what projects are available, select File | New | Project, as shown in Figure 1-27.

NOTE

If you've set your environment up for VB, you'll notice right away that the option to select is File | New Project, which is only two menu choices, rather than 3 for C#. While the exact wording and placement of options won't always match, you can rely on the functionality being the same, except for when I explain otherwise.

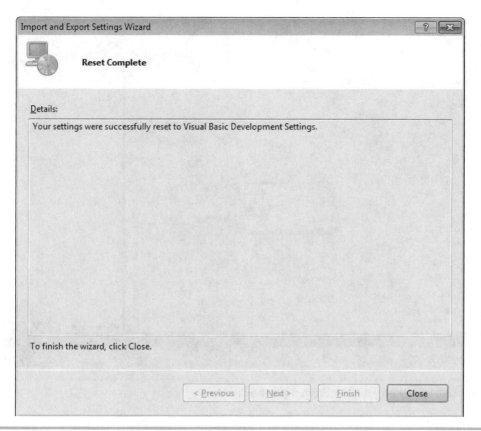

Figure 1-26 Reset Complete window

In addition to a new project, Figure 1-27 shows that you can create a new Web site, just open a file for editing, or open a wizard that creates a new project from existing files. We'll look at many of these options later in the book, but let's take a look at the New Project window, Figure 1-28, which opened as a result of selecting File | New | Project.

The New Project window in Figure 1-28 shows that there are many projects to select from, including Windows, Web, Office, SharePoint, Cloud, Reporting, Silverlight, Test, WCF, and Workflow. Some of these project types don't appear in Figure 1-28, but if you scroll down the Templates list in the New Project window, you'll see them. Figure 1-28 also shows the appearance for C# projects, but there are also similar projects for other programming languages that ship with VS; including VB, C++ (pronounced see-plus-plus), and F# (pronounced f-sharp). If you had selected VB settings during the setup process,

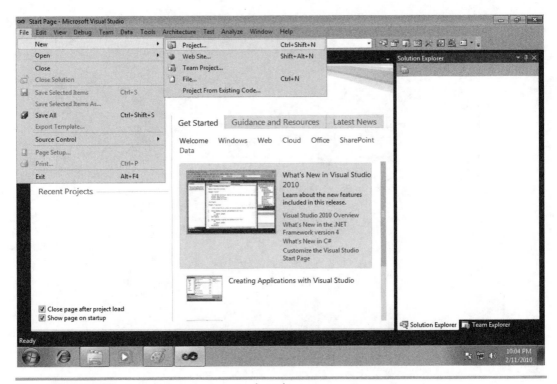

Figure 1-27 Selecting a New Project via the File menu

earlier in this chapter, the default set of project types would have been VB and C# projects would be listed in the Other Languages branch. The following sections describe the types of projects available, some of which you'll learn how to create later in this book.

Windows Projects

Selecting Windows Projects will show you a list of project types that can be created for desktop applications, including Windows Presentation Foundation (WPF), Windows Forms, and Console. Console applications are for building applications that don't need a graphical user interface (also known as GUI and pronounced "goo-ee") and are generally for creating utilities that administrators can write scripts with or for writing a quick test for your program. You'll be using Console applications when learning VB and C# languages later in this book because it is a simple way to concentrate on the language without any distractions. Windows Forms is an older desktop GUI technology. The new desktop GUI technology for .NET is called WPF, which is covered in a later chapter in this book.

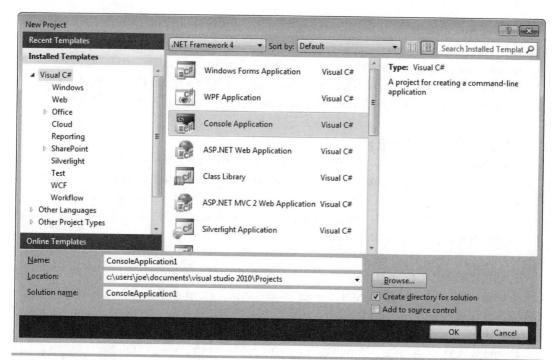

Figure 1-28   New Project window

Other windows projects include Windows Services, which are applications that are always on and run as a service in the background without a GUI, Class Libraries for holding reusable code often referred to as middleware, and Control Libraries for holding graphical controls that can be dragged-and-dropped from the Toolbox onto a visual designer within VS.

Web Projects

Web projects include ASP.NET, Server Controls, Web Services, and Dynamic Data. An ASP.NET project allows you to write an application that is hosted by a Web server, such as Internet Information Server (IIS), and runs in a Web browser. A Server Control project enables you to build a library of GUI controls that can be dragged-and-dropped onto the design surface of a Web page in VS. Web Services are reusable components that you can call from across the Internet. An important feature of Web Services is that they use ubiquitous protocols to enable code from any platform to call them, facilitating integration among heterogeneous computing systems. Dynamic Data projects offer a quick way to build a working Web site, based on an existing database schema.

Office Projects

For years, developers have been writing Visual Basic for Applications (VBA) programs to automate Microsoft Office applications. An Office project allows you to automate Office applications through .NET using languages such as VB and C#. Supported Office applications include Excel, Word, Project, PowerPoint, Outlook, Visio, and InfoPath.

SharePoint Projects

SharePoint is a technology for building portal-style Web applications. It is closely associated with Office applications and managing workgroup collaboration. In order to create and run SharePoint projects, the computer you use to run VS will need to be running one of Microsoft's server platforms, such as Server 2008. SharePoint does not run on Windows 7, Vista, or Windows XP.

Database Projects

Database projects include a SQL Server project type, offering close integration with SQL Server for building .NET code that runs inside of SQL Server. For example, you can write stored procedures and functions in either C# or VB and have the benefit of the .NET Framework in your code. VS makes it easy to deploy your code to SQL Server with a single mouse click.

Summary

By knowing the benefits of VS, you have an appreciation for what VS can do for you, increasing your productivity through automatically generated code, rapid coding and visual design, and extensibility. You should be able to install VS, choosing the options that prepare the environment specifically for the work you want to do. Another set of skills you gained was the ability to manipulate the layout of your environment and manage environment settings, including how to get your environment back to the default settings if you've made too many changes. Having grown acquainted with each of the major features of the IDE, you can open VS and find the features that you need. With your knowledge of the advantages of VS, proper installation, and awareness of VS capabilities, you are now ready to start your first software development project, which you'll learn about in the next chapter.

Chapter 2

Learning Just Enough C# or VB.NET: Basic Syntax

Key Skills & Concepts

- Learn Basics of Starting a Project

- Use the VS Editor

- Code Expressions and Statements

The .NET platform supports several different programming languages. Since all of the languages run on the same platform and share the same class libraries, language choice becomes a personal choice of preference. In other words, you can accomplish the same tasks, regardless of what programming language you use. With .NET, you have a choice of language but retain the same benefits of having all of the features of .NET available to you.

Visual Studio (VS) 2010 ships with four programming languages: C#, C++, F#, and Visual Basic.NET (VB). The pronunciation of each of these languages, respectively, is See Sharp, See Plus Plus, Eff Sharp, and Vee Bee. C# and VB are the two most popular .NET programming languages and have the greatest support in VS. Therefore, this book uses both C# and VB in all examples. While you may choose one of these languages as your favorite, there is great benefit in knowing both. Most of what is written online, in magazines, and in books contains examples for either C# or VB, and sometimes, but not always, both. You might not want to miss great content because of a limited language choice.

Chapter 1 danced around projects and what is available. It was important to have that overview, but I'm sure you're eager to see some code. This chapter will be satisfying in that you'll learn how to create a project, see what code is generated, and learn how to add code yourself. This is the first chapter of three that covers language syntax, combining each language feature with tips on how VS helps you code. You'll start off by creating a simple project and then learn about language types and statements.

Starting a Bare-Bones Project

Chapter 1 described the project types that you can create. This chapter takes you a step further; actually creating a project. Because the primary focus of this chapter is on learning C# and VB, the project type will be a Console application. A Console application is very simple, allowing you to read and write text from and to the Command Prompt window. Later chapters introduce you to the project types used most, such as WPF and ASP.NET.

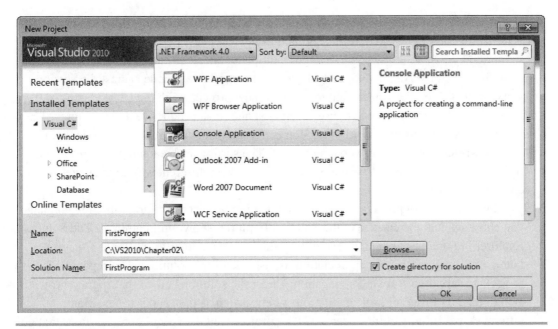

Figure 2-1   The New Project window

To get started, open VS and select File | New | Project. You'll see the New Project window, shown in Figure 2-1. Your first task is to select Console Application as the program type. Then set the program name to **FirstProgram** and specify a location of your choice for where the project will be created. Other features of the New Project window include the ability to specify the .NET Framework version, sorting options, icon size options, and a search capability.

NOTE

It's often useful to choose a project location other than the default. The default is your personal "My Documents" folder, which is long to type, cumbersome to navigate to, and error prone. Choosing a shorter path helps alleviate these problems. If you're working on a team with other developers, it's also helpful to use a common location for projects where everyone has their files in the same location.

NOTE

In the example code that accompanies this book, the projects are named FirstProgramCS (containing C# examples) and FirstProgramVB (containing VB examples). You'll see this convention, specifying the language in the project name suffix, in all of the code examples accompanying this book.

Along the very top center of the dialog shown in Figure 2-1, the .NET Framework is the set of class libraries, runtime, and languages that is the development platform supported by VS. VS allows you to target multiple versions of the .NET Framework, including versions 2.0, 3.0, 3.5, and 4.0. VS will compile your code against the version you choose. Generally, you'll want to begin all new projects with the latest version, 4.0, because you'll want to be able to use the newest and most productive .NET features. The primary reason for using an earlier version is if you must perform work on code that is already written for an earlier version of .NET. The sorting and searching features to the right of this selection enable you to find project types in different ways, whichever is most comfortable for you.

Clicking OK will produce a Console application project in the programming language you chose, which you can see in the Solution Explorer, shown in Figure 2-2. The Solution Explorer in Figure 2-2 contains a solution, which is a container for multiple projects. Later, you'll gain a stronger appreciation for the role of the solution when organizing projects to support a software application. Under the solution is the FirstProgram project. Within the FirstProgram project are project items, such as files and settings. Many different types of project items can go into a project, and the specific project items that go

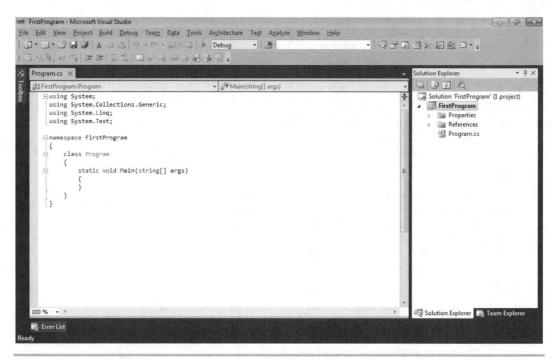

Figure 2-2 A Console application in the Solution Explorer

into a project depend on the project type. For example, there are project items that are part of a WPF application but wouldn't be part of a Console application. Of particular interest in the FirstProgram project is the file named Program.cs (or Module1.vb if programming in VB), which is a code file, as we'll discuss in the next section.

Examining the Code Skeleton

Having run the New Project Wizard for a Console application, you'll see a file named Program.cs (or Module.vb) that contains skeleton code in the editor. VS will create skeleton code using built-in templates for most project types that you create. You're free to add, remove, or modify this code as you see fit. Listing 2-1 contains the skeleton code, which I'll explain next.

Listing 2-1   Console application skeleton code

C#:

```
using System;
using System.Collections.Generic;
using System.Linq;
using System.Text;

namespace FirstProgram
{
    class Program
    {
        static void Main(string[] args)
        {
        }
    }
}
```

VB:

```
Module Module1

    Sub Main()

    End Sub

End Module
```

The skeleton code in Listing 2-1 is what VS created when the new Console application was created. It is there to give you a head start on writing your program. What you now have is a whole computer program. This program doesn't do much of anything at this point, but it will actually run and then end itself. Looking at the whole program, you can see that there are sets of nested curly braces in the C# code. The VB code has *Module* and *Sub* with corresponding *End* identifiers to indicate the boundaries of a block. The braces in C# code always come in pairs and define a block. The following explanation works from the inside out to help you understand what this code means.

The Main Method

The innermost block of the C# code is the static void *Main(string[] args)* definition, which is called a *method.* The method in VB is called *Sub Main* and is identical in purpose. You'll learn later that methods are one way you can group code into logical chunks of functionality. You can think of methods as actions where you, as the method author, tell the computer what to do. The name of this particular method is *Main,* which is referred to as the *entry point* of the program, the place where a Console application first starts running. Another way of thinking about *Main* is that this is the place your computer first transfers control to your program. Therefore, you would want to put code inside of *Main* to make your program do what you want it to.

In C#, *Main* must be capitalized. It's also important to remember that C# is case-sensitive, meaning that *Main* (capitalized) is not the same as *main* (lowercase). Although VS capitalizes your code for you if you forget to, VB is not case-sensitive. Capitalization is a common gotcha, especially for VB programmers learning C#.

In C#, methods can return values, such as numbers, text, or other types of values, and the type of thing they can return is specified by you right before the method name. In VB, a *Sub* (a shortened keyword derived from the term subroutine) does not return a value, but a *Function* does, and you'll see examples soon. Since *Main,* in the C# example, does not return a value, the return type is replaced with the keyword *void.* Methods can specify parameters for holding arguments that callers pass to the method. In the case of *Main,* the parameter is an array of strings, with a variable name of *args.* The *args* parameter will hold all of the parameters passed to this program from the command line.

One more part of the C# *Main* method is the *static* keyword, which is a modifier that says there will only ever be a single instance of this method for the life of the program. To understand instances, consider that methods are members of object types where an object can be anything in the domain of the application you're writing, such as a Customer, Account, or Vehicle. Think about a company that has multiple customers. Each customer is a separate instance, which also means that each Customer instance contains methods that belong to each instance. If an object such as Customer has methods that belong to each instance, those methods are not static. However, if the Customer object type has a method that is static, then there would only be a single copy of that method that is shared among all Customer objects. For example, what if you wanted to get a discount price for all customers, regardless of who the customer is; you would declare a static method named *GetCustomerDiscount*. However, if you wanted information that belonged to a specific customer, such as an address, you would create an instance method named *GetAddress* that would not be modified as static.

VB uses the term *shared,* which has the same meaning as static. Modules are inherently shared, and all module methods must be shared. Therefore, the VB *Main* method is shared.

In C#, the curly braces define the begin and end of the *Main* method. In VB, *Main* begins with *Sub* and is scoped to *End Sub.* Next, notice that the C# *Main* method is enclosed inside of a set of braces that belong to something called a *class* that has been given the name *Program.* The VB *Main* method is enclosed in something called a *module.* You'll learn about the enclosing class and module next.

The Program Class

Methods always reside inside of a type declaration. A type could be a class or struct for C# or a class, module, or struct in VB. The term *type* might be a little foreign to you, but it might be easier if you thought of it as something that contains things. Methods are one of the things that types contain. The following snippet, from Listing 2-1, shows the type that contains the *Main* method, which is a class in C# and a module (in this example) in VB:

```
class Program
{
    // Main Method omitted for brevity
}
```

VB:

```
Module Module1
    ' Main omitted for brevity
End Module
```

Most object types you create will be a class, as shown in the previous C# example. In VB, you would replace *Module* with *Class.* Although VS uses *Module* as the default object type for a new project, it's a holdover from earlier versions of VB. In practice, you shouldn't use the VB Module but should prefer *Class.* The *Program* class contains the *Main* method. You could add other methods to the *Program* class or *Module1* module, which you'll see many times throughout this book. The Console application defined the skeleton code class to have the name *Program.* In reality you can name the class anything you want. Whatever names you choose should make sense for the purpose of the class. For example, it makes sense for a class that works with customers to be named *Customer* and only contain methods that help you work with customers. You wouldn't add methods for working directly with invoices, products, or anything other than customers because that would make the code in your *Customer* class confusing. Classes are organized with namespaces, which are discussed next.

The FirstProgram Namespace

A *namespace* helps make your class names unique and therefore unambiguous. They are like adding a middle name and surname to your first name, which makes your whole name more unique. A namespace name, however, precedes the class name, whereas your middle name and surname follow your first or given name. A namespace also helps you organize code and helps you find things in other programmers' code. This organization helps to build libraries of code where programmers have a better chance to find what they need. The .NET platform has a huge class library that is organized into namespaces and assemblies; this will become clearer the more you program. The main .NET namespace is *System,* which has multiple sub-namespaces. For example, guess where you can find .NET classes for working with data? Look in *System.Data.* Another quick test: Where are .NET classes for working with networking protocols like TCP/IP, FTP, or HTTP? Try *System.Net.*

Another benefit of namespaces is to differentiate between classes that have the same name in different libraries. For example, what if you bought a third-party library that has a *Customer* class? Think about what you would do to tell the difference between *Customer* classes. The solution is namespaces, because if each *Customer* has its own namespace, you can write code that specifies each *Customer* by its namespace. Always using namespaces is widely considered to be a best practice.

The *Program* class in Listing 2-1 belongs to the *FirstProgram* namespace, repeated here for your convenience (in C#):

```
namespace FirstProgram
{
    // Program class omitted for brevity
}
```

You can put many classes inside of a namespace, where inside means within the beginning and ending braces for a namespace.

The *using* directives at the top of the C# part of Listing 2-1 are really a shortcut that makes it easier for you to write code. For example, the *System* namespace contains the *Console* class. If the *using System* directive were not present, you would be required to write *System.Console.WriteLine* instead of just *Console.WriteLine*. This was a short example, but *using* directives can help clean up your code and make it more readable.

A VB module must be declared at the global level, meaning that it can't be added to a namespace that you create. The following example demonstrates what a VB namespace looks like:

```
Namespace FirstProgram
    Public Class Customer

    End Class
End Namespace
```

In this example, you can see that the *FirstProgram* namespace contains a *Customer* class. The next task you'll want to take on is writing code, but before doing so, let's look at some of the features of the VS Code editor.

An Overview of the VS Code Editor

The VS Code editor is where you'll be performing much of your coding work. This section will point out a few features you will be interested in and show you how to perform customizations. Figure 2-3 shows the editor with the Console application skeleton code from the C# part of Listing 2-1.

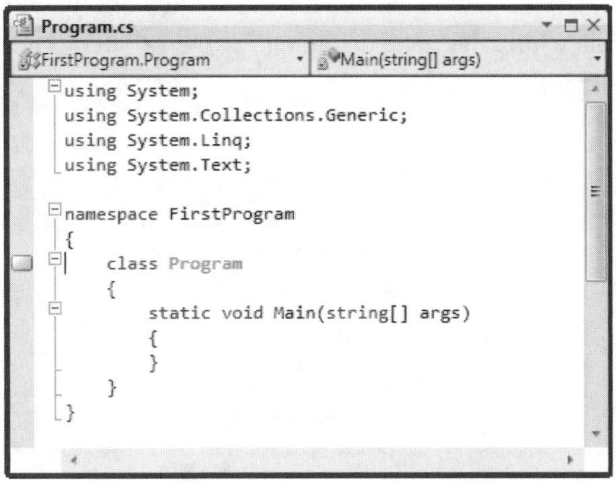

Figure 2-3   The VS Code editor

The following sections examine various elements of the Code editor, starting with class and member locators.

Class and Member Locators

The two drop-down lists, class locator and member locator, at the top of the editor are for navigating the code. If you have multiple classes in your file, you can use the class locator drop-down list on the left to select the class you want to find, and the editor will move you to the first line of that class declaration. In practice, I only put a single class within a single file, so the class locator doesn't get much attention. However, you will have VS wizards that automatically generate code and put many classes in the same file, and the class locator is very useful if you want to find a particular class and learn about what the automatically generated code is doing. The member locator drop-down list on the top right contains a list of methods and other members for the class selected in the class locator. The only class member we've discussed so far is the method, but there are more, as you'll learn in upcoming chapters. Selecting a member causes the editor to move you to the first line of that class member. Whenever you find yourself scrolling through a large file, remember that the member locator will help you find what you're looking for quickly.

The vertical bar on the left side of the editor is called the indicator margin, where you'll see icons for features such as bookmarks and debug breakpoints. The next section discusses bookmarks.

Bookmarks

Figure 2-3 shows a bookmark on the line for the program class. Bookmarks allow you to navigate code quickly without manual navigation when working with multiple documents or multiple locations within the same document. Table 2-1 shows a list of keyboard commands for bookmarks.

Key Code	Meaning
CTRL-B, T	Toggle a bookmark on or off
CTRL-B, N	Move to next bookmark
CTRL-B, P	Move to previous bookmark
CTRL-B, C	Clear all bookmarks
CTRL-W, B	Open the Bookmarks window

Table 2-1 Bookmark Shortcut Keys

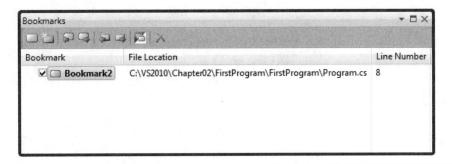

Figure 2-4   The Bookmarks window

One of the entries in Table 2-1, CTRL-W, B opens the Bookmarks window shown in Figure 2-4, allowing you to manage bookmarks throughout your application.

The bookmark has a toolbar, which is the same toolbar that appears in VS when the editor window is active. The actions on the toolbar include the items from Table 2-1, plus the ability to move between folders.

Within the Bookmark list, you can check to make a bookmark active or inactive. When the bookmark is inactive, previous and next navigation will not stop at the bookmark. You can change the name of the bookmark by clicking the name twice. The File Location and Line Number tell you where the bookmark is located.

Setting Editor Options

The editor is very configurable, and there are more options available than many people realize. You can view available options by selecting Tools | Options to show the Options window in Figure 2-5. As you can see from the figure, selecting Environment | Fonts And Colors allows you to change the appearance of VS. Regarding our current discussion of the editor, this is where you can customize the coloration of code elements that appear in the editor.

TIP

If you want to share your custom editor settings, you can use the Import and Export Settings Wizard that you learned about in Chapter 1. There is also an Import And Export Settings branch right below Fonts And Colors in the Options window.

Most editor customizations are in a language-specific branch of the Options window. Figure 2-6 shows the options available for C# programmers.

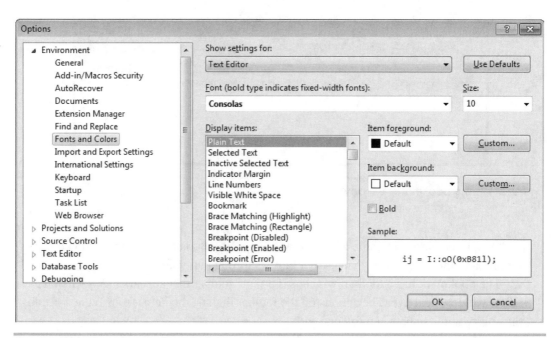

Figure 2-5   The Options window

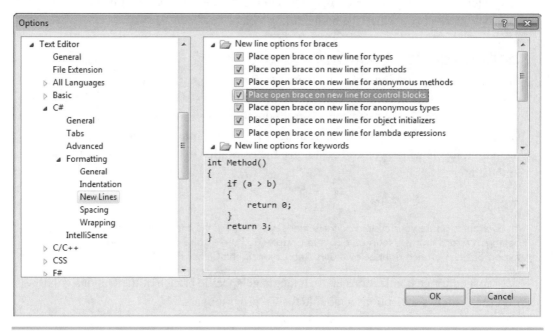

Figure 2-6   C# code editor options

The Options window in Figure 2-6 is opened to Text Editor, C#, Formatting New Lines. As you can see, there are very detailed settings for even how the editor automatically formats new lines and where braces appear. If the code doesn't format the way you want it to, visit this page to set the options to what you please.

Saving Time with Snippets

Snippets are important to learn because they will save you time. A *snippet* is a set of keystrokes that form a template for a piece of code. The code for a snippet is typically something that is common in normal programming. You'll see many common statements and blocks of code in this chapter, many of which have associated snippets. This section shows you the mechanics of using snippets, and you'll see more examples throughout the rest of this chapter.

To use a snippet, begin typing the snippet prefix until the snippet acronym appears in the Intellisense completion list, press the TAB key twice, and fill in the snippet form while tabbing through each field. Press ENTER when you're done.

Since you've already learned about namespaces, I'll show you the namespace snippet. To start, open any code file and click to start typing in a part of the file outside of all code blocks, such as directly below any *using* statements but above any existing *namespace* statements. Type the letter **n** and watch the completion list go straight to the namespace element. Type an **a** and you'll see the namespace alone in the completion list, as shown in Figure 2-7.

NOTE
The CTRL-ALT-SPACE keystroke in Figure 2-7 switches between the Intellisense modes Consume First and Standard mode. In Standard mode, which shows CTRL-ALT-SPACE, typing characters automatically selects keywords. However, there are situations where you are trying to type a word that doesn't exist yet and Intellisense is too aggressive by adding the selected completion list item, instead of what you typed. In those cases, you can press the CTRL-ALT-SPACE keys to go to Consume First mode and what you've typed will be selected. You can still use the DOWN ARROW key on your keyboard in Consume First mode to select the highlighted term in the completion list.

Figure 2-7   Using snippets

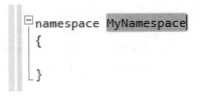

Figure 2-8 Filling in the Snippet template

You can identify snippets in the completion list by the torn paper icon. At this point, you can press the TAB key to complete the namespace keyword. Then press TAB again to produce a template where you can fill out the highlighted fields. Figure 2-8 shows the results of creating a namespace snippet by typing **n** and pressing TAB, TAB.

As shown in Figure 2-8, you would type in the *Namespace* name in the highlighted form field to replace *MyNamespace,* which is placeholder text. For templates with more fields, you would press the TAB key to move between fields. In the case of the namespace shown in Figure 2-8, there is only one field in the template to complete.

VB offers a couple of ways to add snippets: by typing prefixes or via a pick list. To see how VB snippets work, place your carat inside of the *Module1* module, underneath *End Main* (not inside of the *Main* block). Type **Su** and press TAB, and notice that VS creates a *Sub* (method) along with a template containing a field for filling out the *Sub* snippet.

Another way to add VB snippets is to type a **?** and press TAB. You'll receive a pick list, as shown in Figure 2-9. You can navigate this pick list to find the snippet you need, as classified in one of the folders. VB ships with many more built-in snippets than for C#.

Now that you know how to use snippets, let's move on to the different types of statements you can have in C# and VB and how snippets work with those statements.

```
Insert Snippet:

Module
        📁 Application - Compiling, Resources, and Settings
        📁 Code Patterns - If, For Each, Try Catch, Property, etc
        📁 Data - LINQ, XML, Designer, ADO.NET
        📁 Fundamentals - Collections, Data Types, File System, Math
        📁 Office Development
        📁 Other - Connectivity, Crystal Reports, Security, Workflow
        📁 Windows Forms Applications
        📁 Windows System - Logging, Processes, Registry, Services
        📁 WPF
```

Figure 2-9 VB snippet pick list

Coding Expressions and Statements

There are various types of statements you can write with both C# and VB, including assignment, method invocations, branching, and loops. We'll start off by looking at primitive types, such as integers and strings, and then I'll show how to build expressions and set values by performing assignments. Then you'll learn about branching statements, such as if and switch in C# or the case statement in VB. Finally, you'll learn about various loops, such as for and while. I describe these language features in general terms because they differ between C# and VB, but you'll learn that the concepts are essentially the same.

Before writing any code, you should know how Intellisense works; it is an important productivity tool that reduces keystrokes for common coding scenarios.

Making Intellisense Work for You

Previously, you saw how snippets work. Snippets use Intellisense to show a completion list. Intellisense is integrated into the VS editor, allowing you to complete statements with a minimum number of keystrokes. The following walkthrough shows you how to use Intellisense, as we add the following line to the *Main* method. Don't type anything yet; just follow along to see how Intellisense works:

C#:

```
Console.WriteLine("Hello from Visual Studio 2010!");
```

VB:

```
Console.WriteLine("Hello from Visual Studio 2010!")
```

The following steps show you how VS helps you save keystrokes:

1. Inside the braces of the *Main* method, type **c** and notice how the Intellisense window appears, with a list of all available identifiers that start with **c**. This list is called a completion list.

2. Type **o** and notice that the completion list filters all but those identifiers that begin with **co**.

3. Type **n** and you'll see that the only identifier available is **Console**. This is what we want, and you only needed to type three characters to get there.

4. At this point most people press the ENTER or TAB key to let VS finish typing Console, but that is effectively a waste of a keystroke.

You know that there is a dot operator between *Console* and *WriteLine*, so go ahead and type the period character, which causes VS to display "**Console.**" in the editor and show you a new completion list that contains members of the *Console* class that you can now choose from.

NOTE
So, I'll admit that I spent a couple paragraphs trying to explain to you how to save a single keystroke, but that's not the only thing you should get out of the explanation. The real value is in knowing that there are a lot of these detailed options available to increase your productivity. Every time you take advantage of a new VS option, you raise the notch of productivity just a little higher.

5. Now type **write** and notice that both *Write* and *WriteLine* appear in the completion list. Now type the letter **l** and notice that *WriteLine* is the only option left in the completion list.

NOTE
If you've typed **WriteLine** a few times, you'll notice that the completion list goes straight to *WriteLine* after a few characters, rather than just *Write*. This is because Intellisense remembers your most frequently used identifiers and will select them from the list first. If you continue to type, Intellisense will then highlight those identifiers with exact matches. Notice the checked option in Figure 2-10; Intellisense preselects most recently used members, showing that this behavior is turned on by default.

6. Save another keystroke and press the (key to let VS finish the *WriteLine* method name.

7. At this point, you can finish typing the statement, resulting in a *Main* method that looks like this:

C#:

```
static void Main(string[] args)
{
    Console.WriteLine("Hello from Visual Studio 2010!");
}
```

VB:

```
Sub Main()
    Console.WriteLine("Hello from Visual Studio 2010!")
End Sub
```

If you're a C# developer and want to change Intellisense options, open Tools | Options and select Text Editor | C# | Intellisense, and you'll see the Intellisense options in Figure 2-10. This option isn't available for VB.

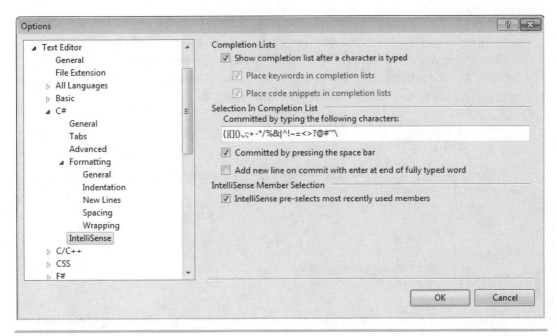

Figure 2-10   Intellisense options

Notice that there is a text box titled "Committed by typing the following characters," which contains a set of characters that will cause VS to type the rest of the selected identifier in the completion list plus the character you typed. Referring back to Step 4, this is how you know that a period commits the current selection.

You now have a program that does something; it can print a message to the console. The next section will explain how you can run this program.

Running Programs

In VS, you can run a program either with or without debugging. *Debugging* is the process of finding errors in your code. If you run with debugging, you'll be able to set break points and step through code, as will be described in Chapter 6. Running without debugging allows you to run the application, avoiding any breakpoints that might have been set.

To run without debugging, either select Debug | Start Without Debugging or press CTRL-F5. This will run the Command Prompt window, where you'll see the words "Hello from Visual Studio 2010!" or whatever you asked the computer to write, on the screen. The Command Prompt window will stay open until you press ENTER or close the window.

To run with debugging, either select Debug | Start Debugging or press F5. Because of the way the application is coded so far, the Command Prompt window will quickly run and close; you might miss it if you blink your eyes. To prevent this, you can add a *Console.ReadKey* statement below *Console.WriteLine,* which will keep the window open until you press any key. Here's the updated *Main* method:

C#:

```
static void Main(string[] args)
{
    Console.WriteLine("Hello from Visual Studio 2010!");
    Console.ReadKey();
}
```

VB:

```
Sub Main()
    Console.WriteLine("Hello from Visual Studio 2010!")
    Console.ReadKey()
End Sub
```

Pressing F5 will show "Hello from Visual Studio 2010!" on the Command Prompt window, just as when running without debugging.

To understand why there are two options, think about the difference between just running a program and debugging. If you run a program, you want it to stay open until you close it. However, if you are debugging a program, you have most likely set a breakpoint and will step through the code as you debug. When your debugging session is over, you want the program to close so that you can start coding again right away.

Now that you know how to add code to the *Main* method and run it, you can begin looking at the building blocks of algorithms, starting in the next section.

Primitive Types and Expressions

The basic elements of any code you write will include primitive types and expressions, as explained in the following sections.

Primitive Types

You can define variables in your programs whose type is one of the primitive types. *Variables* can hold values that you can read, manipulate, and write. There are different types of variables, and the type specifies what kind of data the variable can have. In .NET there are primitive types (aka built-in) and custom types. The custom types are types that you create yourself and are specific to the program you are writing. For example, if you are writing a program to manage the customers for your business, then you would create a type that could be used as the type of a variable for holding customer types. You'll

VB	C#	.NET	Description
Byte	byte	Byte	8-bit unsigned integer
SByte	sbyte	SByte	8-bit signed integer
Short	short	Int16	16-bit signed integer
UInt16	ushort	UInt16	16-bit unsigned integer
Integer	int	Int32	32-bit signed integer
UInt32	uint	UInt32	32-bit unsigned integer
Long	long	Int64	64-bit signed integer
UInt64	ulong	UInt64	64-bit unsigned integer
Single	float	Single	32-bit floating point
Double	double	Double	64-bit floating point
Boolean	bool	Boolean	true or false
Char	Char	Char	16-bit Unicode character
Decimal	decimal	Decimal	96-bit decimal (used for money)
String	string	String	String of Unicode characters

Table 2-2   Primitive Types

learn how to create custom types later. First, you need to learn about primitive types. The primitive types are part of the programming languages and built into .NET. A primitive type is the most basic type of data that you can work with in .NET, which can't be broken into smaller pieces. In contrast, a custom type can be made up of one or more primitive types, such as a Customer type that would have a name, an address, and possibly more bits of data that are primitive types. Table 2-2 lists the primitive types and descriptions.

Looking at Table 2-2, remember that C# is case-sensitive and all of the primitive types are lowercase. You can also see a third column for .NET types. Occasionally, you'll see code that uses the .NET type, which aliases the C# and VB language-specific types. The following example shows how to declare a 32-bit signed integer in both C# and VB, along with the .NET type:

C#:

```
int age1;
Int32 age2;
```

VB:

```
Dim age1 as Integer
Dim age2 as Int32
```

Consistent with Table 2-2, C# uses *int* and VB uses *Integer* as their native type definitions for a 32-bit signed integer. Additionally, you see age defined in both C# and VB using the .NET type, *Int32*. Notice that the .NET type is the same in both languages. In fact, the .NET type will always be the same for every language that runs in .NET. Each language has its own syntax for the .NET types, and each of the language-specific types is said to *alias* the .NET type.

Expressions

When performing computations in your code, you'll do so through *expressions,* which are a combination of variables, operators (such as addition or multiplication), or referencing other class members. Here's an expression that performs a mathematical calculation and assigns the result to an integer variable:

C#:

```
int result = 3 + 5 * 7;
```

VB:

```
Dim result As Int32 = 3 + 5 * 7
```

A variable that was named result in this example is a C# type *int* or a VB type *Int32,* as specified in Table 2-2. The variable could be named pretty much anything you want; I chose the word *result* for this example. The type of our new variable *result* in the VB example is *Int32,* which is a primitive .NET type. You could have used the VB keyword *Integer,* which is an alias for Int32 instead. The expression is *3 + 5 * 7,* which contains the operators + (addition) and * (multiplication) and is calculated and assigned to *result* when the program runs. The value of *result* will be 38 because expressions use standard algebraic precedence. In the preceding example, *5 * 7* is calculated first, multiplication has precedence, and that result is added to 3.

You can modify the order of operations with parentheses. Here's an example that adds 3 to 5 and then multiplies by 7:

C#:

```
int differentResult = (3 + 5) * 7;
```

VB:

```
Dim differentResult As Int32 = (3 + 5) * 7
```

Because of the grouping with parentheses, *differentResult* will have the value 56 after this statement executes.

The Ternary and Immediate If Operators

The C# ternary and VB immediate if operators allow you to test a condition and return a different value depending on whether that condition is true or false. Listing 2-2 shows how the ternary and immediate if operators work.

Listing 2-2   A ternary operator example

C#:

```
int bankAccount = 0;
string accountString = bankAccount == 0 ? "checking" : "savings";
```

VB:

```
Dim accountString As String =
    IIf(bankAccount = 0, "checking", "saving")
```

The conditional part of this operator evaluates if *bankAccount* is equal to 0 or not when the program runs (commonly known as "at runtime"). Whenever the condition is true, the first expression, the one following the question mark for C# or following the comma for VB, "checking" in this case, will be returned. Otherwise, if the condition evaluates to false, the second expression, following the colon for C# or after the second comma for VB, will be returned. That returned value, either the string "checking" or "savings" in this case, is assigned to the *accountString* variable that was declared.

NOTE
In earlier versions of the VB programming language, you were required to place an underline at the end of a statement that continued to the next line. In the latest version of VB, line continuations are optional. If you've programmed in VB before, the missing statement continuation underline might have caught your attention, but it is now perfectly legal.

Enums

An *enum* allows you to specify a set of values that are easy to read in code. The example I'll use is to create an enum that lists types of bank accounts, such as checking, savings, and loan. To create an enum, open a new file by right-clicking the project, select Add | New Item | Code File, call the file BankAccounts.cs (or BankAccounts.vb), and you'll have a blank file. Type the enum in Listing 2-3.

Listing 2-3 An example of an enum

C#:

```
public enum BankAccount
{
    Checking,
    Saving,
    Loan
}
```

VB:

```
Enum BankAccount
    Checking
    Saving
    Loan
End Enum
```

Listing 2-4 shows how you can use the *BankAccount* enum:

Listing 2-4 Using an enum

C#:

```
BankAccount accountType = BankAccount.Checking;

string message =
    accountType == BankAccount.Checking ?
        "Bank Account is Checking" :
        "Bank Account is Saving";
```

VB:

```
Dim accountType As BankAccount = BankAccount.Checking

Dim message =
    IIf(accountType = BankAccount.Checking,
        "Bank Account is Checking",
        "Bank Account is Saving")
```

The *accountType* enum variable is a *BankAccount* and is initialized to have the value of the *Checking* member of *BankAccount.* The next statement uses a ternary operator to check the value of *accountType,* evaluating whether it is *Checking.* If so, *message* is assigned with the first string. Otherwise, *message* is assigned with the second string. Of course, we know it's the first string because the example is so simple that you can see it is coded that way.

Branching Statements

A branching statement allows you to take one path of many, depending on a condition. For example, consider the case for giving a customer a discount based on whether that customer is a preferred customer. The condition is whether the customer is preferred or not, and the paths are to give a discount or charge the entire price. Two primary types of branching statements are *if* and *switch* (*Select Case* in VB). The following sections show you how to branch your logic using *if* and *switch* statements.

Expressions

If statements allow you to perform an action only if the specified condition evaluates to true at runtime. Here's an example that prints a statement to the console if the contents of variable *result* is greater than 48 using the > (greater than) operator:

C#:

```
if (result > 48)
{
    Console.WriteLine("result is > 48");
}
```

VB:

```
If result > 48 Then
    Console.WriteLine("Result is > 48")
End If
```

C# curly braces are optional if you only have one statement to run after the *if* when the condition evaluates to true, but the curly braces are required when you want two or more statements to run (also known as "to execute") should the condition be true. The condition must evaluate to either a Boolean true or false. Additionally, you can have an *else* clause that executes when the *if* condition is false. A clause is just another way to say that an item is a part of another statement. The *else* keyword isn't used as a statement

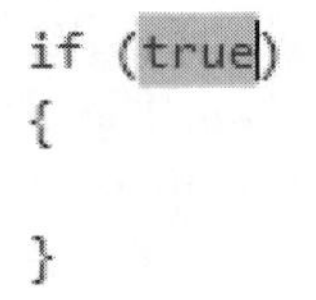

```
if (true)
{

}
```

Figure 2-11 The C# *if* statement snippet template

itself, so we call it a clause because it can be part of an *if* statement. An example of an *else* clause is shown here:

C#:

```
if (result > 48)
{
    Console.WriteLine("result is > 48");
}
else
{
    Console.WriteLine("result is <= 48");
}
```

VB:

```
If result > 48 Then
    Console.WriteLine("Result is > 48")
Else
    Console.WriteLine("Result is <= 48")
End If
```

As the preceding example shows, if *result* is not greater than 48, then it must be less than or equal to 48.

if and *else* Snippets

The *if* snippet creates a template for you to build an *if* statement. To use the *if* snippet, type **if** and press TAB, TAB; you'll see the template in Figure 2-11 for C# or Figure 2-12 for VB.

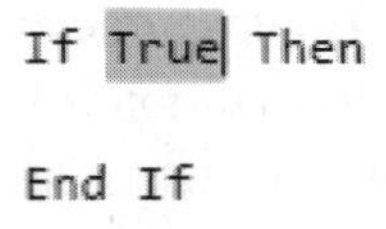

```
If True Then

End If
```

Figure 2-12 The VB *if* statement snippet template

As shown in Figure 2-11, the template brings you to a highlighted field for specifying the condition of the *if* statement. For C#, type the condition you want evaluated and press ENTER; the snippet completes by placing your carat within the *if* statement block. For VB, just place your cursor where you want to begin typing next.

In C#, the *else* statement snippet is similar to *if.* Type **else** and press TAB, TAB—the *else* template appears with the carat between the blocks of the *else.* There isn't a VB *else* snippet; just type **Else** between the last statement of the *If* and the *End If.*

Switch/Select Statements

A *switch* statement (*Select Case* statement for VB) tells the computer to evaluate one or many conditions and branch appropriately. Here's an example that will perform different actions depending on the value of a name variable:

C#:

```csharp
var name = "Megan";

switch (name)
{
    case "Joe":
        Console.WriteLine("Name is Joe");
        break;
    case "Megan":
        Console.WriteLine("Name is Megan");
        break;
    default:
        Console.WriteLine("Unknown Name");
        break;
}
```

VB:

```vb
Dim name As String = "Megan"

Select Case name
    Case "Joe"
        Console.WriteLine("Name is Joe")
    Case "Megan"
        Console.WriteLine("Name is Megan")
    Case Else
        Console.WriteLine("Unknown name")
End Select
```

In the C# example, you can see the keyword *switch* with the value being evaluated in parentheses. The code to execute will be based on which *case* statement matches the switch value. The *default* case executes when there isn't a match. The *break* keyword

```
switch (switch_on)
{
      default:
}
```

Figure 2-13 A switch snippet template

is required. When the program executes a *break* statement, it stops executing the *switch* statement and begins executing the next statement after the last curly brace of the *switch* statement.

For the VB example, the *Select Case* statement uses *name* as the condition and executes code based on which case matches *name*. The *Case Else* code block will run if no other cases match.

Switch Statement Snippets

There are two scenarios for *switch* statement snippets: a minimal *switch* statement and an expanded switch with enum cases. First, try the minimal *switch* statement by typing **sw** and pressing TAB, TAB, resulting in the *switch* statement in Figure 2-13.

You would replace the *switch_on* in Figure 2-13 with a value you want to use in the switch statement. After pressing ENTER, you'll see the snippet expand to a *switch* statement with a default case, as follows:

```
switch (name)
{
    default:
        break;
}
```

VB Select statements work similar to the C# *switch*; type **Se** and press TAB, TAB; you'll see the VB template shown in Figure 2-14.

```
Select Case VariableName
       Case 1

       Case 2

       Case Else
```

Figure 2-14 The Select Case snippet template

In C#, you normally just add the *case* statements you need. However, there is a special feature of the switch snippet that makes it even more efficient to use enums, creating a case for each enum value automatically. In the following example, we use the *accountType* variable of the enum type *BankAccount* from Listing 2-3. To see how the *switch* statement works with enums, type **sw** and press TAB, TAB ; you'll see the switch template with the condition field highlighted. Type **accountType** in the field and press ENTER. The switch snippet will automatically generate cases for each of the *BankAccount* enum members as follows:

```
switch (accountType)
{
    case BankAccount.Checking:
        break;
    case BankAccount.Saving:
        break;
    case BankAccount.Loan:
        break;
    default:
        break;
}
```

The enum comes through as a convenience that is easy to read and minimizes potential spelling mistakes when using strings. Now that you know how branching statements work, let's move on to loops.

Loops

You can perform four different types of loops: *for, for each, while,* and *do.* The following sections explain how loops work.

For Loops

For loops allow you to specify the number of times to execute a block of statements. Here's an example:

C#:

```
for (int i = 0; i < 3; i++)
{
    Console.WriteLine("i = " + i);
}
```

VB:

```
For i As Integer = 0 To 2
    Console.WriteLine("i = " & i)
Next
```

```
for (int i = 0; i < 3; i++)
{
    Console.WriteLine("i = " + i);
}
```

Figure 2-15 The C# for loop snippet template

In the preceding C# loop, *i* is a variable of type *int,* the loop will continue to execute as long as *i* is less than 3, and *i* will be incremented by one every time after the loop executes. The condition, *i < 3,* is evaluated before the loop executes, and the loop will not execute if the condition evaluates to false.

The VB *For* loop initializes *i* as an integer, iterating (repeating) three times from 0 to 2, inclusive.

The *for* Loop Snippet

To use the C# *for* loop snippet, type **fo** and press TAB, TAB; you'll see the snippet template in Figure 2-15.

NOTE
The + and & operators from the preceding code example perform string concatenation. Although *i* is an integer, it will be converted to a string prior to concatenation.

The same key sequence (**fo,** TAB, TAB) works for VB *For* loop snippets too, except that you'll see the snippet template in Figure 2-16.

The C# *for* loop snippet template is different from previous templates in that you have two fields to fill out. First, name your *indexer,* which defaults to *i,* and then press TAB, which moves the focus to the loop size field, containing *Length* as the placeholder. If you like the variable name *i,* which is an understood convention, just press the TAB key and set the length of the loop. You'll end up with a *for* loop and the carat inside of the block.

For Each Loops

For each loops let you execute a block of code on every value of an array or collection. Arrays store objects in memory as a list. Collections are more sophisticated than arrays

```
For index As Integer = 1 To 10

Next
```

Figure 2-16 The VB *For* loop snippet template

and hold objects in memory in different forms, which could be Stack, List, Queue, and more. Here's an example that loops on an array of strings:

C#:

```
string[] people = { "Megan", "Joe", "Silvia" };

foreach (var person in people)
{
    Console.WriteLine(person);
}
```

VB:

```
Dim people = {"Megan", "Joe", "Silvia"}

For Each person As String In people
    Console.WriteLine(person)
Next
```

In this example, *people* is an array of strings that contains three specific strings of text. The block of the loop will execute three times, once for each item in the array. Each iteration through the loop assigns the current name to *person*.

The *For Each* Loop Snippet

To add code using a *for each* snippet in C#, type **fore** and press TAB, TAB, which results in the snippet template shown in Figure 2-17.

The *for each* loop snippet gives you three fields to complete. The *var* is an implicit type specifier that allows you to avoid specifying the type of item; the compiler figures that out for you, saving you from some keystrokes. The item field will be a collection element type. You may leave *var* as is or provide an explicit type, which would be *string* in this case. You can tab through the fields to add meaningful identifiers for the item and collection you need to iterate through.

To execute the VB *For Each* snippet, type **?**, TAB, **C**, ENTER, **C**, ENTER, **f**, ENTER and you'll see the *For Each* loop template shown in Figure 2-18.

```
foreach (var item in collection)
{

}
```

Figure 2-17   The C# *for each* loop snippet template

```
For Each Item As String In CollectionObject

Next
```

Figure 2-18 The VB *For Each* loop snippet template

While Loops

A *while* loop will allow a block of code to execute as long as a specified condition is true. Here's an example that does a countdown of numbers:

C#:

```csharp
int count = 3;

while (count > 0)
{
    Console.WriteLine("count: " + count);
    count--;
}
```

VB:

```vb
Dim count As Integer = 3

While count > 0
    Console.WriteLine("count: " & count)
    count -= 1
End While
```

The *while* loop executes as long as *count* is greater than 0. Since *count* is 3 and will decrement by one each time through the loop, the value will change from 3 to 2 to 1 and then the loop won't execute anymore. Be careful not to create endless loops.

The *while* Loop Snippet

To create a *while* loop snippet, type **wh** and press TAB, TAB; and you'll see the snippet template in Figure 2-19 (C#) or Figure 2-20 (VB).

For C#, filling in the condition and pressing ENTER places the carat inside the *while* loop block.

```csharp
while (true)
{

}
```

Figure 2-19 The C# while loop snippet template

```
While True

End While
```

Figure 2-20   The VB while loop snippet template

Do Loops

You can use a *do* loop if you want the code in the loop to execute at least one time. Here's an example that demonstrates a simple menu that obtains user input:

C#:

```
string response = "";

do
{
    Console.Write("Press 'Q' and Enter to break: ");
    response = Console.ReadLine();
} while (response != "Q");
```

VB:

```
Do
    Console.Write("Press Q and Enter to break: ")
    response = Console.ReadLine()
Loop While response <> "Q"
```

In this example, you'll always get the prompt for **Press 'Q' and Enter to break:**. The *Console.ReadLine* reads the user input, which is of type *string*. If the input is a string that contains only a capital **Q**, the loop will end.

VB has another variation of loops that use the *Until* keyword, as follows:

```
Do
    Console.Write("Press Q and Enter to break: ")
    response = Console.ReadLine()
Loop Until response = "Q"
```

In this code, you can see that the *Until* condition will continue looping while the condition is not true, which is opposite of the *Do Loop While*.

The Do Loop Snippet

To use the *do* loop snippet, type **do** and press TAB, TAB; you'll see the *do* loop template shown in Figure 2-21.

```
do
{

} while (true);
```

Figure 2-21   The C# *do* loop snippet template

```
Do

Loop While True
```

Figure 2-22 The VB *do* loop while snippet template

Fill in the condition on the *do* loop and press ENTER, placing the carat in the *do* loop block.

For a VB *Do* snippet type **?**, TAB, **C**, ENTER, **C**, ENTER, and use an arrow key to select the variant of *Do* loop that you want. Figure 2-22 shows an example of the Do Loop While template.

Summary

Working with languages is a core skill when building .NET applications. Two of the most used languages in .NET are C# and VB, which is why this chapter is dedicated to those two languages. You learned about types, expressions, statements, code blocks, conditions, and branching. Additionally, you learned some of the essential features of VS for writing code, such as the code editor, bookmarks, Intellisense, and snippets.

Chapter 3 takes you to the next step in your language journey, teaching you about classes and the various members you can code as part of classes.

Chapter 3

Learning Just Enough
C# and VB.NET:
Types and Members

Key Skills & Concepts

- Create Classes

- Write Methods

- Code Fields and Properties

A *type* is a general term for classes, modules, enums, and more. This chapter will specifically discuss the class type, which allows you to create your own custom types. You'll also see the value of a class when you learn about class members. You'll see how the field, method, and property class members can be used. We'll start with learning how to create and use classes.

Creating Classes

Previously, you learned about the primitive types, which are built into languages and alias the underlying .NET types. You can also create your own types, via classes, which you can instantiate and create objects with. The following section explains how to create a class and then instantiate an object from it.

Class Syntax

To create a new custom class definition, right-click the project, select Add | Class, name the class **Employee** for this example, and type the file extension **.cs** for C# or **.vb** for VB; then click Add (VS will add this file extension for you if you don't). You'll see a file with the same code as Listing 3-1.

Listing 3-1   A new Employee class

C#:

```
using System;
using System.Collections.Generic;
using System.Linq;
using System.Text;

namespace FirstProgram
```

```
{
    public class Employee
    {
        public string FirstName;
    }
}
```

VB:

```
Public Class Employee
 Public Dim FirstName As String
End Class
```

The C# *Employee* class is nearly the same as the *Program* class that you created in the preceding chapter, except that the class name here is *Employee*. In VB, you've only created a module before, and the *Employee* class is your first class for this book. You can add members to a class, which could be events, fields, methods, and properties. Listing 3-1 shows an example of a field, *FirstName,* and you'll learn about events, methods, and properties in later sections of this chapter. A *field* is a variable in a class that holds information specific to that class.

Listing 3-2 shows how to instantiate an object of type Employee, which is your new custom type, and use it. You would put this code inside of *Main* or another method. You'll learn more about methods in the later section "Writing Methods."

Listing 3-2   Code that uses a class

C#:

```
Employee emp = new Employee();
emp.FirstName = "Joe";
```

VB:

```
Dim emp As New Employee
emp.FirstName = "Joe"
```

In Listing 3-2, you can see that *emp* is a variable declared as type *Employee.* The C# *new Employee()* or VB *New Employee* clause creates a new instance of *Employee,* and you can see that this new instance is being assigned to *emp.* With that new instance, via the *emp* variable, you can access the Employee object, including its instance members. In Listing 3-2, the *FirstName* field of that particular instance of Employee is assigned a string value of "Joe". Here you see that an object can contain data.

Now that you can define a new class, create an instance from that class, and use it, the next section shows you another feature of classes called inheritance.

Class Inheritance

One class can reuse the members of another through a feature known as *inheritance*. In programming terms, we say a child class can derive from a parent class and that child class will inherit members (such as fields and methods) of the parent class that the parent class allows to be inherited. The following example will create a *Cashier* class that derives from the *Employee* class. To create this class, right-click the project, select Add | Class, and name the class **Cashier**. Listing 3-3 shows the new class and modifications for implementing inheritance.

Listing 3-3   Class inheritance

C#:

```
using System;
using System.Collections.Generic;
using System.Linq;
using System.Text;

namespace FirstProgram
{
    public class Cashier : Employee
    {
    }
}
```

VB:

```
Public Class Cashier
    Inherits Employee

End Class
```

The C# inheritance relationship is indicated by the colon after the *Cashier* identifier, followed by the class being derived from, *Employee*. In VB, you write the keyword *Inherits,* on a new line, followed by the class being derived from. Essentially, this means that *Cashier* has all of the same members as *Employee*. Listing 3-4 demonstrates the benefits of inheritance.

Listing 3-4   Code using inheritance

C#:

```
Cashier cashr = new Cashier();
cashr.FirstName = "May";
```

VB:

```
Dim cashr As New Cashier
cashr.FirstName = "May"
```

According to Listing 3-4, *Cashier* does not have a field named *FirstName*. However, *Employee* does have a *FirstName* field and *Cashier* derives from *Employee*. Because of inheritance, *Cashier* automatically inherits *FirstName*, and the code in Listing 3-4 is perfectly legal. Inheritance can be thought of as specialization in the sense that, in this example, Cashier is a specialized kind of Employee. To take advantage of this specialization, you could add a new field to your new Cashier class called "assignedCashRegister" where now, not only does the Cashier class have the fields and methods of Employee, it is able to hold the value for a specific cash register name or number. An instance of the Employee class would not be able to contain this information. The .NET Framework uses inheritance extensively to offer you reusable class libraries.

TIP
You can often use the phrase "is a" to describe the relationship between inherited classes when starting from the child class. For example, you can say "Cashier *is an* Employee." If you apply this phrase technique to your software design and the sentence sounds logically correct, then you've probably used inheritance correctly.

The class Snippet
C# has a class snippet, but VB doesn't. Before using the class snippet, create a new class file by right-clicking the project, select Add | New Item | Code File, and name the file **Manager**. You'll now have a blank file to work with. To use the class snippet, type **cl** and press TAB, TAB; and you'll see the snippet template in Figure 3-1.

Figure 3-1   The C# class snippet template

Just type in the class name in the field and press ENTER. The carat will locate to the inside of the class block. Now that you know how to create classes, you'll need to know how to add members, starting with methods.

Writing Methods

You can divide your algorithms into blocks of code called *methods.* In different programming languages, methods are called functions, procedures, or subroutines. I'll use the term method as a generic term, except when I need to be more specific. You've already used methods when coding *Console.WriteLine,* where *WriteLine* is a method of the *Console* class. A method contains one or more statements. Reasons for creating methods include the ability to modularize your code, isolate complex operations in one place, or group a common operation that can be reused in multiple places. The following sections show you how to declare and use methods.

Declaring and Using a Method

To start off, I'll show you a very simple method so that you can see the syntax and understand the program flow. Listing 3-5 will move the *Console.Writeline* statement from the *Main* method discussed in Chapter 2 into a new containing method and then add a statement to the *Main* method that calls the new method.

Listing 3-5   Declaring and calling a method

C# (Program.cs)

```csharp
using System;
using System.Collections.Generic;
using System.Linq;
using System.Text;

namespace FirstProgram
{
    class Program
    {
        static void Main(string[] args)
        {
            MessagePrinter msgPrint = new MessagePrinter();
            msgPrint.PrintMessageInstance();
        }
    }
}
```

C#: (MessagePrinter.cs)

```csharp
using System;
using System.Collections.Generic;
using System.Linq;
using System.Text;

namespace FirstProgram
{
    class MessagePrinter
    {
        public static void PrintMessageStatic()
        {
            Console.WriteLine("Hello from a static method.");
        }

        public void PrintMessageInstance()
        {
            Console.WriteLine("Hello from an instance method.");
        }
    }
}
```

VB (Module1.vb):

```vbnet
Module Module1
    Sub Main()
        MessagePrinter.PrintMessageShared()

        Dim msgPrint As New MessagePrinter()
        msgPrinter.PrintMessageInstance()
    End Sub
End Module
```

VB (MessagePrinter.vb)

```vbnet
Public Class MessagePrinter
    Public Shared Sub PrintMessageShared()
        Console.WriteLine("Hello from a shared method.")
    End Sub

    Public Sub PrintMessageInstance()
        Console.WriteLine("Hello from an instance method.")
    End Sub
End Class
```

Listing 3-5 has two types of methods, static and instance. In VB, shared methods are the same as static. You can tell which type of method each is because static methods have the *static* modifier (*shared* in VB), but instance methods don't have a static (or shared in VB) modifier. First, let's look at the static (shared) method declaration, and then you'll see how it's called.

The static (shared in VB) method, *PrintMessageStatic* (*PrintMessageShared* in VB) has a public access modifier, which means that any other code using the containing class, *MessagePrinter,* will be able to see the method. If you didn't include the public access modifier, the method would automatically default to being private and only other code residing within the *MessagePrinter* class would be able to use that method.

PrintMessageStatic has a *void* keyword, meaning that this method does not return a value. In VB, you indicate that a method does not return a value by making it a *Sub,* as was done in Listing 3-5. Later, you'll learn how to create a method that does return values to its calling code that invokes this method. The empty parameter list appended to the *PrintMessageStatic* (*PrintMessageShared* in VB) means that there are not any parameters for this method. Parameters allow callers to pass information to the method; a subject we'll discuss soon.

Within the method block, you can see that there is a *Console.WriteLine* statement. You can add as many statements as you need for the purpose of the method. Next, we'll examine how *PrintMessageStatic* (*PrintMessageShared* in VB) is called, which the following code repeats from Listing 3-5:

C#:

```
Program.PrintMessageStatic();
```

VB:

```
MessagePrinter.PrintMessageShared()
```

Viewing the preceding example, which shows a statement inside of the *Main* method, you can see the call to *Program.PrintMessageStatic* (*PrintMessageShared* in VB). Notice that the class (aka type) that contains all the methods is named *MessagePrinter.* In C#, a static method is called through its containing type, which is why you call *PrintMessageStatic* with the *Program* prefix. In VB, you can invoke shared methods through either the method's type or an instance of that type. We discuss instance methods next.

The next method, *PrintMessageInstance,* is an instance method; it has no static modifier. The rest of the method definition mirrors that of the *PrintMessageStatic* method.

Since *PrintMethodInstance* is an instance method, you call it differently; through an instance of its containing type, which the following code repeats from Listing 3-5:

C#:

```
MessagePrinter msgPrint = new MessagePrinter();
msgPrint.PrintMessageInstance();
```

VB:

```
Dim msgPrint As New MessagePrinter()
msgPrinter.PrintMessageInstance()
```

As this example shows, the type of *msgPrint* is *MessagePrinter.* Using the statement *new MessagePrinter* creates a new instance of *MessagePrinter* at runtime, which is assigned to the *msgPrint* variable. Now that you've created an instance of a *MessagePrinter* and *msgPrint* has a reference to that instance, you can call the instance method, *PrintMessageInstance,* via the *msgPrint* variable. Next, let's look at how to add parameters to a method and discuss why that's important.

Declaring Parameters and Passing Arguments

Passing parameters to a method is a great way to make code more reusable. For example, what if you had a method that printed a report containing the names of all customers? It wouldn't make sense to create one method for each customer, especially when the list changes all the time. Listing 3-6 shows a method that takes a list of customers and prints a report with customer names.

Listing 3-6   Declaring a method that takes parameters

C# (Program.cs):

```
using System;
using System.Collections.Generic;
using System.Linq;
using System.Text;

namespace FirstProgram
{
    class Program
    {
        static void Main(string[] args)
```

```
        {
            MessagePrinter msgPrint = new MessagePrinter();

            string[] customerNames = { "Jones", "Smith", "Mayo" };
            string reportTitle = "Important Customer Report";

            msgPrint.PrintCustomerReport(customerNames, reportTitle);
        }
}
```

C# (MessagePrinter.cs):

```
using System;
using System.Collections.Generic;
using System.Linq;
using System.Text;

namespace FirstProgram
{
        public void PrintCustomerReport(
            string[] customers, string title = "Customer Report")
        {
            Console.WriteLine(title);
            Console.WriteLine();

            foreach (var name in customers)
            {
                Console.WriteLine(name);
            }
        }
    }
}
```

VB (Module1.vb):

```
Module Module1
    Sub Main()
        Dim msgPrint As New MessagePrinter()

        Dim customerNames = {"Jones", "Smith", "Mayo"}
        Dim reportTitle As String = "Important Customer Report"

        msgPrint.PrintCustomerReport(customerNames, reportTitle)
    End Sub
End Module
```

VB (MessagePrinter.vb):

```
Public Class MessagePrinter
    Sub PrintCustomerReport(ByVal customers As String(), ByVal title
As String)
        Console.WriteLine(title)
        Console.WriteLine()

        For Each name In customers
            Console.WriteLine(name)
        Next
    End Sub
End Class
```

Parameters are a comma-separated list of identifiers, along with the type of each identifier, which clearly indicates what type of parameter the method is expecting. In Listing 3-6, the *PrintCustomerReport* method has two parameters: *title* of type string and *customers* of type string array. The method displays the title in the console window when you run the program, displays a blank line, and then iterates through the list, displaying each customer name to the console.

You can see how the *Main* method creates a new instance of *MessagePrinter,* which *msgPrint* points to, and then calls *PrintCustomerReport* using *msgPrint.* The arguments being passed, *reportTitle* and *customerNames,* match the position and types of the parameters for *PrintCustomerReport,* which are of the correct types that the *PrintCustomerReport* method is expecting.

In the preceding example, the calling code must provide arguments, actual data, for all parameters. However, you can specify parameters as being optional, allowing you to omit arguments for the optional parameters if you like. Here's a modification to *PrintCustomerReport* where the title becomes an optional parameter:

C#:

```
public void PrintCustomerReport(
    string[] customers, string title = "Customer Report")
{
    Console.WriteLine(title);
    Console.WriteLine();

    foreach (var name in customers)
    {
        Console.WriteLine(name);
    }
}
```

VB:

```
Sub PrintCustomerReport(
    ByVal customers As String(),
    Optional ByVal title As String = "Customer Report")

    Console.WriteLine(title)
    Console.WriteLine()

    For Each name In customers
        Console.WriteLine(name)
    Next
End Sub
```

The preceding code requires callers to pass an array of customers, but it does not require a title. When writing methods, optional parameters must be listed last. Here's a method call without the optional parameter:

C#:

```
custProg.PrintCustomerReport(customerNames);
```

VB:

```
msgPrint.PrintCustomerReport(customerNames)
```

Because the caller didn't pass an argument for *title,* the value of *title* inside of *PrintCustomerReport* becomes the default value assigned to the *title* parameter.

In addition to passing arguments to methods, you can receive values returned from methods.

Returning Data and Using Method Results

It is common to call methods that return values. To demonstrate the proper syntax, Listing 3-7 contains a method that accepts an *int* and returns the squared value of that *int.* Calling code then assigns the return value from the method to a variable and displays the value on the console window. Create a new class named *Calc.cs* or *Calc. vb* to hold the new method.

Listing 3-7   Returning values from methods

C# (Program.cs):

```
using System;
using System.Collections.Generic;
using System.Linq;
using System.Text;
```

```
namespace FirstProgram
{
    class Program
    {
        static void Main(string[] args)
        {
            Calc mathProg = new Calc();

            int squaredInt = mathProg.SquareInt(3);
            Console.WriteLine("3 squared is " + squaredInt);

            Console.ReadKey();
        }
    }
}
```

C# (Calc.cs):

```
using System;
using System.Collections.Generic;
using System.Linq;
using System.Text;

namespace FirstProgram
{
    public class Calc
    {
        public int SquareInt(int number)
        {
            return number * number;
        }
    }
}
```

VB (Module1.vb):

```
Module Module1

    Sub Main()
        Dim mathProg As New Calc()
        Dim squaredInt As Integer = mathProg.SquareInt(3)
        Console.WriteLine("3 squared is " & squaredInt)
    End Sub
End Module
```

```
Sub MySub()

End Sub
```

Figure 3-2   The VB sub snippet template

VB (Calc.vb):

```
Public Class Calc
    Public Function SquareInt(ByVal number As Integer) As Integer
        Return number * number
    End Function
End Class
```

For the C# example, notice how the return type of the *SquareInt* method is type *int,* rather than the keyword *void* that was used in our methods before. Whenever you specify a return type, the method must return something whose type is the same as the return type declared. In the preceding example, the return type is declared as *int*; therefore, the method guarantees that the result of the calculation is type *int*. The *Main* method has a couple of statements that invoke this method and display the results to the console.

In the VB example, the method is now a *Function*. *Sub* methods don't return values. Notice how the function signature appends *As Integer* after the parameter list, which indicates that the return type of the function is *Integer.*

Method Snippets

C# doesn't have snippets for writing methods (although you could create your own snippets), but VB does. In VB, type **Sub**, TAB, TAB; producing the template shown in Figure 3-2; or **Fun**, TAB, TAB; producing the template shown in Figure 3-3.

```
Function MyFunc() As Integer
    Return 0
End Function
```

Figure 3-3   The VB function snippet template

Coding Fields and Properties

A *field* is a variable that is a member of a class (type), as opposed to variables that are declared inside of methods, which are called *local variables* or locally scoped variables. *Properties* are type members that give you functionality that is a cross between fields and methods. You can read and write to a property just as you can to a field. Additionally, you can define code that runs whenever you read to or write from a property, similar to methods. The following sections define fields and properties.

Declaring and Using Fields

As stated, a field is a variable that is a member of a class (or some other container, such as a *struct,* which is very similar to a class). This provides the benefit of having the field and the data it contains available to all of the other members of the class (as well as to any deriving classes, via inheritance, depending on the field's access modifier). To demonstrate how a field is declared and used, the example in Listing 3-8 simulates a bank account that has a field of type decimal named *currentBalance,* which holds an account balance. The class has two methods: *Credit* and *Debit. Credit* increases the value of *currentBalance,* and *Debit* decreases the value of *currentBalance.*

Listing 3-8   Using fields and properties

C#:

```
using System;
using System.Collections.Generic;
using System.Linq;
using System.Text;

namespace FirstProgram
{
    class Program
    {
        private decimal accountBalance = 100m;

        static void Main(string[] args)
        {
            Program account = new Program();
            account.Credit(100m);
            account.Debit(50m);
            Console.WriteLine("Balance: " + account.CurrentBalance);

            Console.ReadKey();
        }
    }
}
```

```csharp
        public void Credit(decimal amount)
        {
            accountBalance += amount;
        }

        public void Debit(decimal amount)
        {
            accountBalance -= amount;
        }

        public decimal CurrentBalance
        {
            get
            {
                return accountBalance;
            }
            set
            {
                if (value < 0)
                {
                    // charge fee
                }
                accountBalance = value;
            }
        }
    }
}
```

VB:

```vb
Module Module1
Private Dim accountBalance As Decimal = 100
    Sub Main()          Credit(100)
        Debit(50)
        Console.WriteLine("Balance: " & CurrentBalance)

        Console.ReadKey()
    End Sub

    Sub Credit(ByVal amount As Decimal)
        accountBalance += amount
    End Sub

    Sub Debit(ByVal amount As Decimal)
        accountBalance -= amount
    End Sub
```

```
    Public Property CurrentBalance() As Decimal
        Get
            Return accountBalance
        End Get
        Set(ByVal value As Decimal)

            If value < 0 Then
                ' charge fee
            End If

            accountBalance = value
        End Set
    End Property
End Module
```

Look at where *accountBalance* is declared: at the beginning of the *Program (Module1* in VB) class block. It is at the same scope as *Main* and other methods, meaning that it is a member of *Program (Module1* in VB), just like *Main, Credit,* and *Debit.* When variables like *accountBalance* are declared as class members, as opposed to local variables that are declared inside of method blocks, they are called fields. The *accountBalance* is type decimal, which is a good choice for holding financial values.

The *accountBalance* field has a *private* modifier, which means that it can only be used by members of the same class. The implementations of *Credit* and *Debit,* respectively, increase and decrease the value of *accountBalance.* Since *Credit* and *Debit* are members of the same class as *accountBalance,* they're allowed to read from and write to *accountBalance.*

Main invokes *Credit* and *Debit* to change the value of the *accountBalance* field. Additionally, *Main* displays the value of *accountBalance* in the console window through a property named *CurrentBalance.* The next section explains how the *CurrentBalance* property works.

Declaring and Using Properties

Properties are class members that you use just like a field, but the difference is that you can add specialized logic when reading from or writing to a property. Listing 3-8 contains an example of a property, *CurrentBalance,* repeated as follows for your convenience:

C#:

```
public decimal CurrentBalance
{
    get
    {
        return accountBalance;
    }
```

```
    set
    {
        if (value < 0)
        {
            // charge fee
        }
        accountBalance = value;
    }
```

VB:

```
Public Property CurrentBalance() As Decimal
    Get
        Return accountBalance
    End Get
    Set(ByVal value As Decimal)

        If value < 0 Then
            ' charge fee
        End If

        accountBalance = value
    End Set
End Property
```

Properties have accessors, named *get* and *set,* that allow you to add special logic when the property is used. When you read from a property, only the *get* accessor code executes, and the *set* accessor code only executes when you assign a value to a property. In the preceding example, the *get* accessor returns the value of *currentBalance* with no modifications. If there were some logic to apply, like calculating interest in addition to the current balance, the *get* accessor might have contained the logic for that calculation prior to returning the value. The *set* accessor does have logic that checks the value to see if it is less than zero, which could happen if a customer overdrew his or her account. If the value is less than zero, then you could implement logic to charge the customer a fee for the overdraft. The *value* keyword contains the value being assigned to the property, and the previous *set* accessor assigns *value* to the *accountBalance* field. The following statement from the *Main* method in Listing 3-8 reads from *CurrentBalance,* effectively executing the get accessor, which returns the value of *currentBalance*:

C#:

```
Console.WriteLine("Balance: " + account.CurrentBalance);
```

VB:

```
Console.WriteLine("Balance: " & CurrentBalance)
```

Since the *CurrentBalance* property returns the value of the *accountBalance* field, the *Console.WriteLine* statement will print the value read from *CurrentBalance* to the command line.

Many of the properties you'll write will simply be wrappers around current object state with no other logic, as in Listing 3-9.

Listing 3-9   Property that wraps object state with no logic

C#:

```csharp
private string m_firstName;

public string FirstName
{
    get
    {
        return m_firstName;
    }
    set
    {
        m_firstName = value;
    }
}
```

VB:

```vb
Private m_firstName As String
Public Property FirstName() As String
    Get
        Return m_firstName
    End Get
    Set(ByVal value As String)
        m_firstName = value
    End Set
End Property
```

In Listing 3-9, you can see that *m_firstName,* commonly referred to as a backing field, is a private variable and that the *FirstName* property only returns *m_firstName* from the *get* accessor and assigns the value to *m_firstName* in the *set* accessor. Since this is so common, you can save syntax by using an automatic property, as shown in Listing 3-10.

Listing 3-10   Auto-implemented properties

C#:

```
public string FirstName { get; set; }
```

VB:

```
Public Property FirstName As String
```

```
public int MyProperty { get; set; }
```

Figure 3-4   The C# property snippet template

The automatic property, *FirstName,* is logically equivalent to the expanded *FirstName* with accessors and backing field. Behind the scenes, the compiler produces the expanded version where the backing field is guaranteed to have a unique name to avoid conflicts. Do not overlook that when you use automatic properties, you cannot add your own code that runs inside the *get* or *set* accessors.

The Property Snippet

To create a property snippet, type **pro** and press TAB, TAB; and you'll see the property snippet template shown in Figure 3-4 for C# or Figure 3-5 for VB.

A C# property snippet template creates an automatic property by default, but the VB snippet template is a normal property with full *get* and *set* accessors.

```
Private newPropertyValue As String
Public Property NewProperty() As String
    Get
        Return newPropertyValue
    End Get
    Set(ByVal value As String)
        newPropertyValue = value
    End Set
End Property
```

Figure 3-5   The VB property snippet template

Summary

You are now able to create classes to define your own custom types. After learning how to create classes and use class instances, also known as objects, you learned how to add fields, methods, and properties to your class definition. The methods discussion was more in-depth, showing you how to define parameters and return values. You also learned how to define both auto-implemented and normal properties, and you learned a little about class inheritance.

The next chapter moves you up a level in language skills by showing you how to create another type, called an interface. You'll also learn how to add another type of class member, events.

Chapter 4

Learning Just Enough C# and VB.NET: Intermediate Syntax

Key Skills & Concepts

- Use Delegates and Events

- Implement Interfaces

- Code with Arrays and Generics

I n previous chapters, you learned basic syntax and how to create your own types. This chapter rounds out the bare essentials of what you need to know with delegates and events, interfaces, and a quick introduction to arrays and generics. This material doesn't attempt to be too advanced, but gives you enough information to understand the language concepts involved. You'll see all of these language features being used throughout the book, and it's good to have some background on what they mean. Let's start off with delegates and events.

Understanding Delegates and Events

Sometimes you need to write flexible code that performs general operations. For example, when the designers of the .NET Framework created user interfaces, they added reusable controls, such as buttons, list boxes, and grids. When writing these controls, the framework designers didn't know how we would use them. For example, how would anyone know what we wanted our code to do when a user clicks a button on the user interface? So, these controls have interaction points built in so that they can communicate with your program; these interaction points are called events. These events fire whenever a user performs an action such as a button click or a list box selection. We write code to hook up these events to some other code in our program that we want to run when that event happens, such as when the user clicks a button, and this is what delegates are used for.

An *event* defines the type of notifications that a object can provide, and a *delegate* allows us to connect the event to the code we want to run.

This section will show you the mechanics of how delegates and events work, but you should understand that the mechanics may seem somewhat abstract at first. Delegates and events are most often used when you're working with .NET Framework technologies that use them, such as Windows Presentation Foundation (WPF), Silverlight, and ASP.NET. What you'll want to do is get a feel for the mechanics right now and then refer back to this discussion when you encounter delegates and events in later chapters.

The next section will add more logic to the *set* accessor in *CurrentBalance* in the next listing and raise an event for the calling code.

Events

An event is a type of class member that allows your class or class instance to notify any other code about things that happen within that class. To help you understand the use of events, this section will associate an event with the *accountBalance* of an account. Listing 4-1 is a modified version of Listing 3-8 from Chapter 3. It additionally has an event and logic that raises the event.

To see how an event can be useful, consider a program that uses a class that manages accounts. There could be different types of accounts, such as checking or savings. If a customer performs an overdraft, the consequences probably vary by what type of account is being used. However, all you want is a generalized account class that can be used by any bank account type and doesn't know what the overdraft rules are, which makes the class more reusable in different scenarios. Therefore, you can give the account class an event that will fire off a notification whenever an overdraft occurs. Then, within your specialized checking account class instance, for example, you can register something called an event handler so that the instance of the class knows each time the overdraft event occurs via the handler.

In Listing 4-1, the *CurrentBalance* property is modified to raise (or fire off) an *OverDraft* event whenever the assigned value is less than 0. The *Main* method hooks up another method that will run whenever that event occurs. I'll explain the event first and then follow up with a discussion of how to hook up a method that listens for when the event is raised and receives the message sent by the event.

Listing 4-1 Event demo

C#:

```
using System;
using System.Collections.Generic;
using System.Linq;
using System.Text;

namespace FirstProgram
{
    class Program
    {
        private decimal accountBalance = 100m;

        static void Main(string[] args)
```

```csharp
    {
        Program account = new Program();
        account.OverDraft += new EventHandler(account_OverDraft);
        account.CurrentBalance = -1;

        Console.ReadKey();
    }

    public decimal CurrentBalance
    {
        get
        {
            return accountBalance;
        }
        set
        {
            if (value < 0)
            {
                if (OverDraft != null)
                {
                    OverDraft(this, EventArgs.Empty);
                }
            }
            accountBalance = value;
        }
    }

    static void account_OverDraft(object sender, EventArgs e)
    {
        Console.WriteLine("Overdraft Occurred");
    }

    public event EventHandler OverDraft;
    }
}
```

VB:

```vb
Module Module1
    Private Dim accountBalance As Decimal = 100

    Sub Main()
        AddHandler OverDraft, AddressOf AccountOverdraft
        CurrentBalance = -1
```

```
            Console.ReadKey()
        End Sub

        Public Event OverDraft As EventHandler

        Public Sub AccountOverdraft (ByVal sender As Object, ByVal e As
    EventArgs)
            Console.WriteLine("Overdraft Occurred")
        End Sub
    End Module
```

Listing 4-1 has an event named *OverDraft*. The *OverDraft* event is *public* and is declared with the *event* keyword. The *EventHandler* is a delegate, which we'll discuss soon, but it basically allows you to define the type of method that can be called by the event. It defines the communication contract that must be adhered to by any code that wishes to listen for the event to fire.

Look at the *set* accessor of the *CurrentBalance* property, inside of the *if* statement where it determines if value is less than 0. The C# example has another *if* statement to see if the *OverDraft* event is equal to *null*.

In C# when an event is equal to *null,* it means that nothing has subscribed to be notified by the event—in essence, no other code is listening. However, when the C# event is not *null,* then this indicates that some code somewhere has hooked up a method to be called when the event fires. That method is said to be listening for the event. So, assuming that the caller has hooked up a method, the *OverDraft* event is fired. This check for *null* is important. If nothing is listening for the event (and our code knows this to be the case when the event is *null*), and we raise or fire the event by calling *OverDraft(this, EventArgs.Empty),* an error (null reference exception) would occur at runtime whenever a value is set into the *CurrentBalance* property. The arguments to the C# event mean that the current object (which is the *Program* class instance), *this,* and an empty *EventArgs* will be passed as the event message to any other methods that were hooked up to this event. It is interesting to note that many methods can be hooked up to your event (or none at all), and each will be notified in turn when your event fires. You should start to see that events really are a form of almost spontaneous communication within your program.

In VB, you don't need to check for *Nothing* (equivalent to C# *null*).

The preceding discussion talked about a method that is hooked up to the event and executes (receives a message) whenever the event fires. The next section explains how to use a delegate to specify what this method is.

Delegates

Delegates let you hook up methods as the receiver to specific events. The delegate specifies the allowable signature, the number of arguments, and their types, of a method that is allowed to be hooked up to the event as a listener or handler. The *EventHandler* delegate type for the *OverDraft* event specifies what the signature of a method should be, as follows:

C#:

```
public event EventHandler OverDraft;
```

VB:

```
Public Event OverDraft As EventHandler
```

This *EventHandler* is a class that belongs to the .NET Framework class library, and it, by definition, specifies that any methods hooked up to the *OverDraft* event must define two parameters: an *object* of any type and an *EventArgs* class. *EventHandler* also specifies that the method does not return a value explicitly. The following method, *account_OverDraft* (*AccountOverdraft* in VB), matches the predefined *EventHandler* signature:

C#:

```
static void account_OverDraft(object sender, EventArgs e)
{
    Console.WriteLine("Overdraft Occurred");
}
```

VB :

```
Public Sub AccountOverdraft(ByVal sender As Object, ByVal e As
EventArgs)
    Console.WriteLine("Overdraft Occurred")
End Sub
```

Notice that the C# *account_OverDraft* (*AccountOverdraft* in VB) doesn't return a value and has two parameters that are type *object* and *EventArgs,* respectively. The *account_OverDraft* (*AccountOverdraft* in VB) method is hooked up to the *OverDraft* event in the *Main* method in Listing 4-1, repeated as follows for your convenience:

C#:

```
account.OverDraft += new EventHandler(account_OverDraft);
account.CurrentBalance = -1;
```

VB:

```
AddHandler OverDraft, AddressOf AccountOverdraft
CurrentBalance = -1
```

In the C# example, the += syntax is for assigning a delegate to an event (using a bit of programmer slang, this syntax is commonly said to "wire up an event"). The VB example uses *AddHandler* and *AddressOf* to assign the *AccountOverDraft* method to the *OverDraft* event. In the C# example, the delegate is a new instance of *EventHandler* and the event is *OverDraft*. If you remember, the delegate type of *OverDraft* is *Eventhandler*, which defines the precise message contract.

The next piece of the puzzle is the method to be notified when the event happens. This method is the parameter given to the new *EventHandler* delegate instance. You saw earlier where the *account_OverDraft* (*AccountOverDraft* in VB) method had the signature specified by the *EventHandler* class, making it possible for our method to be specified as the new *EventHandler* parameter. With that one line of code (the one with the += statement), *account_OverDraft* (*AccountOverdraft* in VB) is now hooked up to the *OverDraft* event. This means that when the value of *CurrentBalance* is set to less than zero via the *set* accessor of *CurrentBalance,* the *OverDraft* event gets fired because the *OverDraft(this, EventArgs.Empty)* is called, which then invokes the *account_OverDraft* (*AccountOverdraft* in VB) method (the method we wired up to the event), which in turn executes its code.

One more note about events: you'll see them used extensively in graphical user interface (GUI) code. Think about the GUI code that has reusable components, like buttons and list boxes. Every time the user clicks a button or selects an item in the list box, you want code to execute and do something, like perhaps save the user's data somewhere. You do this through events: a *Click* event for the button and a *SelectedItemChanged* for the list box. This is the standard way that you program GUIs; you have an event and you define a method to hook up to that event so that your running program can do some work in reaction to the user.

Event, Delegate, and Handler Code Completion

While there isn't a snippet, per se, to create an event or delegate, in C# there is Intellisense Code Completion support for hooking a delegate up to an event, which also generates the handler method. The process takes two steps: delegate and handler creation. To get started, type the reference to the event's containing instance, the event name, and +=. As soon as you type the = sign, you'll see a tooltip like the one in Figure 4-1.

```
account.OverDraft +=
```
new EventHandler(account_OverDraft);   (Press TAB to insert)

Figure 4-1   Code completion for delegate assignment

Figure 4-2 Code completion for handler method creation

As you can see, the Editor pops up a tooltip instructing you to type TAB to create a new delegate instance. Type TAB and Code Completion will pop up another tooltip for creating the handler method, as shown in Figure 4-2.

In Figure 4-2, you can see that Code Completion is suggesting a method name for you. You have a choice of pressing TAB or changing the method name and then pressing TAB. Either way, you have a fast way to hook up a handler method to an event via the event's delegate type.

Just as a delegate provides an interface to a method that is a contract basically to describe how to communicate, you can also define interfaces to classes to communicate with them in a specified way, and these are intuitively named . . . interfaces.

Implementing Interfaces

Another language feature that gives you flexibility is interfaces. An *interface* can be useful if you want to have a group of classes that can be interchanged at any time, yet you need to write the same operations for each of these classes. Essentially, you want to write the code that uses the class only one time, but still switch what the actual class is. That's where interfaces come in. The interface creates a contract that each of the interchangeable classes must adhere to. So, if the interface says that all classes that implement the interface have method A and property B, then every class that implements the interface must have method A and property B; the compiler enforces this like a contract that cannot be broken. The following sections show you how to write an interface and then build a couple of classes that implement that interface. Finally, you'll see how to write code against the interface.

One important fact to remember about interfaces is that they don't have any code other than definitions of members. This definition of members is the contract of the interface. You are the one who must to write a class that contains the members of the interface, and you must write the code that provides an implementation of the interface members. A common point of confusion is that an interface does not have any executable code, but the classes that implement the interfaces do.

The following sections show you how to create an interface, how to create a class that has code (that you've written) to implement the interface contract, and how to write code that operates on the classes that implement (guarantee the contract of) the interface.

Creating an Interface

To create an interface, right-click the project in Solution Explorer, select Add | New Item, select Code under the language branch in Installed Templates, and select the Interface item. Name the Interface **IAccount** and click Add. By standard convention, you will always name any interface class you create with a name that starts with an uppercase letter *I*. You'll see the interface in Listing 4-2 added to your project:

Listing 4-2   An interface

C#:

```
using System;
using System.Collections.Generic;
using System.Linq;
using System.Text;

namespace FirstProgram
{
    public interface IAccount
    {
        void Credit(decimal amount);
        void Debit(decimal amount);
        decimal CurrentBalance { get; set; }
    }
}
```

VB:

```
Public Interface IAccount
    Sub Credit(ByVal amount As Decimal)
    Sub Debit(ByVal amount As Decimal)
    Property CurrentBalance As Decimal
End Interface
```

After you've added the interface, you'll need to make modifications to make the code match Listing 4-2. Notice that the *IAccount* members don't have an implementation and so appear incomplete because they have no lines of code. Also, each member doesn't have a public modifier, because interface members are implicitly public. The following sections show you how to build the classes that implement the *IAccount* interface; there, you should begin to see the benefit that an interface can bring.

Making Classes Implement the Interface

To create a class, right-click the project in Solution Explorer, select Add | New Item, select Code under the language branch in Installed Templates, and select the Class item. Name the class **Checking** and click Add. Using the same procedure as Checking, add another class, but name it **Saving**. Listings 4-3 and 4-4 show the two new classes.

Listing 4-3 Checking class that implements IAccount interface

C#:

```csharp
using System;
using System.Collections.Generic;
using System.Linq;
using System.Text;

namespace FirstProgram
{
    class Checking : IAccount
    {
        public void Credit(decimal amount)
        {
            // implement checking logic
            CurrentBalance += amount;
            Console.Writeline("Added " + amount.ToString() +
                                    " to Checking Account");
        }

        public void Debit(decimal amount)
        {
            // implement checking logic
            CurrentBalance -= amount;
            Console.Writeline("Debited " + amount.ToString() +
                            " from Checking Account");
        }

        public decimal CurrentBalance { get; set; }
    }
}
```

VB:

```vbnet
Public Class Checking
    Implements IAccount

    Public Sub Credit(ByVal amount As Decimal) Implements IAccount.
Credit
```

```vb
    ' Implement Checking logic
    CurrentBalance += amount
        Console.Writeline("Added " & amount.ToString() &
                        " to Checking Account")
End Sub

Public Sub Debit(ByVal amount As Decimal) Implements IAccount.Debit
    ' Implement Checking logic
    CurrentBalance -= amount
        Console.Writeline("Debited " + amount.ToString() +
                        " from Checking Account")
End Sub

Public Property CurrentBalance As Decimal Implements IAccount.
CurrentBalance
End Class
```

Listing 4-4   Saving class that implements IAccount interface

C#:

```csharp
using System;
using System.Collections.Generic;
using System.Linq;
using System.Text;

namespace FirstProgram
{
    class Saving : IAccount
    {
        public void Credit(decimal amount)
        {
            // implement savings logic
            CurrentBalance += amount;
            Console.Writeline("Added " + amount.ToString() +
                            " to Saving Account");
        }

        public void Debit(decimal amount)
        {
            // implement savings logic
            CurrentBalance -= amount;
            Console.Writeline("Debited " + amount.ToString() +
                            " from Saving Account");
        }
```

```
            public decimal CurrentBalance { get; set; }
        }
    }
```

VB:

```
Public Class Saving
    Implements IAccount

    Public Sub Credit(ByVal amount As Decimal) Implements IAccount.
Credit
        ' Implement Saving logic
        CurrentBalance += amount
            Console.Writeline("Added " & amount.ToString() &
                            " to Saving Account")
    End Sub

    Public Sub Debit(ByVal amount As Decimal) Implements IAccount.Debit
        ' Implement Saving logic
        CurrentBalance -= amount
            Console.Writeline("Debited " + amount.ToString() +
                            " from Saving Account")
    End Sub

    Public Property CurrentBalance As Decimal
        Implements IAccount.CurrentBalance
End Class
```

In both Listings 4-3 and 4-4, notice that the *Checking* and *Saving,* respectively, implement the *IAccount* interface, repeated as follows:

C#:

```
class Checking : IAccount
```

and

```
class Saving : IAccount
```

VB:

```
Public Class Checking
    Implements IAccount
```

and

```
Public Class Saving
    Implements IAccount
```

In the C# listing, following the class name by a colon and then the interface name specifies that the class will implement the interface. The VB listing uses the *Implements* keyword to indicate that *Checking* and *Saving* classes implement the *IAccount* interface. Looking at both *Checking* and *Saving,* you can see that they have the *Credit, Debit,* and *CurrentBalance* members that are specified in *IAccount.* The primary difference is that *IAccount* doesn't have an implementation, but you wrote an implementation for *Checking* and *Saving.* Listings 4-3 and 4-4 simplify the implementation of the interface so that you don't have to read a lot of code that doesn't add to the purpose of the listing to show you how a class implements an interface. In reality, the code in the methods would be different for *Checking* and *Saving* because they are different account types with different business rules.

You've created an interface and written classes to implement the contract of that interface. The next section gives you a couple of examples to help clarify the practical use of interfaces.

Writing Code That Uses an Interface

One of the best ways to understand the value of interfaces is to see a problem that interfaces solve. In this section, I'll show you some code that accesses the *Checking* and *Saving* classes individually, essentially duplicating code. Then I'll show you how to write the code a single time with interfaces. The particular example runs a payroll by obtaining instances of *Checking* and *Saving* classes and crediting each class, which is synonymous with employees being paid. Starting with the bad example, Listing 4-5 shows how this code works.

Listing 4-5 Processing payroll with explicit checking and saving class instances

C#:

```
public void ProcessPayrollForCheckingAndSavingAccounts()
{
    Checking[] checkAccounts = GetCheckingAccounts();

    foreach (var checkAcct in checkAccounts)
    {
        checkAcct.Credit(500);
    }
```

```csharp
        Saving[] savingAccounts = GetSavingAccounts();

        foreach (var savingAcct in savingAccounts)
        {
            savingAcct.Credit(500);
        }
    }

    public Checking[] GetCheckingAccounts()
    {
        Checking[] chkAccts = new Checking[2];

        chkAccts[0] = new Checking();
        chkAccts[1] = new Checking();

        return chkAccts;
    }

    public Saving[] GetSavingAccounts()
    {
        int numberOfAccounts = 5;
        Saving[] savAccts = new Saving[numberOfAccounts];

        for (int i = 0; i < numberOfAccounts; i++)
        {
            savAccts[i] = new Saving();
        }

        return savAccts;
    }
```

VB:

```vb
Sub ProcessPayrollForCheckingAndSavingAccounts()
    Dim checkAccounts As Checking() = GetCheckingAccounts()

    For Each checkAcct In checkAccounts
        checkAcct.Credit(500)
    Next

    Dim savingAccounts As Saving() = GetSavingsAccounts()

    For Each savingAcct In savingAccounts
        savingAcct.Credit(500)
    Next
End Sub
```

```
Function GetCheckingAccounts() As Checking()
    Dim chkAccts(1) As Checking

    chkAccts(0) = New Checking()
    chkAccts(1) = New Checking()

    Return chkAccts
End Function

Function GetSavingsAccounts() As Saving()
    Dim numberOfAccounts As Integer = 5
    Dim savAccts(numberOfAccounts) As Saving

    For i As Integer = 0 To numberOfAccounts
        savAccts(i) = New Saving()
    Next

    Return savAccts
End Function
```

To save space, I haven't included the entire application in Listing 4-5, which is available with the source code for this book via the McGraw-Hill Web site. To understand how it works, imagine that you've written the following code in the *Main* method:

C#:

```
Program bank = new Program();
bank.ProcessPayrollForCheckingAndSavingAccounts();
```

VB:

```
ProcessPayrollForCheckingAndSavingAccounts()
```

Walking through the code, let's start at the *ProcessPayrollForCheckingAndSaving Accounts* method. You can see how the algorithm calls *GetCheckingAccounts* to retrieve an array of *Checking* objects. If you recall, an array is a list of elements of a specified type, that type being *Checking* in this case. The algorithm goes on to iterate through the *Checking* objects, invoking *Credit* on each to add 500 to the account. Some employees want their paychecks in *Checking,* but others might want their paychecks to go into *Saving* (or some other account). Therefore, the algorithm calls *GetSavingsAccounts* to get a list of those accounts for employees who want their paychecks to go into their savings. You'll notice that the algorithm inside of *GetSavingsAccounts* is different from

GetCheckingAccounts, which I did on purpose so that you'll see different ways to use loops; but this doesn't affect the calling code because it's encapsulated in individual methods. The point to make here is that *GetCheckingAccounts* will only return *Checking* class instances and *GetSavingsAccounts* will only return *Saving* class instances. The rest of the algorithm in the *ProcessPayrollForCheckingAndSavingAccounts* method mirrors the processing for *Checking.*

What should catch your attention is the duplication of code in the *ProcessPayroll ForCheckingAndSavingAccounts* method. Although the *Credit* methods of *Checking* and *Saving* should have different implementations, the code calling *Credit* can be the same, eliminating duplication. Listing 4-6 shows how to take advantage of the fact that both *Checking* and *Saving* implement the same interface, *IAccount.* You'll see how to call *Credit* on any *IAccount*-derived type with one algorithm, eliminating the duplication you saw in Listing 4-5.

Listing 4-6   Processing payroll through the IAccount interface

C#:

```
public void ProcessPayrollForAllAccounts()
{
    IAccount[] accounts = GetAllAccounts();

    foreach (var account in accounts)
    {
        account.Credit(1000);
    }
}

public IAccount[] GetAllAccounts()
{
    IAccount[] allAccounts = new IAccount[4];

    allAccounts[0] = new Checking();
    allAccounts[1] = new Saving();
    allAccounts[2] = new Checking();
    allAccounts[3] = new Saving();

    return allAccounts;
}
```

VB:

```vb
Sub ProcessPayrollForAllAccounts()
    Dim accounts As IAccount() = GetAllAccounts()

    For Each account In accounts
        account.Credit(1000)
    Next
End Sub

Function GetAllAccounts() As IAccount()
    Dim allAccounts(3) As IAccount

    allAccounts(0) = New Checking()
    allAccounts(1) = New Saving()
    allAccounts(2) = New Checking()
    allAccounts(3) = New Saving()

    Return allAccounts
End Function
```

You can call the code in Listing 4-6 from the *Main* method like this:

C#:

```csharp
Program bank = new Program();
bank.ProcessPayrollForAllAccounts();
```

VB:

```vb
ProcessPayrollForAllAccounts()
```

Examining Listing 4-6, you can see that *accounts* is an array of *IAccount*. While you can't instantiate an interface by itself, you can assign an instance of the class that implements that interface using a variable simply declared as the interface type. In this case, *GetAllAccounts* returns a list of objects that implement *IAccount*.

Looking inside of the *GetAllAccounts* method, you can see how an array is being built with both *Checking* and *Saving* objects. Since *Checking* and *Saving* implement *IAccount,* which you saw in Listings 4-3 and 4-4, instances of *Checking* and *Saving* can be directly assigned into elements of an *IAccount* array.

Back in the *ProcessPayrollForAllAccounts* method, you can see a loop iterate through each *IAccount* instance, calling *Credit*. The reason you can call *Credit* like this is that *IAccount* defines a contract for the *Credit* method. Calling *Credit* on each instance really

```
interface IInterface
{

}
```

Figure 4-3   The C# interface snippet template

invokes the *Credit* method on the runtime *Checking* or *Saving* instance. Your code that you wrote for *Checking.Credit* and *Saving.Credit* will execute as if your code called them directly as in Listing 4-5. Also observe that we've eliminated the duplication because one algorithm, namely *IAccount.Credit( )* in our example, works on both *Checking* and *Saving* objects.

Now you can see that interfaces help you treat different types of objects as if they were the same type and helps you simplify the code you need to write when interacting with those objects, eliminating duplication. Imagine what would happen if you were tasked with adding more bank account types to this algorithm without interfaces; you would need to go into the algorithm to write duplicate code for each account type. However, now you can create the new account types and derive them from *IAccount*; the new account types automatically work in the same algorithm.

The interface Snippet

Before using the interface snippet, open a new file by right-clicking your project in VS Solution Explorer, select Add | New Item | Code File, and name the file **IInvestment.cs** (or **IInvestment.vb** in VB). You'll have a blank file to work with. To use the interface snippet, type **int** and press TAB, TAB; you'll see a snippet template similar to Figure 4-3 (C#) or Figure 4-4 (VB).

Because prefixing interfaces with *I* is an expected convention, the template highlights the identifier after *I*.

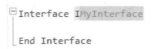

```
Interface IMyInterface

End Interface
```

Figure 4-4   The VB interface snippet template

Applying Arrays and Generics

Whatever code you write will typically need to group objects into a single collection of that object type. For this, you can use an array, which is a container that can have zero or many elements, each holding an instance of a particular type. You'll soon see how to use an array to locate the elements (items) you want. There are also generic collection classes in the .NET Framework that are even more powerful than arrays. You'll learn how to use both arrays and generic collections in this section.

Coding Arrays

You've already seen several examples of arrays being used previously in this chapter. You declare a variable of the array type, instantiate the array to a specified size, and then use the array by indexing into its elements. Listing 4-7 shows an example that demonstrates the mechanics of creating and using an array.

Listing 4-7   Creating and using an array

C#:

```
private void ArrayDemo()
{
    double[] stats = new double[3];

    stats[0] = 1.1;
    stats[1] = 2.2;
    stats[2] = 3.3;

    double sum = 0;

    for (int i = 0; i < stats.Length; i++)
    {
        sum += stats[i];
    }

    Console.WriteLine(
        stats[0] + " + " +
        stats[1] + " + " +
        stats[2] + " = " +
        sum);
}
```

VB:

```
Sub ArrayDemo()
    Dim stats(2) As Double

    stats(0) = 1.1
    stats(1) = 2.2
    stats(2) = 3.3

    Dim sum As Double = 0


    For i As Integer = 0 To 2
        sum += stats(i)
    Next

    Console.WriteLine(
        stats(0) & " + " &
        stats(1) & " + " &
        stats(2) & " = " &
        sum)
End Sub
```

In the C# example of Listing 4-7, you can see that the *stats* variable is declared as *double[ ]*, an array of type double. You must instantiate arrays, as is done by assigning *new double[3]* to *stats*, where 3 is the number of elements in the array. C# arrays are accessed via a 0-based index, meaning that *stats* has three elements with indexes 0, 1, and 2.

The VB example declares *stats* as an array of type double. Notice that the rank of the array is 2, meaning that 2 is the highest index in the array. Since the array is 0-based, *stats* contains indexes 0, 1, and 2; three elements total.

Assigning values to an array means that you use the name of the array and specify the index of the element you want to assign a value to. For example, *stats[0]* (*stats(0)* in VB) is the first element of the stats array, and you can see from the listing how each element of the stats array is assigned the values 1.1, 2.2, and 3.3. The *for* loop adds each element of the array to the *sum* variable. Finally, you can see how to read values from an array by examining the argument to the *Console.WriteLine* statement. Using the element access syntax, you can see how to read a specific element from the stats array.

An array is a fixed-size collection, and therefore somewhat limited in functionality. In practice, you'll want to use more sophisticated collections, like the *List* class, which is referred to as a generic collection. Not all collection classes in the .NET Framework are generic collections; however, generic collections are now the preferred kind of collection to use in most cases.

Coding Generics

Generics are language features that allow you to write a piece of code that will work with multiple types efficiently. A generic class definition has a placeholder for the type you want it to represent, and you use this placeholder to declare the type you want to work with. There is an entire library of generic collections in .NET as well as generic types across the entire .NET Framework Class library. Because of the volume of information required for comprehensive coverage of generics, this section will only serve as a brief introduction, giving you an example of generic use that you're most likely to see in the future. Listing 4-8 demonstrates how to declare a generic *List*. The code specifies the type of the list as a *Checking* account and then proceeds to populate the generic list and perform operations on the *Checking* elements of the generic list. Remember to include a *using* directive (*imports* for VB) for the *System.Collections.Generic* namespace near the top within your file.

Listing 4-8   Coding a generic list collection

C#:

```csharp
private void ListDemo()
{
    List<Checking> checkAccts = new List<Checking>();

    checkAccts.Add(new Checking());
    checkAccts.Add(new Checking());

    for (int i = 0; i < checkAccts.Count; i++)
    {
        Console.WriteLine(checkAccts[i].CurrentBalance);
    }
}
```

VB:

```vbnet
Sub ListDemo()
    Dim checkAccts As New List(Of Checking)

    checkAccts.Add(New Checking())
    checkAccts.Add(New Checking())


    For i As Integer = 0 To checkAccts.Count - 1
        Console.WriteLine(checkAccts(i).CurrentBalance)
    Next
End Sub
```

In .NET, the generic *List* type is declared as *List<T>*, or *List(Of T)* in VB. The *T* is a type placeholder, where you can specify any type you want. For example, you could create a *List<int>* for integers or a *List<string>* for strings, which would be *List(Of Integer)* and *List(Of String)* in VB, respectively. In Listing 4-8, you can see that *checkAccts* is declared as *List<Checking>* (*List(Of Checking)* in VB). Since a list grows dynamically to accommodate any number of elements, you use the *Add* method to add elements to the *List*. Once elements are in the *List,* you can use element access syntax, as shown in the *for* loop, to access the elements one at a time. Collections such as *List* are convenient because they have multiple convenience methods, such as *Clear, Contains, Remove,* and more.

In addition to *List,* the *System.Collections.Generic* namespace has several other generic collections, such as *Dictionary, Queue,* and *Stack.* Each generic is initialized by replacing the type parameters with the types you want to work on and then by using the specialized methods of that collection. Whenever you see the type parameter syntax, you should recognize that a generic is being used and you will have an idea of what the code means and how to read it in the documentation.

Summary

What you learned in this chapter were essential skills for upcoming chapters in the rest of the book. Knowing how delegates and events work helps you with event-driven development that is common to GUI application development. Understanding interfaces directly relates to being able to build Web services, among other uses. You'll also make regular usage of arrays and generics, and this chapter gave you the essentials to know what collections are.

Remember that this was only an introduction to C# and VB and that there is much more to learn about these languages. Of course, this book is about VS and not languages, so the next chapter is where you'll learn to build VS projects.

Part II

Learning the VS 2010 Environment

Chapter 5
Creating and
Building Projects

Key Skills & Concepts

- Work with Projects and Solutions

- Set Properties in the Properties Window

- Reference and Use Class Libraries

- Compile and Run Projects

- Use the Class Designer

Projects and solutions are VS's way of helping you organize your code for both development and deployment. For development, you have a hierarchical structure that is flexible and allows you to organize your code in a way that makes sense for you and your team. For deployment, you can build different project types that will result in executable or library files (often referred to as assemblies) that run your program when executed.

While reading this chapter, you'll learn how to use solutions and projects. You'll learn how to find settings and options for customizing projects, how to reference assemblies, and different options for compiling code. As an extra bonus, you'll learn how the Class Designer allows you to obtain a high-level visualization of your code and perform some design work. We'll begin with learning about solutions and projects.

Constructing Solutions and Projects

With VS, you can build applications that range in size and sophistication. At the most basic level, you can start a console project that contains one or more files with code, which is very simple. At higher levels of complexity, you can build enterprise-scale applications consisting of many projects of various types, organized to support large teams of developers working in unison.

VS uses a hierarchical model to help you organize your code and gives you flexibility in how a project is set up. Some features, such as solutions and projects, are well defined, but you have the freedom to add folders that help customize the arrangement of files to meet your needs.

Two organizing principles of solution and project organization will always be true: you will work with only one solution at a time and that solution will always have one or more projects. For simplicity, I'll use the term "project," but that still means that we have a project inside of a solution. Different project types have unique settings and options, but we'll start by creating a Console application, which will reduce unnecessary detail and help focus on the common features of all project types.

Creating a New Project

As a shortcut, press CTRL-SHIFT-N to open the New Project window, shown in Figure 5-1. CTRL-N will only open a single file, which you can't compile, so don't forget the SHIFT key. Of course, you can always use the menu to created a new project.

Chapter 2 describes the features of the New Project window. The process is the same any time you create a new project. VS remembers your last project type, which could be helpful if you are creating multiple projects of the same type. Make sure you select Console Application as your project type.

The way you create and name VB and C# projects are different in that all of the decisions for C# projects are made at one time, but VB divides creation into initial project creation and then saves additional information when you save the project for the first time.

C# projects allow you to configure Name, Location, Solution, and Solution Name as shown in Figure 5-1. In C#, the Name field is the name of the project you are creating, and the Solution Name field is the name of the solution. While typing the project name,

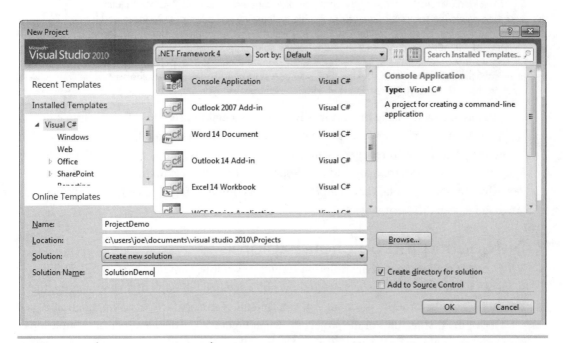

Figure 5-1 The New Project window

VS will update the Solution Name with the same name. In a multiproject solution, this might not make sense. So, first type the project name and then you can provide a name for the solution that is more appropriate. In Figure 5-1, you can see that the project is named ProjectDemo and the solution is named SolutionDemo. VS allows you to put spaces in the names. A consequence of this is that the default namespace for a project will use the project name with spaces translated to underlines; something to be aware of if your coding conventions don't allow underlines in identifier names.

If you have a very simple project and want all project files in the same folder, uncheck Create Directory For Solution. However, most applications you build will have multiple projects and leaving this box checked makes more sense because it maintains consistency between folder and solution organization. In any case, when an additional project is added to your solution, VS will always put the new project into a separate subfolder.

If you check Add To Source Control, VS will open a window for you to configure source control. Source control is a repository for you to check code into. This is especially useful for teams where each developer can check in his or her code for a common repository of source code for this solution when you create the solution. Click OK to create the solution.

TIP

If you accidentally start a project type that you didn't intend, select File | Close Solution and then delete the solution folders from the file system. VS will often put OS locks on files, so it's important to close the solution so that you will be able to delete files. The VS Recent Projects list will have an entry with the name of the solution you just deleted, but you can click that entry and VS will recognize that the solution no longer exists, prompting you to remove the entry from the list. After that, you can start over again and use the same solution/project name you intended, but with the right project type.

Starting a new Console project in VB, you only need to provide a Name parameter, which is the name of the project to create. Once the project is created, the first time you create the project, you'll receive a window that asks you for Name, Solution Name, Location, Create Directory, and Add To Source Control options that work the same as described for the previous C# example. You've accomplished the same task, regardless of language, but in different ways.

Navigating the Solution Explorer

VS creates a new project in the Solution Explorer window, shown in Figure 5-2. While other VS windows provide specialized views into specialized parts of an application, the Solution Explorer window is where you can find all of the artifacts of an application.

One of the first features of the project shown in Figure 5-2 is the hierarchical relationships. You will have only one solution. VB doesn't show the solution file by default, but you can

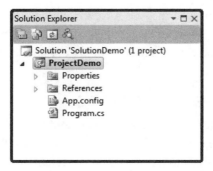

Figure 5-2 The Solution Explorer window

change this by selecting Tools | Options | Projects And Solutions and checking the box for Always Show Solution.

You can add multiple projects to a solution, as well as folders for organizing the projects. Right-click the solution name in the Solution Explorer and select Add | New Project, and you can add more projects. Add | Existing Project allows you to add a project that already exists to your opened solution. The reason this option exists is that while VS solutions associate one or more projects together as a solution unit, any single project could optionally be associated with other solutions. In other words, a single project could be shared with other solutions.

Select Add | New Solution Folder to add a folder to a solution. You can add a hierarchy of folders to a solution for organizing projects. One thing to remember about solution folders is that unlike creating folders inside a project that become physical file system folders, solution folders are logical and don't create a physical folder in your file system. If you want your file system layout to match the Solution Explorer layout with solution folders, you must create the file system folders yourself. To avoid confusion, remember that it is possible for the physical location of projects to differ from the Solution Explorer layout.

Besides organizing projects, solution folders are also useful for associating specific artifacts with your project. While solution folders are not tied to physical file system folders, they are included with source control providers, such as Visual Source Safe and Team System. One potential use of a solution folder is to include a copy of an external class library that you've built your project with. This way, whenever other members of the team check the solution out of source control, they all are working with the same files and versions. Solution folders can also be used for any type of file, including project documentation or anything else that you want to keep organized in a single place.

Depending on project type, VS hides various files associated with a project. The Solution Explorer toolbar has a Show All Files button that will show these hidden files. If you have the solution selected, all you'll see is the Add A New Solution Folder button, so you'll need to select a project before the Show All Files button will display. An example of a hidden file is the bin folder hierarchy that contains the output of your project when you compile.

Examining Property Settings

Each project has associated settings that you can configure. When you first create a project, these settings are configured for common values for that project type. However, you can modify these settings to meet your needs. Each project has a logical folder named Properties, shown previously in Figure 5-2, which will open a property setting window when you double-click the Properties (My Project in VB) folder in a project, shown in Figure 5-3.

There are multiple tabs, each with related properties grouped to the subject of each tab. Depending on project type, you might see additional tabs, but some of the tabs are common

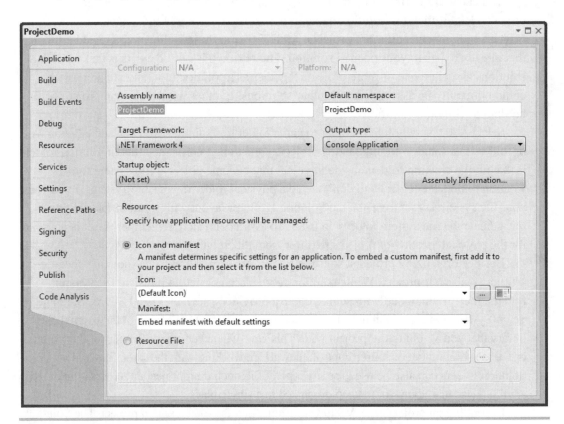

Figure 5-3 The Project Properties window

to all projects. The following sections describe each of the features of the Application settings tab.

Assembly Name

VS projects create either *.dll or *.exe assemblies. The assembly name provides the filename for this project and defaults to the name of your project. From Figure 5-3, you can see that Assembly Name is set to ProjectDemo. Since this is a Console application, the output would be a *.exe. It follows that the filename would be ProjectDemo.exe. Had the project type been a Class Library, the filename would have been ProjectDemo.dll.

Default Namespace

The *Default* namespace (*Root* namespace in VB) setting determines what the namespace will be defined automatically as whenever you add a new code file to your project. It's initially set to the name of your project. If you want the namespace of new files to be different, set the namespace here.

Target Framework

VS has .NET Framework multitargeting support, where you can work with any version of .NET between v2.0 and v4.0. Select the .NET version you need in the Target Framework combo box. VB includes this option on the Compile tab when clicking the Advanced Compile Options button. Remember to set the VB project from .NET Framework 4.0 Client Profile to .NET Framework 4.0 because later we'll be referencing a class library that is set to .NET Framework 4.0 and the target frameworks must be compatible for one assembly to reference another.

Since you can have multiple versions of .NET on the same machine as VS 2010, you can switch freely between different projects that use different .NET versions. This is particularly useful if you're a consultant working on different projects with different versions or if you're providing maintenance support on older versions of a product while doing active development work in a different project using .NET 4.0.

Output Type

An Output type (Application type in VB) is the type of assembly created when you build your project. The three types of output are Windows Application, Console Application, and Class Library. You already know how to create a Console application, which produces a *.exe assembly. Later in this chapter, you'll learn how to create a Class Library project, which produces a *.dll assembly. In Chapter 8, you'll learn how to create a Windows Application project, which is a *.exe.

TIP

If you have a WPF project, its Output Type is set to Windows Application. If you switched the Output Type of a WPF application to Console Application, you would see the Console window appear also. This might be useful for some intermediate debugging where you could emit Console.WriteLine messages. Of course, VS provides excellent debugging tools, which you'll learn about in Chapter 6, including an Output window, but this is just another option if you ever wanted it.

Startup Object

You could add multiple *Main* methods to a Console application or a WPF application, but only one *Main* method can be active at a time. The Startup object allows you to specify which class contains the *Main* method you want to use as the entry point to your application. One of the reasons you might want to do this is to start your application in different configurations, which might facilitate testing by allowing you to go straight to a part of the program without too much navigation.

Icon and Manifest

By clicking the ellipses button on the right of the icon drop-down list, you can browse to an icon file, *.ico, that will appear as your application icon.

TIP

VS ships with system icons that you can use in your own applications. Navigate to C:\Program Files\Microsoft Visual Studio 10.0\Common7\VS2010ImageLibrary\1033 and you'll see a Zip file named VS2010ImageLibrary. Your path might be different if you chose to install VS2010 somewhere other than the default. Unzip this VS2010ImageLibrary and you'll see a plethora of resources with images, audio, animations, and icons that are common to Microsoft operating systems and applications.

The manifest allows you to specify Microsoft Windows User Access Control (UAC) settings or to support a form of deployment called Click-Once, where a WPF application can be deployed from a Web page and run locally on your desktop machine. The manifest describes the application and deployment features of your Click-Once application. Since these manifests are automatically generated when you publish a Click-Once application, you normally won't ever manually build manifest files yourself; this is considered an advanced practice and includes knowledge beyond what a beginner's guide would include.

In VB, there is a UAC Settings button that allows you to directly modify the app .manifest file. This is an advanced technique that requires knowledge of the operating system UAC settings.

If you select the Resources option, you can include a Win32 resources file, which you can then access through code in your application. This is another advanced scenario beyond the scope of this book.

Assembly Information

Clicking Assembly Information shows the window in Figure 5-4. This information is included in the assembly metadata when you build your project. Most of the information in this window is self-explanatory. Since assemblies can comprise multiple files, you are allowed to vary the assembly (all files) and this file's assembly version numbers.

With .NET, you can have two-way communications with Component Object Model (COM) applications. You can enable this by allowing your assembly to have a Globally Unique Identifier (GUID) so that COM can find it, and check the COM visible box.

Leave the Neutral Language as None, unless you want the default locality to be something other than en-US, which is the locale for US English.

To see what these settings look like, press F6 to build the application, and then navigate to the location in the file system where you created the project. The location on my machine for this demo is C:\VS2010\Chapter05\SolutionDemo\ProjectDemo\bin\Debug, but yours could be different if you created your project in a different location. Regardless, you'll find the ProjectDemo.exe file in the bin\Debug folder. Right-click ProjectDemo.exe, select Properties, and click the Details tab of the ProjectDemo Properties window, shown in Figure 5-5.

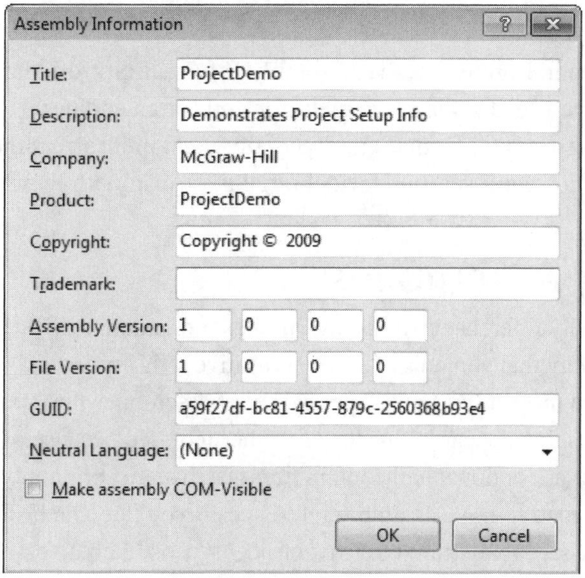

Figure 5-4   Assembly Information

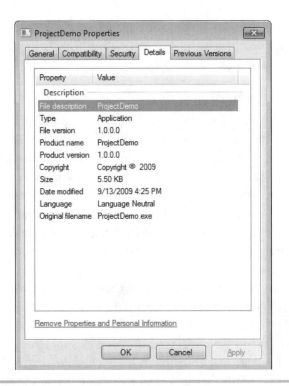

Figure 5-5   File Properties window

As you can see in Figure 5-5, the Assembly Information from the project properties is included with the file. This is convenient for you (or an end user) to be able to open the file and read pertinent information, especially version information, to know you're working with the correct assembly, for debugging, or just to know what is on your system.

Referencing Assemblies

All projects normally reference external assemblies. For example, System.dll is a .NET Framework assembly that contains all of the primitive .NET types and is normally included in every project. Each project type has a specific set of assemblies that appear in the References list. The assemblies that appear in this list are either required because of the type of project you are building or are optional and contain libraries that are commonly used for that type of project. You are free to remove assembly references if you like, but be aware that removing a reference to an assembly required for that project type is likely to result in your code not being able to compile.

Assembly references are added to a project to tell the compiler where to find the types it is using in an application. When your compiler runs, it will know what types you have in your code and looks through the set of referenced assemblies to find that type. Adding an assembly reference doesn't add all of the code from the referenced assembly to your code; it just tells the compiler where to look.

NOTE

There is often confusion around the relationship between assembly references and namespaces. A namespace *using* statement (*Imports* in VB) allows your code to be written without fully qualifying type references for types in an assembly. However, the assembly reference is just a way to tell the compiler in which specific external assembly to look to find those types: two different purposes. This confusion is exacerbated by the fact that you get the same error message from the compiler when you either are missing an assembly reference or don't have a using (Imports for VB) directive in your code for a namespace that a type resides in. Just remember to ensure that you have an assembly reference first and then add a using (Imports) directive at the top of your file.

Adding a .NET Assembly Reference

You can add references to your project by right-clicking the project and clicking Add Reference. You'll see the Add Reference window, shown in Figure 5-6. On the .NET tab of this window, you'll see a list of assemblies from the Global Assembly Cache

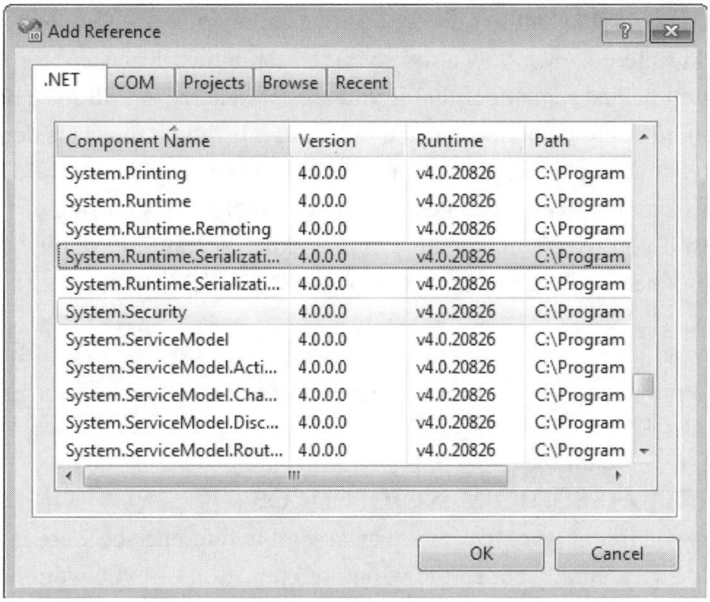

Figure 5-6 The Add Reference window

(GAC), which is a shared repository of assemblies. Microsoft and third parties will place assemblies in the GAC to make it easier to share them by any programs.

The COM tab shows all of the COM applications currently registered on your computer. For example, if you wanted to communicate with Excel, you would click the COM tab and add a reference to the version of Microsoft Office Excel that you are working with. Adding a reference to a COM object causes VS to automatically generate a new assembly, called an Interop assembly, that has stub methods that make it easy for you to perform operations on that COM object. You would need to reference the documentation for the COM object/application to determine what operations are possible, but this is a very powerful way to work with legacy applications and Microsoft Office applications that expose a COM interface.

CAUTION

If you're adding an assembly reference for a VB project, remember to open My Projects on ProjectDemo, go to the Compile tab, click the Advanced Compile Options button, and ensure that the Target Framework is set to .NET Framework 4.0 (not .NET Framework 4.0 Client Profile). The reason is that the class library project is automatically set to .NET Framework 4.0 and the target framework for both the referencing and referenced assemblies must be the same.

The Recent tab has a list of references that you've recently added to a project, which is a convenience based on the probability that if you added a reference to one project in a solution, you might want to quickly add that same reference to others. The Browse tab of the Add Reference window allows you to search the file system for a *.dll file to add as a reference. Just remember that if you are referencing a *.dll for a project in the same solution, it would be better to use the Project tab, which manages dependencies and ensures that your project is updated if the referenced project changes. File references can't know if the external *.dll changed because the external *.dll is outside of your solution. In most cases, if you're referencing an external *.dll, you don't have the code, so a project reference won't be possible. The next section explains more about project references.

NOTE

The New Projects window, CTRL-N, contains Office project types that can help you get started building Microsoft Office applications.

Managing Assembly References

Occasionally, you might want to remove an assembly reference because it isn't necessary or because you accidentally added the wrong reference. In C#, you would open the References folder, select the reference to remove, and press DELETE. In VB, you would

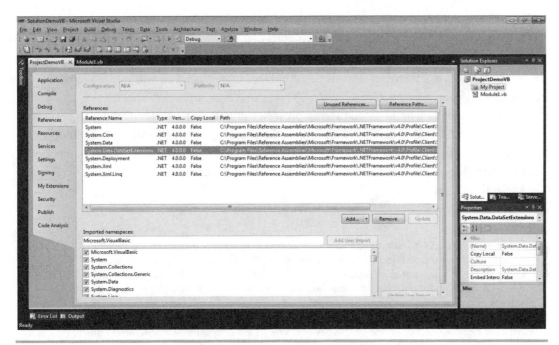

Figure 5-7   The VB My Project References tab

open the Properties window by double-clicking My Project, click the References tab,
select the reference to delete, and click Remove. Figure 5-7 shows the VB References tab.

VB includes additional functionality on the References tab. For example, you can
click Add to add a reference. You also click Unused References to remove references for
assemblies that are not being used in your code. Clicking Reference Paths allows you to
specify a folder that VS will look in to find assemblies you want to reference.

C# has a separate tab on the Properties window for managing Reference Paths. When
VS looks for referenced assemblies, it will search the current project directory, then in
the folders identified in Reference Paths, and then in folders for the list of assemblies
specified by the Add References window.

Referencing Your Own Class Libraries

There are various reasons for creating your own code libraries. For example, you might
have reusable code or want to keep your code organized into separate assemblies. To
do this, you would create Class Library projects, and then reference those class library
projects from other code. First, let's create a Class Library project and then create a
reference to the Class Library project from a Console application.

Within the SolutionDemo solution, we'll create a new project for a class library. Right-click SolutionDemo and select Add | New Project. This time, select Class Library instead of Console Application and name it **ClassLibraryDemo**. Clicking OK will add a new Class Library Project to your SolutionDemo Solution. You will now have two projects in your solution.

To use the code in the ClassLibrary project, right-click the ProjectDemo project and select Add Reference. This time, select the Project tab, which will contain all of the projects that belong to the same solution. Select the ClassLibraryDemo project and click OK. You'll see the reference to ClassLibraryDemo appear in the References folder in the ProjectDemo project.

TIP

Resetting References for Renamed Projects. You can rename any project by right-clicking the project and selecting Rename. However, that doesn't change the physical folder name. If you want to change the physical folder name, close the solution (select File | Close Solution) and then change the project folder name. When you re-open the solution, Solution Explorer won't be able to load the project. This is because the folder name for the project in the solution file hasn't changed. To fix this, select the project in Solution Explorer and open the properties window. In the properties window, select the file path property and either type the newly changed path or click the ellipses button to navigate to the *.csproj file. Navigate back to Solution Explorer, right-click the project that didn't load, and select Reload Project.

Now that you have a reference to a class library, you'll want to write code that uses the objects in the class library, which you'll learn about next.

Using Code in Class Libraries

To use class library code, you need to ensure you have a reference to the class library. If using C#, you can add a using directive, and in VB you can add an Imports directive, which allows you to use the types in the class library without fully qualifying them.

After referencing the class library assembly and ensuring namespaces are managed properly, you can use class library classes and instantiate these externally referenced objects and access or invoke the members as if they were part of the code in your own assembly. The .NET CLR will take care of making sure that your calls to the class library object work transparently behind the scenes. The preceding section showed you how to create the reference from one project to another, allowing the compiler to find the other assembly. This section will explain how to write the code that specifies which objects in the class library to use.

Assuming that you were building an educational application, you might have a class library that helped you keep track of students. To facilitate this scenario, you can rename the Class1.cs or Class1.vb file in the ClassLibraryDemo project to Student.cs or Student.vb.

If you're using C# when you do this, VS will ask if you want to change the class filename from Class1 to Student. VB will make the class name change automatically, without asking. This is a convenient way to keep your classes and filenames in sync. It is common to create only one class per file. Listing 5-1 shows the new student file after renaming and adding code to make it functional.

Listing 5-1 Class library code

C#:

```
using System;
using System.Collections.Generic;
using System.Linq;
using System.Text;

namespace ClassLibraryDemo
{
    public class Student
    {
        public List<int> GetStudentGrades(string studentName)
        {
            return new List<int> { 80, 100, 95 };
        }
    }
}
```

VB:

```
Public Class Student
    Public Function GetStudentGrades(ByVal studenName As String) As
List(Of Integer)
        Dim intList As New List(Of Integer)
        intList.Add(80)
        intList.Add(100)
        intList.Add(95)
        Return intList
    End Function
End Class
```

The important parts of Listing 5-1, for the current discussion, is that *Student* is a class inside of the *ClassLibraryDemo* namespace. You'll need to remember the namespace so that you can obtain a reference to a *Student* instance from the calling code. Listing 5-2 shows how. Remember that the VB namespace is implicitly set to whatever is defined as the namespace setting on the My Project page, which defaults to the project name.

Listing 5-2   Application code calling class library code

C#:

```csharp
using System;
using System.Collections.Generic;
using System.Linq;
using System.Text;

using ClassLibraryDemo;

namespace ProjectDemo
{
    class Program
    {
        static void Main(string[] args)
        {
            string studentName = "Joe";
            Student myStudent = new Student();
            List<int> grades = myStudent.GetStudentGrades(studentName);

            Console.WriteLine("Grades for {0}:", studentName);
            foreach (int grade in grades)
            {
                Console.WriteLine(" - " + grade);
            }

            Console.ReadKey();
        }
    }
}
```

VB:

```vbnet
Imports ClassLibraryDemoVB

Module Module1

    Sub Main()
        Dim grades As List(Of Integer)
        Dim studentName As String = "Joe"
        Dim myStudent As New Student

        grades = myStudent.GetStudentGrades(studentName)

        Console.WriteLine("Grades for {0}:", studentName)
```

```
    For Each grade In grades
        Console.WriteLine(" - " & grade)
    Next

    Console.ReadKey()
End Sub

End Module
```

One item to draw your attention to in Listing 5-2 is the *using* directive (*Imports* in VB), specifying that you can use the types in the *ClassLibraryDemo* namespace without fully qualifying them. After that, you can see how Listing 5-2 creates instances of *Student* and *myStudent* and calls *GetStudentGrades*.

TIP

The call to *Console.ReadKey* in Listing 5-2 causes program execution to stop until the user presses a key on their keyboard. If *Console.ReadKey* was not present, the program would finish the *Main* method, which would close the application before you had the chance to see the output.

Next, you'll want to compile the code to see if the syntax is good and then run the program to see if it operates properly. The next section explains how compiling and running works with VS.

Compiling Applications

You'll find several compilation options on the Build menu. Because there are so many options, it isn't always intuitive which option you should use. The options are scoped to either the current project or the entire solution. The top portion of the menu applies to the entire solution, and the second section is context-sensitive, applying to the currently selected project. The following sections describe each set of options, including build, rebuild, and clean for both projects and solutions.

Building Solutions/Projects

Building typically means that you run the compiler to compile source code files. Sometimes the build includes more than compilation. For example, if you are writing ASP.NET applications, VS will generate code based on the Web controls on the page and then that generated code will be compiled with normal code. Therefore, the term build is more accurate than compile.

During a normal build, VS will only build the items in a project or solution that are out of date. More specifically, only projects that have changes and edits will be rebuilt, but projects that are untouched will be reused as is. A build is typically the fastest option during normal development because building only items that are out of date means that there are likely items that don't need to be built. Be aware, though, that you'll occasionally need to build everything to make sure you aren't accidentally working with old code.

Rebuilding Solutions/Projects

A rebuild performs the same actions as a build, except that it forces the build of all items belonging to a project or solution. Reasons for a rebuild include ensuring new code you've written works with existing code, creating a fresh build for deployment, and ensuring important items are built when a normal build doesn't work.

Many developers, including myself, like to pull the latest changes from source control into my solution every morning before starting work. This ensures that the current code in the solution will build with whatever was in source control. This keeps the code in your local solution from differing too much from what is in source control.

Before you deploy an application, you'll want to perform a rebuild to ensure all of the code builds. Depending on your process, you will want to test the code that was just rebuilt, prior to deployment. The rebuild ensures that the application you are preparing for deployment is the most current.

Sometimes your normal build doesn't work correctly or you're seeing bugs that seem to be associated with code that you've already written. While VS is a great tool and manages dependencies between projects, there are still complex situations where everything doesn't build correctly. At these times, you can try a rebuild, which forces the build on all items of a project or solution.

A rebuild takes more time to perform because all items in a project must be rebuilt. If you have a small project, you might not notice the differences. However, if you have a fairly large solution, with dozens of projects, a steady pattern of rebuilds throughout the day could cut into your productivity. A rebuild on a project is often not much more work than a build on the project, but there are probably edge cases where the difference in time would be noticeable. It is the rebuild on the solution that will most likely get your attention. That said, each version of VS has progressively improved the performance of the build process, so you should interpret the performance as a relation between build and rebuild, rather than as a statement about VS compared to any other tool.

Cleaning Solutions/Projects

A clean operation will delete project outputs, which include *.dll, *.exe, or other items produced by the build process. You would often perform a clean operation to guarantee that all outputs are fresh or to obtain a smaller copy of the project.

Normally, a full rebuild ensures that you have the most up-to-date outputs available. You could also perform a clean operation to ensure all outputs were removed and then perform a build to see which outputs were created. This might give you insight into whether the build on a solution was including all of the projects. In normal circumstances, VS manages all of your dependencies for you, as described in the next section. However, in advanced scenarios, some developers might occasionally change these dependencies. Cleaning is a tool to help you know whether a project is really being built. From a practical perspective, this is rare and you could inspect file dates to tell the same thing, but cleaning is another path you can take.

A more common use of clean is to remove outputs from the project to make it smaller. You might want to compress a project or solution and e-mail it to another person, requiring that you minimize the size of the attachment. While code files normally compress very well, *.dll and *.exe files can take up some file space, even when added to a compressed file. If you perform a clean before compressing the files, you will use much less file space.

Managing Dependencies and Build Order

A dependency describes to VS which other projects a given project depends on to operate properly. For the example in this chapter, the ProjectDemo project references ClassLibraryDemo and uses the code in ClassLibraryDemo. Therefore, ProjectDemo has a dependency on ClassLibraryDemo. VS adds this dependency automatically, which is good because when VS builds your solution, it will keep all projects up-to-date. VS manages a tree of dependencies. Whenever you perform a rebuild, VS looks at the dependency tree and builds all projects that don't have dependencies. Then, VS builds all projects that depend on the last set of projects that were rebuilt. This process continues until the entire solution is rebuilt and all projects at the top of the tree reference updated versions of all referenced projects.

You can manually manage dependencies by right-clicking a project or the solution in Solution Explorer and selecting Project Dependencies. Figure 5-8 shows the Project Dependencies window.

In the Project Dependencies window, you can select (from the drop-down list) the project to set dependencies upon. There is a list of projects that you can set dependencies on. As shown in Figure 5-8, the ProjectDemo project has a dependency on ClassLibraryDemo. VS created this dependency automatically.

Project dependencies directly affect the build order of a project. If you recall from the previous discussion, projects that have dependencies upon them will be built before the depending projects. From the Project Dependencies window, shown in Figure 5-8, you can click the Build Order tab to manage the order of the build. You could also get to the Build Order tab by right-clicking a project or the solution in Solution Explorer and selecting Project Build Order. You can see the Build Order tab in Figure 5-9.

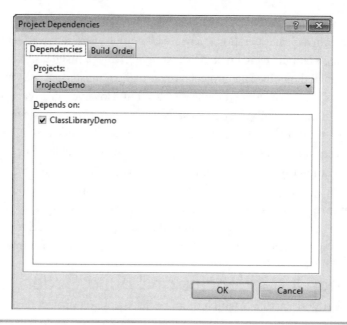

Figure 5-8 Project Dependencies window

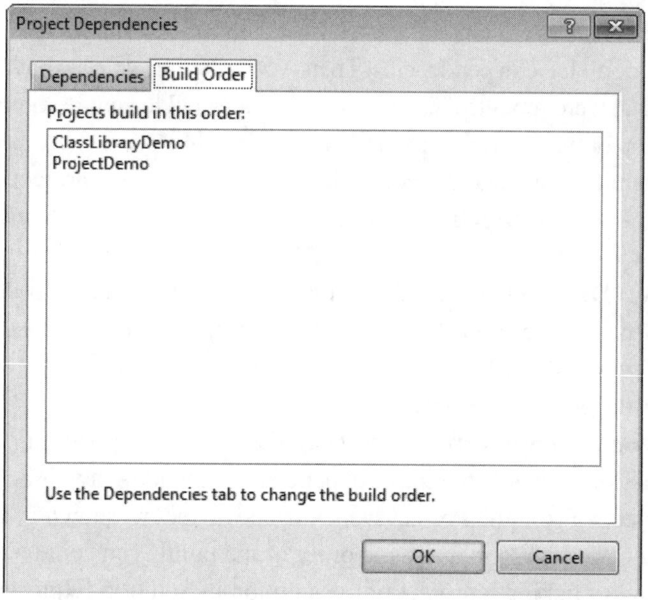

Figure 5-9 The Project Build Order tab

CAUTION

Don't alter project dependencies unless you really know what you are doing. The results could be severe in that it can take a long time to fix dependencies in a large project. The automatic dependency management provided by VS is very dependable, and you should rely upon it whenever possible.

Managing Compilation Settings

The project property pages include a tab for compiler settings. You set compiler settings for each individual project. Figure 5-10 shows the C# tab, which you can open by double-clicking the Properties folder on a project. Some of these settings are advanced topics that are out of the scope of this book. For example, this book doesn't discuss COM Interop, unsafe code generation, or serialization assemblies. I'll simply mention the setting with a quick explanation so that you'll know it's there if you ever run into one of these scenarios in the future.

The DEBUG and TRACE compilation constants enable you to use the Debug and Trace classes, respectively, that are members of the .NET Framework *System.Diagnostics*

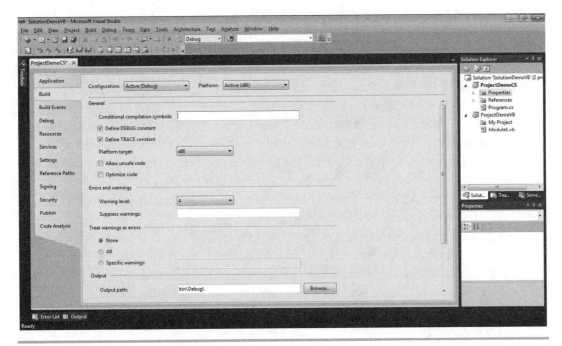

Figure 5-10   C# Compiler Options

namespace. You can also build code that depends on your own custom constants by adding your own constants to the Conditional Compilation Symbols box as a comma-separated list of strings.

C# allows you to write code that is classified as unsafe, meaning that you can use pointers and other features in an unsafe context. Unsafe code is still managed code (managed by the CLR). However, the CLR can't verify that the code is safe because unsafe code can contain pointers. This is an advanced feature and the box is unchecked, ensuring that you must check it to opt in to enable this type of coding.

All warning messages are associated with a level, and the Warning level is set to 4 by default, which includes all compiler warnings. Setting this to a lower level would suppress the display of all warnings at that level or higher. You can also suppress specific warnings by adding them to a comma-separated list in the Suppress Warnings box. You really shouldn't suppress warnings, as this setting could cover up an error that would be hard to detect otherwise.

When you build an application, your program will run even if warnings are present but will not run if the compiler encounters errors. Sometimes warnings are so important that you might want to treat them as errors, and the Treat Warnings As Errors section gives you flexibility in handling warning-as-error scenarios.

The output path of an application defaults to bin\Debug under the project folder for Debug builds and bin\Release for release builds. You can change this location if you like.

Checking the XML Documentation file will cause XML Documentation comments to be extracted from your code into an XML file that you specify. Checking this box increases the time of the build process, so you won't necessarily want to leave it on during Debug builds, when you are doing most of your coding. The XML documentation file can be input into third-party tools that automatically build technical documentation for you.

You would only check the Register For COM Interop box if you were building a .NET Assembly that was being called from a COM application.

If you're doing XML serialization of types in an assembly, you can turn on the Generate Serialization Assembly to speed the serialization process.

C# has another group of settings on the Build Events tab. You can run code before or after the build for each project. You can set the conditions upon when the build occurs, which could be always, on a successful build, or only when an update occurs. The build events have a set of macros you can access that give you information on the current build process.

VB has options that are specific to the VB compiler on its Compile page, shown in Figure 5-11.

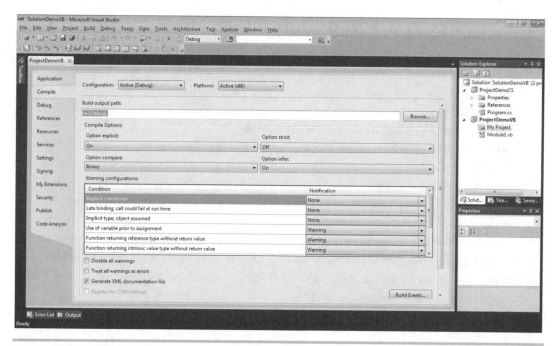

Figure 5-11   The VB Compile Options page

Most of the VB and C# compiler options are similar, except for Option Explicit, Option Strict, Option Compare, and Option Infer. In VB, variable declaration before use can be turned off. When Option Explicit is on, you must declare any variables before use. You can also assign any type to another by default, but Option Strict, if turned on, will force you to use code that performs a conversion from a larger type to a smaller type, often referred to as a narrowing conversion.

Option Compare causes comparison of strings to be done in a binary fashion. However, when working with different languages, you'll want to consider changing Option Compare to text so that the comparison will consider culture-specific issues affecting string comparisons. Option Infer will allow a variable to assume its type based on what is being assigned to the variable, rather than explicitly declaring the variable type. Here's an example of interred type on a variable:

```
Dim studentName = "Joe"
```

In this example, the type of "Joe" is clearly a String. Since Option Infer is turned on, this syntax is valid and *studentName* becomes a String because that is the type of the value being assigned.

Navigating a Project with Class View

An alternate way to work with projects is via Class view, which allows you to view solutions and project artifacts through the logical layout of the code. In C#, you can open Class view by pressing CTRL-W, C or select Class View from the View menu. In VB you can open Class view by pressing CTRL-SHIFT, C or select View | Other Windows | Class View. Figure 5-12 shows the Class View window.

In Class view, you have a hierarchy of nodes that start at the project, include references and namespaces, and contain classes under those namespaces. Under each class you have Base Types, which contains a list of base classes derived from and implemented interfaces for that specific class. Notice how I selected the Student class in Figure 5-12, which shows the members of the class in the bottom pane.

As shown in the Class View toolbar, you can create new folders, use the arrows to navigate up or down the hierarchy, or choose options of what to display in the hierarchy. There is also a button with a glyph of objects that indicate how to create a class diagram, which is discussed in the next section.

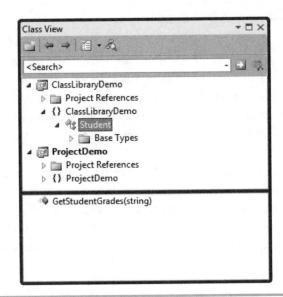

Figure 5-12 The Class View window

Using the Class Designer

When working with a project, it can sometimes be helpful to have a high-level view of the project contents, especially if someone else has created the project and you haven't worked with that project before. This is where the Class Designer can help. In addition to code visualization, another capability of the Class Designer is to give you a basic tool to perform some design yourself. We'll look at visualizing existing classes first.

Class Designer Visualization

Whenever you select a project in Solution Explorer, you'll see the Class Designer button appear in the Solution Explorer toolbar. The Class Designer button also appears on the Class View window. Clicking View Class Diagram will produce a diagram of classes in your solution, shown in Figure 5-13.

As you can see in Figure 5-13, VS produces a new file, named ClassDiagram1.cd, with a visual representation of your code. You can see that the properties window is open, allowing you to view information about the selected *Program* class. Additionally, the

Figure 5-13 Visualizing code with the Class Designer

Class Details window provides additional details on the members of the *Program.cs* class. Figure 5-13 is a minimal diagram of one class with a single method, *Main,* and you would have seen all of the classes in the current project if there were more. This could be a good way to help you learn about an existing base of code.

In addition to code visualization, you have the ability to perform some light design with the Class Designer, as discussed in the next section.

Class Designer Code Generation

The Class Designer allows you to generate code graphically. On the left-hand side of Figure 5-13, you'll see a tab for the Toolbox. Hovering over that tab, you'll see a group of images for code items, such as Class, Enum, Inheritance, and more. Figure 5-14 shows the results of using Toolbox items to enhance the existing Figure 5-14 diagram.

In Figure 5-14, you can see the Toolbox with options for what type of items you can add to a class diagram. Each of the Toolbox items matches some type of code that you would normally write. The class diagram itself has additional items, including an abstract

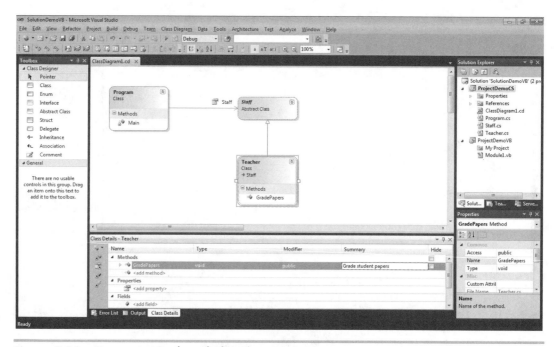

Figure 5-14 Generating code with the Class Designer

class named *Staff*, a normal class named *Teacher*, an inheritance relationship where *Teacher* derives from *Staff*, and an association from *Program* to *Staff*.

To create a new object, drag-and-drop the object from the Toolbox to the Class Designer surface; you'll see an input window similar to Figure 5-15.

The New Abstract Class window in Figure 5-15 is typical of most of the Class Designer objects you can add to a diagram where you fill in the initial data for naming the class and specifying the file the code will be added to. Not all Toolbox options work this way, though; associations and inheritance work by selecting the item in the Toolbox, selecting the object where the line begins in the Class Designer, and dragging the line to the object in the Class Designer being referenced.

The other two places you can modify data are in the Class Details and Properties windows. You can see how I added the *GradePapers* method in Class Details. You can add members to an object yourself by clicking the object in Class Designer, and then adding the member in Class Details. The *GradePapers* method also has a Summary comment for documentation and a parameter named *papers* with a type of *List<string>*.

The Properties window is context-sensitive, showing you what options are available for whatever you have selected in the Class Designer. In Figure 5-14, the *Teacher* class is selected in Class Designer and the Summary property in the Properties window was filled in with a comment. Listing 5-3 shows the code from the Teacher.cs (Teacher.vb in VB) file that was generated after all of these actions in the graphical designer.

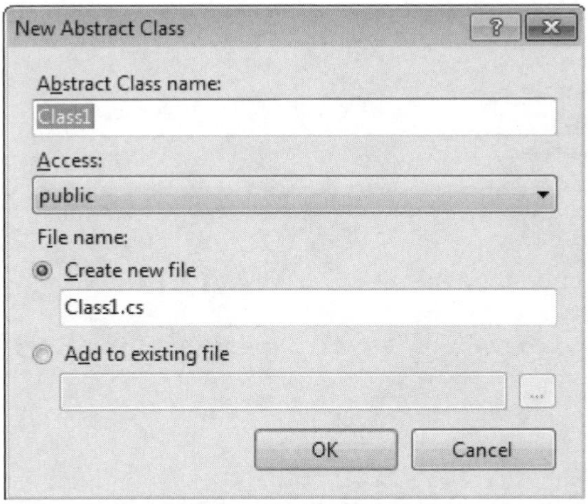

Figure 5-15   Adding a new object to the Class Designer

Listing 5-3   Code generated from the Class Designer

C#:

```csharp
using System;
using System.Collections.Generic;
using System.Linq;
using System.Text;

namespace ProjectDemo
{
    /// <summary>
    /// Teaches Classes
    /// </summary>
    public class Teacher : Staff
    {
        /// <summary>
        /// Grade student papers
        /// </summary>
        /// <param name="papers">Papers to grade</param>
        public void GradePapers(List<string> papers)
        {
            throw new System.NotImplementedException();
        }
    }
}
```

VB:

```vb
''' <summary>
''' Teaches Classes
''' </summary>
Public Class Teacher
    Inherits Staff

    ''' <summary>
    ''' Grade student papers
    ''' </summary>
    Public Sub GradePapers(ByVal papers As List(Of String))

    End Sub

End Class
```

As shown in Listing 5-3, code generated from the Class Designer includes default *using* directives and the namespace as specified in project properties. The class name, *Teacher,* is the same as the visual object in the class diagram, and the *GradePapers* method is the same as specified in the Class Details window. You can also see the comment on *Teacher* as specified in the Property window. All that's left for you to do is replace the call to *throw new System.NotImplementedException* with your own code in C# or just add your code to *GradePapers* in VB.

Summary

You should now know how to create a solution and a project. You can set project properties and add new members to projects. Additionally, you are able to add class libraries to a project and reference those class libraries from other projects that use those libraries. If you prefer a more formal design process, VS offers the Class Designer, which you learned to use for both visualization and code generation. The next chapter builds upon the coding process with VS by showing you how to debug code.

Chapter 6
Debugging with
Visual Studio

Key Skills & Concepts

- Exploring Available Debugging Tools

- Setting Breakpoints

- Inspecting Program State

- Solving Problems with VS Debugging Tools

More often than we would like, our code has bugs. Fortunately, when bugs do happen, you have a lot of help with VS. This chapter shows you how to use the VS debugger to fix problems by setting breakpoints, stepping through code, and inspecting program state. There's also a section on development-time tools to inspect the structure of your code. Beyond setting breakpoints, you'll learn how to customize breakpoints and how to manage a list of breakpoints. Then you'll see the options VS has for stepping through code. This chapter also shows you many ways to see what the values of variables are in your code and the various tools available for inspecting your code. First, we'll start with some example code you can use to practice the concepts learned in this chapter.

Example Code for This Chapter

It would take many pages of code to show a complete program with all of the complexity of a real-world scenario, which might be hard to follow for the purposes of this chapter. So, the example you'll see simulates the environment of a full application. When performing debugging, you'll need to traverse hierarchies in code, where one method calls another, which could go multiple levels deep, depending on the program. The example code will have multiple levels of method calls so that you can see how to use VS to debug code.

Listing 6-1 shows the example code for this chapter. It's a console application, just like all of the applications created in previous chapters. You create a console project by selecting File | New | Project, select the Console Application project, give the project a name, and generate the project by clicking OK. The application in Listing 6-1 calculates a discount for a customer, based on a special discount percentage for that customer and what that customer ordered.

Listing 6-1   Example code for chapter

C#: Program.cs

```csharp
using System;

namespace DebugAndTestDemo
{
    class Program
    {
        static void Main()
        {
            Customer cust = new Customer();
            cust.Discount = .1m;

            Order ord = new Order();
            ord.AddItem(5.00m);
            ord.AddItem(2.50m);

            cust.Order = ord;
            decimal discount = cust.GetOrderDiscount();

            Console.WriteLine("Customer Discount: {0}", discount);
            Console.ReadKey();
        }
    }
}
```

C#: Customer.cs

```csharp
namespace DebugAndTestDemo
{
    class Customer
    {
        public decimal Discount { get; set; }
        public Order Order { get; set; }

        public decimal GetOrderDiscount()
        {
            return Order.Total * Discount;
        }
    }
}
```

C#: Order.cs

```csharp
using System.Collections.Generic;
```

```csharp
namespace DebugAndTestDemo
{
    class Order
    {
        private List<decimal> orderItems = new List<decimal>();

        public decimal Total
        {
            get
            {
                decimal amount = 0;

                foreach (var item in orderItems)
                {
                    amount = amount + item;
                }

                return amount;
            }
        }

        public void AddItem(decimal amount)
        {
            orderItems.Add(amount);
        }
    }
}
```

VB: Module1.vb

```vb
Module Module1

    Sub Main()
        Dim cust As Customer = New Customer()
        cust.Discount = 0.1D

        Dim ord As Order = New Order()
        ord.AddItem(5D)
        ord.AddItem(2.5D)

        cust.Order = ord

        Dim discount As Decimal = cust.GetOrderDiscount()

        Console.WriteLine("Customer Discount: {0}", discount)
        Console.ReadKey()
    End Sub

End Module
```

VB: Customer.vb

```
Class Customer
    Property Discount As Decimal
    Property Order As Order
    Function GetOrderDiscount() As Decimal
        Return Order.Total * Discount
    End Function
End Class
VB: Order.vb
Class Order
    Private orderItems As New List(Of Decimal)

    Public ReadOnly Property Total() As Decimal
        Get
            Dim amount As Decimal = 0

            For Each item In orderItems
                amount = amount + item
            Next

            Return amount
        End Get
    End Property

    Sub AddItem(ByVal item As Decimal)
        orderItems.Add(item)
    End Sub
End Class
```

A quick look at the code in Listing 6-1 tells you that this program is more sophisticated than the examples you've encountered in previous chapters. To understand what is happening, start at the *Main* method, the entry point of the application. There are two objects instantiated in *Main,* namely *Customer* and *Order.*

After instantiating *Customer,* you can see that the *Discount* property on *cust* is being set to *.1* (10%). This means that each instance of *Customer* can have a unique discount amount, which could be useful if you wanted to reward good shopping habits.

Next, you can see the instantiation of *Order* and subsequent calls to *AddItem* on the object reference *ord.* This code only adds the order amount, but in a real scenario it would likely be a class with more fields to carry the specific details of the order item. The *Customer* class has an *Order* property, which the code then passes our *Order* instance, *ord,* to. Now, you have a *Customer* with a discount amount and it has a reference to our specific *Order,* which in turn has items (represented here by the items' monetary amount only for brevity).

This program calculates the total monetary discount that a customer would receive for that order by calling the *GetOrderDiscount* method on the *Customer* instance, which then returns the calculated discount amount to be subsequently displayed on the console. Essentially, we created a couple of object instances, *cust* and *ord,* gave the object instances the data they needed, and told the object instances to do some work for us. The result is a special discount monetary amount for a given customer, based on the customer's items ordered.

All of the code in the *Main* method is at the first level of the call hierarchy. The methods and properties in *Customer* and *Order* are at the second level of the hierarchy. Looking at *Order,* you can see that there is a *Total* property and an *AddItem* method. *AddItem* adds the *item* parameter to its *orderItems* collection. *Total* iterates through the *orderItems* collection, first calculating then returning the sum of all items. Notice that the *Customer* class has a *Discount* property that holds a decimal value that will be used as a percentage. The *GetOrderDiscount* method in *Customer* multiplies the *Discount* by the *Total* in *Order* to return the discount of the order.

It's important for you to study this example and understand the relationships and communication between various objects. Observe that each class has a distinct purpose, relating to how it is named. The purpose of the class helps decide what data and methods that class will have; *Order* has *Total* and *AddItem*, and the class *Customer* has *Discount* and *GetOrderDiscount*. Each object communicates with other objects, cooperating to perform a task. For example, it is *Customer*'s responsibility to calculate a discount because the *Customer* class knows what the discount should be (because we told it what the discount was in *Main*). However, *Customer* must communicate with *Order* because *Order* is the only object that knows about the order items and how to calculate the total.

Although I've shown you the code and explained how it works, it's often useful to see the flow of logic of the actual running program yourself. VS includes various visualization and debugging tools that help you understand the flow of logic, which are discussed next.

Development-Time Code Tools

One of the new features of VS 2010 is Call Hierarchy, which allows you to see what code calls a method and which methods are being called by your code. First, I'll explain why call hierarchy is important, and then I'll show you how to use it. Figure 6-1 shows what the Call Hierarchy window looks like, and the following discussion will explain the motivation for and use of the Call Hierarchy feature.

The call hierarchy tells you several things about code, including the degree of reuse, impact of a change, and potential importance of a routine. To help understand the discussion, a call site is code that invokes another class member. For example, in Listing 6-1, the *Main* method is the call site and the *GetOrderDiscount* method is the called code.

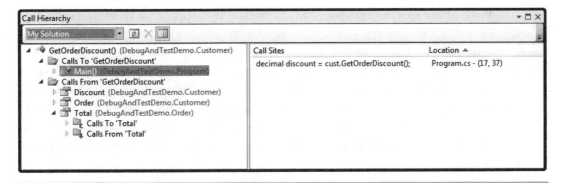

Figure 6-1   The Call Hierarchy window

From the perspective of reuse, many call sites to a method could indicate that the method is relatively generic and reusable. While a low number of call sites might not indicate the reusability of a method, zero call sites certainly indicates that the method is not being used and can potentially be eliminated.

A lot of call sites could also indicate that a change to a method can have a significant impact. Looking at the number of call sites that a method has could be informative from the perspective of passing different values or seeing how many changes will be required in called methods.

The previous discussion is to help you understand how call hierarchy might be useful. Now, let's look at how call hierarchy works. First, remember that call hierarchy is context-sensitive, meaning that whatever code in the editor has focus defines your point of view. The point of view for this example will be the *GetOrderDiscount* method in the *Customer* class, and we want to see the call sites of *GetOrderDiscount* and what statements inside of *GetOrderDiscount* are call sites. To use call hierarchy, either right-click the *GetOrderDiscount* method in the editor and select View Call Hierarchy, or select *GetOrderDiscount* in the editor and press CTRL-K, T. VS shows the Call Hierarchy window in Figure 6-1.

The Call Hierarchy window in Figure 6-1 shows *Calls To* and *Calls From* for the *GetOrderDiscount* method. *Calls To* is a list of call sites to the *GetOrderDiscount* method. *Calls From* is a list of statements within *GetOrderDiscount* that are call sites for other class members.

The drop-down list at the top left of Figure 6-1, with *My Solution* selected, identifies how far Call Hierarchy will look to find Calls To and Calls From call sites. The options are My Solution, Current Project, and Current Document, which are self-explanatory.

If you've been working on your code and want to update the Call Hierarchy window, click Refresh. Every time you view Call Hierarchy, the selected item is added to the list. You can use the Remove Root button to delete an item from the list. The Toggle Details Pane button shows and hides the Details pane, which shows the code and location of the call site. In Figure 6-1, the *Main* method is selected, which shows the call to *GetOrderDiscounts* off the *cust* instance of *Customer* from Listing 6-1. The actual code line is shown also. You can double-click the statement to navigate the editor to the location of that statement. In fact, you can double-click any call site in the Call Hierarchy to navigate to the location of the call site in the editor.

The Call Hierarchy shows all of the possible paths you can take through a specific point in code. While quite useful, it's limited to providing a static view of your code, and it does not provide the detailed insight into your running program that debugging may require. When debugging, you typically need to view the running state of an application at a specific point in time. The following sections show you various features of the debugger that help you inspect the runtime behavior of code.

Configuring Debug Mode

By default, VS creates projects with Debug mode enabled, which specifies project settings that make it possible for you to debug your application. The VS toolbar shows you the current configuration settings you're using; clicking the drop-down list will show Debug and Release configurations. The Release configuration defines settings for your program that you want to use when you deploy it for production (actual) use. You can also create a custom configuration that allows you to set project properties how you want. For the purposes of this chapter, we will use the Debug configuration.

To understand what the Debug configuration gives you, ensure that the Debug configuration is selected in the toolbar; you'll need to have a project open to do this. Then double-click the properties folder of your project and click the Build tab as shown in Figure 6-2.

Figure 6-2 shows that optimizations are turned off and both *TRACE* and *DEBUG* are defined. Figure 6-2 shows the properties for a C# project, but in VB, the tab is called Compile. When optimizations are turned on, the compiler will perform extra processing on the code that makes it smaller and faster, altering the structure of the code. When debugging, you don't want optimizations because you need the code you're stepping through to match what the compiler produces. Compiler constants (also known as compiler directives) such as *TRACE* and *DEBUG* are used by the compiler to enable or disable blocks of code. For example, the System.Diagnostics namespace has a Debug class that will only work if *DEBUG* is defined.

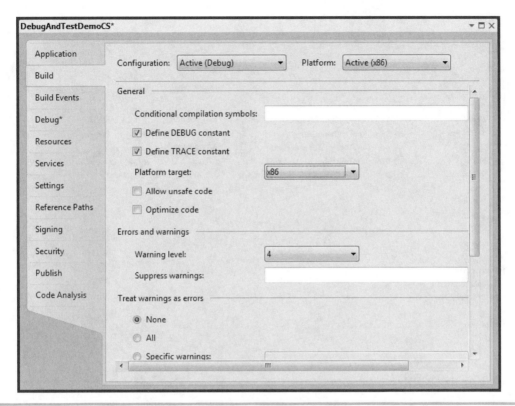

Figure 6-2   The Build (C#) and Compile (VB) Properties tab

Do a build of your application, which will produce various files suitable for debugging. To view these files, right-click the solution, project, or folder in Solution Explorer and select Open Folder in Windows Explorer. Then navigate to the bin\Debug folder, which should look similar to Figure 6-3.

There are four files in Figure 6-3, two for the application and two to support running in the debugger. DebugAndTestDemoCS.exe is the executable console application, which you might have already expected. A *.pdb file is a symbol file that helps synchronize the identifiers in your code with the executable file, making it easier to step through code with the VS debugger.

There are two files with vshost in their name, which are instrumental to the debugging process. A *.vshost file makes your application load faster during debugging, gives you the ability to test your application with different security configurations, and allows you to evaluate expressions while debugging. The vshost files are for debugging only, so you

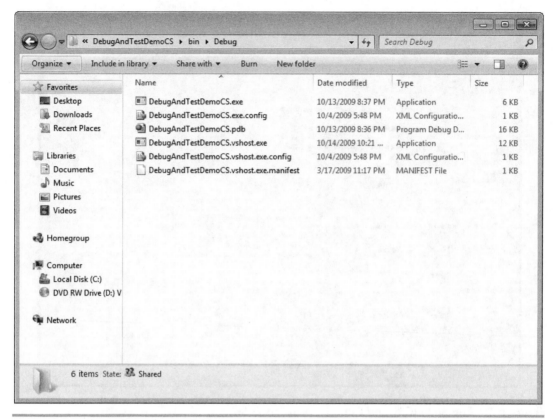

Figure 6-3 The Debug Output folder

should not deploy them with your application; they would just take up extra space and not serve a purpose. You normally want vshost files in place when debugging in VS. There are various debugger settings you can configure in VS that affect your session and modify the vshost configuration files. Open the properties page and click the Debug tab, shown in Figure 6-4.

In Figure 6-4, you can see that the Configuration is set to Debug and the Platform is set to x86. The Platform target can be Any CPU, x86, x64, or Itanium, depending on the CPU you are building the application on. The compiler will perform optimizations for the CPU type you select. If you're running VS on a 64-bit operating system, your Active solution platform may show as Active (Any CPU).

The Start Action section of the Debug tab determines how the debugging session begins. Start Project is the default, Start External Program allows you to attach your VS debugging session to an already-running application, and Start Browser With URL lets you debug a

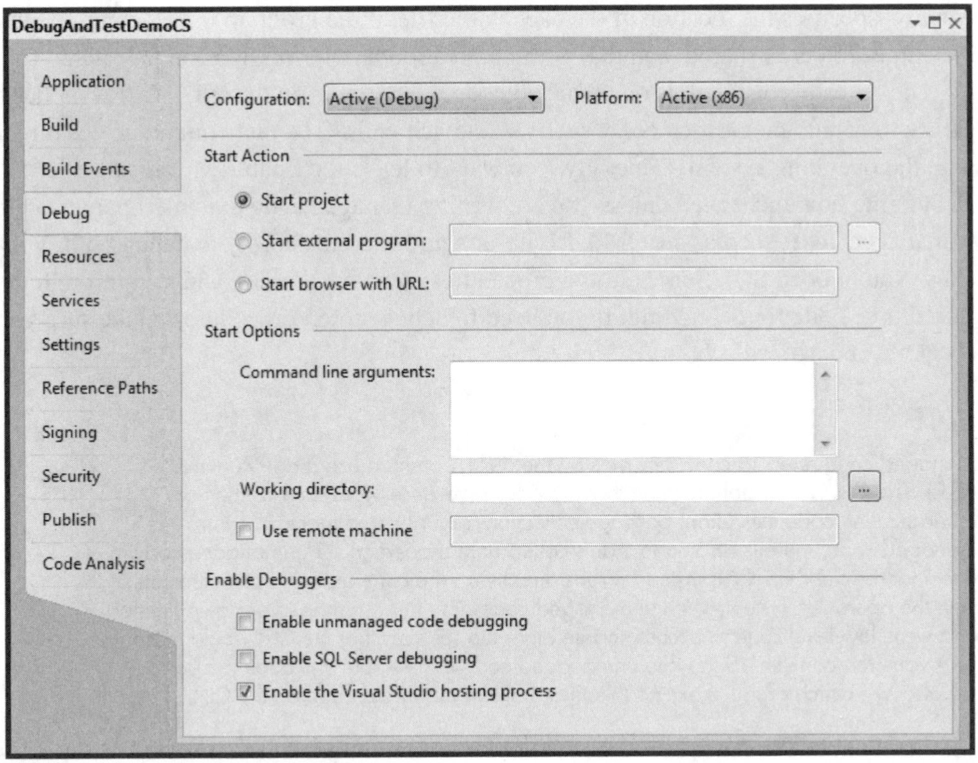

Figure 6-4   Debug properties

Web application. Generally, you'll only use Start Project for a desktop application. The property pages change for Web applications, which automatically run in a browser.

You can add a space-separated list of values for command-line arguments. If you're building an application that needs to be run from a command window or from a command script, this method is very useful to test and debug a specific command-line configuration. You can then read the values you've entered into the Command Line Arguments text box by reading them from the *args* array passed to the *Main* method.

A working directory is the root location of where your program reads and writes files. By default, this location is bin\Debug for Debug configurations and bin\Release for Release configurations. You can change the working directory location by putting a file path in the Working Directory property box.

Use Remote Machine is an advanced scenario where you can debug an application running on a remote machine. To do this, you would need to install remote debugging software on the remote machine, ensure the Output path of the Build tab of the Properties window specifies the location of the executable file of the program to be debugged, that the output folder is shared, and that your application has permissions on the shared folder.

The focus of this book is on managed code, which runs on the .NET CLR. VS has the ability to debug unmanaged code, such as that written in C++ that communicates directly with the operating system. Generally, you want to leave the Enable Managed Code Debugging box unchecked unless you are writing managed code that interoperates with unmanaged code, such as a COM DLL library, and need the ability to debug both. VS will allow you to open SQL Server stored procedures, set a breakpoint, and step through the stored proc code for debugging. If you need to debug stored procedures, make sure you check this box.

NOTE

Managed code refers to code that runs on the .NET Common Language Runtime (CLR). The CLR is a virtual machine that provides several services such as memory management, code execution, garbage collection, security, and more. In contrast to managed code, there is also code that is called *unmanaged code.* Unmanaged code does not use the .NET CLR; instead it runs directly on the computer and communicates with the operating system. With unmanaged code, you must manage your own memory and write low-level code to accommodate all of the services that the CLR would normally give you. You can use VS to write unmanaged code in C++, but this book focuses on C# and VB, which produce executable files that run managed code on the CLR.

The Enable The Visual Studio Hosting Process setting is what caused the vshost files to be generated in the output folder. Normally, you want to leave this box checked because of the benefits of vshosts, described previously. The only exception might be if you had a unique situation where the services provided by the vshosts process conflicted with the code you were running, which would be an advanced and rare scenario.

TIP

In earlier versions of VS, you would occasionally get a file permission error on the vshosts file, which was caused by the fact that there were file locks on the file. This can occur if you have attached to the running process from another instance of VS or the process shut down improperly in a sequence that didn't release the file lock on vshosts. One of the work-arounds is to uncheck the Enable The Visual Studio Hosting Process box, rebuild, recheck the Enable The Visual Studio Hosting Process box, and build again. You also have the choice of restarting your OS, whichever you find easier. This scenario doesn't point to a deficiency in VS or the operating system, because the file locks are necessary when an application is running. Rather, the scenario is a consequence of having a bug in your code or improperly shutting down an application.

In addition to property settings, you have a plethora of options available via the Options window, which you can open by selecting Tools | Options, as shown in Figure 6-5.

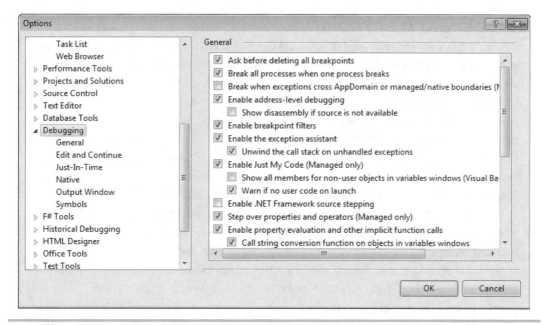

Figure 6-5   Debugging options

As you can see in Figure 6-5, there are a variety of options that allow you to configure debugging. The primary difference between project settings and Options settings is that project settings are for that one project, but Options settings let you change the settings for all projects and have those settings, when applicable, apply to any new projects you create. Therefore, if there are default settings you want on all projects, visit the Options settings to set them first. The options are much too numerous to list here, and many of them deal with advanced scenarios that are out of scope of this book. If you ever have a question about whether a capability is available or if you need to save settings, you should visit the Options window to see if that capability is available. Now that your system is configured for debugging, you can set breakpoints and start the debugging process.

Setting Breakpoints

Breakpoints are places in your code where you want the program to automatically pause from running, similar to when you push the pause button while watching a movie with your home DVD or Blu-ray player. Once your program hits (stops on) your breakpoint, you will be able to perform debugging tasks, which could be viewing the values of variables at this frozen point in time (program state), evaluating expressions, or editing code and continuing execution. The following discussion shows you how to create and manage breakpoints in your application.

Creating a Breakpoint

To create a breakpoint, you need to open a project and have a code file open in the editor. A good project choice would be the example application with code from Listing 6-1. In the VS editor, there is a margin on the left side. If you click in this margin, VS will set a breakpoint on the matching code statement. Clicking a statement in code to give it the focus and pressing F9 sets a breakpoint too. You'll see a red dot in the margin and the matching statement highlighted in red, as shown in Figure 6-6. Note that you may only set a breakpoint on code that actually gets executed at runtime. If you try to select a line of code that does not, such as a namespace name definition, the red dot will not appear and you'll see a message at the bottom of VS saying, "A breakpoint could not be inserted at this location."

To ensure VS stops on a breakpoint, the application must be running in debug mode. You can start the program running in debug mode by selecting Debug | Start Debugging, pressing F5, or clicking the Start With Debugging toolbar button (the one with the green arrow). The breakpoint in Figure 6-6 is on the call to *GetOrderDiscount* in the *Main* method. When the program hits the breakpoint, the breakpoint line will turn yellow and there will be a yellow arrow on the red dot in the margin. Clicking the Continue button (which is the same green arrow button used to start debugging) or pressing F5 will cause VS to resume execution. Any time you want to stop debugging, select Debug | Stop Debugging, press F5, or click the Stop Debugging toolbar button (small blue square).

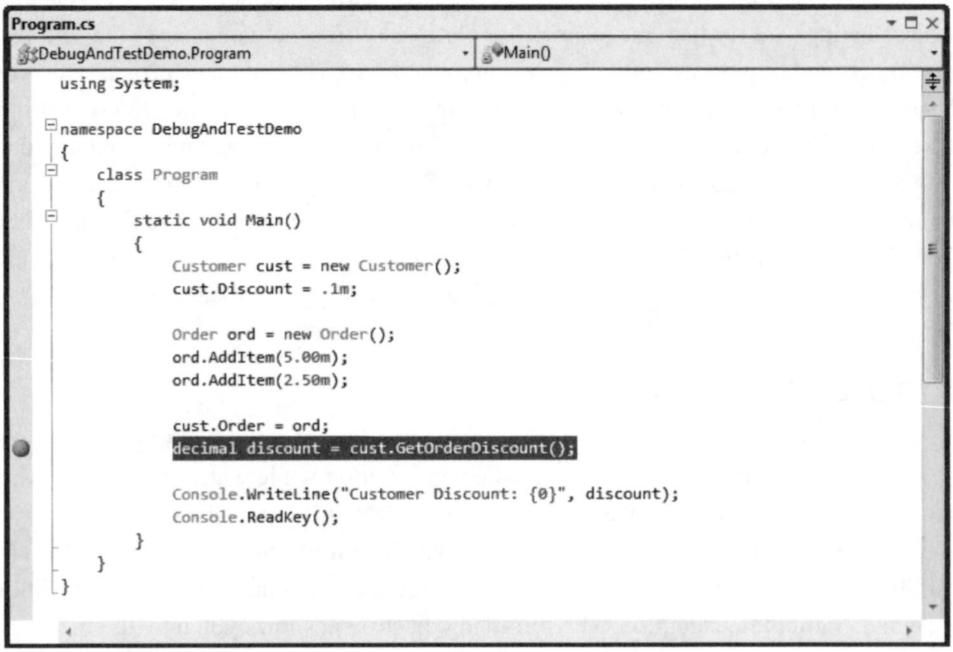

```csharp
Program.cs
DebugAndTestDemo.Program                              Main()
    using System;

    namespace DebugAndTestDemo
    {
        class Program
        {
            static void Main()
            {
                Customer cust = new Customer();
                cust.Discount = .1m;

                Order ord = new Order();
                ord.AddItem(5.00m);
                ord.AddItem(2.50m);

                cust.Order = ord;
                decimal discount = cust.GetOrderDiscount();

                Console.WriteLine("Customer Discount: {0}", discount);
                Console.ReadKey();
            }
        }
    }
```

Figure 6-6 A breakpoint

TIP

If you write a program that is doing a lot of work, or very little work but is stuck in an endless loop that you inadvertently created, you can pause execution by selecting the blue pair of vertical bars button found to the left of the square blue stop button. When you do this, your program stops at whatever line of code it was executing at the moment you selected the pause button. You can then resume from that point. This button works much like the pause button on a remote control or a personal media player.

Customizing a Breakpoint

The preceding explanation described how to set a location breakpoint, where execution stops on a designated line in code. However, you can make a program stop executing based on various criteria, such as hit count, conditions, and more. To see what else is available, set a location breakpoint and then right-click the dot in the margin to view the context menu. Table 6-1 describes each of the breakpoint options available from the breakpoint context menu.

You can also set a function breakpoint by clicking on the method to break on and selecting Debug | New Breakpoint | Break At Function or pressing CTRL-D, N.

Option	Meaning
Delete Breakpoint	Removes the breakpoint.
Disable/Enable Breakpoint	If you don't want to delete the breakpoint because you'll use it again, you can disable the breakpoint and then enable it later when you want to use it again.
Location	This is set when you click in the margin. You can change features of the location through a dialog window.
Condition	Allows you to enter an expression that can cause the program to stop if either the expression evaluates to true or the value of a variable has changed. The expression is based on variables in your code.
Hit Count	Makes the program break on that line every time, after a number of times the line has executed, when the count is a multiple of a number (i.e., every *n*th time), or when the number of hits is greater than or equal to a number.
Filter	The breakpoint will only be hit (causing execution to pause) for any combination of machine, process, or thread choice that you set.
When Hit	Sets a tracepoint that prints a message to the output window. The message is configurable to include output of various system values like function, thread, and more. You can view the message in the Output window by selecting View	Output Window or pressing CTRL-ALT-O. You also have the option of running a macro when the breakpoint is hit.
Edit Labels	You can associate breakpoints with labels to help organize breakpoints into groups.
Export	Lets you export breakpoints into an external XML file.

Table 6-1   Options from the Breakpoint Context Menu

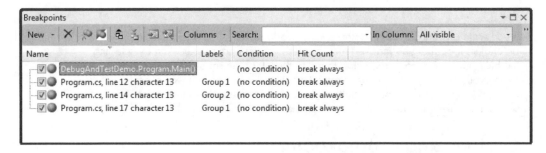

Figure 6-7 The Breakpoints window

Managing Breakpoints

Over time, breakpoints can be set across many locations in your project. You can manage all of these breakpoints in a central location by selecting Debug | Windows | Breakpoints, which will show the window in Figure 6-7.

Much of the functionality of the Breakpoints window has been explained already, except that the toolbar options apply to all of the breakpoints that are currently checked. Clicking a column sorts the contents. The Search box helps you filter breakpoints, and the In Columns box helps focus on what the search applies to. There are export and import buttons on the toolbar that allow you to respectively save and retrieve breakpoints to and from an XML file. Double-clicking any breakpoint takes you to the location in the editor where the breakpoint is set. Right-clicking a breakpoint shows a context menu with options that have already been discussed in this section.

Once you set a breakpoint, you can step through code to see what the execution flow of the program is, as is discussed in the next section.

Stepping Through Code

Stepping through code is the process of executing one or more lines of code in a controlled manner. At the most granular level, you can step through code line-by-line. While moving line-by-line is often necessary, it could also be cumbersome, so there are ways to step over multiple lines of code, allowing them to silently and quickly execute.

To step through code, open a project, set a breakpoint, and run with debugging until the program hits the breakpoint. At that point in time, you can perform various operations such as step, step over, and step out. Table 6-2 explains the stepping operations that are available. The explanations in the table assume that a breakpoint has been hit with your executing program now paused before performing the step operation.

Operation	Explanation
Step Over	Executes the code in the current line and moves to the next line of code where it again pauses, waiting for your instruction. Perform a Step Over by selecting Debug I Step Over, pressing F10, or clicking the Step Over button in the toolbar. You can also right- click and select this option. Most Visual Studio developers will have the F10 shortcut memorized in short order.
Step Into Specific	When the current line is on a method call, a Step Into will move control to the first line of the method being called and execution will pause there. Perform the Step Into by selecting Debug I Step Into, pressing F11, or clicking the Step Into button in the toolbar. F11 is the fastest way for you to do this operation.
Step Out	If you're in a method, you can move back to the caller by performing a Step Out operation. Perform a Step Out by selecting Debug I Step Out, pressing SHIFT-F11, or clicking the Step Out button on the toolbar. Note that no lines of code are skipped inside the function; they still run following your program's logic. Your program will automatically pause at the line of code following this function's return.
Run to Cursor	Sometimes you want to execute a block of code and stop at a certain line. You could set another breakpoint and run until you hit the breakpoint. However, a quicker way when you don't want to keep a new breakpoint around is to right-click the line you want to stop at and select Run To Cursor. Again, no lines of code are skipped; the program will merely pause when it gets to the line you placed your cursor on. Optionally, you can click the line to run to and press CTRL-F10. This is particularly useful if you don't feel like stepping through every iteration of a loop.
Set Next Statement	You can skip forward and backward over multiple lines of code without executing the skipped code. For example, it's easy to step over a method, only to realize that you really wanted to step into that method. You don't want to restart the application unless you need to. To get back to that line of code so that you can step into the method call, select the yellow arrow in the margin and drag it back up to the method call. Then you can do a Step Into. Alternatively, if you have one or more statements that you don't want to execute, drag the yellow arrow in the margin to the statement following the code you don't want to run and then use stepping operations to resume your debugging session. This technique is also quite handy when you are using the Edit and Continue feature, where you can change your program on the fly, experiment with different coding ideas you may have, and rerun those lines of code instantly. Note that VS does not reset variables back to initial states, so you may have to manually reset values in order to get the results you expect.

Table 6-2   Step Operations

A Step Over operation executes the code in the current line and moves to the next. You can perform a Step Over by selecting Debug | Step Over, pressing F10, or clicking the Step Over button in the toolbar.

You now know how to step through code, which is useful. However, the ability to see the values of variables and watch them change is an important skill, which you learn about in the next section.

Inspecting Application State

Application state is the value of variables in your code, the current path of execution, or any other information that tells you what your program is doing. While debugging, it's important to be able to view application state and compare what is really happening to what you expected to happen. VS gives you various windows for viewing application state, which you'll learn about in this section.

NOTE
When inspecting the state of your application, you'll need to keep the concept of scope in mind. When a variable is in scope, you will be able to see the variable's value. Scope is defined within a block. In C#, the block is defined with curly braces, and VB defines a block with begin and end statements. A couple examples of scope involve class fields and local variables. A private class field would be in scope for all the methods of that class but not in another class. A local variable would be in scope for all statements of the method it is defined in, but would be out of scope for other methods. Another scenario is a for loop that defined a variable in its body—the variable would be in scope for the body of the loop but out of scope outside of the loop body.

Locals and Autos Windows

The Locals and Autos windows show you the variables in your system at the current breakpoint. Locals gives you a list of all variables that the current statement could access (also referred to as in scope). The Autos window shows variables from the current and previous lines. You can open the Locals and Autos windows from the Debug | Windows menu when your VS debug session is active and paused at a breakpoint. These windows may have already been placed for you at the bottom left of Visual Studio next to the Output window if you've not rearranged your VS layout.

As shown in Figure 6-8, the Locals window shows all of the variables in scope for the *Main* method from Listing 6-1. The Locals window is a coarse-grained view, and the

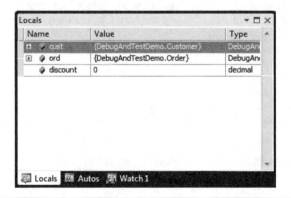

Figure 6-8   The Locals window

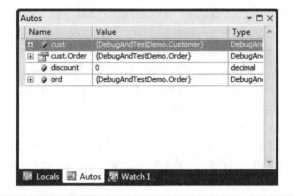

Figure 6-9 The Autos window

list can be quite long, depending on how many variables are in scope. You would want to use the Locals window to find any variables being affected by the current algorithm. In comparison, Figure 6-9 shows the Autos window.

Notice that the Autos window provides a more fine-grained view of both variables and the properties of objects from the current and previous lines. You would want to use Autos for a more targeted view of what is currently happening in the code.

Watch Windows

A Watch window allows you to create a custom list of variables to watch. You can drag and drop variables from the editor or type a variable name in the Watch window. Selecting Debug | Windows | Watch will display a list of four Watch windows, where you can have four different sets of data to inspect at one time. Figure 6-10 shows a Watch window with a variable.

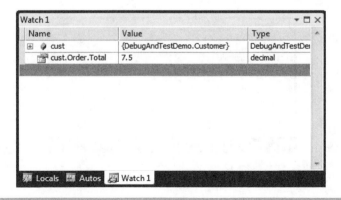

Figure 6-10 The Watch window

The Locals and Autos windows can sometimes become crowded with too many variables and slow you down as your code gets more complex, especially when the variables you're interested in are at the bottom of the list or so far apart that you must scroll between them. Another benefit of the Watch window is that you can drill down into an object to show a value without continuously expanding the tree view. An example of this is to type **cust.Order.Total** as shown in Figure 6-10, to see the results of the *Totals* property of the *Order* property of the *cust* instance. In addition, you can edit the values of your variables and properties in this window by either double-clicking the current value shown in the Value column or right-clicking the variable name and choosing Edit. When the value changes, it changes color from black to red to let you know it has changed. This technique of editing your values on the fly comes in quite handy, especially when you find yourself sliding the yellow arrow up to previous lines of code in order to re-run them without restarting your program. These techniques should prove to be a huge time saver.

The Immediate Window

While debugging, it's often useful to type an expression to see the results at the current time. The Immediate window allows you to type in variable names and many other types of statements. You can access the Immediate window by selecting Debug | Windows, or it may open for you automatically during debugging at the bottom-right side of VS. You can see the Immediate window being used in Figure 6-11.

The Immediate window in Figure 6-11 has three statements, showing that you can read a property, execute a method, or evaluate an expression. I typed these statements in myself, and you can do the same, writing nearly any code you want.

When evaluating an expression in VB, prefix the statement with a question mark, *?*.

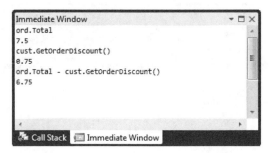

Figure 6-11   The Immediate window

The Call Stack Window

If you recall from the previous section on design-time tools, the Call Hierarchy window gives you a view of the code at design time. On a related note, you also have the ability to view the path of execution during runtime via the Call Stack window. During debugging, you may find the Call Stack window already open on the right-bottom of VS in a tab next to the Immediate window if you've not changed your layout and depending upon your initial VS environment setup. Otherwise, you can open this window by selecting Debug | Windows | Call Stack from the top menu bar. With the Call Stack window, you can view the current execution path of the application from *Main* to where your current line of execution is. Figure 6-12 shows the Call Stack window. To understand why it's called a Call Stack, notice that each method call is stacked on the other with the current method at the top, the entry point at the bottom, and subsequent calls in between; it's like a stack of plates where the last plate is at the top.

In the Call Stack window, shown in Figure 6-12, you can see that I've stepped into the *GetOrderDiscount* method. Double-clicking another method in the Call Stack window brings you to the call site where a given method was called. This is a very important and powerful tool because it allows you to visit calling code and inspect application state at the call site, giving you valuable information about how calculations were formulated before the current method was called.

The Quick Watch Window

The Quick Watch window allows you to quickly view an expression. It offers Intellisense when writing the expression, allowing you to reevaluate the expression and add the expression to a Watch window. You can open the Quick Watch window by selecting Debug | Quick Watch or pressing CTRL-D, Q. If you've selected an expression in the editor,

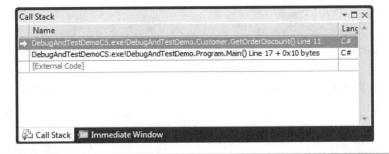

Figure 6-12   The Call Stack window

Figure 6-13 The Quick Watch window

the Quick Watch window will show that expression. Figure 6-13 shows the Quick Watch window in use.

Clicking the Reevaluate button, shown in Figure 6-13, will show the results of evaluation in the Value area. The Value area will only hold the current expression. If you want to save an expression, click Add Watch, which will load the expression into a Watch window. Be aware that closing the Watch window will remove your expression, but the expression will be part of a history list that you can select from.

Watching Variables with Pin To Source

While debugging, you can hover over any variable to see its value, but when you move the mouse away, the tooltip with the value goes away. The Pin To Source feature goes a step further by displaying the value all the time. To use Pin To Source, right-click the variable and select Pin To Source. Alternatively, you can hover over the variable in the debugger and click the push-pin that shows with the tooltip. Figure 6-14 shows a pinned value.

Once you've pinned a value, you can continue debugging and scroll back up to the variable to read its current value. In addition to seeing the value, you can add a comment by clicking the chevron that appears when you hover over the pinned value. The pinned value is commented with "product of discount and sum of order items."

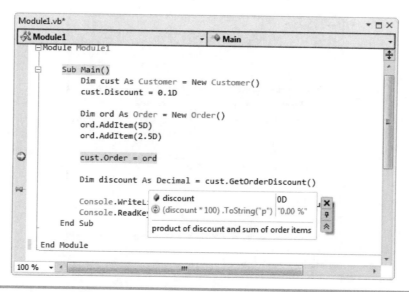

Figure 6-14 A pinned value

VS will locate the pinned value after the line, and you might not see the value if it occurs on a long line that exceeds the width of your screen. Fortunately, you can click the pinned value and drag it to where you want on the screen. To avoid confusion, remember to keep the pinned value located close to the variable whose value is displayed.

Right-click the pinned value to display a context-sensitive menu with options for Edit Value | Hexadecimal Display | Add/Remove Expression. Figure 6-14 shows how I added the expression *(discount * 100) .ToString("p")* to show the value as a percentage. Adding expressions can make the value more readable or allow you to add related expressions to see how the value produces other computed results on the fly.

You can close the pinned value by hovering over the pinned value and clicking the *X* (close icon).

Working with IntelliTrace

The IntelliTrace window gives you a view of all the changes that occurred in an application during a debugging session. As you step through code, the IntelliTrace window displays each step of your debugging session. Through the IntelliTrace toolbar, you can set the view for Diagnostic Events or Call View. Diagnostic events allow you to filter by Category or Thread. Clicking each of the items of the IntelliTrace window allows you to view application state at that point in time. Figure 6-15 shows you the IntelliTrace window.

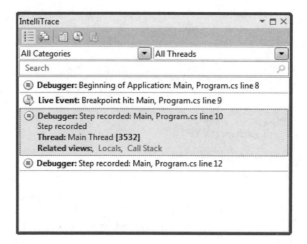

Figure 6-15 The Debug History window

IntelliTrace could be useful if you stepped over a statement that changed the value of a variable and needed to go back to see what the variable value was before you stepped. Figure 6-15 shows this scenario, where the highlighted event, Breakpoint hit: Main, allows you to view Locals or Call Stack. The important distinction is that the values shown are for the point in time when that event occurred, not the current time, which can be very valuable information. Another important application of IntelliTrace is to inspect IntelliTrace log files that were produced by another developer or the new Microsoft Test and Lab tool that records a tester's testing session.

You can configure IntelliTrace options by selecting Tools | Options | IntelliTrace. IntelliTrace will create a log file that exists as long as VS is running. When VS stops, the log file is deleted, so it's important that you copy this file before shutting down VS. The location of the log file is on the Advanced branch of IntelliTrace in Tools | Options.

If you receive a log file from another developer, you can load it by selecting File | Open | Open New. Then you can view debugging history to view the state of the application during each event of the session.

Solving Problems with VS Debugger

Previously, you've seen how the VS tools work and gathered a few tips on debugging. This section builds upon what you've learned and steps you through a couple of real-world scenarios that demonstrate how to use the VS debugger to solve problems: finding and handling bad data and fixing null references. The program itself is not particularly sophisticated, but it contains just enough logic to lead you down a rat hole and show you how to work your way out. First, we'll look at the program, and then we'll follow up with two bug-fixing exercises.

A Program with Bugs

The code in this section contains bugs, and it's important that you type it in as listed or use the downloadable code for this book from the McGraw-Hill Web site. I'll describe each piece of code and try not to give away all of the secrets of the bugs just yet. Later, I'll guide you through a process of discovery to find and fix the bugs. The program is a search application that takes the first name of a person and searches for that person through a list of customers. If the program finds the customer being searched for, it will print the customer's first and last name. Otherwise, the program will print a message stating that it did not find the customer.

The program is divided into three major parts: a class to hold customer information, a class that will return a list of customers, and the class containing the *Main* method that runs the program. The following sections describe each of these classes.

The Customer Class

Any time you are working with data, you'll have a class to hold that data. Since this application works with customers, the natural approach is to have a *Customer* class, as follows:

C#:

```csharp
public class Customer
{
    public string FirstName { get; set; }
    public string LastName { get; set; }
}
```

VB:

```vb
Public Class Customer
    Property FirstName As String
    Property LastName As String
End Class
```

This is the minimal information required for this demo, and any class that you build will have more properties. Notice that both properties are type string.

The CustomerRepository Class

In this program, we create a class that is solely responsible for working with data. This is a common pattern, which is called the Repository pattern. The following *CustomerRepository* class has a method that returns a list of *Customer* objects:

C#:

```csharp
using System.Collections.Generic;

public class CustomerRepository
{
    public List<Customer> GetCustomers()
    {
        var customers = new List<Customer>
        {
            new Customer
            {
                FirstName = "Franz",
                LastName = "Smith"
            },
            new Customer
            {
                FirstName = "Jean "
            },
            new Customer
            {
                FirstName = "Wim",
                LastName = "Meister"
            }
        };

        return customers;
    }
}
```

VB:

```vb
Public Class CustomerRepository
    Public Function GetCustomers() As List(Of Customer)
        Dim customers As New List(Of Customer) From
            {
                New Customer With
                {
                    .FirstName = "Franz",
                    .LastName = "Smith"
                },
                New Customer With
```

```
        {
            .FirstName = "Jean "
        },
        New Customer With
        {
            .FirstName = "Wim",
            .LastName = "Meister"
        }
    }

    Return customers

  End Function
End Class
```

The *GetCustomers* method returns a *List<Customer>* (*List(Of Customer)* in VB). For the purposes of this discussion, how the *GetCustomers* method works won't matter. Such a method could easily get customers from a database, Web service, or other object. For simplicity, *GetCustomers* initializes a *List* with *Customer* objects. The part of this method that is particularly important is the customer whose *FirstName* property is set to *"Jean "*. Notice the blank space appended to the name, which is required to make this scenario behave as designed (i.e., to intentionally create a bug). It's also conspicuous that the *Customer* object with a *FirstName* property set to *"Jean "* also does not have a *LastName*.

The Program with Bugs

The following is a search program that uses *CustomerRepository* to get a list of *Customer* objects. The logic will iterate through the results, checking to see if the result is equal to the search term. When the result is equal, the program prints the full name of the customer. If no matching customers are found, the program indicates that the customer wasn't found:

C#:

```
using System;

class Program
{
    static void Main()
    {
        var custRep = new CustomerRepository();

        var customers = custRep.GetCustomers();

        var searchName = "Jean";
        bool customerFound = false;
```

```csharp
        foreach (var cust in customers)
        {
            // 1. First Bug
            if (searchName == cust.FirstName)
            {
                Console.WriteLine(
                    "Found: {0} {1}",
                    cust.FirstName,
                    cust.LastName);
                customerFound = true;
            }
        }

        if (!customerFound)
        {
            Console.WriteLine("Didn't find customer.");
        }

        Console.ReadKey();
    }
}
```

VB:

```vb
Module Module1

    Sub Main()
        Dim custRep As New CustomerRepository

        Dim customers As List(Of Customer)
        customers = custRep.GetCustomers()

        Dim searchName As String = "Jean"
        Dim customerFound As Boolean = False

        For Each cust As Customer In customers
            ' 1. First Bug
            If (searchName = cust.FirstName) Then

                Console.WriteLine(
                    "Found: {0} {1}",
                    cust.FirstName,
                    cust.LastName)
                customerFound = True

            End If
        Next
```

```
        If (customerFound = False) Then
            Console.WriteLine("Didn't find customer.")
        End If

        Console.ReadKey()

    End Sub

End Module
```

Notice that the *searchName* variable is set to *"Jean"*. Within the loop, the *searchName* is compared with the *FirstName* property of each *Customer* instance for equality. Here's the output from when the program runs:

```
Didn't find customer.
```

What is supposed to happen is that the program should find the matching record and print it out, but that's not what happens. Here is the first bug, and the following discussion describes how to find the cause of the bug using the VS debugger.

Finding the Bug

At this point, we know there is a bug and it's reproducible, meaning that we can use VS to debug and find the cause of the problem. In this situation, the program is saying that it didn't find a *Customer* record or, in other words, there is no record with a *FirstName* of *Jean*. However, we know for a fact that the data does include a customer whose *FirstName* is *Jean*. We need to find out why the program cannot find it. The following steps show how the VS debugger can help isolate the problem.

1. Start by setting a breakpoint on the foreach loop in the *Main* method. This wasn't an arbitrary decision. Instead, considering the nature of the problem, I selected a part of the program that is likely to begin providing a cue to what the problem is. Looking at the program, one of the reasons that the program might not find the *searchName* is that we aren't getting data, causing the program to not execute the body of the foreach loop.

2. Press F5 to run the program in debug mode. This will execute the program and make it stop on the foreach loop, making it possible to look at program state.

3. After VS hits the breakpoint, hover over *customers* to see if there are any values. You'll observe that *customers* does have three values. The fact that there are customers indicates that the foreach loop is executing and we've eliminated that as a possibility.

4. Next, set a breakpoint on the *if* statement, right-click the breakpoint, and set the condition as follows:

C#:

```
cust.FirstName == "Jean"
```

VB:

```
cust.FirstName = "Jean"
```

The goal here is to see what happens when the *if* statement finds the record matching the *searchName*. At this point, we're assuming that *Jean* does exist in the data. Working with a small program, you can use windows such as Autos, Locals, or Watch to find this record. However, many real-world scenarios will give you a list with many more records. Therefore, rather than waste time drilling down through dozens of records, use the VS debugger to help find the record quickly. Keep in mind that all the best plans don't always work out, as you'll soon see, but the primary point is taking the most productive step first. Setting a conditional breakpoint demonstrates how you can set conditions that can avoid eating up time caused by stepping through loops.

5. Press F5 to run the program. You expect to hit the breakpoint, but that won't happen. Confusing? We know that there isn't anything wrong with the logic, because the *if* statement condition is a simple equality operator. Perhaps we've looked in the database or whatever source the data came from, but it's given in this scenario that Jean is definitely in the data. However, this illustrates a common problem where the quality of data you work with is less than desired.

6. This time, change the breakpoint condition on the *if* statement as follows and re-run the program:

C#:

```
cust.FirstName.Contains("Jean")
```

VB:

```
cust.FirstName.Contains("Jean")
```

Remember, we suspect bad data, so the call to *Contains* on the string assumes that there might be some extraneous white space or other characters around the name in the data. Hover over *cust.FirstName* or look at *cust* in one of the debug windows to verify it is the record you are looking for. This breakpoint will pause on any records that contain the sequence of characters *"Jean"*, such as Jean-Claude. So, you might have multiple matches that aren't what you want. The benefit is that the number of records you must look at is much fewer and you can save time. If you have multiple records, you can press F5 and the breakpoint will pause on each record, allowing you to inspect the value. In this case, the record set is so small that we hit the right record immediately.

7. Press F10 to step over the *if* condition. This will tell us whether the condition is being evaluated properly. In this case, VS does not step into the *if* statement but instead moves to the end of the *if* statement, meaning that *searchName* and *cust.FirstName* are not equal. This means you need to take a closer look at *cust.FirstName* to see what the problem is with the data.

8. Next, we'll use a couple of the VS debugger tools to inspect *cust.FirstName* and find out why the equality check is not working. Open the Immediate window (CTRL-D, I) and execute the following expression:

```
cust.FirstName
```

which will return this:

```
"Jean "
```

Here, you can see that the result has a trailing space—dirty data. Clearly, *"Jean"* does not equal *"Jean "* because of the extra character in the data. There are various non-printable characters that could show up, and VS can help here too.

9. Open a Memory window (CTRL-D, Y), type **cust.FirstName** into the Address box, and press ENTER. This will show the hexadecimal representation of the data at the memory location of the variable, shown in Figure 6-16.

The layout of the Memory window starts with an address on the left, which is scrolled down to the line where the data in *cust.FirstName* variable first appears. In the middle is the hex representation of the data. The final column has a readable

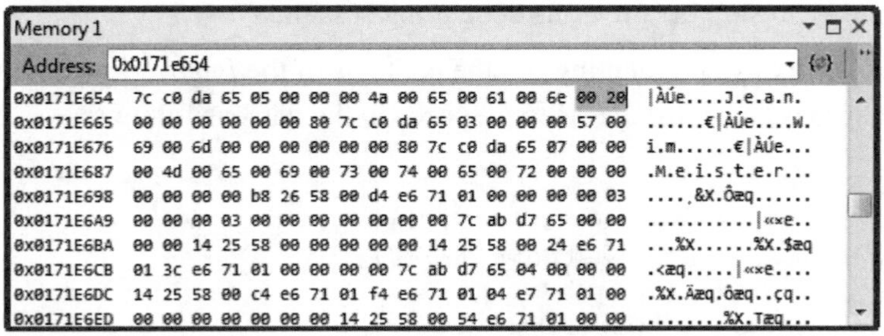

Figure 6-16 The Memory window

representation of the data where any characters that don't have a readable representation appear as dots. You can see *".J.e.a.n."* on the first line of the third column. .NET characters are 16-bit Unicode, and the data for the character only fills the first byte, resulting in the second byte being set to 00, causing the dots between characters you see in the first column. If the data used another character set, such as Japanese Kanji, you would see data in both bytes of the character. The hex representation of this data in the second column is *"00 4a 00 65 00 61 00 6e 00 20"*. Looking at the Unicode representation, which you can find at http://unicode.org/, you'll see that the hex and visual representation of the characters match.

You can see that I've highlighted the *00 20* at the end of the first line of the second column in Figure 6-16, which proves that *Jean* is followed by a Unicode space character. Knowing this information might help you share information with someone who is responsible for the data, letting them know that there are extraneous spaces in the data. Some computer or software systems might even use other types of characters, perhaps a proprietary delimiter for separating data, and accidentally save the data with the delimiter.

Fixing the First Bug

While you might have bad data and it might not be your fault, the prospect of fixing the problem by fixing the data source is often illusive, meaning that you need to apply a fix in your code. In this section, we'll apply a fix. However, we'll put a convoluted twist in the solution where we discover a new bug when fixing the first. The purpose is twofold: to illustrate the real-world fact that there are often multiple problems with a given piece of code and to show a completely different type of bug that you will encounter when writing your own code. The following steps lead you through the fix and subsequent discovery of the new bug:

1. Press SHIFT-F5 to stop the previous debugging session.

2. Implement a fix by commenting out the contents of the *foreach* loop and replacing with code that protects against extraneous spaces in the data, as follows:

   C#:

   ```
   var firstName = cust.FirstName.Trim();
   var lastName = cust.LastName.Trim();

   if (searchName == cust.FirstName)
   ```

```
    {
        Console.WriteLine(
            "Found: {0} {1}",
            firstName,
            lastName);
        customerFound = true;
    }
```

VB:

```
    Dim firstName As String = cust.FirstName.Trim()
    Dim lastName As String = cust.LastName.Trim()

    If (searchName = cust.FirstName) Then

        Console.WriteLine(
            "Found: {0} {1}",
            cust.FirstName,
            cust.LastName)
        customerFound = True

    End If
Next
```

Notice that the fix was to use the string.*Trim* method to remove the extraneous space from the data, assigning the clean results to local variables. *Trim* defaults to using the space character but has overloads that allow you to specify a different character, just in case the actual character you saw in Figure 6-16 was something other than a space. The rest of the logic uses variables with the clean data.

3. Press F5 to run the program and see if the fix works. Unfortunately, you're stopped in your tracks by the fact that a new error occurs: a *NullReferenceException*. Unlike runtime errors that give you wrong data, VS helps greatly by breaking on exceptions when they occur in the code. The next section describes this error, the *NullReferenceException*, in greater detail and provides information to help you deal with the problem when it occurs in your programs.

Debugging and Resolving NullReferenceException Problems

Encountering a *NullReferenceException* in your code is a common occurrence, deserving some discussion to help you deal with these problems effectively. As described in Step 3 in the preceding section, VS will pause on a *NullReferenceException* when running the program. In this particular example, VS pauses on the line that cleans *LastName* properties, repeated here for your convenience:

C#:

```
var firstName = cust.FirstName.Trim();
var lastName = cust.LastName.Trim();
```

VB:

```
Dim firstName As String = cust.FirstName.Trim()
Dim lastName As String = cust.LastName.Trim()
```

If you recall, the reason for calling *Trim* on the *FirstName* and *LastName* properties was to clean the data prior to performing further operations on that data. While we were concerned about *FirstName,* we also called *Trim* on *LastName* as well to help protect against invalid data there too, just to be safe. The following steps show you how to use VS to analyze the current situation and make an effective decision on an appropriate fix.

1. If VS isn't running, restart the program and let it run until VS pauses with a NullReferenceException.

2. Hover the cursor over *cust.LastName* to view the value. Alternatively, you can look in one of the debugging windows to see the value. Observe that *LastName* is *null.*

   This is the critical point in the analysis, finding the value that is *null.* It was clear that *cust* is not *null* because the previous statement, cleaning *FirstName,* executed without error as verified by inspecting the *firstName* variable. This example makes it very easy to find the *null* value because it occurred on the line where VS paused. In more challenging situations, you could be passing an object to a method in a third-party library where you don't have the code and VS will pause on the line with the method call. In that case, you have to inspect the values being passed to the method to see if any are *null.*

   Once you've found the *null* value, you must understand why the code raised the *NullReferenceException* error. A *null* value is the absence of a value; nothing is assigned to the variable. If you try to reference a variable with *null* assigned to it, you will receive a *NullReferenceException.* This makes sense because you are trying to perform an operation on a variable that has no definition. In this particular example, *LastName* is *null,* but we're still referencing *LastName* by calling the *Trim* method. This is illogical because there is not a string to trim; the string variable is set to *null.*

You want the *NullReferenceException* to be raised because it protects you from performing an invalid operation in your code. After you've found the *null* value and ascertained the reason, it's time to find out why the value is *null* in order to make an informed decision on a fix.

3. In the Immediate window, type the following command:

C#:

customers.IndexOf(cust)

VB:

?customers.IndexOf(cust)

This will return *1,* which is the index of the current *Customer* record, *cust,* in the collection *customers.* This will save a lot of time when trying to find this object in the data.

4. The debugger is currently paused on the line that cleans *LastName,* where the *NullReferenceException* occurred and there is a yellow arrow on the breakpoint. With your mouse, drag the yellow error up to the line that calls *GetCustomers.* We're currently attempting to answer the question of where this value became *null.* If lucky, we can stop this at the source and possibly find a bug where the value is inadvertently set to *null.*

5. Press F11 to step into the *GetCustomers* method. VS will navigate to the first line of the *GetCustomer* method.

6. Press F10 twice to see what values are being returned. This example is so simple that you can visually see the data. However, in real scenarios, you will probably be running code that makes the query to a database, or other data source, and might prepare that data in a form digestible by any potential callers. In Chapter 7, you'll learn more about how to perform database queries, but we want to keep things simple for now so that you won't be distracted by details unrelated to the point of this exercise, which is debugging. Therefore, we need to inspect the data to see if it is the source of the null data by typing the following command into the Immediate window:

C#:

customers[1].LastName

VB:

?customers(1).LastName

Additionally, you can drill down into the customers collection in one of the debugging windows, such as Autos, Locals, or Watch, inspecting the *Customer* object at index 1. If you recall from Step 3 in the preceding sequence, the *Customer* object we're interested in is at index 1. This result tells us that *LastName* for this *Customer* was set to *null* at the data source and there is nothing we can do to keep it from being set to *null*; another case of bad data. If you see a trend, you would be correct; never trust data whether it comes from a user on the front end or from the database on the back end. At this point, we have all the information we need to fix the problem and make sure we don't accidentally call methods on null data.

Press SHIFT-F5 to stop debugging.

7. In this example, we'll fix the problem by checking for *null* before using a variable and then replacing *null* with a default value. Comment out the contents of the *foreach* loop and replace it with the following code:

C#:

```csharp
string firstName = string.Empty;
if (cust.FirstName != null)
{
    firstName = cust.FirstName.Trim();
}

string lastName =
    cust.LastName == null ?
    "" : cust.LastName.Trim();

if (searchName == firstName)
{
    Console.WriteLine(
        "Found: {0} {1}",
        firstName,
        lastName);
    customerFound = true;
}
```

VB:

```vb
Dim firstName As String = String.Empty

If (cust.FirstName IsNot Nothing) Then
    firstName = cust.FirstName.Trim()
End If

Dim lastName As String
```

```
If cust.LastName Is Nothing Then
    lastName = ""
Else
    lastName = cust.LastName.Trim()
End If

If (searchName = firstName) Then

    Console.WriteLine(
        "Found: {0} {1}",
        cust.FirstName,
        cust.LastName)
    customerFound = True

End If
```

This code fixes the problem two different ways, giving you more than one way to solve the problem, depending on the style you prefer. In essence, the solution checks the *FirstName* and *LastName* properties to see if they are *null* (*Nothing* in VB). If they are not *null,* we know the properties have valid strings and are safe to work with. Otherwise, we return an empty string.

In VB, you use the *Is* and *IsNot* operators when working with *Nothing,* rather than the respective == and *!=* for working with C# *null.* Also, the VB *Iif,* which is the equivalent of the C# ternary operator, evaluates both true and false expressions, resulting in a *NullReferenceException* even if the false condition doesn't execute. Therefore, the preceding VB example uses the more verbose *If Then Else* syntax.

The choice to default to an empty string is specific to this example only. In practice, you'll have to look at your own situation to see if it makes sense to use a default value. For example, the presence of a *null* value might represent an erroneous condition and you might prefer to log the condition and not allow the user to continue with the current operation. Another strategy might be to skip this record, processing all the others, and then show the user a list of records that weren't processed. You might want to fix the problem with any or none of the ideas I have here, but my point is that you should think about what working with a *null* value means to your particular situation and not think that the only way to fix a *null* reference bug is the way we did here.

8. Press F5 to run the program. It will provide the following output:

```
Found: Jean
```

Victory!

Summary

You are now able to debug code. The section "Development-Time Code Tools" explained how to view the structure of your code at development time. You learned how to set breakpoints along with the many conditions available for breakpoint customization. The section "Stepping Through Code" explained how to navigate through your application, stepping into and out of methods and changing the executable location of your application. You can also open several windows and inspect the state of your application. In particular, you learned how to use the Debug History window that lets you see the state of an application at various stages of a debugging session.

In the next chapter, we migrate from a pure focus of working with code to using the features of VS that allow you to work with .NET technologies. More specifically, the next chapter shows how VS makes it easy to work with data.

Chapter 7
Working with Data

Key Skills & Concepts

- Work on SQL Server Databases with Visual Studio 2010
- Query Data with Language Integrated Query (LINQ)
- Use LINQ to SQL to Query and Manipulate SQL Server Data

Most of the work we do each day involves data, and most of the data we work with comes from databases. Because of the importance of data in our applications, this chapter introduces how to work with data in VS. It's very important to learn the concepts in this chapter because it will affect all of the work you do when programming. You'll also see many examples of working with data throughout the rest of this book, underscoring the importance of data in software engineering.

While you're free to work with any data source you want, Microsoft has several versions of SQL Server from free Express versions to Enterprise level. Since SQL Server Express ships with VS, we'll use that for all of the examples in this chapter and the rest of the book. Don't worry; the development experience for Express is similar to all other versions, so what you learn will be applicable to other versions of SQL Server.

Data operations are so important that you also have support in the programming languages for working with data called Language Integrated Query (LINQ). You can use LINQ to query many types of data sources, whether it is objects, XML, or relational data. This chapter will show you how to use LINQ for querying data from SQL Server.

Working with Databases

VS provides several tools for working directly with databases. The free Express versions of VS, such as Visual C# Express and Visual Basic Express, don't have this built-in support. However, you can visit MSDN and download the free SQL Server Express for database work alongside the Express versions. What I'll show you in this chapter will be available in VS Professional or later, which includes support for working with SQL Server directly in the VS IDE.

Introduction to Server Explorer

You don't need to open a project to perform any database work. To start working with databases in VS, you need to start VS and then open Server Explorer by clicking

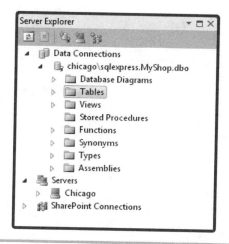

Figure 7-1 Server Explorer

View | Server Explorer or pressing CTRL-ALT-S. Server Explorer, shown in Figure 7-1, allows you to work with databases, servers, and SharePoint. Servers give you access to the various types of services for managing an operating system, such as Event Logs, Performance Counters, and Services. It is very convenient to be able to access these services in VS during development. For example, if you need to restart an operating system service, you can do it quickly. SharePoint is out of the scope of this book, but the relevant part of Server Explorer is the Data Connections section at the top, which you can see in Figure 7-1.

The Data Connections section will have a list of databases that you can select and work with. Initially, the list will be empty and you must add connections yourself, which you can do by right-clicking Data Connections and configuring the database settings. Since the process of connecting to an existing database is similar to the task for creating a database, I'll show you how to create a brand new database instead, which is covered in the next section.

Creating a Database

All of the examples in this chapter will use a database that we will create in this section. Therefore, we need to create a database to work with. With VS Standard and higher, you don't need external tools to create a simple database because there is built-in support for getting started. That said, there are advanced scenarios where a database administrator would want to use the SQL Server tools to create the database themselves, meaning that you would only want to connect to the database they created. For many cases, you can just create the database yourself to get started.

Figure 7-2 Create New SQL Server Database

To create a database, right-click Data Connections in Server Explorer, and select Create New SQL Server Database. This will show the Create New SQL Server Database window, shown in Figure 7-2.

In Figure 7-2, the server name is .\sqlexpress. The dot before the backslash represents the current machine name, and the sqlexpress is the name for the SQL Server Express database. Server names will vary, depending on the location of the server and the name given to the database server instance. For example, if you were deploying an application to a shared Web hosting site, the server name would look something like sql02.somedomain. com, which is established by the hosting provider you are using.

Your authentication options include Windows and SQL Server. Here, I'm choosing Windows authentication because it's the simplest option. The database created here is local, but you might have a database already created on a server at another location. The database on another server might have a SQL login, which is another method of authentication.

After adding the database name, click OK to create the database. As shown in Figure 7-2, we've called this database MyShop, representing an application that supports customers who order products from a store. You'll see the new database under Data Connections in Server Explorer, similar to what you see in Figure 7-1. Now you're ready to add tables.

Adding Tables

The database itself will hold data for customers, orders, and order details that we introduced in the preceding chapter. The data will be held in tables that we'll create in this section. In later sections, I'll show you how to perform Create, Read, Update, and Delete (CRUD) operations on this data. Right now, you'll learn how to create the tables.

To create a table, right-click the Tables branch under the database in Server Explorer and select Add New Table; you'll see a Table Designer similar to Figure 7-3. Yours won't have the *CustomerID* or *Name* columns yet; that's coming up next.

The Table Designer allows you to add columns and configure the data type (such as integer, date, float, or character) and other details of each column and the table. Figure 7-3 shows a table with two columns, *CustomerID* of data type *int* and *Name* of data type *nvarchar(50)*. Ensure that Null is unchecked for each column to avoid errors in code that doesn't check for *null* later in this chapter.

NOTE

Databases, such as SQL Server, have their own type system, which doesn't always match the .NET type system perfectly. That said, there are types that match very well; for instance, a SQL *int* is the same as a C# *int* or VB *Integer*. A SQL *nvarchar(50)* can be matched with a C# *string* or VB *String*. However, the *nvarchar* is limited to 50 characters, or whatever length is specified in parentheses, but the C# *string* and VB *String* don't have a specified size. A full discussion of SQL types is out of scope, but you should be aware that there are differences between SQL and .NET types.

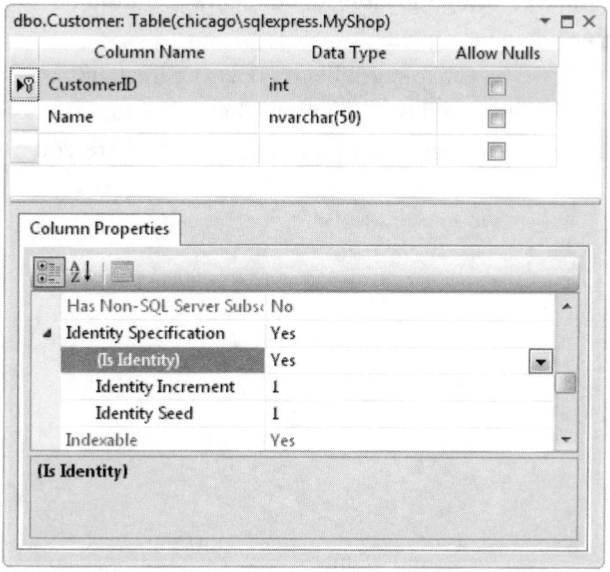

Figure 7-3 The Customer table

The *CustomerID* has a primary key symbol, which is created by right-clicking the column and selecting Set Primary Key. If you needed a composite key (multiple columns that define a key), which you don't in this simple example, you would press CTRL and click each column that belongs to the key and then right-click and select Set Primary Key.

NOTE
When working with LINQ, which we discuss later in this chapter, it is absolutely essential that you give every table a primary key.

In addition to setting the primary key, it's helpful to make the key number auto-increment so that it will have a unique value for every record you insert. In Figure 7-3, you can see that *CustomerID* is selected and Column Properties has scrolled down to the Identity Specification property. By default, Identity Specification is collapsed and set to No. You'll need to expand the Identity Specification property by selecting the arrow on the left, and change the value to Yes by selecting the drop-down arrow on the right of the "(Is Identity)" setting, which by default is No. This will also enable Identity Increment, which specifies the number to add for each new record, and the Identity Seed, which specifies what the first number will be. The effect of setting Identity Increment is that the first record added to the table will have a *CustomerID* with the value 1 (Identity Seed) and subsequent records will have a *CustomerID* with the values 2, 3, 4, and so on (Identity Increment). The value for *CustomerID* in each record creates a unique value that identifies the record and makes it easy to program data applications.

When you're done creating the table, click the Save button on the toolbar and name the table **Customer** when prompted.

You can add data to the Customer table by opening the database in Server Explorer, navigate to the Tables folder in the MyShop database, right-click Customer, and select Show Table Data. You'll see a grid similar to Figure 7-4 where you can enter some

Figure 7-4 Adding data to a table

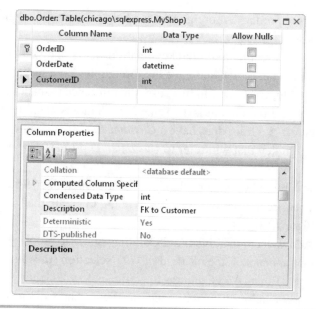

Figure 7-5 The Order table

customer data. Notice that you need only type a name in the *Name* column (replacing the word *NULL*) and do not need to enter a value for the *CustomerID,* since we've made the *CustomerID* column auto-increment.

In a database of any sophistication, you have multiple tables. In the MyShop database, a Customer has an Order. So, create a new table named **Order**, shown in Figure 7-5, that has Primary Key *OrderID,* a *datetime* field called *OrderDate,* and an *int* field called *CustomerID.*

The Description in the Column Properties for the *CustomerID* field says *FK to Customer. FK* is an abbreviation for foreign key, which is used to create a relationship between a parent table and a child table. The next section explains more about what a foreign key is and how to create one.

Relating Tables with Foreign Keys

Foreign keys allow you to establish a relationship between two tables. You can think of this relationship as being parent/child, master/detail, or one-to-many; each analogy being equal, I'll use parent/child. The preceding section shows how to create Customer and Order tables. The relationship between these two tables is that Customer is the parent and Order is the child. One record in Customer can have many records in Order; customers can have zero or more orders. A foreign key can help manage the relationship between Customer and Order.

The mechanics of creating a foreign key relationship is that you put the foreign key column in the child table, Order, and have the foreign key column refer to the primary key of the parent table, Customer. In this case, the reference is made simply by matching the integer value; if the ID number is the same in both tables, then the records are related. As shown in Figure 7-5, Order does have a *CustomerID* column, of type *int,* and we will make this the foreign key that will refer to *CustomerID* primary key in Customer, shown in Figure 7-3.

To create this foreign key relationship in VS, right-click the *CustomerID* column in the Order table and select Relationships. We're going to create the foreign key relationship that you see in Figure 7-6.

Next, click Add, select the Tables And Columns Specific property, and click the ellipses button that appears on the far right of your selection (the ellipses does not appear until you first click "Tables And Columns Specific" below "(General)" in the Foreign Key Relationships dialog window. This will open the Tables And Columns window shown in Figure 7-7.

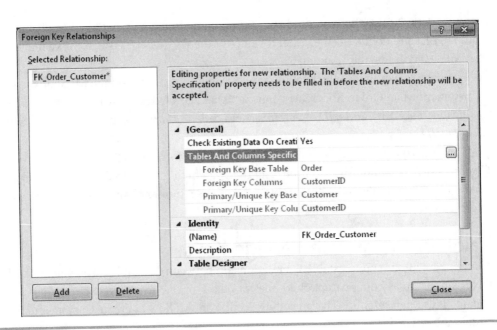

Figure 7-6 Managing a foreign key relationship

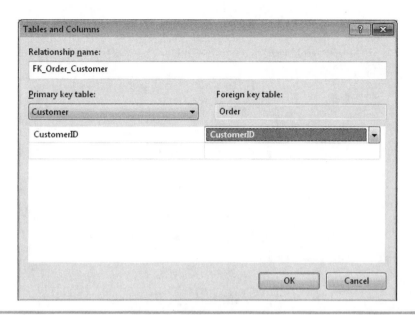

Figure 7-7 Configuring a foreign key relationship

In the primary key table drop-down, shown in Figure 7-7, select *Customer,* which automatically selects the primary key, *CustomerID.* (Note: If you don't see this behavior, check to see that you've set your primary key columns and saved those table changes as described earlier.) In the list, under Foreign Key Table in Figure 7-7, you'll initially see *OrderID,* which is the primary key of the order table. Select *OrderID* and change it to *CustomerID* as the foreign key column. Click OK to exit and click Close to finalize creation of the foreign key relationship. When you click Save to save the new foreign key relationship, you'll see a warning message similar to Figure 7-8, listing the tables participating in the change. Select Yes to make your changes to the SQL Server tables. You can uncheck the Warn About Tables Affected box if you don't want to see this message anymore, but the message does serve as a safety net to make sure you don't accidentally save unintended changes to SQL Server, which is an external product to VS 2010.

Once the foreign key is in place, you can add a few records to the Order table, much as you did with the Customer table, but remember that the *CustomerID* must match an existing *CustomerID* in the Customer table because of the foreign key relationship. Forcing the child to refer to its parent is good because it maintains the integrity of the database, demonstrating the value of a foreign key.

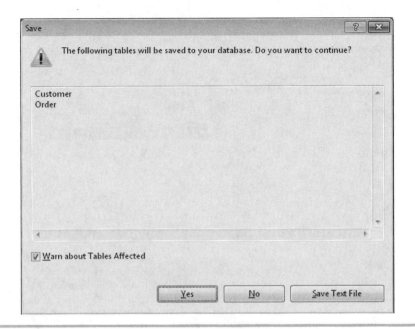

Figure 7-8 Foreign key relationship Save warning message

TIP

Figure 7-7 shows an editable Relationship Name field. In many cases, you won't care what this name is because it follows a standard convention of FK_Child_Parent. However, sometimes you have multiple relationships between the same tables, which means that VS appends an incremental number to the end of the name. Thus, for instance, the next foreign key relationship between the same two tables would be FK_Child_Parent1. In those cases, it would be smart to plan ahead and change the name to something meaningful so that you can later understand or quickly recall what relationship rules the foreign keys are enforcing. To see what I mean by enforcing rules, go ahead and enter a new record in the Order table, but enter an integer in the CustomerID column that does not exist already in the Customer table, like 9999. Try to save that record and then read the error message presented to you.

Working with multiple tables, you might want to have a better feel for the database structure and relationships. Database diagrams could be helpful in this case. To create a database diagram, right-click the Database Diagrams folder under the database in Server Explorer and click Add New Diagram. Click Yes when you receive an information message requesting the creation of objects for database diagramming. In the Add Table window, press the CTRL key so that you can select multiple rows, click to select each table, and click Add. You'll see a new database diagram similar to Figure 7-9 (you may see Order appear above Customer in your diagram, which is fine; the position of

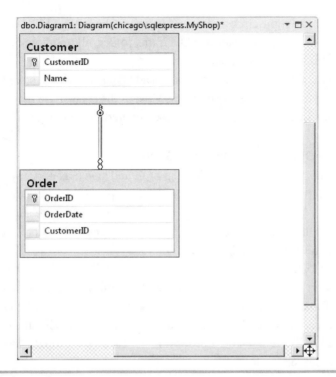

Figure 7-9 A database diagram

the symbols—the key and the infinity symbol at the end of the line connecting the two tables—is what is important).

As shown in Figure 7-9, the database diagram shows you tables, columns, and relationships. You can use this window to add new tables and relationships. When you want to create a new table, right-click the design surface, select Add Table, and use the Visual Designer to configure the table, as in previous examples. What is helpful with this designer is the ease in which foreign key relationships can be created as compared to the method we used earlier to accomplish the same thing. To create a foreign key relationship, click the foreign key column in the child table, drag the carat to the parent table, and drop the carat on the primary key of the parent table. When you're finished with creating the database diagram, VS will prompt for the diagram name; you can reply with a name of your choice and click OK to save the diagram.

Other features of the database diagram include navigation, printing, and multiple diagrams. When you have a database diagram larger than the screen size, click the symbol with the four arrow heads at the lower right-hand corner of the database diagram, and move your mouse to quickly navigate through the document. If you want a permanent copy of the diagram, right-click and copy to clipboard or select File | Print. You can also add multiple diagrams to the Database Diagrams folder, allowing you to have multiple different views for your convenience.

In addition to tables and diagrams, you can add database views, stored procedures, functions, synonyms, types, and assemblies. Most of these database items are for advanced scenarios, but it's important that you know about stored procedures, which are covered next.

Adding Stored Procedures

A *stored procedure* is code that is written in SQL and saved as part of a database. It is a method stored in the database itself, and not in your program code; hence the term stored procedure. In this section, I'll show you how to create and execute a stored procedure. Later sections of this chapter will show you how to execute this stored procedure, which runs a data query, through LINQ to SQL.

To create a stored procedure, right-click the Stored Procedure folder for the database in Server Explorer and select Add New Stored Procedure. You'll see an editor appear with skeleton code for a stored procedure. Modify the code so that it retrieves all of the data from the Customer table, as shown in Listing 7-1. After modifying the template code, click Save and you'll see the stored procedure appear in the Stored Procedures folder of the database in Server Explorer.

Listing 7-1   Stored procedure example

```
CREATE PROCEDURE GetCustomers
AS
declare @cust_count int
select @cust_count = count(*) from Customer
if @cust_count > 0
begin
    select [Name] from Customer
end
return
```

Listing 7-1 declares a variable named *@cust_count* and runs a *select* statement to assign the number of customers, *count(*),* to *@cust_count*. If *@cust_count* is larger than 0, there are customers and the stored procedure queries for customer names. Teaching TSQL (Microsoft's dialect of SQL) syntax is outside the scope of this book, but you can download SQL Server Books Online for free and purchase McGraw-Hill's *Microsoft SQL Server 2008: A Beginner's Guide, Fourth Edition* by Dusan Petkovic (McGraw-Hill/Professional, 2008) to get started.

To execute this stored procedure, right-click the stored procedure in the database in Server Explorer and click Execute. You'll see output similar to the following if there are records in the customer table:

```
Running [dbo].[GetCustomers].

Name
--------------------------------------------------
Meg
Joe
May
No rows affected.
(3 row(s) returned)
@RETURN_VALUE = 0
Finished running [dbo].[GetCustomers].
```

In addition to execution, you can debug the stored procedure in VS. To debug, set a breakpoint on any line in the stored procedure, right-click the stored procedure in Server Explorer, and select Step Into Stored Procedure or click ALT-F5. If you need more help debugging, visit Chapter 6 for a refresher on VS debugging capabilities.

Configuring Database Options

VS has many database configuration settings that you can view via the Tools | Options menu and selecting Database Tools, as shown in Figure 7-10. For example, one of the

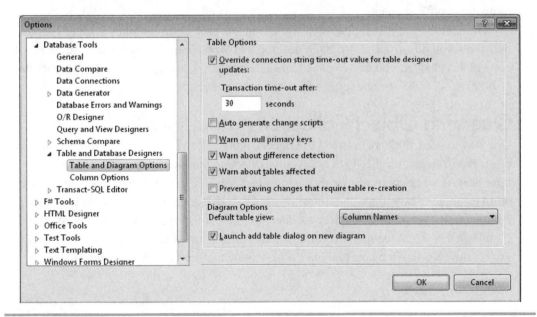

Figure 7-10   Database Tools options

options found after clicking the arrow button to expand Database Tools and then selecting Table And Database Designers is "Prevent saving changes that require table re-creation." VS will not allow you to save a foreign key change to existing tables. However, by unchecking "Prevent saving changes that require table re-creation," you'll be able to save foreign key changes to an existing table.

As with so many other features of VS, there are literally dozens of database settings; most are intuitive if you already understand SQL Server. Other options differ, depending on the version of VS you have, and your Options screen might not look the same as Figure 7-10.

Now that you know how to create databases, tables, and stored procedures, you'll need to know how to use your database from code. The rest of this chapter shows you how to use LINQ to work with data. First, we'll look at the basic syntax of LINQ through LINQ to Objects and then follow with working with SQL Server through LINQ to SQL.

Learning Language Integrated Query (LINQ)

LINQ is a set of features built into programming languages, such as C# and VB, for working with data. It's called Language Integrated Query because the LINQ syntax is part of the language, as opposed to being a separate library. This section will show you the essentials of LINQ with LINQ to Objects, a LINQ provider for querying in-memory collections of objects. The great news is that the syntax you learn here is not only applicable to LINQ to Objects, but to all other LINQ providers, such as LINQ to SQL and more, that you'll encounter.

The examples in this chapter will use a Console project for simplicity. Later chapters will show you how to display data in desktop and Web applications. If you want to run the code in this chapter, you can create a Console application and type the examples into the *Main* method, as has been explained in each previous chapter of this book.

Querying Object Collections with LINQ

One way to use LINQ is via LINQ to Objects, which allows you to query collections of objects. You can use LINQ to query any collection that implements the *IEnumerable* interface. As you may recall, we discussed interfaces in Chapter 4; now you can see one more example of how important interfaces are to .NET development. Listing 7-2 shows a program that uses LINQ to query a collection. The object type is a custom class, named *Customer.* The *Main* method creates a generic list of *Customer* and uses a LINQ query to extract the *Customer* objects that have a first name that starts with the letter *M.*

Listing 7-2   A program demonstrating how to make a LINQ to objects query

C#:

```csharp
using System;
using System.Collections.Generic;
using System.Linq;

class Customer
{
    public string FirstName { get; set; }
    public string LastName { get; set; }
}

class Program
{
    static void Main(string[] args)
    {
        List<Customer> custList = new List<Customer>
        {
            new Customer
            {
                FirstName = "Joe",
                LastName = "Zev"
            },
            new Customer
            {
                FirstName = "May",
                LastName = "Lee"
            },
            new Customer
            {
                FirstName = "Meg",
                LastName = "Han"
            }
        };

        var customers =
            from cust in custList
            where cust.FirstName.StartsWith("M")
            select cust;

        foreach (var cust in customers)
        {
            Console.WriteLine(cust.FirstName);
        }
```

```
            Console.ReadKey();
        }
    }

    VB:

Class Customer
    Property FirstName As String
    Property LastName As String
End Class

Module Module1

    Sub Main()
        Dim custList As New List(Of Customer) From
        {
            New Customer With
            {
                .FirstName = "Joe",
                .LastName = "Zev"
            },
            New Customer With
            {
                .FirstName = "May",
                .LastName = "Lee"
            },
            New Customer With
            {
                .FirstName = "Meg",
                .LastName = "Han"
            }
        }

        Dim customers =
            From cust In custList
            Where cust.FirstName.StartsWith("M")
            Select cust

        For Each cust In customers
            Console.WriteLine(cust.FirstName)
        Next

        Console.ReadKey()
    End Sub

End Module
```

Both the C# and VB examples from Listing 7-2 contain similar LINQ queries. To clarify, the following examples show both the C# LINQ query:

```
var customers =
    from cust in custList
    where cust.FirstName.StartsWith("M")
    select cust;
```

and the VB LINQ query:

```
Dim customers =
    From cust In custList
    Where cust.FirstName.StartsWith("M")
    Select cust
```

The *customers* variable in the LINQ queries references a new collection that holds the result of running the LINQ query, which contains all of the customers where the first letter of the *FirstName* property is the letter *M*. The *from* clause specifies the range variable that you name, *cust* is the name I chose, and the collection object to query, *custList,* was created and populated in the previous line of code. The range variable is what you use to specify parameters of the LINQ query. In the preceding example, we use the *where* clause to filter the results of the query. This *where* clause calls the *StartsWith* method on each *FirstName* property of the *cust* range variable to specify the filter.

The *select* clause specifies that each individual customer object is returned into our new customers collection, which we declared as type *var* (*Dim* in VB), which means our *customers* variable winds up being whatever collection type is returned from our LINQ query. This also means that the resulting customers collection will contain zero or more *Customer* type instances, depending on the filter we specified and whether our *custList* contained any Customer objects in the first place as a result of the *Select cust* portion of the LINQ statement. The *select* clause for C# queries is required, but the *select* clause for VB queries is optional and will return the range variable instance if omitted.

What our LINQ statement is essentially saying in English is "Create a new collection object and assign it to our variable customers (we don't really care what type of object customers turns out to be as long as we can use it later), then go through every object in our previously defined and loaded *custList* collection, selecting only the ones that have for their FirstName property a string that begins with the letter *M,* and ignore all the rest, then take the ones that match this filter and stuff them into whatever collection you created for me earlier that you assigned to my variable customers."

Creating a LINQ Projection with Anonymous Types

You can customize what is returned by the select clause by using what is called an anonymous type. This customization of return values is called a *projection*. Anonymous types facilitate custom projections, allowing you to return the results of a LINQ query in a form that you specify without needing to declare a new type ahead of time. Here's an example of creating a query that declares a new anonymous type for combining the *FirstName* and *LastName* properties of Customer into a variable, *FullName*, that is created as a string-type property associated with the object returned into *cust* in the foreach statement:

C#:

```
var customers =
    from cust in custList
    where cust.FirstName.StartsWith("M")
    select new
    {
        FullName =
            cust.FirstName + " " +
            cust.LastName
    };

foreach (var cust in customers)
{
    Console.WriteLine(cust.FullName);
}
```

VB:

```
Dim customers =
    From cust In custList
    Where cust.FirstName.StartsWith("M")
    Select New With
    {
        .FullName =
            cust.FirstName & " " &
            cust.LastName
    }

For Each cust In customers
    Console.WriteLine(cust.FullName)
Next
```

In both the C# and VB select clauses you see a *new* statement (*New With* in VB) that defines the anonymous type. The new anonymous type has a single property, *FullName,* that is the combination of *FirstName* and *LastName* in *Customer,* but the new type will only have a *FullName* property. Notice how the *foreach* loop uses the *FullName* property, instead of the *FirstName* property from Listing 7-2. The beauty of this anonymous type is that we don't really care what type of object is generated for us by the LINQ query, as long as that object has the new property associated with it that we specified, *FullName* in this case, which it does.

The variable, *cust,* in the preceding listing is used in two different scopes: the LINQ query and the foreach statement. Although the identifier, *cust,* is the same, the two usages are separate instances. Although you might not use the same practice in your own code, I wanted to demonstrate this so that you can see that range variables, such as *cust,* are scoped to the query they are defined in.

Another nuance of the preceding code is that *cust,* in the foreach loop, is not type *Customer.* Rather, it is an instance of the anonymous type created by the projection (select clause) of the LINQ query. Therefore, *FullName* is the only property each anonymous type instance, *cust,* contains.

Using LINQ to Sort Collection Results

Another common task you'll want to perform with data is sorting so that you can put objects in a certain order. The following example modifies the example from Listing 7-2 to sort items from the customer List in descending order:

C#:

```
var customers =
    from cust in custList
    orderby cust.FirstName descending
    select cust;
```

VB:

```
Dim customers =
    From cust In custList
    Order By cust.FirstName Descending
    Select cust
```

The *orderby* (*Order By* in VB) clause specifies the properties to sort on. This example sorts the list by the *FirstName* property in descending order.

This was a quick taste of what you could do with LINQ, and there is much more. In fact, I wrote an entire book on the subject titled *LINQ Programming* (McGraw-Hill/ Professional, 2008). The remaining section of this book takes what you've learned here and expands, showing you more samples of LINQ queries. The difference will be that you will be working with SQL Server data instead of in-memory objects.

Handling Data with LINQ to SQL

The LINQ to SQL provider allows you to communicate with SQL Server databases. There are many other types of providers, such as LINQ to Entities for generic databases (which includes SQL Server), LINQ to XML for XML data sources, and LINQ to Oracle for Oracle databases. The preceding section showed you how to use the in-memory provider, LINQ to Objects. However, LINQ to SQL is the easiest database provider to learn and ships with VS. Once you learn LINQ to SQL, the journey to other providers is easier. The following sections will show you how to set up LINQ to SQL, perform queries, and modify data.

Setting Up LINQ to SQL

Setting up LINQ to SQL involves running the LINQ to SQL Wizard and adding classes and methods. Behind the scenes, LINQ to SQL generates code, saving you a lot of work. The result of setting up LINQ to SQL is that you will have a *data model,* which is an environment with classes that you can use to query and modify database data and call methods for invoking stored procedures.

Before setting up LINQ to SQL, you'll need to create a project (a Console project for the purposes of this chapter). See Chapter 5 if you need a refresher on how to set up a Console project. Select Add | New Item, select LINQ to SQL Classes, name the file **MyShop.dbml,** and click Add. This will show you the LINQ to SQL Designer, with two surfaces for classes and methods. Figure 7-11 shows the LINQ to SQL Designer with a couple of classes and a method.

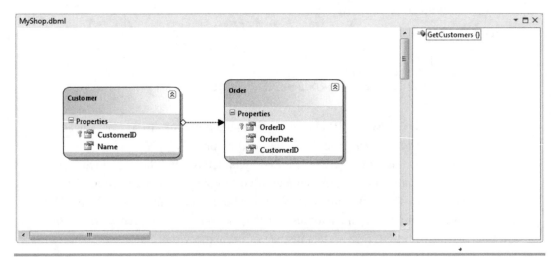

Figure 7-11 The LINQ to SQL Designer

To add entities to the LINQ to SQL Designer, open Server Explorer, select a database, and open the Tables folder. Then drag and drop the Customer and Order tables from Server Explorer to the left surface of the LINQ to SQL Designer. You can see the Customer and Order classes in Figure 7-11, along with properties corresponding to the fields of each table in the database.

The line between Customer and Order is called an *association.* As you might guess from reading the previous discussion on class relationships, the association defines the relationship between two classes. Although a relationship between tables is constrained by a foreign key in a child that refers to the primary key of that child's parent, an association is the reverse direction; it is a property of a parent class that refers to all of the children of that class. When coding, you can use this association to navigate between parent and child objects.

NOTE

Features, such as the difference between foreign key relationships in relational databases and associations in object-oriented code, are often referred to as an impedance mismatch, a term taken from electrical engineering, between data and objects. LINQ is designed to reduce the impedance mismatch by allowing you to work with data from an object-oriented point of view, rather than doing all of the low-level work yourself such as copying data records into data transfer objects, DTOs, that you design and create.

On the right pane of Figure 7-11, you can see a *GetCustomers* method, which allows you to call the *GetCustomers* stored procedure. You can put stored procedures, such as *GetCustomers,* onto the design surface by opening the Stored Procedures folder of the database in Server Explorer and dragging and dropping that stored procedure onto the right pane of the LINQ to SQL Designer.

If your database has views and functions, you can add them the same way as you did for classes and functions previously. Before showing you how to use these new classes and views, I'll show a little more about what you can do with the LINQ to SQL Designer.

Working with the LINQ to SQL Designer

While the most important part of the LINQ to SQL Designer is being able to add classes and methods, you should also know about some if its features such as the Methods pane hiding, zooming, and auto-layout. You'll see these options through the design surface context menu (right-click).

Most of the time working with the Designer is with classes, and you want as much screen real estate as possible. You can achieve this goal by hiding the Methods pane. Just right-click the design surface and select Hide Methods Pane. Similarly, select Show Methods Pane to make the Methods pane reappear.

The default zoom level for the Designer is 100%, but you can change this by right-clicking, select Zoom, and select a zoom level percent. This might be useful if you wanted a higher-level view where you could fit more objects onto the screen at one time.

If you right-click and select Layout Diagram, VS will automatically lay out your diagram so that classes with relationships can physically reside in the same area with minimal overlapping of association lines, a feature I call auto-layout. After you've performed auto-layout, you will be able to manually change the location of classes by selecting and dragging each class to a new location, a feature I call manual layout.

TIP

Be careful of executing auto-layout after you have your layout the way you want. I tend to perform an auto-layout after the first time working with the LINQ to SQL Designer on a database. Then I follow up with manual layout to make working with classes even easier. Using auto-layout after manual layout will result in a lot of lost work.

It's common in development to add new tables to a database that you also want in the Designer. In that case, drag and drop the tables from Server Explorer as you did for Customer and Order earlier. If a table changes, you can select its corresponding class in the Designer and delete that class and then drag and drop the new table onto the design surface. Any foreign key references will result in associations on the Designer if classes for both tables reside in the Designer too.

An important part of working with the Designer is properties. Right-click the Designer, select Properties, and you'll see the Properties window, similar to Figure 7-12.

Figure 7-12 The LINQ to SQL Class Designer Properties window

LINQ to SQL generates a lot of code for you, and the Properties window allows you to modify parts of that code through the Code Generation section. To see this section, be sure your Properties window has the "Categorized" button selected near the top left side, and not the Alphabetical "AZ" button. You can also see the database connection string, which is created when you dragged and dropped from Server Explorer to the Designer and saved.

In addition to properties for the Designer itself, you view properties on objects such as classes, associations, and methods. Select the object you want to work with, right-click that object, and select Properties to show the Properties window for that object.

You now have a data model to work with. The following sections show you how to work with this data model to query, insert, update, and delete data.

Introduction to Querying LINQ to SQL

Previously, you learned how to use LINQ through the LINQ to Objects provider. All of what you learned with LINQ to Objects is applicable to other LINQ providers, including LINQ to SQL. This section combines the nuances of LINQ to SQL with what you've already learned to query database data. Listing 7-3 shows a LINQ query with LINQ to SQL that retrieves values from the Customer table of the MyShop database, which contains the tables added previously in this chapter.

Listing 7-3 Querying data with LINQ to SQL

C#:

```csharp
using System;
using System.Linq;

namespace LinqToSqlDemoCS
{
    class Program
    {
        static void Main()
        {
            var myShop = new MyShopDataContext();

            var customers =
                from cust in myShop.Customers
                where cust.Name != "Joe"
                select cust;

            foreach (var cust in customers)
            {
                Console.WriteLine("Name: " + cust.Name);
            }
```

```
                     Console.ReadKey();
            }
        }
    }
```

VB:

```
Module Module1

    Sub Main()
        Dim myShop As New MyShopDataContext

        Dim customers =
            From cust In myShop.Customers
            Where cust.Name IsNot "Joe"
            Select cust

        For Each cust In customers
            Console.WriteLine("Name: " & cust.Name)
        Next

        Console.ReadKey()
    End Sub

End Module
```

And here's the output using my data:

```
Name: Meg
Name: May
```

Other than the obvious fact that we're now getting our data from a real database, the difference between Listing 7-3 and the LINQ to Objects examples you saw earlier are that you have to use the *System.Linq* namespace (C# only), declare the *MyShopDataContext* data context, and query *Customers* from the data context. In C#, the *using* directive for the *System.Linq* namespace is required. If you left it out, the compiler will give you the following error message:

"Could not find an implementation of the query pattern for source type 'System. Data.Linq.Table<LinqToSqlDemoCS.Customer>'. 'Where' not found. Are you missing a reference to 'System.Core.dll' or a using directive for 'System.Linq'?"

Remember this message because any time you add a new file to a C# project where you are coding LINQ queries, this will be an indication you need to add a *using* directive for the *System.Linq* namespace.

A *data context* is the code that is generated by VS when you run the LINQ to SQL item wizard. The *Main* method instantiates *MyShopDataContext,* which is the data context. The name came from when the LINQ to SQL item wizard ran and your naming of the *.dbml file.

LINQ to SQL queries are made with the data context, which contains a property that holds a collection of the class type that the property is named after, *myShop.Customers* and *myShop.Orders* in this case. The LINQ query in the *Main* method uses the *myShop* data context instance to access the *Customers* collection in the from portion of the query.

NOTE
The LINQ to SQL provider uses pluralized data context properties. However, the results are not perfect; for example, Deer becomes Deers, which is incorrect in English. Additionally, pluralization is designed for English and will produce strange results in languages other than English. If the pluralization generated by the LINQ of a class is incorrect, you can either double-click the class name in the Designer or change the class name via the Properties window.

This section introduced you to what goes into creating a LINQ to SQL query, but your queries will likely need to work with multiple tables, as discussed in the next section.

Performing Queries on Multiple Tables

Until now, all queries have been from a single data source or table, like *Customers* in Listing 7-3. Often, you need to combine the results from multiple tables, which is where select many and join queries are useful. To demonstrate how joins work, we'll define a scenario where you need to know the dates of all orders made and the name of the customer who made the order.

The select many lets you join tables based on associations in the LINQ to SQL Designer. From the parent object, you navigate to the child object and are able to access the properties of both parent and child. The following code shows how to perform a select many query that gets data from the Customer and Order tables and repackages it into a collection of data transfer objects:

C#:

```
var myShop = new MyShopDataContext();

var customers =
    from cust in myShop.Customers
    from ord in cust.Orders
    select new
    {
        Name = cust.Name,
        Date = ord.OrderDate
    };
```

```
foreach (var custOrd in customers)
{
    Console.WriteLine(
        " Name: " + custOrd.Name +
        " Date: " + custOrd.Date);
}
```

VB:

```
Dim myShop As New MyShopDataContext

Dim customers =
    From cust In myShop.Customers
    From ord In cust.Orders
    Select New With
    {
        .Name = cust.Name,
        .Date = ord.OrderDate
    }

For Each custOrd In customers
    Console.WriteLine(
        " Name: " & custOrd.Name &
        " Date: " & custOrd.Date)
Next
```

And here's the output:

```
Name: Joe Date: 1/5/2010 12:00:00 AM
Name: May Date: 10/5/2010 12:00:00 AM
Name: May Date: 10/23/2010 12:00:00 AM
```

Imagine that the preceding code is sitting in the *Main* method, like what you saw in Listing 7-3. The different part of this query that makes it a select many type of query is the second *from* clause. Consider the parent/child relationship between Customer and Order, which is represented by *cust* and *ord* in this query. The second *from* clause uses the *cust* instance to specify the orders to query, which will be all orders belonging to each customer. The *ord* instance will hold each order belonging to its associated *cust*. To make this data useful, the projection is on an anonymous type that pulls together the name of the customer and the date of that customer's order.

In the database, I created two orders for May, one order for Joe, and zero orders for Meg. Since there wasn't an order for Meg, you don't see any items from Meg in the output. Later, I'll show you how to add a parent record, even when that parent record has no child records.

The select many query is fine for simple queries but becomes harder to use in more complex queries. In this case, a join query emerges as an easier option. Like a select many query, a join query will combine two tables that have matching keys. Here's an example of a join query that accomplishes the exact same task as the preceding select many query:

C#:

```
var myShop = new MyShopDataContext();

var customers =
    from cust in myShop.Customers
    join ord in myShop.Orders
        on cust.CustomerID equals ord.CustomerID
    select new
    {
        Name = cust.Name,
        Date = ord.OrderDate
    };

foreach (var custOrd in customers)
{
    Console.WriteLine(
        " Name: " + custOrd.Name +
        " Date: " + custOrd.Date);
}
```

VB:

```
Dim myShop As New MyShopDataContext

Dim customers =
    From cust In myShop.Customers
    Join ord In myShop.Orders
        On cust.CustomerID Equals ord.CustomerID
    Select New With
    {
        .Name = cust.Name,
        .Date = ord.OrderDate
    }

For Each custOrd In customers
    Console.WriteLine(
        " Name: " & custOrd.Name &
        " Date: " & custOrd.Date)
Next
```

The difference between this query and the select many is that there is a *join* clause instead of a second *from*. The *join* identifies a range variable, *ord,* and operates on the *Orders* property of the data context. You also must specify which keys of the table join, mentioning the parent first, *cust.CustomerID,* and then the child, *ord.CustomerID*. Remember to use the *equals* keyword because the equality operator will not work.

The select many and join clauses are synonymous with SQL inner joins because there must be a foreign key in a child table that matches a parent in the parent table before any records for the parent will be returned. To address the issue of needing to get parents that don't have children, you must perform a *left outer join*. To perform the equivalent of a SQL left outer join in LINQ, you must use a standard operator called *DefaultIfEmpty*. The following query gets a record for all customers, regardless of whether they have orders or not:

C#:

```csharp
var myShop = new MyShopDataContext();

var customers =
    from cust in myShop.Customers
    join ord in myShop.Orders
        on cust.CustomerID equals ord.CustomerID
        into customerOrders
    from custOrd in customerOrders.DefaultIfEmpty()
    select new
    {
        Name = cust.Name,
        Date = custOrd == null ?
            new DateTime(1800, 1, 1) :
            custOrd.OrderDate
    };

foreach (var custOrd in customers)
{
    Console.WriteLine(
        " Name: " + custOrd.Name +
        " Date: " + custOrd.Date);
}
```

VB:

```vb
Dim myShop As New MyShopDataContext

Dim customers =
    From cust In myShop.Customers
    Group Join ord In myShop.Orders
        On cust.CustomerID Equals ord.CustomerID
        Into customersOrders = Group
    From custOrd In customersOrders.DefaultIfEmpty()
    Select New With
    {
        .Name = cust.Name,
        .Date = IIf(custOrd Is Nothing,
                    New DateTime(1800, 1, 1),
                    custOrd.OrderDate)
    }
```

```
For Each custOrd In customers
    Console.WriteLine(
        " Name: " & custOrd.Name &
        " Date: " & custOrd.Date)
Next
```

And the output is

```
Name: Meg Date: 1/1/1800 12:00:00 AM
Name: Joe Date: 1/5/2010 12:00:00 AM
Name: May Date: 10/5/2010 12:00:00 AM
Name: May Date: 10/23/2010 12:00:00 AM
```

For C#, the left outer join is accomplished the same way as a join except for two additional lines: the *into* clause and the second *from* clause. For VB, the left outer join is the same as the join except for three lines: the *Into* clause, the second *From* clause, and the *Group* keyword. The *into* clause specifies an identifier that is used by the *from* clause. In the *from* clause, *DefaultIfEmpty* will return the default value for the continuation variable type. In the preceding example, the continuation variable is *customerOrders* whose type is *Order.* Since LINQ to SQL types are classes and *Order* is a class from the *Orders* entity collection, the default value is *null* (*Nothing* in VB). Notice how I enhanced the projection with a ternary (immediate if in VB) operator to control what value is returned when the parent doesn't have a child. When performing a left outer join, make sure you compare the value against its default value to determine if the parent doesn't have a child and ensure that valid values are set. Not only does the preceding example demonstrate how to check for a default value, but it also shows that you can use expressions in your projections.

In addition to LINQ queries, you can call stored procedures. As you may recall from the previous discussion on working with the LINQ to SQL Designer, I described how to drag and drop a stored procedure from Server Explorer to the design surface. Adding the stored procedure to the design surface also added a method to the data context. Here's how to use that method:

C#:

```
var myShop = new MyShopDataContext();

var customers = myShop.GetCustomers();

foreach (var cust in customers)
{
    Console.WriteLine("Name: " + cust.Name);
}
```

VB:

```
Dim myShop As New MyShopDataContext

Dim customers As IEnumerable =
    myShop.GetCustomers()

For Each custOrd In customers
    Console.WriteLine("Name: " & custOrd.Name)
Next
```

And here's the output:

```
Name: Meg
Name: Joe
Name: May
```

Just call *myShop.GetCustomers* and you'll receive a collection of Customer objects.

There are many more advanced scenarios that you can handle with LINQ, but this is just a beginner's guide. However, you now have a solid base of query techniques that will get you started. In addition to querying a database, you'll need to perform insert operations, which is next.

TIP
LINQ to SQL generates SQL (Structured Query Language) statements to send to the database for your queries. If you would like to see the generated SQL, set a breakpoint on the line after the query and run the program with debugging. When you hit the breakpoint, hover over the variable holding query results and you'll see the SQL statement.

Inserting Data with LINQ to SQL

To insert a new record into a table, you'll need to create an instance of the LINQ to SQL class for that table, call a method to insert, and then call another method to commit the changes. The following example shows how to add a new record to the Customer table:

C#:

```csharp
private static int InsertCustomer()
{
    var cust = new Customer { Name = "Jim" };

    var myShop = new MyShopDataContext();

    myShop.Customers.InsertOnSubmit(cust);

    myShop.SubmitChanges();

    return cust.CustomerID;
}
```

VB:

```vb
Function InsertCustomer() As Integer
    Dim cust = New Customer With
    {
        .Name = "Jim"
    }

    Dim myShop As New MyShopDataContext

    myShop.Customers.InsertOnSubmit(cust)

    myShop.SubmitChanges()

    Return cust.CustomerID
End Function
```

As shown here, each collection property, such as *Customers,* has an *InsertOnSubmit* method that takes an object of the collection's type, *Customer* in this case. Don't forget to call *SubmitChanges,* or else you won't see any changes to your data. The next section discusses updates. Once the insert executes, with *SubmitChanges,* the new object, *cust,* will be updated with the new *CustomerID,* which you read and return to calling code.

Updating Data with LINQ to SQL

To update data, you need to get an object for the record you want to update, change the object you received, and then save the changes back to the database. The following example shows how to update a record:

C#:

```csharp
private static void UpdateCustomer(int custID)
{
    var myShop = new MyShopDataContext();

    var customers =
        from cust in myShop.Customers
        where cust.CustomerID == custID
        select cust;

    Customer firstCust = customers.SingleOrDefault();

    if (firstCust != null)
    {
        firstCust.Name = "James";
    }

    myShop.SubmitChanges();
}
```

VB:

```
Sub UpdateCustomer(ByVal custID As Integer)
    Dim myShop As New MyShopDataContext

    Dim customers =
        From cust In myShop.Customers
        Where cust.CustomerID = custID
        Select cust

    Dim firstCust As Customer =
        customers.SingleOrDefault()

    If (firstCust IsNot Nothing) Then
        firstCust.Name = "James"
    End If

    myShop.SubmitChanges()
End Sub
```

In the previous queries for the customer whose name was *Jim,* change the object to *James* and saves changes. The call to *SingleOrDefault* was necessary because the result of a LINQ to SQL query is a collection, but we only want the first or only record returned. There is also an operator method named *Single,* but using *SingleOrDefault* is favorable because it returns a default value if no records are returned, whereas *Single* will throw an exception. The code uses an *if* statement to protect against the possibility of an exception; otherwise, the code would throw a *NullReferenceException* when *firstCust* is *null* (*Nothing* in VB) and the code tries to access the *Name* property of a null object. Remember to call *SubmitChanges*; otherwise the updates won't be made.

You can now query, insert, and update. Your final skill to learn is deleting data.

Deleting Data with LINQ to SQL

To delete a record from the database, you get a reference to the object for that record, call a method to delete that object, and save changes. Here's an example that deletes a record:

C#:

```
private static void DeleteCustomer(int custID)
{
    var myShop = new MyShopDataContext();

    var customers =
        from cust in myShop.Customers
        where cust.CustomerID == custID
        select cust;
```

```
Customer firstCust = customers.SingleOrDefault();

if (firstCust != null)
{
    myShop.Customers.DeleteOnSubmit(firstCust);
}

myShop.SubmitChanges();
}
```

VB:

```
Sub DeleteCustomer(ByVal custID As Integer)
    Dim myShop As New MyShopDataContext

    Dim customers =
        From cust In myShop.Customers
        Where cust.CustomerID = custID
        Select cust

    Dim firstCust As Customer =
        customers.SingleOrDefault()

    If (firstCust IsNot Nothing) Then
        myShop.Customers.DeleteOnSubmit(firstCust)
    End If

    myShop.SubmitChanges()
End Sub
```

This example is similar to the update example that did a query and then a call to *SingleOrDefault* to get a reference to the requested object. You then use the collection property, *Customers* in this case, to call the *DeleteOnSubmit* method. You need the check for *null* (*Nothing* in VB), or you'll receive an *ArgumentNullException* when *DeleteOnSubmit* executes and the *firstCust* argument is *null* (*Nothing* in VB). Remember to call *SubmitChanges*; otherwise, you won't delete the record.

A final note on the preceding three sections. The code runs in an insert, update, and delete sequence. Notice how the insert methods return an *int,* which is the CustomerID. Whenever you perform a query from a database, you'll often want to get the ID field for the record at the same time. The reason is that the ID is unique to that one record and you can perform subsequent actions with the ID. Both the update and delete methods in preceding examples accepted an *int* parameter that was used to perform a database lookup of the record. Again, using the ID guarantees that we'll only return one record, which is also why I was confident in calling *SingleOrDefault.* Since this chapter is about data, I purposely don't show you how the program handles that ID. However, you'll see IDs being used in multiple later chapters that show you how to build user interfaces. Pay attention to how the UI code holds on to IDs and then uses them when calling code that interacts with the database. You'll see many different examples, but most of the examples that you see and then use in your own programs will be variations of what you've learned here.

Summary

This chapter showed you how to work with the VS database tools. You can create tables, relationships, and stored procedures. The section "Querying Object Collections with LINQ" helped you understand basic LINQ queries. You can now use LINQ to SQL, setting up a designer with classes and methods. Additionally, you can create, read, update, and delete data with LINQ to SQL.

This chapter used Console applications to show you how to work with data. This was to help you concentrate on data access exclusively, minimizing any other distractions. However, real applications require graphical user interfaces (GUIs). Remaining chapters of this book will show you how to create GUI applications that consume data, giving you many more examples of how LINQ to SQL works in an application. The next chapter gets you started in GUI development with WPF.

Part III

Building Programs with VS 2010

Chapter 8
Building Desktop
Applications with WPF

Key Skills & Concepts

- Perform Screen Layout

- Use Controls

- Work with Data in the UI

Windows Presentation Foundation (WPF) is a .NET technology for building desktop applications. The result of building a WPF application is an *.exe file that you can run directly on your computer or deploy and run on any other computer that has .NET installed. With WPF, you can add a graphical user interface (GUI), pronounced "Gooey," that makes it easier for users to work with your program. This chapter will show you how to lay out a screen in WPF and explain the controls, such as Button and TextBox, that you can place on the screen. You'll also learn how to capture events off controls, allowing you to add code that runs based on user input. Since most applications work with data, this chapter builds on what you learned in Chapter 7 and shows how to bind data to controls in the GUI.

This chapter will show you how to build a WPF GUI with the VS Designer, but sometimes you must work at a lower level and manipulate the XAML, pronounced "Zammel," that defines the GUI. XAML is an XML format that WPF and Silverlight use to define a GUI. There are two appendixes in this book that will help you get up to speed in XAML: Appendix A, "Introduction to XML," and Appendix B, "Introduction to XAML." If you aren't familiar with XML, start with Appendix A. However, if you have a good grasp of basic XML syntax, go straight to Appendix B. I'll try to explain WPF in a way that any XAML you see can be understood in its context, but you might want to review the appendixes to avoid any confusion. Once you're familiar with XAML, you can return here and start with the next section, which explains how to start a WPF project.

Starting a WPF Project

In Chapter 5, you learned how to create and build projects. The example explained how to create a Console application. However, what you learned there is generally applicable to most other application types. This section builds upon what you already know about projects and explains what is unique to a WPF application. To get started, open the New Project window; select WPF Application; and fill in the project name, location, and solution name. I'm naming the examples in the chapter as MyShop to continue the idea of customers who buy products that started in Chapter 7 when discussing data. Figure 8-1 shows the new WPF application in VS, including a Toolbox, a Designer, and a Solution Explorer. The Toolbox contains controls, which are user interface (UI) elements, such as Button and Textbox, that you can drag and drop onto the Designer.

NOTE

There is another .NET technology, Windows Forms, for creating desktop applications. This book doesn't discuss Windows Forms because it's an older technology. The way forward for desktop application development is WPF, and the intention of this book is to help guide you in a direction most beneficial to you.

The Designer allows you to lay out the UI of the application; it is divided into Design on the top and XAML on the bottom. The Design surface allows you to visually work with controls and layouts of those controls. The XAML editor allows you to work with the XML representation of the controls on the design surface. The Design and XAML are interrelated because a change in one causes a change in the other. For example, if you add a Button to the Design, you'll see the XML representation of that Button in the XAML.

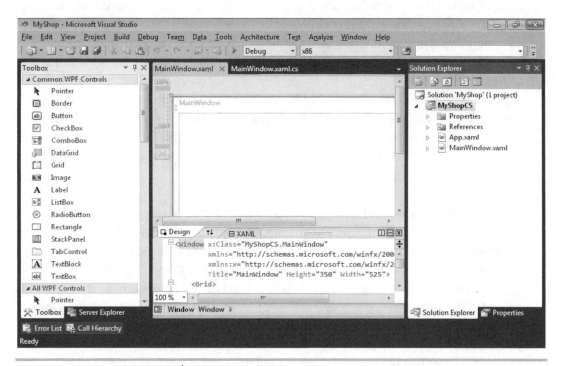

Figure 8-1   A new WPF application project

Similarly, if you add a TextBox element to the XAML, you'll see the visual representation of that TextBox in Design.

You have various controls for manipulating the windows. Both Design and XAML have zoom controls. The zoom tool on Design is a slider in the upper-left corner, and zoom for XAML is a drop-down control in the lower-left corner. You can also zoom by clicking either Design or XAML and moving the mouse wheel. At the upper right of the XAML editor (bottom right of the Design surface), you can switch between horizontal and vertical splits of the window or click the chevron to collapse the XML. The splitter icon below the chevron allows you to split the XAML editor into two if you drag it down. The up-down arrow between the Design and XAML tabs allows you to switch sides so that each panel shows where the other was. Locating the carat in the middle of the separator between Design and XAML allows you to resize each window.

Understanding Layout

A layout defines how you can position and size controls on a screen. WPF windows and controls have a Content (can occasionally be called something else) property that accepts a single control. In some cases, such as a Button control, the content can be text. However, many situations call for the ability to lay out multiple controls. This section concentrates on performing layout in windows, and a Window has a Content property that accepts only one control; that one control should be a layout control, which is the subject of this section.

WPF includes several layout controls, including Grid, StackPanel, DockPanel, WrapPanel, and Canvas. By default, VS will generate a window with a Grid as the layout control. However, you are free to replace the Grid with any other layout control that suits your needs. This section will show you how to use each of these controls.

Grid Layout

Whenever starting a new WPF project, VS adds a Grid. A *Grid* is a layout control that allows you to create a set of rows and columns that hold other controls. You can add rows and columns to a Grid through the Visual Designer by clicking in the middle of a window in design view. Figure 8-2 shows a column being added to a Grid.

The thin vertical line in the middle of the window is a new border between two columns. After clicking the window, you'll see two thick borders on the left and top of the window. While you hover over the top border, VS draws a vertical line that moves left and right as you run your mouse along the top border. You can do the same with the left border, adding rows to the Grid. This is a very quick way to add rows and columns to a Grid.

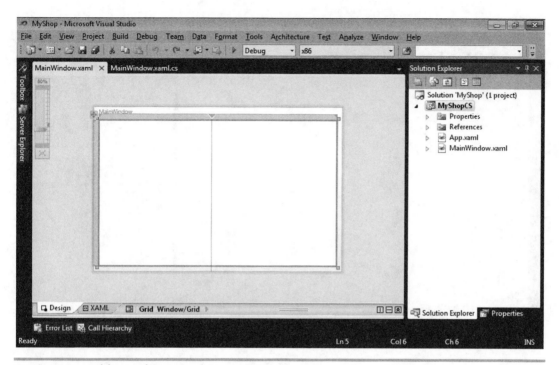

Figure 8-2   Adding columns and rows to a Grid

The arrow in the Grid border allows you to reposition the column or row border. You can remove the column or row border by selecting the arrow in the Grid border and dragging the arrow off the window.

CAUTION
Don't press the DELETE key when you have a border selected. You'll accidentally delete your Grid, which you might have spent some time on. If you want to remove a column or row, grab the arrow for the border you want to remove and drag the border off the window.

Once you've created rows and columns, you can add further customizations that define how much space the column or row can take. There are three sizing customizations: fixed, weighted, and auto. To set each of these options, hover over the column or row border and VS will display a sizing panel, as shown over the left column design border in Figure 8-3.

The diamond icon on the left means fixed, where the size will stay the same. The asterisk icon in the middle is a weighted proportion, where the size stays the same in relation to the other columns. The rightmost icon is auto, meaning that the size will vary according to

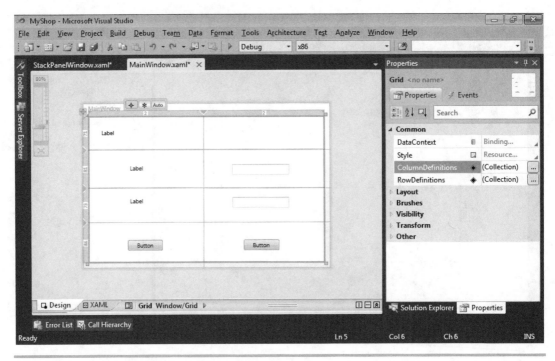

Figure 8-3 Column and row sizing options

whatever space remains after the other columns' sizes are set. After you've added content to your Grid, you can use these sizing options to experiment with the layout that you want.

One thing to notice in Figure 8-3 is the number in the Grid border for each row and column. These numbers tell you the size in pixels for each row and column they appear upon.

Figure 8-3 also shows the Properties window on the right, where you can select and customize the Column and Row collections.

True to the purpose of the Grid, Figure 8-3 shows controls that have been added to the Grid, placed in each cell of the Grid. Another popular layout control is StackPanel, discussed next.

StackPanel Layout

The StackPanel is ideal for when you want to lay out controls each on top of the other, like a stack. You can use a StackPanel by dragging the StackPanel control from the Toolbox onto the design surface. If you want to use the StackPanel as your primary layout, you can

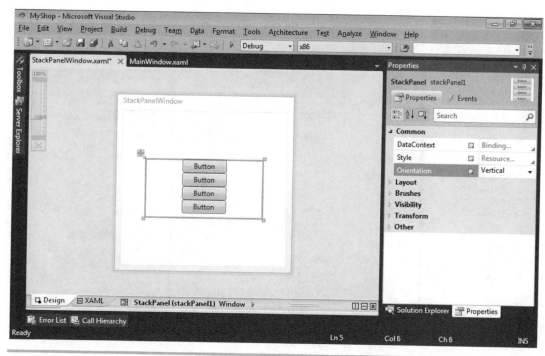

Figure 8-4 Using a StackPanel layout

select the grid, which is added by default to a new project, and delete the Grid. Figure 8-4 shows a StackPanel that contains multiple button controls.

In Figure 8-4, it doesn't matter where you try to lay the buttons—the StackPanel will always lay them out one after the other. In addition to vertical layout, the StackPanel can lay out controls horizontally. Just change the *Orientation* property, shown in the Properties window in Figure 8-4, to Horizontal. Next, you'll learn how to dock controls to the sides of a container.

DockPanel Layout

You've seen how VS allows you to dock windows within the borders of the application. This helps you organize your screen so that you can use many tools at one time. You can lay out your controls the same way with the DockPanel control.

Get started by dragging and dropping a DockPanel control from the Toolbox to the Window in the design surface. You might want to delete the default Grid first. Also, the DockPanel initializes with a Height and a Width, which you'll probably want to remove by selecting the DockPanel, opening the Properties window, and clearing the *Height* and

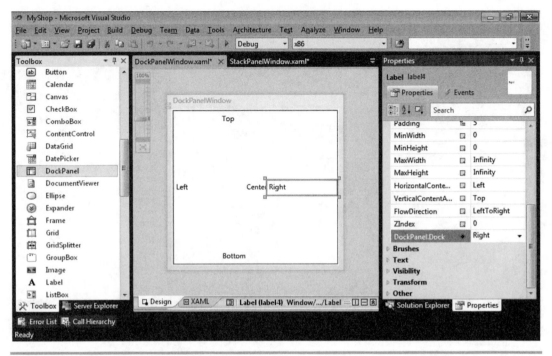

Figure 8-5 DockPanel layout

Width properties. Removing the *Height* and *Width* properties allows the DockPanel to expand and cover the entire window. Figure 8-5 shows a DockPanel with Label controls in each docking position.

Every time you drag and drop a control onto the design surface of a DockPanel, the control will take the center position by default. To specify where the control should dock, open the Properties window and set the *DockLayout.Dock* property. When you add a new control, the new control will become the center control and the other control will dock to the side of the DockPanel you specified in the *Dock* property. The next layout control is WrapPanel.

WrapPanel Layout

Whenever controls should naturally follow each other in sequence and continue wrapping on new lines, you can use a WrapPanel. Examples of when this is useful could be when adding controls that contain text and it's useful to view the controls in sequence. Figure 8-6 shows several CheckBox controls in a WrapPanel.

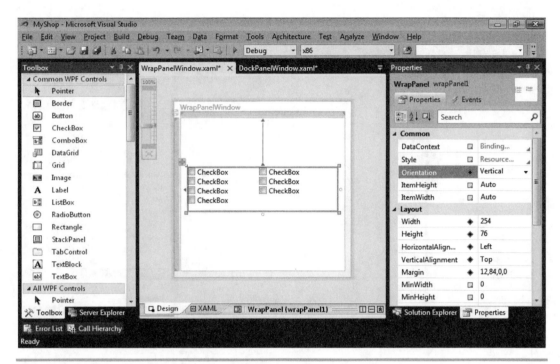

Figure 8-6   The WrapPanel Layout control

Figure 8-6 demonstrates how you can lay out a group of controls to fill an available space. In the case of the CheckBox controls, the Orientation of the WrapPanel is set to Vertical (the default is Horizontal). When the number of CheckBox controls fills the vertical column, remaining CheckBoxes wrap to the next column. Because the sizes of the CheckBox controls are the same, you have a uniform layout, which is easier than trying to do the same thing with a Grid or other layout control. The final layout control we'll discuss is the Canvas, which is next.

Canvas Layout

There are times when you might want to perform explicit layout of controls. If you were building a diagramming application or a drawing program, or if you just wanted to explicitly specify the location of controls, the Canvas layout will work fine. Figure 8-7 shows some controls on a Canvas layout.

The Rectangle and Ellipse controls were dragged and dropped from the Toolbox onto the Canvas control. Notice the *Canvas.Left, Canvas.Top, Width,* and *Height* properties in the Properties window, demonstrating the absolute positioning of the selected Ellipse control.

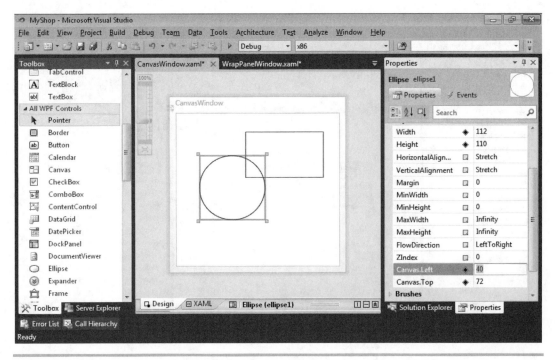

Figure 8-7 The Canvas Layout control

Now that you know how to use the layout controls, the next section takes a closer look at WPF controls in general, giving you tips on how to use them in your application.

Using WPF Controls

WPF includes many controls for helping you build user interfaces. This section groups the controls into categories, including text, selection, containers, information, shapes, and decorators. Data controls are excluded on purpose because the section following controls is "Working with Data in WPF." Before diving into each control, let's do an overview of the VS environment associated with control work.

Managing Windows for Controls

When working with controls, you'll be working with four different windows: Toolbox, Solution Explorer, Designer, and Properties. You learned how to access each of these windows in earlier chapters; but as a convenience, Table 8-1 gives you a quick summary on how to open these windows.

Window	Menu	Keystroke
Toolbox	View I Toolbox	CTRL-W, X
Solution Explorer	View I Solution Explorer	CTRL-W, L
Designer	Double-click *.xaml file in Solution Explorer	SHIFT-F7
Properties Window	View I Properties window	CTRL-W, P

Table 8-1   Primary Windows for Working with Controls

You'll find all of the available controls on the Toolbox, divided into panels where the top panel is Common WPF controls, which makes it easy to find the controls you use the most. The All WPF Controls tab includes the complete list of WPF controls.

You've seen how the Designer can be used in the preceding section, which discussed layout controls. You can open the Designer by double-clicking a *.xaml file in Solution Explorer. To add a control to the Designer, select the control in the Toolbox and drag the control onto the Designer. Figure 8-8 shows a Button that has been dragged and dropped onto the Designer.

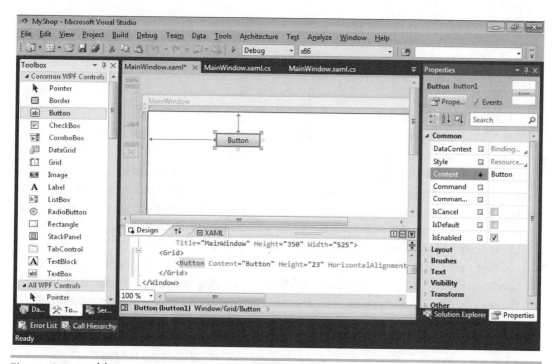

Figure 8-8   Adding a control to the VS Designer

In Figure 8-8, you can see the Toolbox with the Button control selected. The Designer shows a Button control that has been dragged and dropped. In practice, you'll be adding this control into some type of layout control so that you can position it appropriately on the screen.

Below the Designer, the Button control appears in the XAML for this window. If you are uncomfortable looking at XAML, you can review Appendix B as a refresher. The attributes of the Button control in the XAML match the properties in the Properties window.

TIP

It's important to learn how to quickly build UIs using the Visual Designer because it enhances productivity. However, it's also important to be able to read the XAML associated with a window because as you move beyond the beginner content of this book, you'll find scenarios where the Designer alone might not allow you to control every nuance of your visual presentation. A good way to move forward is to experiment on your own by adding each of the controls from the Toolbox to the Designer and then examine the generated XAML.

Setting Properties

The Properties window shows all of the ways that you can configure a control. For button controls, you'll want to change the *Content* property to make the text on the button make sense. In this example, we'll imagine that the purpose of the button is to allow a user to create a new order for a customer. Therefore, set the *Content* property to **New Order**.

Handling Events

In addition to properties, you can handle control events via the Events tab at the top of the Properties window. Figure 8-9 shows the contents of the Events tab.

Controls have literally dozens of events that allow you to manage their behavior in the application. Some events, like Click, are commonly used, while other events, such as Drag Over, only support unique scenarios like drag and drop that you might not ever care about. To handle an event, you can double-click any of the events in the Properties window and VS will wire up that event to a handler method with a default name.

Since the Click event is so common, I'll show how it works. You can implement a handler for the Click event by double-clicking the Click event in the Properties window Events tab. When you double-click, VS opens a file named MainWindow.xaml.cs, assuming the window you're working with is named MainWindow.xaml. MainWindow .xaml.cs is called a code-behind file and is where you can add event handlers. VS also creates a skeleton method in MainWindow.xaml.cs that handles the Button Click event, shown in Listing 8-1.

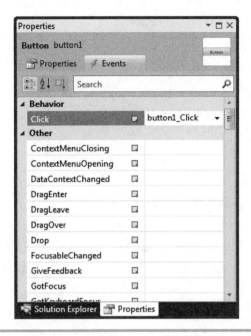

Figure 8-9   The Properties window Events tab

TIP

Controls have default events. The significance of default events is that if you double-click the control in the Designer, VS will generate an event handler for the default event. To be more specific, consider the Button control whose default event is the Click event. If you double-click the Button control in the Designer, VS will generate an event handler for the Click event.

Listing 8-1   A WPF code-behind file

C#:

```
using System;
using System.Collections.Generic;
using System.Linq;
using System.Text;
using System.Windows;
using System.Windows.Controls;
using System.Windows.Data;
using System.Windows.Documents;
using System.Windows.Input;
using System.Windows.Media;
using System.Windows.Media.Imaging;
```

```
using System.Windows.Navigation;
using System.Windows.Shapes;

namespace ControlsCS
{
    /// <summary>
    /// Interaction logic for MainWindow.xaml
    /// </summary>
    public partial class MainWindow : Window
    {
        public MainWindow()
        {
            InitializeComponent();
        }

        private void button1_Click(object sender, RoutedEventArgs e)
        {

        }
    }
}
```

VB:

```
Class MainWindow

    Private Sub Button1_Click(
        ByVal sender As System.Object,
        ByVal e As System.Windows.RoutedEventArgs)
Handles Button1.Click

    End Sub

End Class
```

The Click event handler, just created, is the highlighted method, *button1_Click* (*Button1_Click* in VB), that you see in Listing 8-1. We covered delegates and events in Chapter 4, which you can review for a better understanding of how this method handles the Click event. Notice how the VB code shows another way to handle events in VB, by explicitly specifying *Handles Button1.Click*. Essentially, when a user clicks on the button named *button1*, this handler will be called. This illustrates the concept of *event-driven programming,* where you write handlers, such as *button1_Click,* that run code according to user actions. In addition to creating the event handler in the code-behind, VS adds the method name to the Click event on the Events tab in the Properties window, shown in Figure 8-9.

In addition to creating the handler method and assigning the method name in the Properties window, VS adds the method as an attribute to the Button control in the XAML, shown here. The XAML is independent of programming language and works the same regardless of whether you are coding in C# or VB:

```
<Button Content="Button" Height="23"
        HorizontalAlignment="Left" Margin="76,43,0,0"
        Name="button1" VerticalAlignment="Top" Width="75"
        Click="button1_Click" />
```

Notice the convention being used on the method name, controlName_Event. The controlName part comes from the name of the control, which is *button1*, and the event is the event being handled. The problem with this is that *button1* isn't meaningful and when you return to this code later, you'll be confused by having methods named *button1_Click*, *button2_Click*, and so on. To fix the naming problem, you should name your controls properly before doing anything else with them.

To back out of this, go back to the Events tab of the Properties window. Remember to select the Button in the Designer. The top left of the Properties window contains the ID of the control, which you should change from *button1* to a meaningful name. For example if the purpose of the button was to create a new order for a customer, you could name the button **NewOrderButton**. Then delete the event handler assigned to the Click event of the Button. Figure 8-10 shows these changes in the Properties window. Now the ID and event handler are more readable.

After the event handler is deleted and the control has a new ID, double-click the Click event again. VS will create a new event handler for you, shown here:

C#:

```
private void button1_Click(object sender, RoutedEventArgs e)
{

}

private void NewOrderButton_Click(object sender, RoutedEventArgs e)
{

}
```

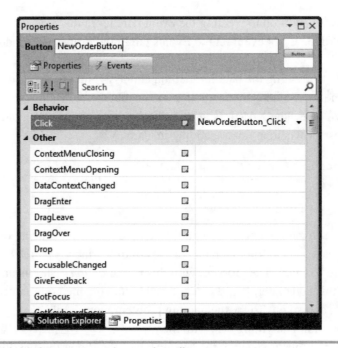

Figure 8-10 Readable button ID and event handler name

VB:

```
Class MainWindow

    Private Sub Button1_Click(
        ByVal sender As System.Object,
        ByVal e As System.Windows.RoutedEventArgs)

    End Sub

    Private Sub NewOrderButton_Click(
        ByVal sender As System.Object,
        ByVal e As System.Windows.RoutedEventArgs) Handles
NewOrderButton.Click

    End Sub

End Class
```

The previous code shows both the old *button1_Click* (*Button1_Click* in VB) event handler and the new *NewOrderButton_Click* event handler. You might wonder why the *button1_Click* event handler wasn't deleted when you deleted it from the Click event in the Properties window, but there's a good reason for this. What if you had already written code in the event handler? VS leans toward the safe side and does not delete your code. Using the previous steps, you have both event handlers sitting side-by-side, which means that you can easily copy your code from *button1_Click* into *NewOrderButton_Click* and then delete the *button1_Click* event handler. So far, we haven't written any code for the event handler, which you'll learn about in the next section.

Coding Event Handlers

One of the tasks you might want to do when a user clicks a button is to open a new window. The first thing you'll need to do is add a new window. To make this work, you would open Solution Explorer, right-click the project you're working with, select Add | New Item, choose Window (WPF), name the window **NewOrder.xaml**, and click Add. This will create a new window open in the Designer.

TIP

The project's Add | New Item context menu includes a Window entry, which can save a couple of clicks when creating a new window.

After the Designer loads, you can quickly open the code-behind by pressing F7. In the code-behind, you'll see the following code:

C#:

```
public partial class NewOrder : Window
{
    public NewOrder()
    {
        InitializeComponent();
    }
}
```

VB:

```
Public Class NewOrder

End Class
```

Notice that the class in this code is named *NewOrder*, illustrating that a window is just another class. As you know, you can instantiate classes and call their methods, which is the technique you'll use to open this window from the *NewOrder_Click* event handler in the code-behind of the *MainWindow* window.

In practice, you'll populate the *NewOrder* window with whatever controls you need to implement a new order. You would populate the window by dragging and dropping controls, just like the *Button* in this example. However, we'll skip that task for now because the current focus is on adding code to the *NewOrderButton_Click* event handler so that you can learn how to code an event handler and open another window. Go back to the *NewOrderButton_Click* event handler in MainWindow.xaml.cs and add the following code:

C#:

```
private void NewOrderButton_Click(object sender, RoutedEventArgs e)
{
    NewOrder newOrd = new NewOrder();
    newOrd.Show();
}
```

VB:

```
    Private Sub NewOrderButton_Click(
        ByVal sender As System.Object,
        ByVal e As System.Windows.RoutedEventArgs)
Handles NewOrderButton.Click

        Dim newOrd As New NewOrder
        newOrd.Show()

    End Sub
```

Since *NewOrder* is a class, you can instantiate it as shown in the preceding code example. To open the window, call the *Show* method.

Now you have a WPF program that handles events and opens new windows. Press F5 to run the program. Click New Order and observe that the New Order window appears. The New Order window isn't very useful because it lacks controls and data management. The next section shows you how to populate window controls with data.

Working with Data in WPF

This section builds upon what you learned in Chapter 7 by showing how to bind data to WPF controls. *Binding* is the process of populating and retrieving data to and from controls. You'll learn how to show data in your user interface. The examples in the following sections show you how to perform create, read, update, and delete (CRUD) operations via WPF. You'll first see how to insert data, using VS tools to construct a data entry screen. Then you'll learn how to read, modify, and delete data through a DataGrid. We'll start with single value binding. To make the examples more interesting, I added extra fields to the tables. You can review Chapter 7 to learn how to add fields to a database and create a LINQ to SQL entity model.

Setting Up a Data Source

Before you can bind to data in the window, you'll need a data source to work with data. To get started, update the Order table, created in Chapter 7, so that it has the following fields:

- OrderID, int, primary key, auto-increment
- CustomerID, int
- OrderDate, datetime
- Location, varchar(50)
- Amount, money

Then update the Customer table with the following fields:

- CustomerID, int, primary key, auto-increment
- Name, nvarchar(50)
- Age, int
- Birthday, datetime
- Income, money

With the database updated, you can add a LINQ to SQL entity model to the project, using the same techniques described in Chapter 7.

To add the data source for binding, open the NewOrder window in the Designer, and select the Data | Add New Data Source menu, which opens the Choose A Data Source Type window, shown in Figure 8-11.

There are different ways to connect to a data source, including directly to the database, via a Web service, via an object, or through SharePoint. This book shows you how to use LINQ to SQL, which is connected by selecting Object and clicking Next, which shows the Select The Data Objects window in Figure 8-12.

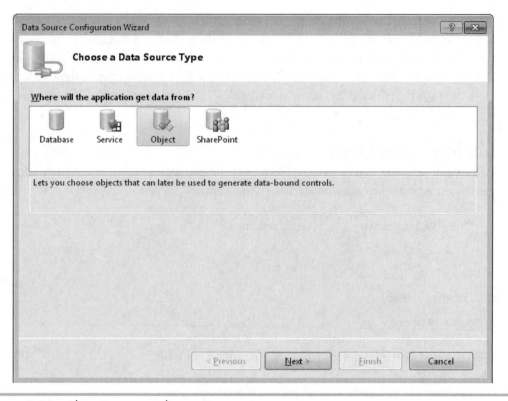

Figure 8-11   Choosing a new data source

On the Select The Data Objects window, check the box next to each object you want to bind in your application. The example in this chapter uses *Customer* and *Order* objects, which you can see checked in Figure 8-12. Clicking Finish will configure the data source for use in the application. You can view data sources by selecting Data | Show Data Sources, shown in Figure 8-13.

The Data Sources window allows you to create controls on a form that are bound to each field of a data source. In the Data Sources window in Figure 8-13, you can see that both *Customer* and *Object* are listed with their fields. What is also evident is the icons associated with each field. The icons describe what type of control should be associated with each data field. For example, *Name* on *Customer* is a TextBox because it is nvarchar(50), but *Birthday* is a calendar because it is a datetime. If you don't like a default control type for a field, you can change it by selecting the field and choosing another control type from the drop-down list, as shown in Figure 8-14.

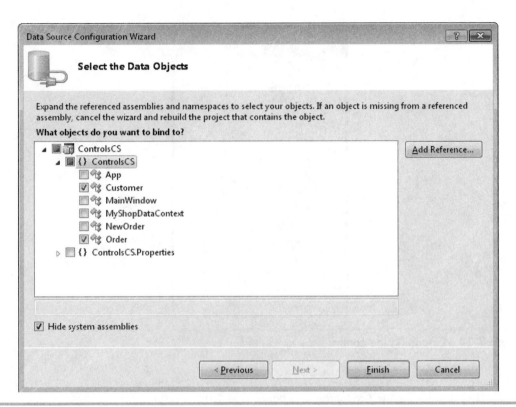

Figure 8-12 Selecting data objects

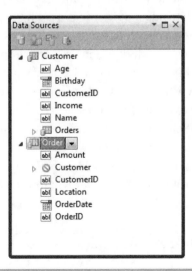

Figure 8-13 The Data Sources window

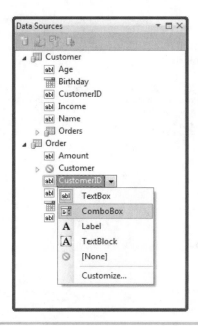

Figure 8-14 Changing the control type for a field

In Figure 8-14, the *CustomerID* is being changed to a ComboBox because it makes more sense to give the user the option of selecting a customer from a list for a new order, rather than typing in an ID number. Also, the object defaults to a Grid control, but in this first example, we only want to add a new order, meaning that the control type should be changed to Detail. To create a new order form with controls bound to order data, select the *Order* object in the Data Sources window and drag and drop the order onto the Designer of the NewOrder window. Figure 8-15 shows this new window.

Figure 8-15 shows how VS added a Grid layout with two columns and a row for each field in the Order table. As explained, the *CustomerID* is a ComboBox and the *OrderDate* is a calendar. VS was smart enough to put spaces between the words in the labels, too. VS didn't put the Save button on the screen, which is something you would need to do to save the data. In addition to adding controls to the Designer, VS added the following *CollectionViewSource* control to the *NewOrder* window's XAML:

```
<Window.Resources>
    <CollectionViewSource x:Key="orderViewSource"
    d:DesignSource="{d:DesignInstance my:Order, CreateList=True}" />
</Window.Resources>
```

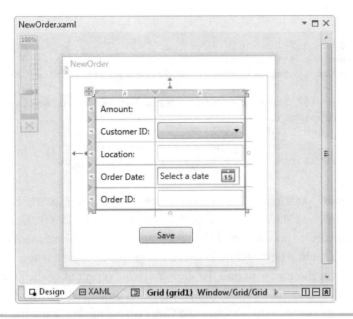

Figure 8-15 Controls bound via a data source

This is another reason it's important to be able to read the XAML for a window, so you can see how objects like this are added and configure them if you need to. In our case, we need to know the name of the *CollectionViewSource,* which is *orderViewSource.* We need to add an *Order* object to the *CollectionViewSource* so that the controls that are bound to it have a place to save data that the user enters. Press F7 to see the code that VS added to the *Window Loaded* event handler, as follows:

C#:

```
private void Window_Loaded(object sender, RoutedEventArgs e)
{
    System.Windows.Data.CollectionViewSource
    orderViewSource =
    ((System.Windows.Data.CollectionViewSource)
    (this.FindResource("orderViewSource")));
    // Load data by setting the
//CollectionViewSource.Source property:
    // orderViewSource.Source = [generic data source]
}
```

VB:

```
Private Sub Window_Loaded(
    ByVal sender As System.Object,
    ByVal e As System.Windows.RoutedEventArgs) Handles MyBase.Loaded

    Dim OrderViewSource As System.Windows.Data.CollectionViewSource
        = CType(Me.FindResource("OrderViewSource"),
            System.Windows.Data.CollectionViewSource)
    'Load data by setting the CollectionViewSource.Source property:
    'OrderViewSource.Source = [generic data source]
End Sub
```

The preceding skeleton code gets a reference to *OrderViewSource,* but that's all. The commented portion of the code suggests how you might populate that control. However, we aren't interested in populating *OrderViewSource* with data because the purpose of this screen is to insert a new record. Instead, the proper approach is to bind an empty object. Later, you'll see how to pull the data from that object after the user fills in the form and clicks on the Save button. In addition to assigning a blank *Order* object to *OrderViewSource*, we need to populate the ComboBox that holds the list of customers and their IDs. The following code is a revision to the *Window_Loaded* event handler that assigns a blank *Order* object to the *OrderViewSource* and binds customers to the ComboBox holding customers:

C#:

```
private void Window_Loaded(object sender, RoutedEventArgs e)
{
    var orderViewSource =
        FindResource("orderViewSource") as CollectionViewSource;
    orderViewSource.Source =
        new List<Order>
        {
            new Order
            {
                OrderDate = DateTime.Now
            }
        };

    customerIDComboBox.ItemsSource =
        from cust in new MyShopDataContext().Customers
        select cust;
}
```

VB:

```
Private Sub Window_Loaded(
    ByVal sender As System.Object,
    ByVal e As System.Windows.RoutedEventArgs) Handles MyBase.Loaded

    Dim OrderViewSource As CollectionViewSource =
        CType(FindResource("OrderViewSource"), CollectionViewSource)
    OrderViewSource.Source =
        New List(Of Order) From
        {
            New Order With
            {
                .OrderDate = DateTime.Now
            }
        }

    CustomerIDComboBox.ItemsSource =
        From cust In New MyShopDataContext().Customers

End Sub
```

The previous re-write of *Window_Loaded* accomplishes two things: assigning an order to *orderViewSource* and populating *customerIDComboBox* with customers. The *Order* object assigned to the *Source* property of *orderViewSource* is empty, except assigning today's date to *OrderDate,* demonstrating how you can set default values. When the user fills out the form on the page, WPF will populate this Order with data because it is data bound, through *orderViewSource*, to the controls on the screen. This section showed you how the data is assigned to the controls, but some controls require even more attention to ensure they display the data correctly. The next section expands upon what you must do to get the ComboBox to work.

Configuring a ComboBox

A couple of the particularly more complex controls to configure are ComboBox and ListBox. The reason is that they have a few different properties that must be set to ensure that whatever is selected can be read and correctly referenced back to the original data source. This section doesn't try to teach you about WPF binding because there are entire books with multiple chapters related to the subject. Instead, you'll learn an essential skill for helping you figure out how to set the right properties on a ComboBox control. In so doing, you'll get a better feel for the features of VS that help you perform the task of setting up controls.

The previous example assigns the results of a LINQ query for *Customer* objects to the *customerIDComboBox,* but this is only the first step to getting the combo box to work properly; you must specify which property of *Customer* must display, which property of *Customer* maps to *Order,* and which property of *Order* to bind the selected item to. To do this binding, open the NewOrder.xaml file in the Designer, select the combo box, and set the properties as specified in Table 8-2.

The following XAML shows the results of the settings you should make in the Properties window, based on Table 8-2:

```
<ComboBox DisplayMemberPath="Name"
          SelectedValue="{Binding Path=CustomerID}"
          SelectedValuePath="CustomerID"
          Grid.Column="1" Grid.Row="1"
          Height="23" HorizontalAlignment="Left"
          Margin="3" Name="customerIDComboBox"
          VerticalAlignment="Center" Width="120">
</ComboBox>
```

DisplayMemberPath and *SelectedValuePath* are names of the properties from the *Customer* objects bound to the *ComboBox.* However, the *SelectedValue* syntax uses a binding expression, where *Path* identifies the property of the Order that will be assigned to with *SelectedValuePath.* The binding for *SelectedValue* is based on the *Order* object

Property	Explanation
ItemsSource	We set this through code in the *Window_Loaded* event. It holds the collection of objects that will appear in the combo box. You need two properties, one to display and one for the key of the object being displayed. The key will be used to map the object back to the database or associate the object in a relationship with another object. In the case of the *Customer* list, the properties of interest are *Name* for display and *CustomerID* for key. Since we are creating a new Order, the *CustomerID* for the Name selected in the combo box will be assigned to the *CustomerID* field of the Order. That way, when the Order is saved, its database record will have the *CustomerID* for the customer the user selected.
DisplayMemberPath	This is the *Name* property from each *Customer* object bound to the combo box.
SelectedValuePath	As explained for *ItemsSource*, you need to associate the selected *Customer* with the *Order* being created. *SelectedValuePath* is the name of the *Customer* object's key, which is *CustomerID* in our example.
SelectedValue	When saving the *Order*, you must have the key associated with the selected customer. The *SelectedValue* is a binding to the property of the *Order* that will be set with the key from the selected *Customer*.

Table 8-2 ComboBox Properties for Data Binding

that was assigned to the Source property of the *orderViewSource* in *Window_Loaded*. Coming full circle, the *orderViewSource* is what the default binding of the containing Grid layout is based on; it was set when dragging and dropping the *Order* data source onto the Design surface.

Now you have an input form that displays data, allowing the user to enter new order information. After the user fills in the form, you need to save the data, which is discussed next.

Reading and Saving Data

Next, you'll want to save the order when a user clicks Save. To do this, add a Button control to the form, set its Content property to **Save**, and set its Name property to **SaveButton**, which you learned how to do earlier in this chapter. Then double-click Save to create a Click event handler like this:

C#:

```csharp
private void SaveButton_Click(object sender, RoutedEventArgs e)
{
    CollectionViewSource orderViewSource =
        FindResource("orderViewSource") as CollectionViewSource;

    List<Order> ordList =
        orderViewSource.Source as List<Order>;
    Order ord = ordList.FirstOrDefault();

    var ctx = new MyShopDataContext();

    ctx.Orders.InsertOnSubmit(ord);

    ctx.SubmitChanges();

    MessageBox.Show("Order Saved!");
}
```

VB:

```vb
Private Sub SaveButton_Click(
    ByVal sender As System.Object,
    ByVal e As System.Windows.RoutedEventArgs)
    Handles SaveButton.Click

    Dim OrderViewSource As CollectionViewSource =
        CType(FindResource("OrderViewSource"), CollectionViewSource)
```

```
    Dim ordList As List(Of Order)
    ordList = CType(OrderViewSource.Source, List(Of Order))
    Dim ord As Order
    ord = ordList.FirstOrDefault()

    Dim ctx As New MyShopDataContext

    ctx.Orders.InsertOnSubmit(ord)
    ctx.SubmitChanges()

    MessageBox.Show("Order Saved!")
End Sub
```

Before the *SaveButton_Click* event handler ends, it shows a message box to the user with a status message, Order Saved. The *MessageBox* class has several overloads of the *Show* method that allows you to specify buttons, icons, and more.

So far, you've learned how to create an input form for adding a new record to the database. The next section will build upon this by showing you how to view, modify, and delete records with the DataGrid.

Using the DataGrid

The DataGrid is the best option for working with data that must be shown with multiple rows and columns. This section will show you how to show, update, and delete items with a Grid. First, we'll display orders.

We'll build off the data source created in the previous example to show data in a Grid. First, you'll need to open the Data Source window by selecting Data | Open Data Sources. The preceding section specified the CustomerID as a ComboBox. If you're following along, you'll want to change CustomerID to a TextBox by clicking on CustomerID for the Order object in the Data Sources window and selecting TextBox. Change the control type of Order from a form to a Grid by selecting the combo box for the *Order* object in the Data Sources window and selecting the DataGrid option. Open the MainWindow .xaml file in the Designer and drag and drop Order from the Data Sources window to the Designer. Remember there is a New Order button that you'll want to move to the bottom of the form. Also, add another button, set its Name property to **UpdateButton**, and set its Content property to **Update**. Position the New Order and Update buttons at the bottom of the form. Resize and move controls and form so they look like Figure 8-16.

Just as with the form view in the preceding section, VS added a CollectionViewSource to the window when adding the Order to the Designer. The following *Window_Loaded* event handler provides the Order data to display in the Grid:

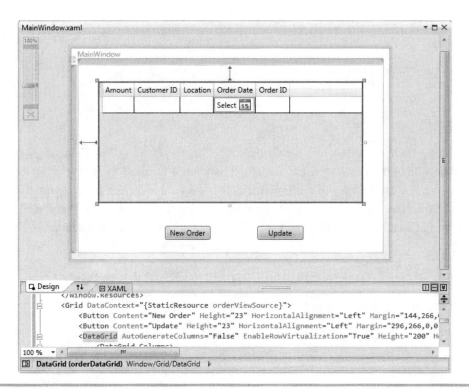

Figure 8-16 Displaying information in a Grid

C#:

```csharp
private MyShopDataContext m_ctx = new MyShopDataContext();

private void Window_Loaded(object sender, RoutedEventArgs e)
{
    CollectionViewSource orderViewSource =
        FindResource("orderViewSource") as CollectionViewSource;

    orderViewSource.Source =
        from ord in m_ctx.Orders
        select ord;
}
```

VB:

```vb
Dim m_ctx As New MyShopDataContext

Private Sub Window_Loaded(
    ByVal sender As System.Object,
    ByVal e As System.Windows.RoutedEventArgs)
    Handles MyBase.Loaded
```

```
Dim OrderViewSource As CollectionViewSource =
    CType(FindResource("OrderViewSource"), CollectionViewSource)

OrderViewSource.Source =
    From ord In m_ctx.Orders
    Select ord
```

```
End Sub
```

This code loads orders into the Grid. Notice that the *MyShopDataContext, m_ctx,* is a field outside of the *Window_Loaded* method handler. It is raised to field level so that the same instance can be used in multiple methods. As you may notice from Figure 8-16, there is also an Update button on the form. Double-clicking the Update button produced the following Click event handler that saves changes, such as updates and deletes, to the Grid:

C#:

```
private void UpdateButton_Click(object sender, RoutedEventArgs e)
{
    m_ctx.SubmitChanges();

    MessageBox.Show("Updates and Deletes Saved!");
}
```

VB:

```
Private Sub UpdateButton_Click(
    ByVal sender As System.Object,
    ByVal e As System.Windows.RoutedEventArgs)
    Handles UpdateButton.Click

    m_ctx.SubmitChanges()

    MessageBox.Show("Updates and Deletes Saved!")
```

```
End Sub
```

When you run the program, you can add new rows, modify the cells of existing rows, or delete a row by selecting the row and pressing DELETE on the keyboard. After making changes to the Grid, click Update, which will call the previous *UpdateButton_Click* event handler.

To understand how this works, remember that the *Window_Loaded* event handler assigned a collection of *Order* objects to the *CollectionViewSource, orderViewSource,* which is data bound to the Grid. Each row of the Grid is bound to an instance of an *Order* object. Each *Order* object is part of the LINQ to SQL *MyShopDataContext.* Since we are using *m_ctx,* which is a field, both the *Window_Loaded* method and the *UpdateButton_Click* method are using the same object instance. When making changes in the Grid, those changes are saved in the Order objects for the changed rows. The *Order* objects notify *MyShopDataContext* that they have changed, which is a service of LINQ to SQL. The *UpdateButton_Click* method uses *m_ctx,* which is the *MyShopDataContext* that knows about the changes to the *Order* objects. Calling *SubmitChanges* on *m_ctx* saves all changes to the database.

You might need to read the preceding paragraph more than one time to understand how this is working. If it's still fuzzy, it might be helpful to review the language chapters earlier in this book to understand how objects are instantiated and used, and review Chapter 7 to ensure you understand the data manipulation picture.

Summary

While there is much more to learn about WPF, this is a beginner's guide and intended to give you the essentials so that you can begin moving in the right direction. You should now be able to create a new WPF project. You learned about layout controls and how they allow you to manage how controls appear on your form. A section explains the windows involved in working with controls. While there are many controls you can use that ship with both WPF and many third-party products, remember that the concepts are relatively the same for using the controls: drag and drop, and configure properties. Most applications work with data, so this chapter builds upon what you know about LINQ to SQL and shows you how to apply this data management knowledge to create user interfaces that users can work with to manage their data.

This chapter introduces you to working with desktop applications, which are still very necessary and popular. However, a lot of today's applications are written for the Internet. The next chapter shows you how to build Web applications with ASP.NET.

Chapter 9

Creating Web
Applications with
ASP.NET MVC

Key Skills & Concepts

- Learn What MVC Means
- Create Models
- Create Controllers
- Create Views
- Work with Data in ASP.NET MVC

ASP.NET is a .NET technology for building Web applications. VS provides support for building a Web application through windows such as the Toolbox, Designer, and Properties windows, as well as the Solution Explorer. This chapter shows you how to use ASP.NET MVC. MVC is an acronym for Model View Controller, which is a well-known design pattern for building applications. You'll learn about how MVC works and how it is implemented in ASP.NET MVC. Let's start by helping you understand what MVC is.

Understanding ASP.NET MVC

The essential piece of knowledge required to be successful with ASP.NET MVC is the Model View Controller pattern. In MVC, the Model, View, and Controller are three separate objects. Table 9-1 describes the purpose of each MVC object.

With MVC, you have a clear separation of concerns where Model, View, and Controller have distinct responsibilities. This makes it easier to write good programs that you can return to later for fixing bugs and adding new features. Besides knowing what each of these three objects is, you must understand their relationship. Figure 9-1 illustrates the Model, the

MVC Object	Purpose
Model	The *Model* is made up of business objects and data.
View	Each MVC application typically has a user interface that displays information to a user and allows the user to input data. The data that the *View* displays is read from a Model, and the data that the user adds to the View is assigned to the Model.
Controller	A *Controller* orchestrates the activities of an application. When a user makes a request for your application, ASP.NET MVC invokes a Controller. The Controller will communicate with the Model and View to ensure the program operates correctly.

Table 9-1 Purpose of MVC Objects

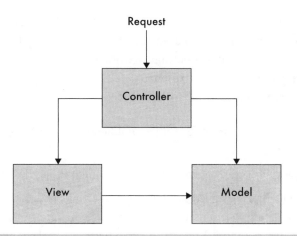

Request

Controller

View ──────▶ Model

Figure 9-1 The Model View Controller pattern

View, and the Controller, including relationships. There are variations of the relationship between Model, View, and Controller, so rather than a theoretically correct depiction of all scenarios, Figure 9-1 is a simplification that should help you get started.

In Figure 9-1, you can see that the Controller references both the View and the Model. This makes sense when you consider that the Controller is managing the operation of the application. The Controller executes in response to a user request. Since the Controller is also responsible for coordinating activity between the Model and the View, you can see the relationship in Figure 9-1 where the Controller references the Model. The View references the Model because the View must bind data to the user interface and needs to know what data is available. The Model does not reference the View or the Controller. The Model is an object that holds data and any other members that help manage that data, such as methods for performing validation.

A typical sequence of operations for an ASP.NET MVC operation starts with a request to a Controller. The Controller will perform the actions requested, working with the Model. The Controller will then give the Model to a View and run the View. The View will display Model data and interact with the user for any screen operations. Based on user interaction with the View, more requests will be made to a Controller to repeat this process. The rest of this chapter shows you how to write the code to make this process work, starting with creating a new ASP.NET MVC project.

Starting an ASP.NET MVC Project

Just as with any other project in VS, you open the New Project window by selecting File | New | Project. Then create an ASP.NET MVC 2 Web Application project named **MyShopCS** (**MyShopVB** for VB). VS will ask if you want to create a test project, and you have the option to choose Yes or No. Choosing Yes will add a unit testing project to the solution. You can choose either option, which won't matter right now because we'll not be covering this topic here, but it is definitely worth exploring on your own. Figure 9-2 shows the new project in Solution Explorer.

VS created several folders with working code:

- The Model, View, and Controller folders hold code for the MVC Models, Views, and Controllers, respectively.

- Previous chapters already explained the purpose of the Properties and References folders.

- The App_Data folder is designed to allow you to ship a local database with your application and is ideal for small programs where you can use the free SQL Express database. See the accompanying note to learn how to add a database in the App_Data folder.

- The Content folder is where you add any Cascading Style Sheets (CSS) files. CSS is a standardized language for defining layout and appearance of a Web site.

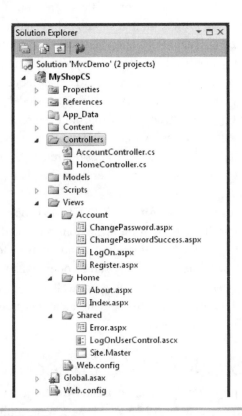

Figure 9-2   A new ASP.NET MVC project

- The Scripts folder holds JavaScript files, which include the jQuery and ASP.NET AJAX client libraries. JavaScript helps make Views more interactive and can be effective in providing a pleasing user experience.

- The Global.asax file holds code that runs at different periods during the application life cycle; we'll investigate this file when looking at routing later in this chapter.

- The web.config file holds configuration information, such as database connection strings and more items that you don't want to hard-code into the application.

NOTE
If you want to ship a local database with your application, you can right-click the App_Data folder for your project, select Add | New Item, navigate to Data, and select SQL Server Database. This will add a blank database *.mdf file under the App_Data folder. You can work with this database through Server Explorer, using techniques learned in Chapter 7, to add tables and other objects. Remember that the server you deploy to must have SQL Server Express installed or your database operations won't work.

The code generated by the New Project Wizard will run, and pressing F5 to execute the application will show you a screen similar to Figure 9-3. Click OK when you see a screen that asks if you want to program to run in debug mode. This will modify the web.config file to allow debugging, which is what you want while developing applications.

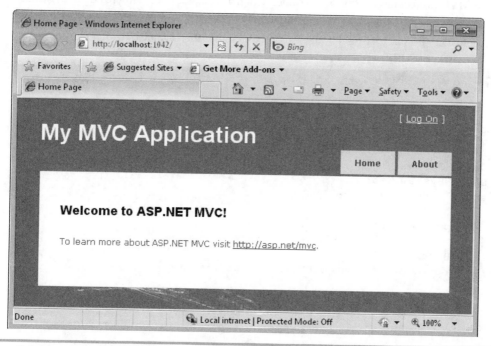

Figure 9-3 Running the default code produced by an ASP.NET MVC project

The skeleton code produced by VS gives you some working examples that you can build on and move forward. One item that VS doesn't produce is the Model, which is discussed next.

Creating the Models

As stated previously, the Model represents the data for the application. The example in this section uses LINQ to SQL to produce the Model for this application. To create the Model, add a LINQ to SQL entity Model by right-clicking the Models folder, selecting Add | New Item, and selecting LINQ to SQL. This creates a *.dbml file that you should add Customer and Order entities to, using the same techniques described in Chapter 7.

In more sophisticated scenarios, you would have additional objects that held business logic or other data that isn't associated with LINQ to SQL. This book keeps tasks at a basic level so that you can understand how to use VS. You can put Model objects in the Models folder or a separate class library. This chapter uses the Models folder.

Building Controllers

Requests come directly to a Controller, which we discussed earlier. As shown in Figure 9-2, the MVC project has a Controllers folder. Controller classes normally reside in the Controllers folder. Figure 9-2 shows two files, AccountController.cs and HomeController.cs, in the Controllers folder. Listing 9-1 shows the contents of the HomeController.cs file.

Listing 9-1   The HomeController class

C#:

```
using System;
using System.Collections.Generic;
using System.Linq;
using System.Web;
using System.Web.Mvc;

namespace MyShopCS.Controllers
{
    [HandleError]
    public class HomeController : Controller
    {
        public ActionResult Index()
        {
            ViewData["Message"] = "Welcome to ASP.NET MVC!";
```

```
            return View();
        }

        public ActionResult About()
        {
            return View();
        }
    }
}
```

VB:

```
<HandleError()> _
Public Class HomeController
    Inherits System.Web.Mvc.Controller

    Function Index() As ActionResult
        ViewData("Message") = "Welcome to ASP.NET MVC!"

        Return View()
    End Function

    Function About() As ActionResult
        Return View()
    End Function
End Class
```

Listing 9-1 demonstrates how closely ASP.NET MVC is tied to conventions. Notice that the class name is HomeController. Appending Controller to a class name is a convention that ASP.NET MVC uses to identify which classes are controllers. Also, the methods in the class are referred to as Actions in ASP.NET MVC. Using the Controllers folder for a Controller, appending the class name with Controller, and available actions are all conventions that you must follow. The following URL, a browser address, demonstrates how these conventions support routing to find a Controller and invoke the About action. You can see this URL if you run the application and click the About tab:

```
http://localhost:1042/Home/About
```

The http://localhost:1042 part of the URL is a Web server that is built into VS and runs the Web application without needing a Web server such as Internet Information Server (IIS). The number 1042 is a random port number generated by the Web server, and your port number is likely to be different.

TIP

You can change your VS Web server's port number. If you open your project's property page by right-mouse clicking on the project in Solution Explorer and select Properties, then select the Web tab on the left, under Servers, you can specify a specific port or make other Web server choices.

For ASP.NET MVC, the important part of the URL is /Home/About. Home is the name of the Controller, and ASP.NET MVC appends Controller to the URL name, looking for the HomeController class, shown in Listing 9-1, physically located in the Controller folder, which is why it's important to ensure you create files in the proper locations. About is an action, which corresponds to the *About* method shown in Listing 9-1. Similar to the *About* method, the Index action is run through the following URL:

```
http://localhost:1042/Home/Index
```

In a later section of this chapter, you'll learn how ASP.NET MVC performs routing, which maps URLs to Controllers.

Both the Index and About actions in Listing 9-1 invoke a method named *View*. This is a convention for invoking a View with the same name as the action method. For example, calling View in the Index action will show a View named Index, and the call to *View* in the About method will show a View named About.

One more item to point out is how the Index action assigns a string to a collection called ViewData. The ViewData collection is one way for a Controller to pass Model data to a View. I'll cover more on Controllers, including how to create your own, in a later part of this chapter, but now, let's do a quick review of Views so that you can see what happens when they are invoked by the Controller.

Displaying Views

A View is what displays in the browser and allows interaction with the user. The View can display any information that a Controller passes to it. For example, notice that the Index action in Listing 9-1 assigns a string "Welcome to ASP.NET MVC!" with the "Message" key in the ViewData collection.

Looking Inside a View

Figure 9-3 shows the View in the browser, displaying the message. Listing 9-2 shows the Hypertext Markup Language (HTML) of the View displaying the message. The View actually has a combination of HTML and ASP.NET markup, sometimes referred to as ASPX, but I'll refer to it as just HTML for the rest of the chapter.

Listing 9-2   A View's HTML

```
<%@ Page Language="C#"
        MasterPageFile="~/Views/Shared/Site.Master"
        Inherits="System.Web.Mvc.ViewPage" %>

<asp:Content ID="indexTitle"
            ContentPlaceHolderID="TitleContent"
            runat="server">
    Home Page
</asp:Content>

<asp:Content ID="indexContent"
            ContentPlaceHolderID="MainContent"
            runat="server">
    <h2><%= Html.Encode(ViewData["Message"]) %></h2>
    <p>
        To learn more about ASP.NET MVC visit
<a href="http://asp.net/mvc"
    title="ASP.NET MVC Website">
    http://asp.net/mvc
</a>.
    </p>
</asp:Content>
```

A quick overview of Listing 9-2 shows that there is a Page directive with a couple of Content containers. The Page directive specifies a MasterPage and Inherits attributes. A MasterPage is a separate file that holds common HTML that can be shown on all pages of a site. You'll see how the MasterPage works soon, but let's stay focused on the current file in Listing 9-2 until then. ASP.NET MVC will compile this HTML into code behind the scenes, and the generated code will derive from the class defined by the Inherits attribute.

The first Content container can hold metadata that goes into an HTML header. The second Content container has the information that will display on the screen. Notice the *Html.Encode(ViewData["Message"])* inside of binding tags *<%=* and *%>*. Any time you add code or need to access ViewData that was passed by the Controller, you will use the binding tags. *Encode* is one of several helper methods of the *Html* class, more of which you'll see soon. The purpose of *Encode* is to translate HTML tags into their encoded representations for security purposes, ensuring that you don't show any harmful JavaScript, or other markup that could possibly execute, to the user. *ViewData["Message"]* should be familiar, as it was set in the Index action in Listing 9-2 but is now being read and displayed on the screen by this View.

Organizing View Files

The file structure in Figure 9-2 shows that Views appear in the Views folder and have a *.aspx file extension. Each subfolder under the Views folder corresponds to a Controller, and the Views within the subfolder correspond generally to Controller actions. When a Controller passes control to a View, by calling *View,* ASP.NET MVC searches for the View in the Views folder with the subfolder named the same as the Controller and the file named the same as the action calling the View.

Notice that there is a Shared folder. Sometimes, you'll want to have a View that is shared by two or more Controller actions, and you can put these shared Views in the Shared subfolder. Whenever ASP.NET MVC doesn't find a View in the Controller-named subfolder, it will search for the View in the Shared folder. An important file in the Shared subfolder is the MasterPage, which is discussed next.

Assigning MasterPage Files

Most sites on the Web have multiple pages, each with common elements. They all have the same header, menu, sidebars, and footers. When you first build a site, you can duplicate this common content with no trouble, but this copy-and-paste type duplication will cause a lot of headaches in the future. The first time you have to change the common elements, you'll need to visit every page. If the site has only a few pages, no problem, but the reality is that most sites of any success grow to dozens or hundreds of pages. It is beyond practical to try to update every page on a site every time the common content changes.

This is where MasterPages help, allowing you to specify the common content in one place where you can have content pages that use the MasterPage. Whenever something changes in the common content, you update the MasterPage, and every page of a site that uses the MasterPage is automatically updated. Listing 9-3 shows the MasterPage, created by ASP.NET MVC, that the content page in Listing 9-2 uses.

Listing 9-3   A MasterPage

```
<%@ Master Language="C#"
         Inherits="System.Web.Mvc.ViewMasterPage" %>

<!DOCTYPE html PUBLIC "-//W3C//DTD XHTML 1.0 Strict//EN"
"http://www.w3.org/TR/xhtml1/DTD/xhtml1-strict.dtd">
<html xmlns="http://www.w3.org/1999/xhtml">
<head runat="server">
```

```
    <title>
        <asp:ContentPlaceHolder ID="TitleContent"
                                runat="server" />
    </title>
    <link href="../../Content/Site.css"
          rel="stylesheet" type="text/css" />
</head>

<body>
    <div class="page">

        <div id="header">
            <div id="title">
                <h1>My MVC Application</h1>
            </div>

            <div id="logindisplay">
<% Html.RenderPartial("LogOnUserControl"); %>
            </div>

            <div id="menucontainer">

                <ul id="menu">
                    <li>
<%= Html.ActionLink("Home", "Index", "Home")%>
                    </li>
                    <li>
<%= Html.ActionLink("About", "About", "Home")%>
                    </li>
                </ul>

            </div>
        </div>

        <div id="main">
          <asp:ContentPlaceHolder ID="MainContent" runat="server" />

          <div id="footer">
          </div>
        </div>
    </div>
</body>
</html>
```

Moving from the top of Listing 9-3 down, you can see the MasterPage directive at the top of the page, which states that this is a MasterPage and ASP.NET MVC will handle the page appropriately. The DTD is a tag that specifies what Web standards this page supports, which is read by browsers to help them determine the best way to display the page.

The rest of the page is framed inside of HTML tags and ASP.NET MVC markup. The *html* tag states that this is an HTML document. HTML documents have two parts, a head and a body, where the head is for metadata describing the page and the body contains display content.

In HTML, a *div* tag blocks off a chunk of HTML and is useful for layout and organization of the page. The *H*x tags, where *x* is a number between 1 and 6, describe headers, where h1 is the largest and h6 is the smallest.

The ContentPlaceHolder controls are instrumental to the success of the MasterPage. If you look at the Content tags in Listing 9-2, you'll see that they have a ContentPlaceHolderID that matches the ID attributes of the ContentPlaceHolder controls in Listing 9-3. What this means is that when the View renders, the MasterPage will display and ASP.NET MVC will inject the Content regions of the content pages into the matching ContentPlaceHolders of the MasterPage. ASP.NET MVC knows which MasterPage to use because the Page directive, as shown in Listing 9-2, specifies the MasterPage attribute.

If you recall from the last section, Listing 9-2 had a binding expression for the *Html Encode* helper method. The MasterPage in Listing 9-3 introduces a couple more *Html* helper methods, *RenderPartial* and *ActionLink*.

The *ActionLink* method has three parameters: *id, controller, and action.* When the *ActionLink* renders in the browser, it will transform into an anchor tag, *a,* with an *id* specified in the first parameter of *ActionLink.* When the user clicks the link in the browser, the application will navigate to the Controller in the third parameter of *ActionLink* and invoke the action in the second parameter of *ActionLink.* So, if the user clicked the link produced by *ActionLink("About", "About", "Home"),* ASP.NET MVC will invoke the About action of the Home Controller. The next section discusses *RenderPartial* in more detail.

Partial Views (a.k.a. User Controls)

It's often the case that you've written View content on one page and need the same identical content on two or more pages. As explained with MasterPages, you want to avoid the maintenance work that comes with updating all of the content that is the same on multiple pages. While MasterPages are good for content that decorates pages across an entire site, a Partial View is ideal for limited reuse of View content on different pages of a site.

A good example of where a Partial View is useful is illustrated in the code produced by the ASP.NET MVC Project Wizard, where it created the LogonUserControl.ascx. The terms Partial View and User Control are synonymous, where the term User Control is familiar to developers who have worked with previous versions of ASP.NET Web Forms. Partial View is consistent with the ASP.NET MVC perspective of Views, where a Partial View is not an entire View, but a chunk of View content that can be reused with multiple Views. It isn't coincidence that this control is physically located in the Views Shared folder, considering that it can be used on multiple pages. Remember, if ASP.NET MVC can't find a file in a View folder named after a Controller, it will look in the Shared folder. Listing 9-4 shows the contents of LogonUserControl.ascx.

Listing 9-4   Contents of a Partial View

```
<%@ Control Language="C#"
            Inherits="System.Web.Mvc.ViewUserControl" %>
<%
    if (Request.IsAuthenticated) {
%>
Welcome <b><%= Html.Encode(Page.User.Identity.Name) %></b>!
  [ <%= Html.ActionLink("Log Off", "LogOff", "Account") %> ]
<%
    }
    else {
%>
[ <%= Html.ActionLink("Log On", "LogOn", "Account") %> ]
<%
    }
%>
```

The Control directive at the top of Listing 9-4 indicates that this is a Partial View. Within the control, you can see an *if* statement, where the language syntax is surrounded by <% and %> binding symbols. The additional syntax to separate code from markup might take a little getting used to, but it is typical in an MVC application to control how markup is rendered. The *IsAuthenticated* property of the *Request* object tells whether the current user is logged in, and the logic ensures the appropriate message displays. The *ActionLink Html* helper methods generate action tags with a URL for actions on the Account Controller. We've barely touched on routing and how a URL matches controllers and actions, but the next section explains how routes work in greater depth.

Managing Routing

ASP.NET MVC has a routing system that matches URLs to controllers with actions and the parameters passed to those actions. When you start a new ASP.NET MVC project, default routing will be established via a file called Global.asax, which is where many events affecting the application are placed. When you run an ASP.NET MVC application, it will use URLs of the form http://domain/controller/action/param1/param2/.../paramN? optionalArg=optionalVal. Here's an example:

```
http://localhost:1042/Home/About
```

In this example, localhost:1042 is the domain, Home is the Controller, and About is the action. When ASP.NET MVC sees this URL, it will instantiate the HomeController class and call the *About* method.

The Global.asax file has an Application_Start event that is called the first time the application runs. This is where routing is set up so that it will be in place for all of the requests while the application is running. Listing 9-5 shows the default routing for an ASP .NET MVC project.

Listing 9-5   Setting up routing

C#:

```csharp
using System;
using System.Collections.Generic;
using System.Linq;
using System.Web;
using System.Web.Mvc;
using System.Web.Routing;

namespace MyShopCS
{
    // Note: For instructions on enabling IIS6 or IIS7 classic mode,
    // visit http://go.microsoft.com/?LinkId=9394801

    public class MvcApplication : System.Web.HttpApplication
    {
        public static void RegisterRoutes(RouteCollection routes)
        {
            routes.IgnoreRoute("{resource}.axd/{*pathInfo}");

            routes.MapRoute(
                "Default",                          // Route name
                "{controller}/{action}/{id}", // URL with parameters
                new {
```

```
                        controller = "Home",
                        action = "Index",
                        id = "" }  // Parameter defaults
            );

        }

        protected void Application_Start()
        {
            RegisterRoutes(RouteTable.Routes);
        }
    }
}
```

VB:

```vb
' Note: For instructions on enabling IIS6 or IIS7 classic mode,
' visit http://go.microsoft.com/?LinkId=9394802

Public Class MvcApplication
    Inherits System.Web.HttpApplication

    Shared Sub RegisterRoutes(ByVal routes As RouteCollection)
        routes.IgnoreRoute("{resource}.axd/{*pathInfo}")

        ' MapRoute takes the following parameters, in order:
        ' (1) Route name
        ' (2) URL with parameters
        ' (3) Parameter defaults
        routes.MapRoute( _
            "Default", _
            "{controller}/{action}/{id}", _
            New With
            {
                .controller = "Home", .action = "Index", .id = ""
            }
        )

    End Sub

    Sub Application_Start()
        AreaRegistration.RegisterAllAreas()

        RegisterRoutes(RouteTable.Routes)
    End Sub
End Class
```

Listing 9-5 shows that the Application_Start event invokes a method named *RegisterRoutes,* passing the *Routes* property of the *RouteTable* class. The *Routes* property is a static RouteCollection, meaning that there is only one copy for the entire application, and it will hold multiple routes. When the application starts, this collection will be empty and the *RegisterRoutes* method will populate the collection with routes for this application.

Routing works by pattern matching, which you can see through the two statements in the *RegisterRoutes* method: *IgnoreRoute* and *MapRoute. IgnoreRoute* is useful for situations where you want to let IIS request the exact URL. In this case, it is any file with the *.axd extension, regardless of parameters.

The *MapRoute* method shows a common pattern for matching URLs to controllers, actions, and parameters. The first parameter is the name of the route. The second parameter describes the pattern, where each pattern match is defined between curly braces. Based on the URL, http://localhost:1042/Home/About, the pattern, {controller}/{action}/{id}, matches Home to {controller} and About to {action}; there is no match for {id}. Therefore, ASP.NET MVC will append "Controller" to the URL segment that matches {controller}, meaning that the Controller name to instantiate is HomeController. *About* is the method inside of HomeController to invoke. Since *About* doesn't have parameters, supplying the {id} is unnecessary.

The third parameter for *MapRoute* specifies default values, where the key matches the pattern parameter and the value assigned to the key is what ASP.NET MVC uses when it doesn't find a pattern match with the URL. Here are a couple of examples:

- http://localhost:1042 invokes the *Index* method of HomeController because no Controller or action matches and the defaults are Home for {controller} and Index for {action}.

- http://localhost:1042/Home invokes the *Index* method of HomeController because no action was specified and the default value for {action} is Index.

You can create your own custom route by using the *MapRoute* method and specifying other default values for the parameters.

Building a Customer Management Application

Now, we'll pull together the ASP.NET MVC concepts you've learned and describe how to build a very simple application that displays, adds, modifies, and deletes customers. In so doing, you'll see how to build up a Model that supports customers, how to create a custom Controller with actions for managing customers, and how to create multiple views to handle interaction with the users as they work with customers.

Creating a Repository

A common pattern for working with data is to build a repository that is responsible for all data-related operations. This is another way to promote separation of concerns so that you isolate logic into specific parts of an application, resulting in easier code to work with. A repository is a class that performs create, read, update, and delete (CRUD) operations on a specific data type. Listing 9-6 shows a repository for working with customer objects. You can create this class by right-clicking the Models folder and selecting Add | Class, and name the class **CustomerRepository**. The code also assumes that you've created a LINQ to SQL *.dbml, named **MyShop**, with a Customer entity for the Customers table in MyShop, which is the database created in Chapter 7.

Listing 9-6   A repository for working with customer data

C#:

```
using System;
using System.Collections.Generic;
using System.Linq;
using System.Web;

namespace MyShopCS.Models
{
    public class CustomerRepository
    {
        private MyShopDataContext m_ctx
            = new MyShopDataContext();

        public int InsertCustomer(Customer cust)
        {
            m_ctx.Customers.InsertOnSubmit(cust);
            m_ctx.SubmitChanges();
            return cust.CustomerID;
        }

        public void UpdateCustomer(Customer cust)
        {
            var currentCust =
                (from currCust in m_ctx.Customers
                 where currCust.CustomerID == cust.CustomerID
                 select currCust)
                 .SingleOrDefault();

            if (currentCust != null)
```

```
        {
            currentCust.Age = cust.Age;
            currentCust.Birthday = cust.Birthday;
            currentCust.Income = cust.Income;
            currentCust.Name = cust.Name;
        }

        m_ctx.SubmitChanges();
    }

    public Customer GetCustomer(int custID)
    {
        return
            (from cust in m_ctx.Customers
             where cust.CustomerID == custID
             select cust)
             .SingleOrDefault();
    }

    public List<Customer> GetCustomers()
    {
        return
            (from cust in m_ctx.Customers
             select cust)
             .ToList();
    }

    public void DeleteCustomer(int custID)
    {
        var customer =
            (from cust in m_ctx.Customers
             where cust.CustomerID == custID
             select cust)
             .SingleOrDefault();

        m_ctx.Customers.DeleteOnSubmit(customer);
        m_ctx.SubmitChanges();
    }
    }
}
```

VB:

```
Public Class CustomerRepository

    Private m_ctx As New MyShopDataContext
```

```vbnet
Public Function InsertCustomer(
    ByVal cust As Customer) As Integer

    m_ctx.Customers.InsertOnSubmit(cust)
    m_ctx.SubmitChanges()
    Return cust.CustomerID

End Function

Public Sub UpdateCustomer(ByVal cust As Customer)

    Dim currentCust =
        (From currCust In m_ctx.Customers
         Where currCust.CustomerID = cust.CustomerID
         Select currCust).SingleOrDefault()


    If Not currentCust Is Nothing Then

        With currentCust
            .Age = cust.Age
            .Birthday = cust.Birthday
            .Income = cust.Income
            .Name = cust.Name
        End With

        m_ctx.SubmitChanges()

    End If

End Sub

Public Function GetCustomer(ByVal custID As Integer) As Customer

    Dim customer =
        (From cust In m_ctx.Customers
         Where cust.CustomerID = custID
         Select cust).SingleOrDefault()

    Return customer

End Function

Public Function GetCustomers() As List(Of Customer)

    Dim customers =
```

```
        (From cust In m_ctx.Customers
         Select cust).ToList()

    Return customers

End Function

Public Sub DeleteCustomer(ByVal custID As Integer)

    Dim customer =
        (From cust In m_ctx.Customers
         Where cust.CustomerID = custID
         Select cust).SingleOrDefault()

    m_ctx.Customers.DeleteOnSubmit(customer)
    m_ctx.SubmitChanges()

    End Sub
End Class
```

You can have more methods in a repository for doing whatever is required with data
for the application, but the items in Listing 9-6 are typical. The LINQ to SQL operations
are consistent with the material covered in Chapter 7, so there's no need to repeat the same
material here. The purpose of the repository is to give the Controller an object to work
with for getting data without filling up Controller methods with data access logic. Let's
see how the Controller works with this repository next.

Creating a Customer Controller

Right-click the Controllers folder, select Add | Controller, or press CTRL-M, press CTRL-
C, and name the file **CustomerController**. Check the box for "Add action methods for
Create, Update, and Details scenarios" as shown in Figure 9-4.

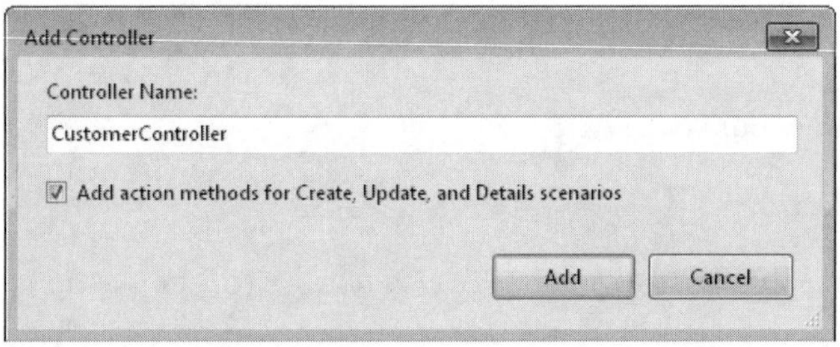

Figure 9-4   Creating a new Controller

This will create a new Controller with several methods for working with Customer data. Listing 9-1 already showed what a Controller looks like, and this is no different, except that it contains more action methods. The following sections explain how to perform various operations on customer data.

Displaying a Customer List

The first thing to do with customers is to display a list that will serve as a starting point for other operations. Listing 9-7 shows the *Index* action method of the CustomerController and how it gets a list of customers to display. The code uses the *CustomerRepository,* created in the preceding section. For C#, you need to add a *using* directive at the top of the file for the MyShopCS.Models namespace.

Listing 9-7   A Controller for displaying a list

C#:

```
public ActionResult Index()
{
    var customers =
        new CustomerRepository()
        .GetCustomers();

    return View(customers);
}
```

VB:

```
Function Index() As ActionResult
    Dim custRep As New CustomerRepository
    Dim customers As List(Of Customer)

    customers = custRep.GetCustomers()
    Return View(customers)
End Function
```

Listing 9-7 shows how the *Index* method uses the CustomerRepository to get the list of customers. You need to pass that list to the View for display.

To create the View, right-click anywhere in the *Index* method and select Add View, which will display the Add View window, shown in Figure 9-5.

The name of the View is Index, corresponding to the name of the action method invoking the View. Naming the View after the action method is the default behavior, but

Figure 9-5 The Add View window

you can name the View anything you want. If the View you need to display is named differently than the action method, you can use the following *View* method overload:

```
View("SomeOtherViewName", customers);
```

We want to use a strongly typed View, meaning that you will have IDE support for referencing the properties of your own object when working in the View. The selected object is *Customer*, which is already defined as a LINQ to SQL entity, which is the same type returned by the call to the *GetCustomers* method in CustomerRepository.

The purpose of this View is to display a list of customers, so we'll select List as View content. This will prepopulate the View with a template for displaying customers. You'll be able to modify the screen as you like. Additionally, if you prefer to write your own code to populate the screen, you can select the Empty option for View content and then code the View manually yourself. Selecting List is a quick way to get started.

You learned about MasterPages earlier in this chapter, and you have the option of selecting a MasterPage of your choice and specifying which ContentPlaceHolder your code will render in.

Click Add to generate the View shown in Listing 9-8.

Listing 9-8   A Customer List View

```
<%@ Page Title="" Language="C#"
         MasterPageFile="~/Views/Shared/Site.Master"
         Inherits="System.Web.Mvc
.ViewPage<IEnumerable<MyShopCS.Models.Customer>>" %>

<asp:Content ID="Content1"
             ContentPlaceHolderID="TitleContent"
             runat="server">
    Index
</asp:Content>

<asp:Content ID="Content2"
             ContentPlaceHolderID="MainContent"
             runat="server">

    <h2>Index</h2>

    <table>
        <tr>
            <th></th>
            <th>
                CustomerID
            </th>
            <th>
                Name
            </th>
            <th>
                Age
            </th>
            <th>
                Birthday
            </th>
            <th>
                Income
            </th>
        </tr>

    <% foreach (var item in Model) { %>

        <tr>
            <td>
                <%= Html.ActionLink("Edit", "Edit",
                    new { id=item.CustomerID }) %> |
                <%= Html.ActionLink("Details", "Details",
                    new { id=item.CustomerID })%>
            </td>
```

```
        <td>
            <%= Html.Encode(item.CustomerID) %>
        </td>
        <td>
            <%= Html.Encode(item.Name) %>
        </td>
        <td>
            <%= Html.Encode(item.Age) %>
        </td>
        <td>
            <%= Html.Encode(String.Format("{0:g}",
                item.Birthday)) %>
        </td>
        <td>
            <%= Html.Encode(String.Format("{0:F}",
                item.Income)) %>
        </td>
    </tr>

<% } %>

</table>

<p>
    <%= Html.ActionLink("Create New", "Create") %>
</p>

</asp:Content>
```

Listing 9-8 organizes the list of Customers in a table. The *tr* tags are rows, *th* are header cells, and *td* are content cells. After specifying the header row, the *foreach* loop iterates on the Model to render each content row. If you recall from Listing 9-7, the *Index* action method called *View* with a *List<Customer>* (*List(Of Customer)* in VB). When creating the View, we specified the object type as *Customer*, which means that the reference to Model in the *foreach* statement is to *List<Customer>* and item contains a *Customer* object.

For each cell being rendered, *item* is the current *Customer* and the property for that cell is referenced by the property of *Customer* that should display. What is particularly important about displaying the data is that each cell uses the *Html.Encode* helper method instead of displaying the data directly. This is a best practice for best security to ensure that any data displayed is not treated as HTML markup or accidentally runs JavaScript that you didn't intend. You see, a malicious hacker could add JavaScript during data entry and when you display that field, the browser would try to run the JavaScript code, which would be bad. Using *Html.Encode* prevents this from happening. The other *Html* helper methods, such as *ActionLink,* already encode output, so you should use *Html.Encode* whenever one of the other helpers isn't used. Notice that the code for the *foreach* loop is enclosed in <% and %> symbols so that it is treated as code and not markup.

Next, you'll want to be able to navigate to the Customer List page from the main menu, so open your MasterPage, Site.Master, and add the Customers ActionLink like this:

```
<ul id="menu">
    <li><%= Html.ActionLink("Customers", "Index", "Customer")%></li>
    <li><%= Html.ActionLink("Home", "Index", "Home")%></li>
    <li><%= Html.ActionLink("About", "About", "Home")%></li>
</ul>
```

The parameters to the new *ActionLink,* from left to right, indicate that the text for the anchor will be Customers, and ASP.NET will invoke the *Index* action method on the *CustomerController* class when the user clicks the link. Figure 9-6 shows what the Customer list looks like when the program runs.

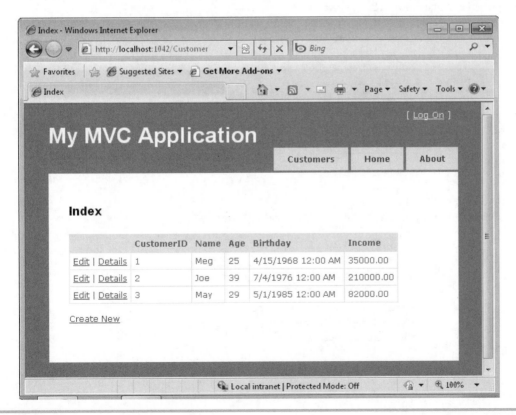

Figure 9-6 Showing a list of objects

As shown in Figure 9-6, the Customer tab appears first on the list, and clicking it shows the list of Customers. In addition to the content you see in the list, there are links, such as Edit and Create. The next section covers the Create operation.

Adding a New Customer

Creating a new customer involves presenting a screen for data entry and saving the new data when submitted. When creating a new object, your Controller needs two methods, a *get* method to initialize an empty Customer and a *post* method to save the new customer data. Listing 9-9 shows the *get* and *post* methods in the *CustomerController* class.

Listing 9-9   Creating a new Customer object

C#:

```
//
// GET: /Customer/Create

public ActionResult Create()
{
    Customer cust = new Customer
    {
        Birthday = new DateTime(1980, 1, 1)
    };

    return View(cust);
}

//
// POST: /Customer/Create

[AcceptVerbs(HttpVerbs.Post)]
public ActionResult Create(Customer cust)
{
    try
    {
        if (string.IsNullOrEmpty(cust.Name))
        {
            ModelState.AddModelError(
                "Name", "Name is required.");
                return View();
        }
```

```csharp
            new CustomerRepository()
                .InsertCustomer(cust);

            return RedirectToAction("Index");
        }
        catch
        {
            return View();
        }
    }
}
```

   VB:

```vbnet
'
' GET: /Customer/Create

Function Create() As ActionResult
    Dim cust As New Customer With
    {
        .Birthday = New DateTime(1980, 1, 1)
    }
    Return View(cust)
End Function

'
' POST: /Customer/Create

<HttpPost()> _
Function Create(ByVal cust As Customer) As ActionResult
    Try
        If String.IsNullOrEmpty(cust.Name) Then
            ModelState.AddModelError(
                "Name", "Name is required.")
        End If

        Dim custRep As New CustomerRepository
        custRep.InsertCustomer(cust)

        Return RedirectToAction("Index")
    Catch
        Return View()
    End Try
End Function
```

In the HTTP protocol, there are different types of verbs for the operation being conducted. Listing 9-9 demonstrates two of these verbs, get and post. A get is typically associated with reading data, and a post is typically associated with writing data. Listing 9-9 shows both *get* and *post* methods in the *Create* method overloads. In ASP.NET MVC, action methods default to get requests and you must use an *HttpVerbs* attribute to specify a post.

The get *Create* action method instantiates a new *Customer* object and passes it to the View. When the user fills in the form and submits, the post *Create* action method will execute and insert the new record into the database.

Notice how I changed the *Create* method parameter from *FormsCollection* to *Customer*. ASP.NET MVC will automatically read the form values and match those values up with matching properties in the object passed to the method. The method also checks to ensure that the name is filled in and adds an error to the ModelState. Whenever an error occurs, you need to return to the same View to ensure the user sees the error and can correct and resubmit. ASP.NET MVC will use this error to display error messages in the View. To create the View, right-click either *Create* method, select Add View, and fill in the values as shown in Figure 9-7.

Figure 9-7 Adding a new Customer

The Add View screen in Figure 9-7 specifies strong typing on the Customer class, but this time it selects Create as the View Content. Listing 9-10 shows the resulting View.

Listing 9-10   View for creating a new Customer

```
<%@ Page Title="" Language="C#"
    MasterPageFile="~/Views/Shared/Site.Master"
    Inherits="System.Web.Mvc.ViewPage<MyShopCS.Customer>" %>

<asp:Content ID="Content1" ContentPlaceHolderID="TitleContent"
    runat="server">
    Create
</asp:Content>

<asp:Content ID="Content2" ContentPlaceHolderID="MainContent"
    runat="server">

    <h2>Create</h2>

    <% using (Html.BeginForm()) {%>

        <fieldset>
            <legend>Fields</legend>

            <div class="editor-label">
                <%= Html.LabelFor(model => model.CustomerID) %>
            </div>
            <div class="editor-field">
                <%= Html.TextBoxFor(model => model.CustomerID) %>
                <%= Html.ValidationMessageFor(
                    model => model.CustomerID) %>
            </div>

            <div class="editor-label">
                <%= Html.LabelFor(model => model.Name) %>
            </div>
            <div class="editor-field">
                <%= Html.TextBoxFor(model => model.Name) %>
                <%= Html.ValidationMessageFor(
                    model => model.Name) %>
            </div>

            <div class="editor-label">
                <%= Html.LabelFor(model => model.Age) %>
            </div>
```

```
        <div class="editor-field">
            <%= Html.TextBoxFor(model => model.Age) %>
            <%= Html.ValidationMessageFor(
                model => model.Age) %>
        </div>

        <div class="editor-label">
            <%= Html.LabelFor(model => model.Birthday) %>
        </div>
        <div class="editor-field">
            <%= Html.TextBoxFor(model => model.Birthday) %>
            <%= Html.ValidationMessageFor(
                model => model.Birthday) %>
        </div>

        <div class="editor-label">
            <%= Html.LabelFor(model => model.Income) %>
        </div>
        <div class="editor-field">
            <%= Html.TextBoxFor(model => model.Income) %>
            <%= Html.ValidationMessageFor(
                model => model.Income) %>
        </div>

        <p>
            <input type="submit" value="Create" />
        </p>
    </fieldset>

    <% } %>

    <div>
        <%=Html.ActionLink("Back to List", "Index") %>
    </div>

</asp:Content>
```

The *ValidationMessageFor Html* helper displays any errors that occur on this page. The error messages are displayed whenever the Controller action method adds the error to the ModelState. When the user clicks the Submit button, this page will post back to the *Create* method with the *AcceptVerbs* attribute for post. Figure 9-8 shows the Create screen when running.

In addition to creating a new Customer, you can edit existing Customers, as is discussed next.

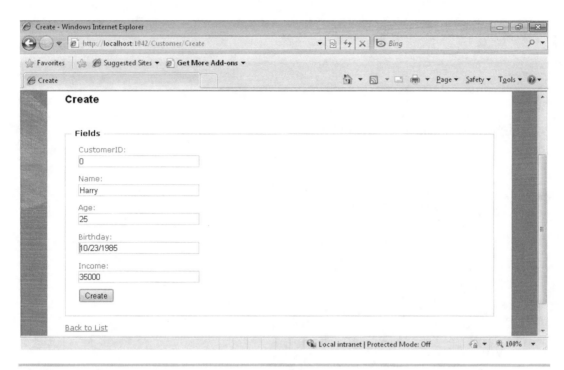

Figure 9-8   The Create screen

Updating Existing Customers

Similar to how we created Customers, you also need two methods for editing a Customer. The *get* method populates an edit form with existing data, and the *post* method saves the changes. Listing 9-11 shows these two methods.

Listing 9-11   Methods for editing Customers

C#:

```
//
// GET: /Customer/Edit/5

public ActionResult Edit(int id)
{
    Customer cust =
        new CustomerRepository()
            .GetCustomer(id);
```

```csharp
        return View(cust);
}

//
// POST: /Customer/Edit/5

[AcceptVerbs(HttpVerbs.Post)]
public ActionResult Edit(Customer cust)
{
    try
    {
        new CustomerRepository()
            .UpdateCustomer(cust);

        return RedirectToAction("Index");
    }
    catch
    {
        return View();
    }
}
```

VB:

```vb
'
' GET: /Customer/Edit/5

Function Edit(ByVal id As Integer) As ActionResult
    Dim custRep As New CustomerRepository
    Dim cust As Customer

    cust = custRep.GetCustomer(id)

    Return View(cust)
End Function


'
' POST: /Customer/Edit/5

<HttpPost()> _
Function Edit(ByVal id As Integer, ByVal cust As Customer)
    As ActionResult
    Try
        Dim custRep As New CustomerRepository
        custRep.UpdateCustomer(cust)
```

```
        Return RedirectToAction("Index")
    Catch
        Return View()
    End Try
End Function
```

In the get *Edit* action method, you need to get a reference to the current record, indicated by the *id* being passed in, and pass that reference to the View for display. The post *Edit* action method accepts the modified customer and passes it to the repository for update in the database. You should also right-click in either of the *Edit* methods and select Add View. Make the View strongly typed, set the class to Customer, and the Content type to Edit.

The final operation to complete is discussed next, how to delete a Customer.

Deleting a Customer

The default template for creating a list added an ActionLink for Details, next to the Edit ActionLink. You can create a read-only details page if you want, or just ensure the list is in the format you want to show each customer record, but for our purposes the Details option is not necessary. So, this example replaces the Details link with one for deleting a record. Listing 9-12 shows the *Delete* Controller method, which replaces the *Detail* Controller method.

Listing 9-12   The Delete Controller method

C#:

```
//
// GET: /Customer/Delete/5

public ActionResult Delete(int id)
{
    new CustomerRepository()
        .DeleteCustomer(id);

    TempData["Result"] = "Customer Deleted.";

    return RedirectToAction("Index");
}
```

VB:

```vb
'
' GET: /Customer/Delete/5

Function Delete(ByVal id As Integer) As ActionResult
    Dim custRep As New CustomerRepository
    custRep.DeleteCustomer(id)

    TempData("Result") = "Customer Deleted."

    Return RedirectToAction("Index")
End Function
```

Besides showing how to use the repository for performing the delete operation, there are a couple of new items in Listing 9-12 that you'll need to know about: *TempData* and specifying a View. *TempData* is a special object for holding data for a single display of a View. So, when the View displays, it can read the current value of *TempData,* but that same value will not be available on the next View unless the Controller explicitly loads it again.

In all of the other calls to *View,* it was assumed that a View named after the Controller method would be returned, so it wasn't necessary to specify the name of the View. However, we don't have a delete View, so we specify Index as the View explicitly.

To accommodate the delete operation, Listing 9-13 shows the modifications on the Index.aspx View for Customers (located under \Views\Customer).

Listing 9-13   Deleting a Customer

C#:

```csharp
... content removed

<h2>Index</h2>

<p>
    <% if (TempData["Result"] != null)
        { %>
            <label><%= Html.Encode(TempData["Result"].ToString() )%>
</label>
    <% } %>
</p>
<table>
```

```
... content removed

<% foreach (var item in Model) { %>

    <tr>
        <td>
            <%= Html.ActionLink("Edit", "Edit",
                new { id=item.CustomerID }) %> |
            <%= Html.ActionLink("Delete", "Delete",
                new { id=item.CustomerID })%>
        </td>
... content removed
```

  VB:

```
... content removed

    <h2>Index</h2>

    <p>
        <% If Not TempData("Result") Is Nothing Then %>
            <label>
                <%= Html.Encode(TempData("Result").ToString())%>
            </label>
        <% End If%>
    </p>
    <p>
        <%= Html.ActionLink("Create New", "Create")%>
    </p>

    <table>

... content removed

    <% For Each item In Model%>

        <tr>
            <td>
                <%=Html.ActionLink("Edit", "Edit",
                    New With {.id = item.CustomerID})%> |
                <%=Html.ActionLink("Delete", "Delete",
                    New With {.id = item.CustomerID})%>
            </td>

... content removed
```

Listing 9-13 has content removed to avoid duplicating code you've already seen. Near the top of the listing, you can see the *if* statement that will check to see if there is a value in *TempData["Result"]* (*TempData("Result")* in VB) and will display that value in a label if present. Next to the Edit ActionLink, the Details ActionLink has been changed to a Delete ActionLink, passing the *id* of the current customer back to the Controller for deletion.

Summary

You now know the essential parts of MVC: Models, Views, and Controllers. You saw how to implement the repository pattern for managing a data access layer and simplify the code. This chapter showed how to create controllers and views. You also learned about routing and how it helps match URLs to controllers, actions, and parameters. Finally, there was a section that demonstrated how to perform CRUD operations with ASP.NET MVC.

Another popular Web technology is Silverlight, which gives you the ability to create rich user experiences. The next chapter helps you get started with Silverlight development.

Chapter 10
Designing Silverlight Applications

Key Skills & Concepts

- Start a New Silverlight Project

- Work with the Silverlight Designer

- Add Controls to an Application

- Play Silverlight Videos

- Deploy Silverlight Applications

Silverlight is a Web technology that allows you to add a rich user experience to Web applications. It uses XAML, just like WPF applications, but runs in a Web page supported by ASP.NET.

Other parts of this book prepare you for working with Silverlight. Since Silverlight uses XAML, you can review Appendixes A and B to get up-to-speed on XAML essentials. Silverlight also has many features in common with WPF. Therefore, it would be useful to review Chapter 8 before reading this chapter. What you'll learn in this chapter is how VS helps you create a Silverlight project, how to add controls to the Silverlight designer, and how to deploy Silverlight applications.

Starting a Silverlight Project

As when starting other projects, you can select File | New | Project or press CTRL-SHIFT-N; you then select a Silverlight application in the New Project window. After you set up the project with a name and folder, VS will display another window for configuring the Silverlight application, shown in Figure 10-1.

Silverlight gives you the option to create a Web site at the same time as you create the Silverlight application. You can opt not to create the Web site, but ultimately, you'll need to host your Silverlight application on a Web page. There is an alternate Web technology based on ASP.NET Web forms, but this book concentrates on the ASP.NET MVC Web development model, discussed in Chapter 9, which is why you see the New Web project type set to ASP.NET MVC Web Project. Click OK to create the Silverlight application, shown in Figure 10-2. You'll also see a screen asking if you want to create a unit test project, which is the same window discussed in Chapter 9. Click OK to continue.

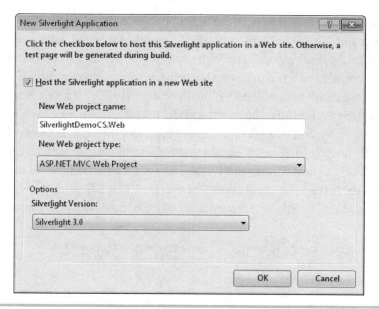

Figure 10-1   Creating a new Silverlight application

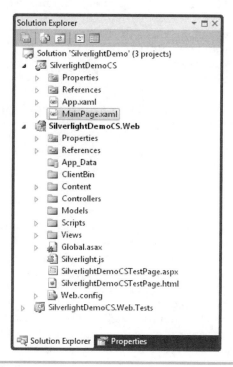

Figure 10-2   A new Silverlight project

Similar to WPF applications, Silverlight applications start with a MainPage.xaml file and an App.xaml file, where App.xaml runs to initialize the application and MainPage .xaml contains the display page. The Web site is a typical ASP.NET MVC application, except that it does have a test page that hosts the Silverlight application, SilverlightDemo CSTestPage.aspx (SilverlightDemoVBTestPage.aspx for VB). There's also a Silverlight DemoCSTestPage.html (SilverlightDemoVBTestPage.html for VB), which performs the same function as the SilverlightDemoCSTestPage.aspx (SilverlightDemoVBTestPage .aspx for VB) hosting Silverlight, except that the *.html version uses JavaScript and the HTML object tag to host Silverlight. Listing 10-1 shows the contents of the test page and how it hosts the Silverlight application. There is no C# or VB version of Listing 10-1 because the code is XAML, which works exactly the same with either language.

Listing 10-1   Hosting a Silverlight application on a Web page

```
<%@ Page Language="C#" AutoEventWireup="true" %>

<!DOCTYPE html PUBLIC
"-//W3C//DTD XHTML 1.0 Transitional//EN"
"http://www.w3.org/TR/xhtml1/DTD/xhtml1-transitional.dtd">
<html xmlns="http://www.w3.org/1999/xhtml" >
<head runat="server">
    <title>SilverlightDemoCS</title>
    <style type="text/css">
    // css styles omitted
    </style>
    <script type="text/javascript" src="Silverlight.js"></script>
    <script type="text/javascript">
        function onSilverlightError(sender, args) {
            // error handling code omitted
        }
    </script>
</head>
<body>
<form id="form1" runat="server" style="height:100%">
<div id="silverlightControlHost">
    <object data="data:application/x-silverlight-2,"
            type="application/x-silverlight-2"
            width="100%" height="100%">
        <param name="source"
                value="ClientBin/SilverlightDemoCS.xap"/>
        <param name="onError" value="onSilverlightError" />
        <param name="background" value="white" />
```

```
        <param name="minRuntimeVersion" value="3.0.40818.0" />
        <param name="autoUpgrade" value="true" />
        <a
href="http://go.microsoft.com/fwlink/?LinkID=149156&v=3.0.40818.0"
style="text-decoration:none">
            <img src="http://go.microsoft.com/fwlink/?LinkId=161376"
                alt="Get Microsoft Silverlight"
                style="border-style:none"/>
        </a>
    </object>
    <iframe id="_sl_historyFrame"
            style="visibility:hidden;height:0px;width:0px;border:0px">
    </iframe>
</div>
</form>
</body>
</html>
```

Listing 10-1 contains an object tag that hosts the Silverlight application. This object tag has various parameters, which are described in Table 10-1.

You can run the application and view the Web page, but there isn't much to see yet. The next section starts you in the direction of making something useful happen with Silverlight by reviewing the Designer.

Parameter	Description
source	In Figure 10-2, you can see a ClientBin folder in the ASP.NET MVC Web application project. When the Silverlight project builds, VS will take the output of that project and place it into the ClientBin folder. The output of a compiled Silverlight project is a *.xap file, which is the same as a compressed *.zip file, but with a different name. Silverlight loads the *.xap file into the browser at runtime and runs the application.
onerror	Listing 10-1 omitted the contents of the onSilverlightError JavaScript function, which is called whenever an error occurs in Silverlight.
background	Sets the control background.
minRuntimeVersion	States that the user must have v3.0.40818.0 or later of the Silverlight plug-in for this application to run. The user receives an error message if she doesn't have the minimum version.
autoUpgrade	If the user doesn't have the minimum version, as specified in minRuntimeVersion, setting this to true will prompt the user to begin the upgrade process.

Table 10-1   Object Tag Parameters for Silverlight

Navigating the Silverlight Designer

The underlying technology for displaying the UI is XML Application Markup Language (XAML), pronounced "Zamel." Appendix A contains an introduction to XML, and Appendix B contains an introduction to XAML if you need to obtain a basic understanding of these two technologies. It would really be helpful for you to review Chapter 8 because you'll find many of the same controls for layout and display in both Silverlight and WPF.

The Silverlight Designer is very similar to the WPF Designer in how you work with controls. Drag and drop from the Toolbox, configure Grids, interact with XAML, and set properties in exactly the same way with Silverlight as with WPF. Since there are so many similarities, I won't repeat the material covered in Chapter 8 but will build upon previous material, showing you what is special about Silverlight.

Using Silverlight Controls

Silverlight has strong multimedia support through streaming audio and video. In fact, the Toolbox has controls that make it easy to host your own videos and control the user experience for playing videos. The following steps show how to design a screen that shows a video, as shown in Figure 10-3.

1. Your project starts out with a page named MainPage.xaml, which you should open so the designer is showing. If the XAML editor is showing, click on the Design tab at the bottom of the designer window.

2. You'll have a default Grid, which you can work with in exactly the same way as the designer for WPF, discussed in Chapter 8. You need to ensure the Grid has two rows, with the top row being large enough to fit the MediaElement and the bottom large enough to fit a single button. Hover over the left margin of the window until you see a grid line appear on the window. Move the grid line vertically until you've created two rows, where the bottom row is large enough to hold a button, as shown in Figure 10-3. Click on the window margin when you have the grid line positioned where you want.

3. Find the MediaElement in the Toolbox and drag it onto the top row of the Window in the designer. If you find that you haven't made the top row large enough, grab the grid line arrow in the left margin and drag it down some more.

4. Set the Name property of the MediaElement control to **VideoPlayer**.

5. The MediaElement control has a Source property that you can set with the URL of a movie. Set the Source property of the MediaElement control to http://mschnlnine .vo.llnwd.net/d1/ch9/8/3/7/0/7/4/OfficeVS10SC1_2MB_ch9.wmv, which is a video that introduces VS 2010.

6. Drag a Button from the Toolbox to the bottom row of the Window in the designer.

7. Set the Name property of the Button to **StartStopButton** and set the Content property of the Button to **Start**.

In Figure 10-3, you can see a Grid with two rows. The top row holds a MediaElement control and the bottom row holds a button. The name of the Video control is VideoPlayer and the name of the button is StartStopButton.

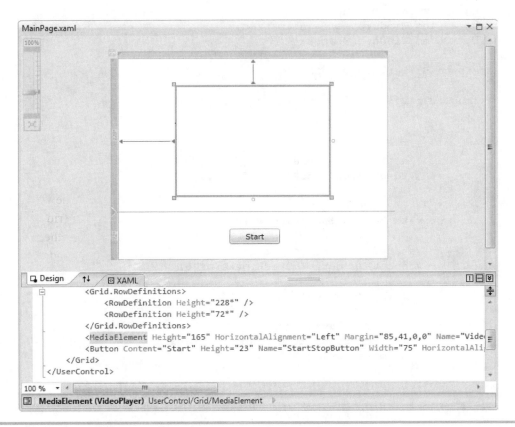

Figure 10-3 Playing Silverlight videos

Double-clicking the StartStopButton control will generate this Click event handler in the code-behind at MainPage.xaml.cs, shown in Listing 10-2.

Listing 10-2   Playing and stopping a video

C#:

```csharp
using System;
using System.Collections.Generic;
using System.Linq;
using System.Net;
using System.Windows;
using System.Windows.Controls;
using System.Windows.Documents;
using System.Windows.Input;
using System.Windows.Media;
using System.Windows.Media.Animation;
using System.Windows.Shapes;

namespace SilverlightDemoCS
{
    public partial class MainPage : UserControl
    {
        public MainPage()
        {
            InitializeComponent();
            VideoPlayer.AutoPlay = false;
        }

        private bool m_isPlaying = false;

        private void StartStopButton_Click(
            object sender, RoutedEventArgs e)
        {
            if (m_isPlaying)
            {
                VideoPlayer.Stop();
                StartStopButton.Content = "Start";
                m_isPlaying = false;
            }
            else
            {
                VideoPlayer.Play();
                StartStopButton.Content = "Stop";
```

```
                m_isPlaying = true;
            }
        }
    }
}
```

VB:

```
Partial Public Class MainPage
    Inherits UserControl

    Public Sub New()
        InitializeComponent()
        VideoPlayer.AutoPlay = False
    End Sub

    Dim m_isPlaying As Boolean = False

    Private Sub StartStopButton_Click(
        ByVal sender As System.Object,
        ByVal e As System.Windows.RoutedEventArgs)
        If (m_isPlaying) Then
            VideoPlayer.Stop()
            StartStopButton.Content = "Start"
            m_isPlaying = False
        Else
            VideoPlayer.Play()
            StartStopButton.Content = "Stop"
            m_isPlaying = True
        End If
    End Sub
End Class
```

By default, the MediaElement starts playing the Source video as soon as the application loads, so I set AutoPlay to false in the code-behind constructor. The *m_isPlaying* field keeps track of whether the MediaElement is playing or not. The Click event handler uses *m_isPlaying* to toggle between playing and stopped.

This is a quick demo of how to work with the MediaElement control, but there's much more you can do, such as pausing, tracking buffering, checking video position, and more. All you need to do is either capture events of the MediaElement control or use controls like buttons and sliders to interact with MediaElement, as the example shows in Listing 10-2. It would be good practice for you to take what you've learned here and add more functionality to the MediaElement control.

Running Silverlight Out-of-Browser (OOB)

A new capability of Silverlight 3 is running out-of-browser, meaning that users can load your application onto their desktop without needing to visit the hosting site. To implement OOB, open the Silverlight application properties by double-clicking the Properties folder in Solution Explorer. You'll see a window similar to Figure 10-4.

Most of the properties in Figure 10-4 have been covered in previous chapters. What's different is the section on Silverlight build options, which allows you to set the version and check the box to reduce the size of the *.xap file through caching. However, leave the option to reduce the *.xap file size unchecked if running OOB because it's not compatible

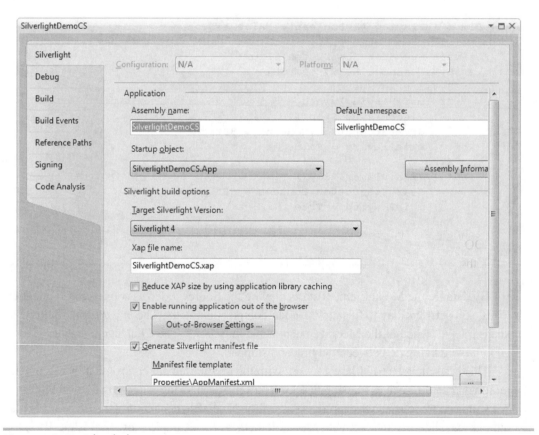

Figure 10-4   Silverlight properties

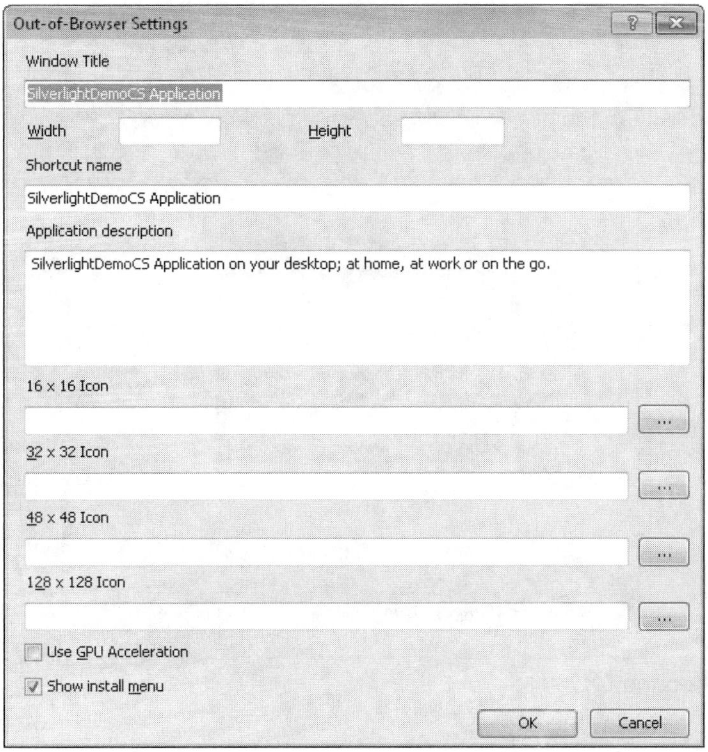

Figure 10-5   Out-of-browser settings

with OOB. The Manifest file describes the contents of the *.xap file. To enable OOB, check the box "Enable running application out of the browser." Then click the Out-Of-Browser Settings button to display the window shown in Figure 10-5.

The OOB settings in Figure 10-5 allow you to set information for the application, the size it will take when running, and variously sized icons that Windows will display. Setting GPU acceleration allows the application to take advantage of the local hardware to optimize graphics.

After you save OOB settings and run the application, the user can right-click the application running in the browser and select Install SilverlightDemoCSApplication Onto This Computer, as shown in Figure 10-6.

Figure 10-6 Choosing OOB

The next window you'll see gives options for adding the application to the Start menu and an icon on the desktop. Figure 10-7 shows that both options are checked.

When you click OK, Silverlight creates a Start menu item and adds the application to the desktop, as shown in Figure 10-8. When you start the application, it will run in a window rather than the browser.

Figure 10-7 Choosing OOB deployment options

Figure 10-8   Executing an OOB application

Deploying Silverlight Applications

You can deploy a Silverlight application to a Web site, as you would an ASP.NET MVC application. However, you'll need to ensure the MIME type and policy is in place to ensure the application will run outside of your development environment.

If you're running IIS 7, Silverlight will already be set up. However, if you're deploying to an IIS 6 server, you must set the MIME type for *.xap files to application/x-silverlight-app as described in the following steps:

1. Open Administrative Tools | Internet Information Services (IIS) Manager.

2. Under Web Sites, in IIS, right-click on the Web site for your Silverlight application and select Properties.

3. Click the HTTP Headers tab, click MIME Types, and click New.

4. Type **.xap** as the Extension and **application/x-silverlight-app** as the MIME type.

Click OK three times to close all windows and close IIS.

Additionally, you must have a policy file in the root folder of your Web site. There are two types of policy files you can use: crossdomain.xml or clientaccesspolicy.xml.

The crossdomain.xml policy was created for Adobe Flash applications and can be used with Silverlight applications too. Here's an example:

```
<!DOCTYPE cross-domain-policy
  SYSTEM "http://www.macromedia.com/xml/dtds/cross-domain-policy.dtd">
<cross-domain-policy>
  <allow-access-from domain="*" />
  <allow-http-request-headers-from domain="*" headers="*" />
</cross-domain-policy>
```

When designing Silverlight, Microsoft recognized that the crossdomain.xml file wasn't flexible enough and added support for another type of policy called clientaccesspolicy.xml. Here's an example:

```
<?xml version="1.0" encoding="utf-8"?>
<access-policy>
  <cross-domain-access>
    <policy>
      <allow-from http-methods="*">"
        <domain uri="*"/>
      </allow-from>
      <grant-to>
        <resource path="/" include-subpaths="true"/>
      </grant-to>
    </policy>
  </cross-domain-access>
</access-policy>
```

This clientaccesspolicy.xml listing allows all domains to access all site content that isn't already secured by other means. You can restrict access by replacing the * in the *domain uri* with an allowable domain. Further, you can replace the resource path with a path on the site to restrict access to specific folders. Add more policy elements to this file to add more domains and paths.

Summary

This chapter explains how to run a Silverlight application. You learned how to use the MediaElement control and how to build UIs using the same techniques as in WPF. The OOB functionality allows you to run Silverlight from your desktop. A section describes deploying the Silverlight application to a Web server.

We've discussed a couple Web technologies already: ASP.NET MVC in Chapter 9 and Silverlight in this chapter. The next chapter shows you another Web technology: WCF Web services.

Chapter 11

Deploying Web Services with WCF

Key Skills & Concepts

- Create a Web Service

- Deploy a Web Service

- Write a Client That Consumes the Web Service

indows Communication Foundation (WCF) is a .NET technology for creating Web services. A *Web service* is software that provides functionality that can be used by any other software application, using any programming language, on any hardware and operating system that can communicate over a network.

The functionality of Web services can be either public or private. Examples of public Web services might be a weather service where you provide the location and you get back a forecast data that you can display on your screen or an address verification application that will validate if a postal address exists or suggest alternatives. Examples of private Web services might be the ability for multiple applications in a large corporation to call a customer Web service with a customer ID and receive that customer's record, or perhaps an ordering system where you can submit a new customer order and the Web service would process the submission in the background for you.

What's common about all of the examples in the preceding paragraph is that, regardless of public or private, the Web service is useful for more than one application or system. Everyone needs the same service from the Web service, so why should each application re-invent the wheel every time? Just set up one service and everyone can work with that one service.

You must be wondering how such a broad claim can be made that one technology is accessible by any system regardless of platform, language, or software. The Web service is separated from the calling system via open standards and a well-defined interface. There are ubiquitous communications protocols, such as HTTP, and data format standards, such as XML, that Web services can use. So, if both systems that communicate use Hypertext Transfer Protocol (HTTP) and XML in the same way, then the Web service can be useful. For example, if an application were built on a Sun workstation running Solaris, saving data in an Oracle database, and written in Java, it could still communicate with your WCF service, which is on an Intel-based server, running Windows 2008, saving data in SQL Server, and written in VB. It doesn't matter because the Java system will translate its call into XML and send the XML data via HTTP to the WCF service. The WCF service understands the XML because it was the WCF service that told the Java application what format to put the XML into. If you're curious about the format, it's called Web Service Description Language (WSDL), which is a contract (or interface) that tells callers how to package the XML and what operations (such as GetWeather) can be called on the Web service. There's more that the WSDL does behind the scenes, but the primary point to make is that clients, such as the Java app, use the WSDL to package their XML and send it to the WCF service. The service translates the XML into a call to a method, runs the method, packages the results back into XML (as defined by the WSDL), and sends the results back to the Java application. Essentially, a WCF service uses open standards so that any other system can use those same open standards to communicate.

This chapter will show you how VS helps you create WCF services, how to create a client that communicates with a WCF service, and how to deploy WCF services. The deployment information in this chapter is also useful to know for other types of Web applications, such as ASP.NET MVC and Silverlight. Let's start off with creating a WCF project.

Starting a WCF Project

To create a new WCF project, press CTRL-SHIFT-N to start a new project, and then select WCF Service Library, name the project **WcfDemo**, and set the location to anywhere you want the project to reside in the file system. This will produce a project similar to Figure 11-1.

Figure 11-1   A WCF Service Library project

The WCF Service Library starts with two files with default names of IService1.cs (IService1.vb for VB) and Service1.cs (Service1.vb for VB), which contain an interface and a class that implements that interface. If you need to brush up on interfaces, review Chapter 4 because an interface is an integral part of WCF development.

Specifying a Contract with WCF Interfaces

The *IService1.cs* (IService1.vb in VB) class in Figure 11-1 contains an interface. As you learned in Chapter 4, interfaces define a set of members that do not have implementations. The actual implementation will be provided by classes that implement the interface. You can consider the interface to be a contract that guarantees a set of operations for a service. In addition to the interface, the types associated with the service are part of the service contract. The contract is important because when you write code that uses the Web service, it is the contract that your code will see and everything that is not in the contract will not be visible. Any application wishing to use a Web service will make calls to the Web service based on what is specified in the contract. In this section, you'll see how to define a WCF contract with an interface, built-in types, and custom types. Later sections will show how to implement and consume the contract, bringing the importance of the contract full circle so that you can see how the contract is defined, implemented, and consumed.

Examining the VS-Generated Contract

You really don't want to work with an interface named *IService1*; it doesn't mean anything. So, rename *IService1.cs* to **ICustomerService.cs** (**IService1.vb** to ICustomerService.vb for VB), because it will be configured to manage customer records. You'll receive a message box for renaming the code, and you should respond affirmatively. When you open the ICustomerService.cs file, you'll see the same code as Listing 11-1, containing an interface and attributes for defining the ICustomerService contract.

Listing 11-1   A WCF service interface

```
using System;
using System.Collections.Generic;
using System.Linq;
using System.Runtime.Serialization;
using System.ServiceModel;
using System.Text;

namespace WcfDemoCS
```

```
{
    // NOTE: You can use the "Rename" command on the
    // "Refactor" menu to change the interface name
    // "IService1" in both code and config file together.
    [ServiceContract]
    public interface ICustomerService
    {
        [OperationContract]
        string GetData(int value);

        [OperationContract]
        CompositeType GetDataUsingDataContract
            (CompositeType composite);

        // TODO: Add your service operations here
    }

    // Use a data contract as illustrated in the sample
    // below to add composite types to service operations
    [DataContract]
    public class CompositeType
    {
        bool boolValue = true;
        string stringValue = "Hello ";

        [DataMember]
        public bool BoolValue
        {
            get { return boolValue; }
            set { boolValue = value; }
        }

        [DataMember]
        public string StringValue
        {
            get { return stringValue; }
            set { stringValue = value; }
        }
    }
}
```

   VB:

```
' NOTE: You can use the "Rename" command on the
' context menu to change the interface name "IService1"
' in both code and config file together.
<ServiceContract()>
```

```
Public Interface ICustomerService

    <OperationContract()>
    Function GetData(ByVal value As Integer) As String

    <OperationContract()>
    Function GetDataUsingDataContract(
        ByVal composite As CompositeType) As CompositeType

    ' TODO: Add your service operations here

End Interface

' Use a data contract as illustrated in the sample below
' to add composite types to service operations

<DataContract()>
Public Class CompositeType

    <DataMember()>
    Public Property BoolValue() As Boolean

    <DataMember()>
    Public Property StringValue() As String

End Class
```

There are two types in Listing 11-1: ICustomerService and CompositeType. Both of these types were generated by VS to provide an example of how you can define a service contract. After explaining the default code, we'll modify the code to make it usable for working with Customer objects.

Starting with the *ICustomerService* interface, the two most important parts of the code are the *ServiceContract* and *OperationContract* attributes. The *ServiceContract* attribute states that this interface defines a contract for a WCF Web service. Without the *ServiceContract* attribute, this interface won't be recognized by WCF. The *OperationContract* attribute specifies methods that are exposed by the WCF service. Without the *OperationContract* attribute, a method will not be visible as part of the WCF service.

A WCF service method can work with any of the built-in types for parameters or return types, demonstrated by the *GetData* method that takes an *int* parameter and returns a string. When working with custom types, you need additional syntax to specify what parts of the type are part of the contract. The types are parameters and return types of the service methods, and are part of the contract in addition to the interface.

The *GetDataUsingDataContract* method illustrates a method that uses a custom type, *CompositeType,* as a parameter and return type. Being a custom type, *CompositeType* has attributes that help define its contract: *DataContract* and *DataMember.* The *DataContract* attribute identifies *CompositeType* as a type that can be included in a WCF service contact. Without the *DataContract* attribute, a type can't be included as part of the service contract. The *DataMember* attribute decorates type members that are part of the contract for this service. Without the *DataMember* attribute, a type member will not be visible as part of the contract.

Creating Your Own Contract

We won't explicitly construct our data types for DataContracts, as shown in the CompositeType in Listing 11-1. Instead, we'll use a built-in capability of LINQ to SQL that gives LINQ to SQL entities a DataContract. To use LINQ to SQL entities, create a new LINQ to SQL item in the same project the WCF service resides in and add the Customer table to the designer. Then click the design surface, not the Customer entity, and view properties. Set Serialization Mode to Unidirectional, as shown in Figure 11-2.

Now, instead of creating a custom type and copying LINQ to SQL entity data into the custom type and returning the custom type, it will be possible to perform a LINQ to SQL query and return the LINQ to SQL entity.

Figure 11-2   Setting the LINQ to SQL Serialization Mode property

We started customizing the contract when changing the name of IService1 to ICustomerService, but we need to continue by defining the methods that will become part of the CustomerService contract: *GetCustomers, GetCustomer, InsertCustomer, UpdateCustomer,* and *DeleteCustomer.* In practice, there will be more methods you'll want, just to customize the contract for the special needs of your application, but these methods depict typical scenarios you'll frequently encounter and are representative of any work you'll perform. Listing 11-2 shows the modifications to ICustomerService to support customer operations. After making the changes in Listing 2, your application won't compile until you implement the *ICustomerService* interface in the next section. Please make the changes, if you're following along, and keep reading until the next section.

Listing 11-2   WCF service contract implementation

C#:

```
[ServiceContract]
public interface ICustomerService
{
    [OperationContract]
    Customer GetCustomer(int custID);

    [OperationContract]
    List<Customer> GetCustomers();

    [OperationContract]
    int InsertCustomer(Customer cust);

    [OperationContract]
    void UpdateCustomer(Customer cust);

    [OperationContract]
    void DeleteCustomer(int custID);
}
```

VB:

```
<ServiceContract()>
Public Interface ICustomerService

    <OperationContract()>
    Function GetCustomer(ByVal custID As Integer) As Customer

    <OperationContract()>
    Function GetCustomers() As List(Of Customer)
```

```
<OperationContract()>
Function InsertCustomer(ByVal cust As Customer) As Integer

<OperationContract()>
Sub UpdateCustomer(ByVal cust As Customer)

End Interface
```

You already know how to specify an interface, and the preceding section explained the purpose of *ServiceContract* and *OperationContract* attributes. Listing 11-2 shows that all you need to do is specify the methods that you want to be included as part of the contract.

There are times when you'll need to return a custom type from a WCF service. For example, if you need to fill in a drop-down list, all you need is a key for the value and a name for the text. So, you can create a custom *CustomerLookup* class, as shown in Listing 11-3, that specifies *DataContract* and *DataMember* attributes. Listing 11-3 demonstrates how a custom type could be coded if you ever needed to do this.

Listing 11-3   A custom type for a WCF service contract

C#:

```csharp
[DataContract]
public class CustomerLookup
{
    [DataMember]
    public int CustomerID { get; set; }

    [DataMember]
    public string CustomerName { get; set; }
}
```

VB:

```vb
<DataContract()>
Public Class CustomerLookup

    <DataMember()>
    Public Property CustomerID() As Integer

    <DataMember()>
    Public Property CustomerName() As String

End Class
```

Using a custom type for the purpose of lookup controls at the UI level, such as the CustomerLookup class in Listing 11-3, opens the potential to only communicate information that is necessary, rather than an entire object where all of the data isn't being used. Considering the potential slowness of network communication, limiting the amount of information transmitted between the Web service and your application can increase the performance of your application.

Now that you have a contract in place, the next step is writing a class that implements that contract.

Implementing Logic with WCF Classes

The contract created in the preceding section was important because it specifies what must be implemented. As you know, interfaces only specify members, which are the contract, but you must write a class that contains code that implements the interface. This section will implement the *ICustomerService* interface with a class named *CustomerService*.

The first thing you should do is rename the Service1.cs (Service1.vb in VB) file to **CustomerService.cs (CustomerService.vb** in VB) and click Yes when VS asks if you want to change the code. Listing 11-4 shows what VS generates as a WCF service class, with the rename applied to the class.

Listing 11-4   Default WCF service implementation class

C#:

```csharp
using System;
using System.Collections.Generic;
using System.Linq;
using System.Runtime.Serialization;
using System.ServiceModel;
using System.Text;

namespace WcfDemoCS
{
    // NOTE: You can use the "Rename" command on the
    // "Refactor" menu to change the class name "Service1"
    // in both code and config file together.
    public class CustomerService : ICustomerService
    {
        public string GetData(int value)
        {
            return string.Format("You entered: {0}", value);
        }
```

```csharp
        public CompositeType GetDataUsingDataContract(
            CompositeType composite)
        {
            if (composite == null)
            {
                throw new ArgumentNullException("composite");
            }
            if (composite.BoolValue)
            {
                composite.StringValue += "Suffix";
            }
            return composite;
        }
    }
}
```

   VB:

```vbnet
' NOTE: You can use the "Rename" command on the
' context menu to change the class name "Service1"
' in both code and config file together.
Public Class Service1
    Implements ICustomerService

    Public Function GetData(
        ByVal value As Integer) As String
        Implements ICustomerService.GetData
        Return String.Format("You entered: {0}", value)
    End Function

    Public Function GetDataUsingDataContract(
        ByVal composite As CompositeType) As CompositeType
        Implements ICustomerService.GetDataUsingDataContract
        If composite Is Nothing Then
            Throw New ArgumentNullException("composite")
        End If
        If composite.BoolValue Then
            composite.StringValue &= "Suffix"
        End If
        Return composite
    End Function

End Class
```

The methods of the *CustomerService* class in Listing 11-4 show skeleton implementations of the *ICustomerService* interface. As you know, Listing 11-2 provided new methods to the *ICustomerService* interface, so the code in Listing 11-4 will not compile because it doesn't implement the *ICustomerService* methods. To fix this problem, delete the *GetData* and *GetDataUsingDataContract* methods from the *CustomerService* class. Then select the ICustomerService identifier in the CustomerService.cs file, which will display an underline on the left of the ICustomerService identifier. Hover over that underline to open a menu with an option to implement the *ICustomerService* interface, which will generate skeleton code for each member of the *ICustomerService* interface inside of the *CustomerService* class. The default method implementations throw a *NotImplementedException* exception, meaning that you need to write the code to implement those methods based on the *ICustomerService* interface. Listing 11-5 shows the implementation of the *ICustomerService* interface in the *CustomerService* class. If using C#, add the code to each method. If using VB, which doesn't have the same interface refactoring support as C#, add all methods and code to the *CustomerService* class as specified in Listing 11-5.

Listing 11-5   A WCF service implementation

C#:

```csharp
using System;
using System.Collections.Generic;
using System.Linq;
using System.Runtime.Serialization;
using System.ServiceModel;
using System.Text;

namespace WcfDemoCS
{
    public class CustomerService : ICustomerService
    {
        public Customer GetCustomer(int custID)
        {
            var ctx = new MyShopDataContext();

            var customer =
                (from cust in ctx.Customers
                 where cust.CustomerID == custID
                 select cust)
                 .SingleOrDefault();
```

```
        return customer;
}

public List<Customer> GetCustomers()
{
    var ctx = new MyShopDataContext();

    return
        (from cust in ctx.Customers
         select cust)
         .ToList();
}

public int InsertCustomer(Customer cust)
{
    var ctx = new MyShopDataContext();

    ctx.Customers.InsertOnSubmit(cust);

    ctx.SubmitChanges();

    return cust.CustomerID;
}

public void UpdateCustomer(Customer cust)
{
    var ctx = new MyShopDataContext();

    var customer =
        (from cst in ctx.Customers
         where cst.CustomerID == cust.CustomerID
         select cst)
         .SingleOrDefault();

    if (customer != null)
    {
        customer.Age = cust.Age;
        customer.Birthday = cust.Birthday;
        customer.Income = cust.Income;
        customer.Name = cust.Name;

        ctx.SubmitChanges();
    }
}
```

```csharp
        public void DeleteCustomer(int custID)
        {
            var ctx = new MyShopDataContext();

            var customer =
                (from cst in ctx.Customers
                 where cst.CustomerID == custID
                 select cst)
                 .SingleOrDefault();

            if (customer != null)
            {
                ctx.Customers.DeleteOnSubmit(customer);

                ctx.SubmitChanges();
            }
        }
    }
}
```

VB:

```vbnet
' NOTE: You can use the "Rename" command on the context
' menu to change the class name "Service1" in both code
' and config file together.
Public Class CustomerService
    Implements ICustomerService

    Public Function GetCustomer(ByVal custID As Integer) As Customer
        Implements ICustomerService.GetCustomer

        Dim ctx As New MyShopDataContext

        Dim customer =
            (From cust In ctx.Customers
             Where cust.CustomerID = custID
             Select cust).SingleOrDefault()

        Return customer

    End Function

    Public Function GetCustomers() As List(Of Customer) Implements
ICustomerService.GetCustomers

        Dim ctx As New MyShopDataContext
```

```vb
        Return (From cust In ctx.Customers
                Select cust).ToList()

    End Function

    Public Function InsertCustomer(ByVal cust As Customer) As Integer
        Implements ICustomerService.InsertCustomer
        Dim ctx = New MyShopDataContext

        ctx.Customers.InsertOnSubmit(cust)

        ctx.SubmitChanges()

        Return cust.CustomerID

    End Function

    Public Sub UpdateCustomer(ByVal cust As Customer)
        Implements ICustomerService.UpdateCustomer
        Dim ctx As New MyShopDataContext

        Dim customer = (From cst In ctx.Customers
                        Where cst.CustomerID = cust.CustomerID
                        Select cst).SingleOrDefault()


        If Not (customer Is Nothing) Then

            With customer
                .Age = cust.Age
                .Birthday = cust.Birthday
                .Income = cust.Income
                .Name = cust.Name
            End With

            ctx.SubmitChanges()

        End If

    End Sub

    Public Sub DeleteCustomer(ByVal custID As Integer)

        Dim ctx As New MyShopDataContext

        Dim customer = (From cst In ctx.Customers
```

```
                        Where cst.CustomerID = custID
                        Select cst).SingleOrDefault()

        If Not (customer Is Nothing) Then

            ctx.Customers.DeleteOnSubmit(customer)

            ctx.SubmitChanges()

        End If

    End Sub

End Class
```

The implementation of CustomerService is similar to what you've seen in previous chapters. The difference is that the implementation is in a Web service, which must be consumed differently. We'll soon get to the section of this chapter that shows how to consume a Web service, but you must understand that a Web service is a component that you communicate with over a network. In previous chapters, you've seen code that works with data integrated with application code. However, Web services must be hosted by a server, such as Internet Information Services (IIS), and consuming code must connect and communicate through calls to IIS. The next section points you in the right direction about hosting a Web service in IIS.

Hosting a WCF Service

The VS development environment will automatically host your service, but eventually you'll need to deploy your service to Internet Information Services (IIS), which is the Web server that hosts .NET applications. The instructions included in this section are general guidance on how the deployment process works. It is very likely that subsequent operating system patches and service packs could change the results for you. It is also possible that the particular operating system and IIS configuration on your computer is different. Additionally, the behavior of software on other operating systems, such as Windows Server 2003 and Windows Server 2008, can differ in subtle, but significant, ways. As such problems are unrelated to VS itself, you should consult your operating system documentation on how to properly configure IIS and operating system security. Although operating system behavior is not a function of VS, the guidance below is intended to point you in the right direction.

Following General Hosting Procedures

For better security, IIS doesn't install with the default installation of the Windows OS. There are different versions of Windows for desktop and server, so I'll provide a general description of what you need to do for installing IIS. The first step is to find the Control Panel in the Windows Operating System (OS). Older Windows versions have a link for Add And Remove Programs, but newer versions call the link Programs And Features, which you need to open. Server OS versions have a control panel you can use to install IIS. Next, search for a link for adding and removing Windows Components (or Windows Features) and click that link. Find IIS and install it and remember to turn on File Transfer Protocol (FTP) support if you want to deploy using FTP. FTP is an Internet protocol that allows you to work with files; it is useful in deployment because it allows moving files from one server to another. You'll need to enable ASP.NET on newer versions of Windows, which I'll explain how to do in a later section.

Once IIS is installed, you can host your application. On desktop versions of Windows, IIS 6 only supports a single Web site, but you can add multiple Web sites to any server OS or IIS 7 and later. To create the Web site, you'll need to either create a virtual directory (in the case of desktop versions of IIS 6) or a Web application. You can do this by opening IIS, which you can find via the Administrative Tools menu; you can often find the Administrative Tools menu from the Control Panel. Find Web Sites, right-click, and select Create New Web Application. If you're using IIS 6 on a desktop, you'll need to go down an additional level, right-click Default Web Site, and select Create Virtual Directory. Don't change any of the default values while stepping through the wizard, but you will need to specify a name for the virtual directory or site name and the physical path. The virtual directory/site name is the location that a user would add to the address bar. The physical path is the location in your file system that you want the application to reside in. This location defaults to c:\inetpub, assuming that your OS is deployed to the c: drive.

Installing IIS 7 on Windows 7

The following is a walk-through for setting up IIS 7 on Windows 7.

1. Select Start | Control Panel | Programs And Features, which will display the Uninstall Or Change A Program window, shown in Figure 11-3.

2. Click the "Turn Windows features on or off" link, which will display the Windows Features window, shown in Figure 11-4.

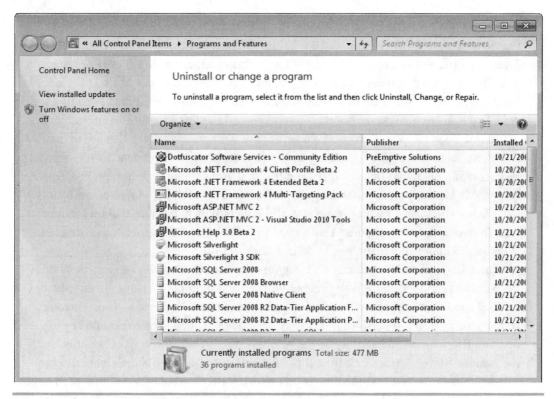

Figure 11-3 The Uninstall Or Change A Program window

Figure 11-4 The Windows Features window

Order of Installations Matter

ASP.NET and WCF Web Services are hosted in IIS and require special configuration to allow hosting by IIS. Therefore, it's helpful if IIS is installed before VS is installed. VS will install all of the ASP.NET and WCF Service settings if IIS is installed. If you install IIS after VS is installed, you can still set up ASP.NET and WCF Service settings with the following commands; first ASP.NET:

"%windir%\Microsoft.NET\Framework\v4.0.21006\aspnet_regiis.exe" –i –enable

and then WCF Services (all on one line):

"%WINDIR%\Microsoft.Net\Framework\v3.0\Windows Communication Foundation\ServiceModelReg.exe" –r

The actual directory name for the aspnet_regiis.exe file might be different because the v4.x.x.x will change in the future, so you might need to open Windows Explorer and search for the actual directory name yourself.

3. This example enables FTP, which is one of the ways you can deploy a Web site. Ensure the option for "Ensure IIS Metabase and IIS 6 configuration compatibility," under the IIS 6 Management Compatibility branch, is selected. When you click OK, the IIS server will be installed.

Creating a Web Site on IIS 7 on Windows 7

Next, you'll need to create a Web site on IIS 7 on Windows 7 by following these steps:

1. Select Start | Control Panel | Administrative Tools, which will display the Administrative Tools window, shown in Figure 11-5.

2. Double-click Internet Information Services (IIS) Manager to display the Internet Information Services (IIS) Manager window, shown in Figure 11-6.

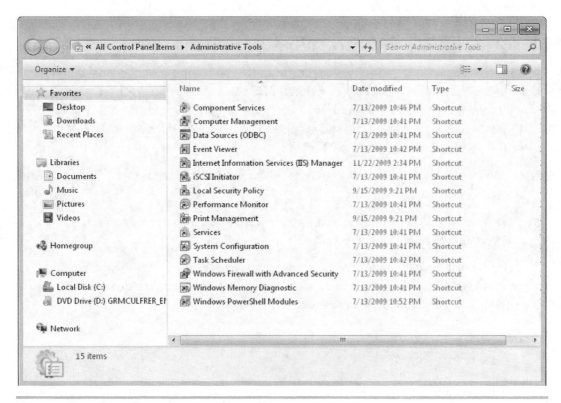

Figure 11-5 The Administrative Tools window

3. Right-click Sites and select Add Web Site, or click the Add Web Site link on the Actions panel to show the Add Web Site window, shown in Figure 11-7.

4. Give the Web site a name and specify the physical location. As shown in Figure 11-7, the name of the site is WcfDemo and the site will be physically located at c:\WebSites\ WcfDemo. Notice that the Port in the Binding section is set to 8080. The default for a Web site port is 80, but you can have only a single site with that port. Alternatively, you could change the host name and keep port 80. In this case, we decided to set the port to 8080 so that the addresses of the Web sites don't overlap. Use a different port number if 8080 is already used on your system. Clicking OK will create the Web site.

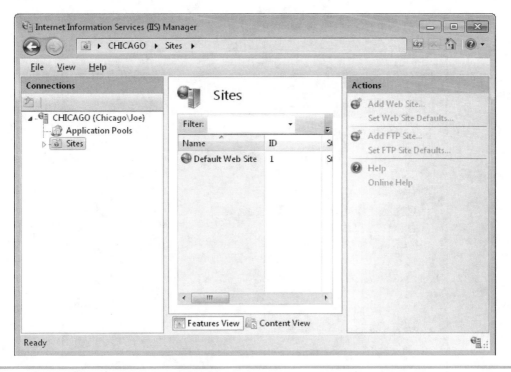

Figure 11-6   The IIS Manager window

5. Ensure that the WcfDemo Web site is selected in IIS Manager and click the Add FTP Publishing link on the Actions pane, which is on the right side of IIS Manager. You'll see the Binding And SSL Settings window, shown in Figure 11-8.

6. Accept the defaults on the Binding And SSL Settings window and click Next to show the Authentication And Authorization window, shown in Figure 11-9.

7. Set options on the Authentication And Authorization window according to who you want to be able to access this Web site. Anonymous allows anyone to access the site and is less secure. A more secure option would be to restrict access to specified users or groups that you trust. Basic authorization shows a login screen when someone connects to the FTP site. Clicking Finish will enable this site for FTP access.

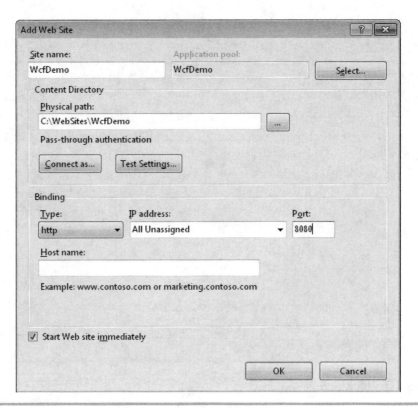

Figure 11-7 The Add Web Site window

8. In IIS Manager, select Application Pools. An application pool is a process that you can assign Web sites to. This gives Web sites protection from each other because if one process crashes, it doesn't bring down Web sites in other processes. IIS created an application pool for your Web site with the same name when creating it previously. Double-click the application pool named after your Web site and set its .NET Framework version to v4. The exact version number could vary in the future, so you want to ensure it's the same .NET Framework version number that you build your application with in VS.

Once your Web site is set up, you can deploy, which is discussed next.

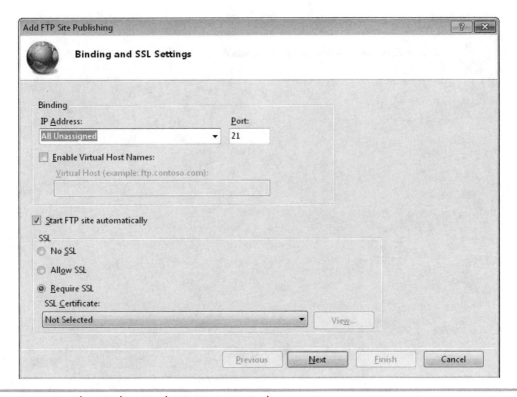

Figure 11-8   The Binding And SSL Settings window

Deploying the WCF Service to IIS

If you want to run the WCF service in VS, you don't have to do anything because VS already set the project up to run with a built-in server. The discussion in this section is intended to help you deploy to IIS on a Windows 2008 server. If you just want to run the Web service in VS, you can skip this section for now and move to the next section on how to build a client that communicates with the Web service. Then return to this section when you're actually ready to deploy to IIS.

To deploy a Web service project, you'll need to obtain the address of the Web site, modify the project configuration file, and use the VS Publish tool.

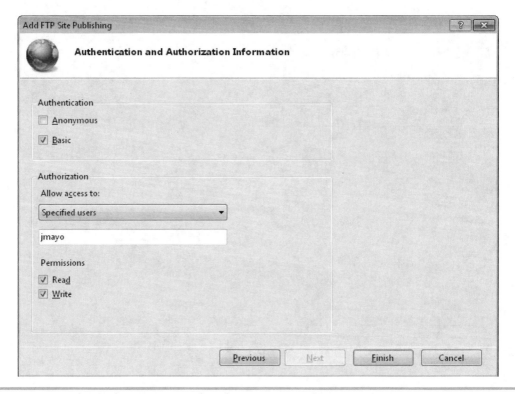

Figure 11-9 The Authentication And Authorization window

TIP

You must run VS as Administrator to publish. To do this, close VS (if running), locate the VS Start menu item (don't click yet), right-click, and select Run As Administrator.

The technique used in the preceding section to create a Web site distinguished the Web site by making it run on port 8080. Although the Web site is named WcfDemo, it's located on the local machine, whose domain is localhost. If you deployed the Web service to a site that already had a domain, you would use that domain name. For example, the domain for the C# Station community site is csharp-station.com, which is addressed as http://www. csharp-station.com. Each Web service at a location is addressed by a *.svc file name and the name that VS creates is called WcfDemoCS.CustomerService.svc. Putting the pieces of WcfDemo site together results in an address of http://localhost:8080/WcfDemoCS. CustomerService.svc.

When you create a new WCF Service project, VS adds a file named app.config to the project, which is a file that belongs only to VS. The app.config file is never deployed with your Web service, but it generates a file named web.config, which is deployed with the project. In WPF projects, VS uses the app.config file to generate a file named projectname.exe.config in the same folder as the projectname.exe file. WCF Service projects don't generate a config file in the output folder, but they do generate a web.config file when you deploy. You'll see web.config soon, after deployment.

During development, you work with the app.config file, which is easy to find and open in your project. The app.config file has a lot of information in it, so Listing 11-6 is a small excerpt that shows you the salient elements of the WCF configuration.

Listing 11-6   The WCF service address in app.config

```xml
<?xml version="1.0" encoding="utf-8" ?>
<configuration>
...
  <system.serviceModel>
    <bindings>
        ...
    </bindings>
    <client />
    <services>
      <service name="WcfDemoCS.CustomerService">
        ...
        <endpoint address="mex" binding="mexHttpBinding"
contract="IMetadataExchange" />
        <host>
          <baseAddresses>
            <add baseAddress=
"http://localhost:8732/Design_Time_Addresses
/WcfDemoCS/CustomerService/" />
          </baseAddresses>
        </host>
      </service>
    </services>
...
  </system.serviceModel>
...
</configuration>
```

Following the path in Listing 11-6—*configuration, system.serviceModel, services, service, host,* and *baseAddresses*—you'll find a *baseAddress* element in bold. The *baseAddress* in Listing 11-6 is split into two lines to fit the book, but remember to combine it into a single line. The *baseAddress* is declaring that applications can communicate with this service via this address. This is a VS development Web server address that was generated for this WCF service. Previously, you saw how we figured out what the deployment address of this application should be. Therefore, when you deploy, comment out the development address and replace it with the deployment address, like this:

```
<baseAddresses>
  <!--<add baseAddress=
"http://localhost:8732/Design_Time_Addresses/WcfDemoCS/Service1/" />-->
  <add baseAddress=" http://localhost:8080/WcfDemoCS.CustomerService
.svc " />
</baseAddresses>
```

The <!-- and --> are comment delimiters, and anything in between them won't be interpreted as part of the configuration. Notice how the deployment address is used (uncommented) as the base address. After deployment, you can comment the deployment address and uncomment the development address so that you can continue working with the WCF service with the VS Web server.

In addition to the *baseAddress,* you need to ensure your database connection is updated for the deployment environment. In the development environment, the default DB connection string defaults to using Integrated Security = true as login credentials, which uses the identity of the currently logged-in user. The result in the deployment environment is that the application will run as the identity of the application pool the Web site is assigned to. The problem with this is that the application pool doesn't have access to your database. The best approach is to create a user for your application only, give that user access to your database, and then set the connection string to use the credentials of that user.

Create a user in your Windows OS that will be used for SQL Server and then give that user access to the database. If you're using an Express version of SQL Server, it can help if you download the free SQL Server Express Management Studio. Because of all the variables that can affect setting up security, refer to SQL Server documentation for more guidance. This chapter uses SQL authentication, so go ahead and create a Windows or SQL user for the MyShop database.

With the user account set up for the database, update the app.config file of the service to use the credentials of that user account, like this. For best security, please remember to change the password:

```
<add name=
"WcfDemoCS.Properties.Settings.MyShopConnectionString"
  connectionString=
"Data Source=.\sqlexpress;Initial Catalog=MyShop;
User ID=MyUserAccount;Password=G7b@H8m2a%lM6y;Pooling=False"
  providerName="System.Data.SqlClient" />
```

To deploy, right-click the Web Services project, WcfDemo, and click Publish, which will display the Publish WCF Service window shown in Figure 11-10.

In the Publish WCF Service window, set the Target Location to the address where the WCF Service is deployed. You saw how to figure out the address earlier in this section. You can choose to either replace only matching files or delete all files in the deployment location. You normally only want to copy files needed to run this application because the deployment will be quicker with fewer files and possibly more secure by only deploying what is necessary. The check box for Include Files From The App_Data Folder is disabled because there isn't an App_Data folder in the WCF Service project. However, this same tool is used to deploy an ASP.NET Web site, which might have an App_Data folder.

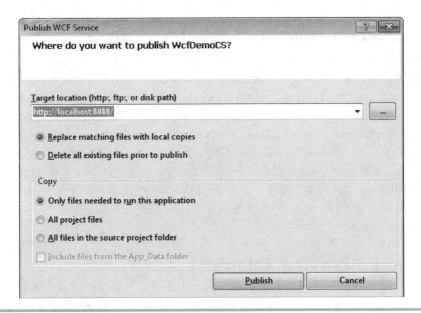

Figure 11-10 The Publish WCF Service window

Normally, you don't want to deploy the App_Data folder because it might hold a database file that is huge and would slow down your application considerably. Of course, if you have SQL Server Express installed at the deployment location and need the database in App_Data to be deployed, check this box to include the database in the deployment. Click Publish to deploy your service.

When deployment is complete, you'll see a message on the VS status bar stating either Publish Succeeded or Publish Failed. If publishing fails, open the Output window, CTRL-W, O, to see the reason why. There are many reasons a deployment can fail, so look at the error message to see if it's something that makes sense to you. Verify that your Web site is properly set up, as explained in the preceding section. Other sources of information include the Microsoft Developer Network (MSDN), at http://msdn.microsoft.com, where you can search for Knowledge Base support articles. Alternatively, you can copy the error message and paste it into your favorite search engine. Many problems with deployment surround IIS setup, so it is worthwhile to learn more about how IIS works. McGraw-Hill offers *Windows Server 2008: A Beginner's Guide,* by Marty Matthews (2008), which does include IIS 7 information. There's also a Windows Server 2003 edition if you are deploying to IIS 6.

Now that you know how to develop and deploy a WCF service, you'll need to know how to write programs that use that service, which is covered next.

Communicating with a WCF Service

Any .NET application can communicate with a Web service. In fact, one of the benefits of having a Web service is to expose functionality that can be used by multiple applications. In theory, any application on any platform can communicate via Web services because the underlying technology relies on open standards, such as HTTP and XML. In practice, the goal of cross-platform communication is an advanced technique accomplished by architects and engineers with detailed knowledge of the inner workings of Web services. For just getting started, it's sufficient to know that you can communicate with Web services with any .NET technology. The following sections show you how to make your applications, clients, communicate with Web services. Let's look at the task of generally creating a reference to a Web service first.

Creating a Service Reference

Regardless of what type of application you're building, you create a reference to a Web service, called a service reference, in the same way. You start off with a project, any project type—Console, WPF, ASP.NET, or Silverlight will do. Right-click the project

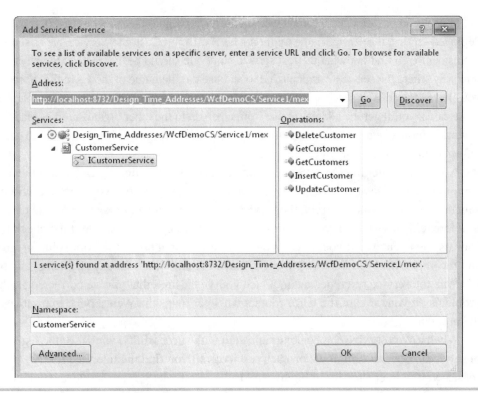

Figure 11-11   The Add Service Reference window

and select Add Service Reference. You'll see the Add Service Reference window, shown in Figure 11-11.

As you may recall from previous discussion in this chapter, we spent some time on setting up a Web service and configuring the Web service address. Now the address comes into focus because it is where the Web service is deployed—you type it into the Address box in the Add Service Reference window, shown in Figure 11-11. If you are using the Web server built into VS to use a Web service project in the same solution, it is convenient to click the Discover button, which will give you a list of Web services in the same solution as the project you are adding the service reference to. The address in Figure 11-11 is different from what you'll see on your computer because the project name, port number, and service name will be different.

If you need to use a deployed Web service, you would put the address of the deployed Web service in the Address box. For example, earlier in this chapter you saw how we deployed a Web service to the local IIS server and that to use that deployed Web service you would put http://localhost:8080/WcfDemo.CustomerService.svc into the Address box. In the deployed service, the service name might not be WcfDemo.CustomerService.svc as shown in this demo. To find out what the real service name file should be, navigate to the physical directory where the service was deployed to and use the file name of the *.svc file. Sometimes, you'll need to use Web services by third parties or another organization in your company. In those cases, you'll get the address to use from a person in the other organization or read their documentation to learn what address to use. If you add your own address, click Go to get more information on the Web service.

After either clicking Discover or adding an address and clicking Go, you'll have one or more services in the Services list. At this point, if you receive an error, it will be because the address is incorrect, the service is experiencing an outage, or (in the case of referencing a service in your own project) the service won't compile. First check the address if you entered it yourself. If you are referencing a project in your solution, go back and recompile the Web Service project to make sure it builds, fix any problems, and try to create the service reference again. Once you've ensured that you've corrected all the problems on your side of the wire, contact whoever owns the Web service to troubleshoot the problem.

When a Web service can be communicated with successfully, you'll see the list of services. You can drill down on each service until you find the interface for the service you're interested in. In Figure 11-11, the ICustomerService is selected, which displays all available operations. Looking back at the previous discussion of creating the CustomerService, you can see the interface that was created and the methods. If you don't see an interface or a method, check the attributes in the code to ensure the interface has a *ServiceContract* attribute and that any methods that should be exposed have an *OperationContract* attribute.

The Web service will create a proxy, which is a class that communicates with the Web service, in your project, using the default namespace declared in the Properties for your project. The namespace in the Add Service Reference defaults to Service1, and you'll want to change that to something meaningful, such as CustomerService, as shown in Figure 11-11. This will result in a proxy class created in *MyProjectNamespace.CustomerService*. This is important to know because you will need to create an instance of the proxy and must know the namespace that the proxy resides in. Click OK to create the service reference such as the one shown in Figure 11-12.

As you can see in Figure 11-12, the project has a new folder, named Service References. The CustomerService reference under ServiceReferences is named after the namespace you specified in the Add Service Reference window.

Figure 11-12   A new service reference in a project

Now that you have a service reference, you can use it in any .NET application. The following section shows you how to write code to communicate with the Web service.

Coding Web Service Calls

This section will explain how to write code that communicates with a Web service. You'll see explanations of the individual statements required to call the Web service and then you'll see the entire listing of all of those statements together. The program that calls the Web service is a Console application. You should create a new Console application and add the code in this section inside of the *Main* method. If you felt like skipping ahead before reading the explanation, you can see the entire code listing of the Console application that calls the Web service in Listing 11-7. However, we'll begin at the first statement and follow until you see all of the code that's required to call and interact with the CustomerService Web service created in the preceding sections.

When creating a service reference, as explained in the preceding section, VS will generate a new class, called a proxy. The proxy looks just like your Web service class but doesn't contain any of the same code. Instead, the proxy will translate calls from the client and communicate with the Web service. The proxy, created after adding the service reference in the preceding section, is named CustomerServiceClient. Remember to add a *using* statement (Imports in VB) for the Web service proxy. Since the default namespace of the example code for this chapter is *CustomerConsole*, the namespace of the Web service proxy is *CustomerConsole.CustomerService*. Here's code that instantiates the proxy:

C#:

```
var svc = new CustomerServiceClient();
```

VB:

```
Dim svc = New CustomerServiceClient
```

The proxy is named after the service reference, with Client appended to the name. As with any other class, you instantiate the proxy, resulting in a reference to the proxy, named svc. Using the proxy makes your code feel like everything is in the same project, but really the proxy makes a call over HTTP, sending an XML package to the Web service. The Web service translates the XML into a method call, executes the code for the method call, and translates the results back into XML. Meanwhile, the proxy is waiting on the Web service and will receive the XML response, translate that response into a .NET object, and pass the object back to your calling code. If the method returns void instead of a type, then there isn't any value to return.

With the service reference, you can begin communicating with the Web service. The following example creates a new customer record, calling the *InsertCustomer* method on the Web service proxy:

C#:

```
var newCust = new Customer
{
    Age = 36,
    Birthday = new DateTime(1974, 8, 22),
    Income = 56000m,
    Name = "Venus"
};

var newCustID = svc.InsertCustomer(newCust);
```

VB:

```
Dim newCust = New Customer

With newCust
    .Age = 36
    .Birthday = New DateTime(1974, 8, 22)
    .Income = 56000
```

```
    .Name = "Venus"
End With

Dim newCustID As Integer

newCustID = svc.InsertCustomer(newCust)
```

At this point, you might be wondering where the *Customer* type came from. As you may recall from the previous section of the chapter that discussed custom objects, the Customer type is a proxy type for the Customer that was defined in LINQ to SQL. Since we set the Serialization Mode of the LINQ to SQL entity model to Unidirectional, the Web service was able to pass the definition of the Customer with the Web service interface, resulting in a Customer proxy.

To perform the insert operation, use the service proxy reference, svc, to pass the instance of the Customer proxy. The following example shows how to get a specified customer from the Web service:

C#:

```
Customer cust = svc.GetCustomer(newCustID);
```

VB:

```
Dim cust As New Customer
cust = svc.GetCustomer(newCustID)
```

Here, the service proxy reference is used to call *GetCustomer* with an ID of the requested customer, returning an instance of the Customer proxy. The next example shows how to update a Customer instance:

C#:

```
cust.Income = 49000m;

svc.UpdateCustomer(cust);
```

VB:

```
cust.Income = 49000

svc.UpdateCustomer(cust)
```

The cust reference in this example is the same reference that was created previously. In this example, we are only changing the Income property. Next, we use the service proxy to call the UpdateCustomer method, passing the Customer proxy reference. If you wanted to see the changes that were made, you could call the GetCustomer method again, like this:

C#:

```
Customer updatedCust = svc.GetCustomer(cust.CustomerID);
```

VB:

```
Dim updatedCust As Customer

updatedCust = svc.GetCustomer(cust.CustomerID)
```

Similarly, you can delete a Customer, as follows:

C#:

```
svc.DeleteCustomer(updatedCust.CustomerID);
```

VB:

```
svc.DeleteCustomer(updatedCust.CustomerID)
```

As in the previous example, we use the service proxy reference to call the *DeleteCustomer* method, passing in an ID from the updated customer. The *updatedCust* reference was from the previous call to *GetCustomer.* If you wanted to get all of the Customer records from the Web service, you could call *GetCustomers,* like this:

C#:

```
Customer[] customers = svc.GetCustomers();
```

VB:

```
Dim customers As Customer()

customers = svc.GetCustomers()
```

While this is similar to other method calls in previous examples, you might notice that the return value from *GetCustomers* here is an array of Customer, *Customer[]* (*Customer()* in VB). However, the Web service defined *GetCustomers* as returning a List of Customer, *List<Customer>* (*List(Of Customer)* in VB), as specified in the *ICustomerService* interface in Listing 11-2 and implemented in the *CustomerService* class in Listing 11-5. As you may recall, the proxy is responsible for translating the XML return value from the Web service into an object, or collection of objects in this case. By default, the proxy translates all collections into an array. However, you can change the return collection type by right-clicking the Service Reference in your project and selecting Configure Service Reference, showing the Service Reference Settings window in Figure 11-13.

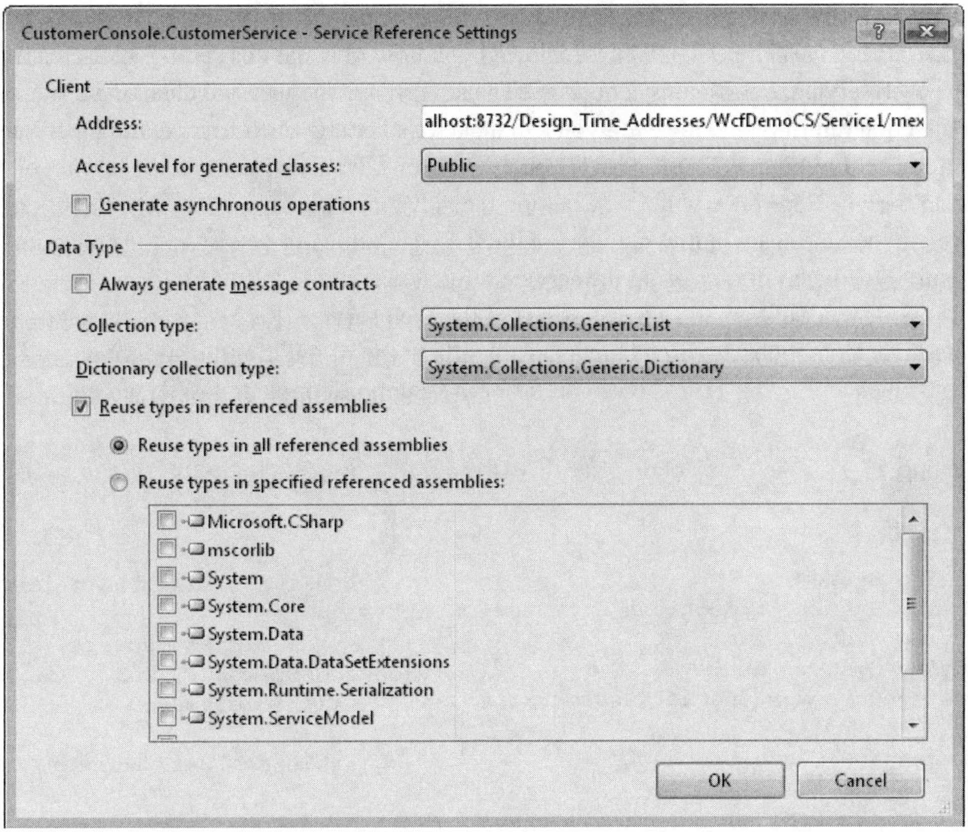

Figure 11-13 The Service Reference Settings window

Most of the items in the Service Reference Settings are advanced options, but focus on the Collection Type setting in the Data Type section. Switch the Collection Type from System.Array to System.Collections.Generic.List and click OK to close. Then change the previous call to *GetCustomers* to the following:

C#:

```
List<Customer> customers = svc.GetCustomers();
```

VB:

```
        Dim cust As New Customer

        cust = svc.GetCustomer(newCustID)
```

This example shows that the proxy will translate the results into a *List<Customer>* (*List(Of Customer)* in VB). While I showed you how to make this setting after creating the Web service, I chose this sequence because it shows the value of changing the collection return type. However, you can make this setting when first creating the Web reference. Looking at Figure 11-11, you can see an Advanced button at the bottom of the Add Service Reference window. Clicking the Advanced button will show you the Service Reference Settings window, shown in Figure 11-13, allowing you to set the collection return type when first creating the service reference.

Now, you've seen all five operations of the Web service. Remember that exactly the same techniques are used here as in any other type of .NET application. For your convenience, Listing 11-7 shows you the entire example for using a Web service.

Listing 11-7   An application using a Web service

C#:

```csharp
using System;
using System.Collections.Generic;
using System.Linq;
using System.Text;
using CustomerConsole.CustomerService;

namespace CustomerConsole
{
    class Program
    {
        static void Main()
        {
            var svc = new CustomerServiceClient();

            var newCust = new Customer
            {
                Age = 36,
                Birthday = new DateTime(1974, 8, 22),
                Income = 56000m,
                Name = "Venus"
            };

            var newCustID = svc.InsertCustomer(newCust);

            Console.WriteLine("New Customer ID: " + newCustID);

            Customer cust = svc.GetCustomer(newCustID);
```

```csharp
        Console.WriteLine("New Customer: " + cust.Name);

        cust.Income = 49000m;

        svc.UpdateCustomer(cust);

        Customer updatedCust = svc.GetCustomer(cust.CustomerID);

        Console.WriteLine("Economic Adjustment: " + cust.Income);

        svc.DeleteCustomer(updatedCust.CustomerID);

        //Customer[] customers = svc.GetCustomers();
        List<Customer> customers = svc.GetCustomers();

        Console.WriteLine("\nAll Customers:\n");
        foreach (var custItem in customers)
        {
            Console.WriteLine(custItem.Name);
        }


        Console.ReadKey();
    }
  }
}
```

VB:

```vbnet
Imports CustomerConsoleVB.CustomerService

Module Module1

    Sub Main()

        Dim svc = New CustomerServiceClient

        Dim newCust = New Customer

        With newCust
            .Age = 36
            .Birthday = New DateTime(1974, 8, 22)
            .Income = 56000
            .Name = "Venus"
        End With

        Dim newCustID As Integer
```

```
        newCustID = svc.InsertCustomer(newCust)

        Console.WriteLine("New Customer ID: " & newCustID)

        Dim cust As New Customer

        cust = svc.GetCustomer(newCustID)

        cust.Income = 49000

        svc.UpdateCustomer(cust)

        Dim updatedCust As Customer

        updatedCust = svc.GetCustomer(cust.CustomerID)

        Console.WriteLine("Economic Adjustment: " & cust.Income)

        svc.DeleteCustomer(updatedCust.CustomerID)

        Dim customers As List(Of Customer)
        'Dim customers As Customer()

        customers = svc.GetCustomers()

    End Sub

End Module
```

Deploying a Client That Consumes a Web Service

When deploying a client that uses a Web service, you need to update the address of the service in the configuration file. The configuration file can vary, based on the type of application you've built. Table 11-1 describes the configuration files for the application types covered in this book.

Application Type	Configuration File
Console	App.config
WPF	App.config
ASP.NET MVC	Web.config
Silverlight	ServiceReferences.ClientConfig

Table 11-1   Configuration Files for Each Application Type

Regardless of the name, each configuration file will have a system.serviceModel element with configuration settings for the Web service. Listing 11-8 shows parts of the configuration file that you should find to change the address of the Web service to communicate with.

Listing 11-8   Web service client configuration

```
<?xml version="1.0" encoding="utf-8" ?>
<configuration>
    <system.serviceModel>
...
        <client>
            <endpoint address="http://localhost:8732
/Design_Time_Addresses/WcfDemoCS/CustomerService /"
                binding="wsHttpBinding"
bindingConfiguration="WSHttpBinding_ICustomerService"
                contract="CustomerService.ICustomerService"
name="WSHttpBinding_ICustomerService">
...
    </system.serviceModel>
</configuration>
```

Following the path system.serviceModel, client, endpoint, you'll find an address attribute. In the preceding example, the address is set to the address of the WcfDemo project inside the same solution. When you deploy your client, you'll want it to communicate with the deployed Web service. The following modification allows this client to communicate with the Web service deployed to IIS as discussed previously in this chapter:

```
<endpoint
address="http://localhost:8080/WcfDemoCS.CustomerService.svc"
binding="wsHttpBinding"
bindingConfiguration="WSHttpBinding_ICustomerService"
contract="CustomerService.ICustomerService"
name="WSHttpBinding_ICustomerService">
```

The address includes a filename, WcfDemoCS.CustomerService.svc, which was automatically generated when deploying the WcfDemo service. You can see the name of this file by looking at the physical folder where the Web service is deployed.

Creating a Web Service in a Web Site

The previous discussion of creating a Web service created a separate project for the Web service. This approach assumes that you have the ability to configure an IIS Web site for the Web service and can have another IIS Web site for your application if you have a Web application as the Web service client. However, this might not be possible if you are deploying to a hosted server by a third-party Internet service provider where you only have a single Web site. In that case, you have the additional option of adding a Web service directly to an existing Web site.

To see how this works, create a new ASP.NET MVC Web site. Right-click the project, select Add | New Item, and create a new WCF Service. What you'll see is an interface file, IService1.cs; an addressable service file; an implementation class, *Service1.svc*; and *Service1.svc.cs,* which you can find under the Service1.svc branch. All of the information you've learned previously in this chapter applies to coding a Web service that is part of the Web application. You should know that this is an option if it fits your needs.

Summary

You've learned how to build a Web service, how to deploy the Web service, and how to write a client that consumes the Web service. The discussion on creating the Web service showed you how to define the Web service contract with an interface and applicable attributes. You saw how to implement the service also. The deployment discussion explained how to host a Web service with IIS and how to use the VS Publish Wizard for deployment. You also saw how to write a client that creates a reference to a Web service and writes code to communicate with the Web service.

Part IV

Enhancing the VS 2010 Experience

Chapter 12
Customizing the Development Environment

Key Skills & Concepts

- Implement Custom Templates
- Create Custom Snippets
- Write Macros

In addition to all the great features you've seen in preceding chapters, VS gives you the capabilities to customize your own environment. The customizations I'll discuss are custom templates, custom snippets, and macros.

Throughout the book, you've started new projects and added items to those projects, using what is available with VS. On some occasions, you might desire to have a special type of project or customize an existing project for your own needs. The same need might apply to project items (such as a special type of class file), where you might change the contents of an item or create a new item.

Chapter 2 showed you how to use snippets, and Chapters 3 and 4 showed how to use several more snippets to quickly code common statements. In addition to using existing snippets, you can create your own. VS also has a management window that allows you to organize snippets, adding, deleting, and rearranging as you see fit.

Whenever you run into repetitive scenarios, it would be nice to capture the actions you perform so that you can quickly complete a task. For example, if you found yourself using the same set of keystrokes, it would be nice to collapse that action down into one command. Macros allow you to collapse repetitive tasks into a single task, saving you time.

Let's start the journey of customizing VS by looking at customizing templates.

Implementing Custom Templates

As you've seen in previous chapters, VS helps you get started with new projects and project items by providing default project items and skeleton code. In most cases, this is a very quick way to get started with a project. As you become more proficient in VS, you might prefer to have projects with different items than those that ship with VS or item templates with different code. This section will show you how to create your own project and item templates.

Creating New Project Templates

If you're working on a single project that lasts a long time, you might be satisfied with using a default template and doing a one-time modification. However, if you are starting new projects on a regular basis, customizing a project template can be very useful. There are various reasons you might want to create a custom project template, such as adding new items that aren't included in the default project template, removing items from the default template that you don't ever use, or changing an existing item for version upgrades. In addition to customizing existing templates, you might want to create a brand new template for a new project type that doesn't yet exist.

The example in this section will show you how to customize the ASP.NET MVC project template. The specific changes made to the template will be to remove much of the default code provided by the template. The assumption is that once you've written a few ASP.NET MVC applications, you won't need the default files as examples and would prefer to start with a more bare-bones template and build the application from the ground up yourself.

Modifying a Project

The easiest way to get started with creating a new project template is to start a new project that is most similar to the project type you want to create. If you wanted a blank project, you might start with a Console project because there aren't many items and it's quicker to delete them all. In the scenario for this section, we want to create a specialized ASP.NET MVC project, so it makes sense to create a new ASP.NET MVC project. The following steps show you how:

1. Press CTRL-SHIFT-N to create a new project and select ASP.NET MVC 2 Web Application. Name the project and solution **Custom ASP.NET MVC Web Application** and set the location for anywhere you like. Click OK to create the project. Next, the Create Unit Test Project window will appear and you should click "No, do not create a unit test project" and click OK. VS will create a new solution with a project. Chapter 9 explains what each of the projects and items are.

2. Open the Controllers folder and delete its contents.

3. Open the Models folder and delete its contents.

4. Open the Views folder but only delete the Account and Home folders.

5. Open the Shared folder, under the Views folder, and delete its contents.

6. Double-click Global.asax and comment out the call to routes.MapRoute in the editor.

7. To make sure your changes are okay, build and run the project. Select Build | Rebuild Solution and ensure you don't receive compiler errors. Then press F5 to run and allow VS to modify the Web.config file. Since you've commented out the route in Global .asax and there aren't any files to locate, you'll receive the message "The resource can't be found" in the browser. This is okay because it's assumed that you want to build your own controllers, models, and views and apply custom routing too.

You now have customized ASP.NET MVC project that allows you to build your application without any preinstalled items. VS is likely to ship with an empty template, but for additional customization, you might replace the CSS file in the Content folder or add your own JavaScript libraries to the Scripts folder. Make any changes you feel are most helpful for starting a new ASP.NET MVC project. Next, you'll learn how to transform this project into a reusable project template.

Exporting the Project Template

After you have a project configured the way you want, you can save it as a project template. The first step is to select File | Export Template, which will display the Choose Template Type window, shown in Figure 12-1. Choose Project Template and click Next.

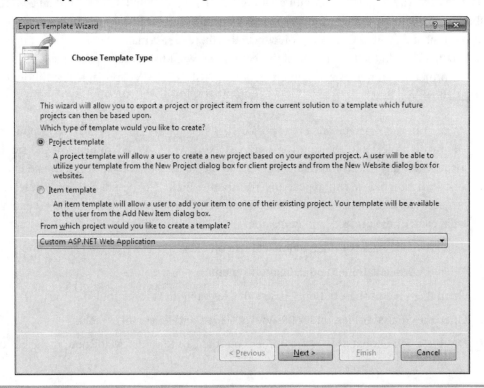

Figure 12-1 The Choose Template Type window

The next window is Select Template Options, shown in Figure 12-2. The Template Name defaults to the name of the project, which you can change. You can see how the filled-in Template description tells what the template is used for. Additionally, if you want to associate an icon or preview, you can click the respective Browse button and select the image you want to be associated with the project. As you may recall, the New Project window has an icon for the project and will display a preview whenever you select the project. The "Automatically import the template into Visual Studio" option will make the project template available via the New Project window. "Display an explorer window on the output files folder" will allow you to access the new file, shown in the Output location. Click Finish to create the template.

After you click Finish, VS does two things: it saves to the output location and makes the template available in VS. The output location is just a place to store the project template, Custom ASP.NET Web Application.zip, which contains all of the information VS needs to display the template and create the project if you select it in the New Projects window.

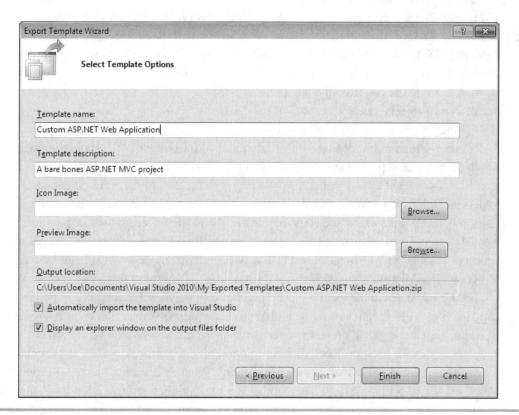

Figure 12-2 The Select Template Options window

You can share the project template with other developers too. The next section shows what to do to get the project template to appear in VS.

Using the New Project Template

The instructions for exporting the project template in the preceding section chose "Automatically import the template into Visual Studio." The use of the word "import" might make you think there is some magic process going on in the background, which there is to some extent. However, all the Export Template Wizard did was copy the Custom ASP.NET MVC Web Application.zip file from the Output location to <My Documents>\Visual Studio 2010\Templates\ProjectTemplates, which I'll call local project templates. The <My Documents> folder location can differ, depending on the version of Windows you're running. Once the file appears in the local project templates folder, you can verify that it's been imported into VS by pressing CTRL-SHIFT-N and observing that Custom ASP.NET MVC Web Application appears in the list.

If you had not checked "Automatically import the template into Visual Studio" (Figure 12-2), then you could have copied the Custom ASP.NET MVC Web Application .zip file to the local project templates folder yourself and the project template would appear in VS. If you share the Custom ASP.NET MVC Web Application.zip file with another developer, she can copy to the local project templates folder also.

If you delete the file from the local project templates folder, it will no longer appear in the VS New Projects window.

Another option for adding project templates is to copy the project templates file to a folder under \Program Files\Microsoft Visual Studio 10.0\Common7\IDE\ProjectTemplates, which I'll call global project templates. There are various folders under global project templates, including CSharp VisualBasic, Web, and more; each folder corresponding to folders in the VS New Project window. Under each folder is a locale code—for instance, English is 1033—and you would copy the file into the locale folder for the category you wanted the project template to appear in. For example, if you wanted the project template to appear in Visual C# | Web in the New Projects window, copy the project template *.zip file to \Program Files\Microsoft Visual Studio 10.0\Common7\IDE\ProjectTemplates\CSharp\Web.

Unlike templates in the local project templates folder, where all you need to do is copy the file, project templates in the global project templates folder don't automatically show up. To test the global project templates scenario, you should remove the project template from your local project templates folder. You must close down VS and execute the following in a command window, which you should open by selecting Start | All Programs | Microsoft Visual Studio 2010 | Visual Studio Tools | right-click on Visual Studio Command

Prompt (2010) and select Run As Administrator. This will take a few minutes to run, but afterward you'll see the project appear in the VS New Project window. This command imports all of the project templates from the global project templates folder into VS:

```
devenv /installvstemplates
```

If later you decide you don't want a given template to appear in the VS New Project window, remove the project template from the global project templates folder(s) and run the preceding command again.

Now you're able to create and use custom project templates. While you might create projects occasionally, it's a common task to create project items, covered next.

Creating New Item Templates

Sometimes, you use certain item templates frequently but often modify the contents of the item for your own purposes. In these cases, it's useful to be able to create a custom item template instead. The example in this section will be to create something that isn't currently an item in VS: a new item template for enums. To create a new item template, we'll create the file for holding the item, save the new item, and then use the new item in a project.

Creating an Item Template

The easiest way to get started with creating a new item template is to start a new project that has an existing item template that is most similar to the one you want to create. For a new enum template, all we need is a class file, so any project that allows you to add a class file template will work. The example in this section will use a Console project, but the project type doesn't matter because we'll only be interested in extracting one file for the item template. The following steps show you how:

1. Press CTRL-SHIFT-N to create a new project and select Console Application. Name the project anything you want and set the location for anywhere you like; name and location don't matter because we are only interested in the item template file and not the project. Click OK to create the project. VS will create a new solution with a project. By now, you've seen plenty of new Console applications in previous chapters, and this will be the same.

2. Right-click the project in Solution Explorer, select Add | New Item, select Code File, name the file **Enum.cs** (**Enum.vb** for VB), and click Add. This will add a new blank file to your project.

3. Add the following code to the file:

C#:

```
/// <summary>
/// Enum description
/// </summary>
public enum MyEnum
{
    /// <summary>
    /// Item 1 description
    /// </summary>
    Item1,

    /// <summary>
    /// Item 2 description
    /// </summary>
    Item2
}
```

VB:

```
''' <summary>
''' Enum description
''' </summary>
Public Enum MyEnum
    ''' <summary>
    ''' Item 1 description
    ''' </summary>
    Item1

    ''' <summary>
    ''' Item 2 description
    ''' </summary>
    Item2

End Enum
```

4. Save the file.

You now have a file that can be used as a skeleton for new enums. The next section shows you how to export this file so that it can be used as an item template.

Exporting the Item Template

After you have a file written the way you want, you can save it as an item template. The first step is to select File | Export Template, which will display the Choose Template Type window, shown in Figure 12-3. Choose Item Template and click Next.

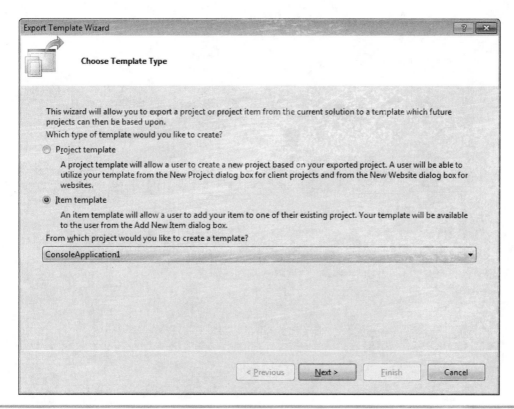

Figure 12-3   The Choose Template Type window

The next window is Select Item To Export, shown in Figure 12-4. The list shows all of the files eligible for creating an item. Check Enum.cs, which is the only file we're interested in for this example. Click Next to continue.

Next, you'll see the Select Item References window, shown in Figure 12-5. These are the assemblies that are part of the project that you're extracting the item template from. Check the assemblies that this item will require. In this case, I want to ensure the System assembly is included. Ignore the warning message, as it is assumed that you will always have the .NET Framework installed and the System.dll assembly will always be available. Click Next to continue.

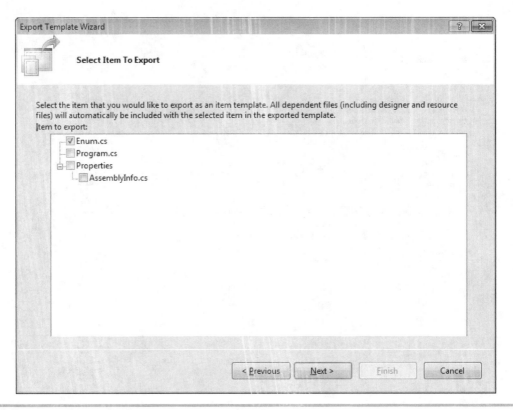

Figure 12-4 The Select Item To Export window

Figure 12-6 shows Select Template Options, where you specify how the item template will appear in the New Items window that appears when selecting Add | New Item on a project. The Template name defaults to the name of the project, which you should change to the item name, by changing the template name to Enum. The description lets the user know the purpose of the item template. If you want to associate an icon or preview, you can click the respective Browse button and select the image you want to be associated with the item. As you may recall, the New Item window has an icon for the item and will display a preview whenever you select the project. The "Automatically import the template into Visual Studio" option will make the item template available via the New Item window. "Display an explorer window on the output files folder" will allow you to access the new file, shown in the Output location. Click Finish to create the item template.

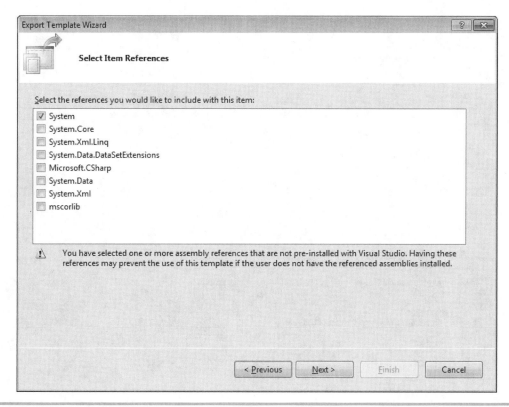

Figure 12-5 The Select Item References window

After you click Finish, VS does two things: it saves to the output location and makes the template available in VS. The output location is just a place to store the item template, Enum.zip, which contains all of the information VS needs to display the template and create the item if you select it in the New Item window. You can share the item template with other developers, too. The next section shows what to do to get the item template to appear in VS.

Using an Item Template

The instructions for exporting the item template in the preceding section chose "Automatically import the template into Visual Studio," copying the Enum.zip file from the Output location to <My Documents>\Visual Studio 2010\Templates\ItemTemplates, which I'll call local item templates. The <My Documents> folder location can differ, depending on the version of Windows you're running. Once the file appears in the local

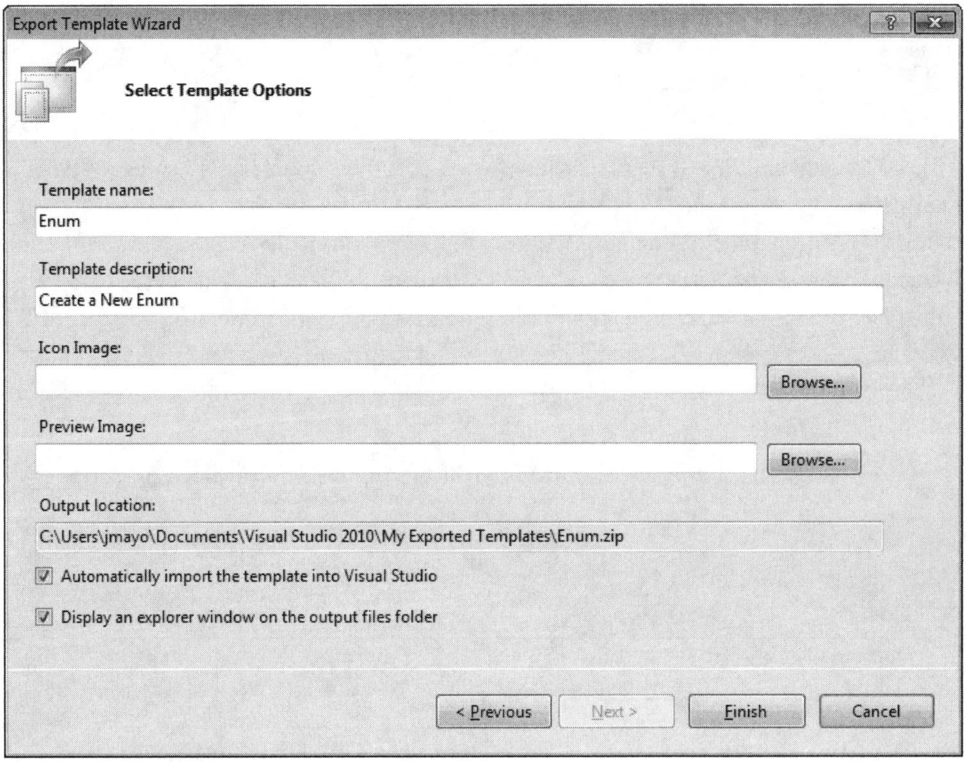

Figure 12-6 The Select Template Options window

item templates folder, you can verify that it's been imported into VS by selecting an open project in Solution Explorer (open a new or existing project if one is not opened), pressing CTRL-SHIFT-A, and observing that Enum appears in the list in the New Item window.

If you had not checked "Automatically import the template into Visual Studio" (Figure 12-6), then you could have copied the Enum.zip file to the local project templates folder yourself and the project template would appear in VS. If you share Enum.zip file with another developer, he can copy to the local item templates folder also.

If you delete the file from the local item templates folder, it will no longer appear in the VS New Item window.

Another option for adding item templates is to copy the project templates file to a folder under \Program Files\Microsoft Visual Studio 10.0\Common7\IDE\ItemTemplates, which I'll call global item templates. There are various folders under global item templates, including CSharp VisualBasic, Web, and more, each folder corresponding to folders in the VS New Item window. Under each folder is a locale code—for instance, English is 1033— and you would copy the file into the locale folder for the category you wanted the project template to appear in.

Unlike templates in the local item templates folder, where all you need to do is copy the file, item templates in the global item templates folder don't automatically show up. To test the global item templates scenario, you should remove the item template from your local item templates folder. You must close down VS and execute the following in a command window, which you should open by selecting Start | All Programs | Microsoft Visual Studio 2010 | Visual Studio Tools | right-click Visual Studio Command Prompt (2010) and select Run As Administrator. This will take a few minutes to run, but afterward you'll see the project appear in the VS New Item window. This command imports all of the item templates from the global item templates folder into VS:

```
devenv /installvstemplates
```

If later you decide you don't want a given template to appear in the VS New Item window, remove the item template from the global item templates folder(s) and run the preceding command again.

This section showed you how to add new project and item templates to VS, but sometimes you just want to add a common bit of code while you're programming. The next section shows you how to add your own custom code snippets to VS.

Creating Custom Snippets

If you've been using VS snippets, as described in Chapter 2, you'll know how much time they can save when writing common blocks of code. In time, you'll wonder why certain items aren't already covered by snippets, especially if you're a C# developer who has noticed that VB has many more snippets. Even if you're a VB developer with the plethora of available snippets, you might find blocks of code that will make you more productive when written in the form of a snippet. This chapter takes you to the next level in working with snippets by showing you how to create and manage your own snippets.

Creating a New Snippet

VB already has a snippet for Sub and Function, but C# doesn't. Since C# doesn't have as many snippets as VB, I'll show you how to create a snippet in C#, but the process is similar for a VB snippet. To create a new snippet, you can either work from an existing snippet file or start from scratch. I'll show you how to find and open existing snippets first.

Examining Existing Snippets

Snippets that ship with VS are located at \Program Files\Microsoft Visual Studio 10.0 under a folder for the language (VC#, VB, XML, and more) you need to find a snippet for. There, you'll either find one or more folders named with language codes (English is 1033) or a folder named Snippets. For some languages, the language code is at a higher level and the Snippets folder is under that or vice versa; regardless, you'll be looking for the Snippets folder that contains items with a .snippet file extension. The file path for C# is \Program Files\Microsoft Visual Studio 10.0\VC#\Snippets\1033. Beneath the Snippets folder, you'll see additional folders that serve to categorize other snippets.

We're going to open the *for* snippet because it contains several features that give you a good idea of how snippets work. It might help if you open a blank file by pressing CTRL-N, selecting Visual C# Class, and naming the file anything you want, and try the *for* snippet before going further; it will give you a good idea of what the snippet is supposed to be doing. Alternatively, you can review the description of the *for* snippet in Chapter 2.

The .snippet extension is registered with VS, so you can double-click the for.snippet file in the Snippets folder and it will open in VS. Listing 12-1 shows what this file looks like.

Listing 12-1   Inside the *for* snippet

```xml
<?xml version="1.0" encoding="utf-8" ?>
<CodeSnippets xmlns=
"http://schemas.microsoft.com/VisualStudio/2005/CodeSnippet">
    <CodeSnippet Format="1.0.0">
        <Header>
            <Title>for</Title>
            <Shortcut>for</Shortcut>
            <Description>Code snippet for 'for' loop</Description>
            <Author>Microsoft Corporation</Author>
            <SnippetTypes>
                <SnippetType>Expansion</SnippetType>
                <SnippetType>SurroundsWith</SnippetType>
            </SnippetTypes>
        </Header>
        <Snippet>
            <Declarations>
                <Literal>
                    <ID>index</ID>
                    <Default>i</Default>
                    <ToolTip>Index</ToolTip>
                </Literal>
```

```
                    <Literal>
                          <ID>max</ID>
                          <Default>length</Default>
                          <ToolTip>Max length</ToolTip>
                    </Literal>
              </Declarations>
              <Code Language="csharp"><![CDATA[for (int $index$ = 0;
$index$ < $max$; $index$++)
                    {
                    $selected$ $end$
                    }]]>
              </Code>
          </Snippet>
      </CodeSnippet>
</CodeSnippets>
```

As shown in Listing 12-1, a snippet is an XML file where all data is defined by begin and end tags arranged in a hierarchy. Inside of the *CodeSnippet* tags are *Header* and *Snippet* elements.

Inside of the *Header* element is a *Shortcut* element that defines the prefix you must type in the VS editor to use the snippet. The *Title* and *Description* tags define what displays for Intellisense in VS when the shortcut is being typed. *Author* tells who wrote the snippet.

The *SnippetTypes* element defines the two ways to use a snippet: *Expansion* and *SurroundsWith*. Chapter 2 describes many snippets that work via *Expansion*. However, *SurroundsWith* snippets are also very useful. To use a *SurroundsWith* snippet, highlight the code that you want to surround, press CTRL-SPACE, and select the snippet. After selecting the snippet, the snippet template will appear in VS, with its blocks surrounding the highlighted text. Since the *for* loop has a block that can contain statements, it makes sense that the *for* snippet is both a *SurroundsWith* and *Expansion* snippet.

The *Snippet* element in Listing 12-1 contains a *Declarations* and *Code* element, where the declarations are used in the code. Thinking about how snippet templates work, remember that your cursor is positioned on blocks of code that you change and tab through to complete the snippet. The blocks of code to be filled in correspond to *Literal* elements in the declaration.

Each *Literal* element has an *ID* that is used in the *Code* to define where the *Literal* is located. *Default* describes the data shown in the template before you start typing. Whenever you're filling in a snippet template, you can hover over the data field and a tooltip will describe what information should go into the data field. This tooltip is defined in the *Tooltip* element of the snippet definition. The *ID* of each literal is defined in the *Code* element.

Inside the *Code* element is the code for the snippet. The variables in the code with $ prefix and suffix help define how the snippet template works. Notice that *$index$* and *max* match *Literal* elements in the *Declarations* element; this is where you must fill in data items when filling in the snippet template in VS. The *end* variable defines where the cursor ends up after the snippet is complete (after pressing ENTER in the snippet template). You'll want to locate *end* where a developer would normally continue typing. The *$selected$* variable is used with *SurroundsWith* snippets, defining the relationship of selected text with where snippet code should be.

Now that you have a basic familiarity with snippets, the next section brings you to the next level as you actually create a new snippet.

Creating New Snippets

To create a new snippet, you can either work from an existing snippet file or start from scratch. If you work from an existing snippet, find and open the snippet closest to what you want to do, using the techniques described in the preceding section. Starting from scratch, there is a quick way to get started using a *snippet* snippet; that's right, there is a snippet that helps you create new snippets.

As you learned in the preceding section, snippets are defined as XML files. Fortunately, VS has a nice XML editor that supports XML snippets. So, when I say that we're going to create a snippet from scratch, that's not quite true, because we're going to leverage VS to get a quick start. In the following steps, I'll show you how to create a snippet you can use to add a C# method to a class quickly:

1. With VS open, press CTRL-N and create a new XML file. If you were opening the file from an existing project, you would need to provide a name, which would be **meth .snippet**. The new XML file has a single line, which is called an XML prefix.

2. Move to the line below the XML prefix, press CTRL-K-X, type **sn** to select *Snippet* in the Intellisense list, and press ENTER. You'll see an XML snippet template with the values for *Title, Author, Shortcut, Description, ID,* and *Default.*

3. Fill in data and tab through the snippet template as follows: *Title* as **Method Snippet**, *Author* as **<your name>**, *Shortcut* as **meth**, *Description* as **Create a New Method**, *ID* as **access**, and *Default* as **public**. Press ENTER when complete.

4. The resulting snippet still needs code and template item definitions, which is accomplished by filling in the *Code* element and adding needed *Literal* elements. First, modify the code element as follows:

```
<Code Language="csharp">
  <![CDATA[$access$ $return$ $methodName$($paramList$)
  {
      $end$
  }
  ]]>
</Code>
```

5. In addition to *access,* the code example in the preceding step includes variables for return, *methodName,* and *paramList.* Add *Literal* elements for each of these variables, where the *ID* is the variable name and the *Default* is set to *return* as **void**, *methodName* as **MethodName**, and *paramList* as **int p1**.

6. Save the file and name it **meth.snippet**. The next section will explain where to put the file, but for now put it in a location that you can remember so you can copy it later. BTW, the Save File dialog box has Snippet Files (*.snippet) for a Save A Type option, which you can use to ensure the snippet has the correct file extension.

You now have a workable snippet. Listing 12-2 shows the snippet in its entirety. Additionally, notice how each *Literal* has a *Tooltip* to help the user of the snippet fill in each data item. Also, notice that the *Language* attribute of the *Code* element is spelled *csharp,* rather than C#. These small nuances, such as the spelling for a language, could make the snippet file invalid. A good troubleshooting technique is to open a similar snippet predefined for VS, as described in the preceding section, and compare formats to see if you might have mistyped something. The next section will explain what to do with this snippet file so that you can begin using it.

Listing 12-2   A custom method snippet

```
<?xml version="1.0" encoding="utf-8"?>
<CodeSnippet Format="1.0.0"
xmlns="http://schemas.microsoft.com
/VisualStudio/2005/CodeSnippet">
  <Header>
    <Title>Method Snippet</Title>
    <Author>Joe Mayo</Author>
    <Shortcut>meth</Shortcut>
    <Description>Create a New Method</Description>
    <SnippetTypes>
      <SnippetType>SurroundsWith</SnippetType>
      <SnippetType>Expansion</SnippetType>
    </SnippetTypes>
  </Header>
  <Snippet>
    <Declarations>
      <Literal>
        <ID>access</ID>
        <Default>public</Default>
        <ToolTip>Access modifier</ToolTip>
      </Literal>
```

```
      <Literal>
        <ID>return</ID>
        <Default>void</Default>
        <ToolTip>Return value</ToolTip>
      </Literal>
      <Literal>
        <ID>methodName</ID>
        <Default>MethodName</Default>
        <ToolTip>Name of Method</ToolTip>
      </Literal>
      <Literal>
        <ID>paramList</ID>
        <Default>int p1</Default>
        <ToolTip>
Comma-separated list of parameters
        </ToolTip>
      </Literal>
    </Declarations>
    <Code Language="csharp">
      <![CDATA[
$access$ $return$ $methodName$($paramList$)
{
    $end$
}]]>
    </Code>
  </Snippet>
</CodeSnippet>
```

Managing the Snippet Library

To use a snippet, you can either copy the snippet into a VS folder or use a VS tool called the Snippet Manager. This section will explain how to make the *method* snippet, created in the preceding section, available to your code.

File Folders Holding Snippets

The local snippets folder is located at \Users\<your name>\Documents\Visual Studio 2010\Code Snippets. You'll see a set of folders for each language/technology, which each have subfolders for organizing snippets. Copy and paste the snippet file into one of these folders, such as Visual C#\My Code Snippets, and the snippet will be immediately available to your code.

The local snippets folder makes a snippet available to your machine login. You can also make the snippet available to everyone who logs on to the machine by copying the snippet to a global snippet folder, located at \Program Files\Microsoft Visual Studio

10.0\. You'll see language technology folders, such as VC# for C# or VB for VB. Within those folders, you'll either see folders for language codes (English is 1033) or a Snippets folder. Drilling down two levels, through the language code folders and Snippet folders (whichever shows first), you'll see more snippets and subfolders that organize the snippets for that language/technology. Copy the snippet into the folder where you feel it belongs. The snippet will be immediately available to your code.

Working with system file folders can be cumbersome, so VS offers a tool to help organize snippets, the Snippets Manager.

Using the Snippets Manager

The Snippets Manager allows you to import new snippets and organize existing snippets. Either select Tools | Code Snippets Manager or press CTRL-K, CTRL-B. You'll see the Snippets Manager window, shown in Figure 12-7.

The Language drop-down shows what type of snippets you can work with. The folders show how snippets are organized. Use the Add and Remove buttons to manage folders. Click the Import button to find and make new snippets available to the application.

As you've seen, snippets give you a well-specified way to quickly write code. However, there is a capability that is even more powerful, which is macros, discussed next.

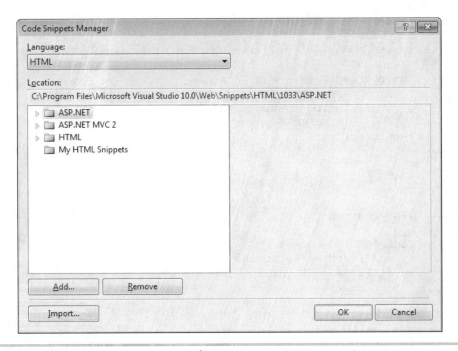

Figure 12-7 The Snippets Manager window

Writing Macros

When the productivity features that ship with VS and custom snippets don't give you enough power, the next step is to consider creating a *macro,* which is a repeatable set of actions that you can record and re-run multiple times. An example of when a macro is useful is whenever you find yourself continuously repeating the same set of actions in VS. This section will show you how to create and run a macro that uses VS features to create a customized block of code for validating strings.

Recording a Macro

When creating business objects, it's common to validate input parameters to ensure they are valid. One such validation is enforcing that calling code pass a required parameter. The example in this section shows you how to write a macro for validating that a string-type parameter is not null, empty, or white space (such as a space or tab). To get started, create a new Console project and add a Class file with the following method to the project, which simulates adding a new customer:

C#:

```csharp
using System;

class Customer
{
    public int AddNewCustomer(string firstName, string lastName)
    {
        int newCustID = 0;

        // Logic to add customer

        return newCustID;
    }
}
```

VB:

```vb
Public Class Customer

    Function AddNewCustomer(
        ByVal firstName As String,
        ByVal lastName As String) As Integer

        Dim newCustID As Integer = 0

        ' Logic to add customer
```

```
        Return newCustID

    End Function

End Class
```

The point of interest in the *AddNewCustomer* method is the *firstName* and *lastName* parameters. Whenever working with data, you'll usually want to ensure that input data is legal. When user input is being processed, it's common to get bad information, even if you have good input validation in your user interface code. For example, the following code calls the preceding *AddNewCustomer* method, passing in bad data as arguments:

C#:

```
class Program
{
    static void Main()
    {
        string firstName = "Joe";
        string lastName = null;

        Customer cust = new Customer();
        cust.AddNewCustomer(firstName, lastName);
    }
}
```

VB:

```
Module Module1

    Sub Main()

        Dim firstName As String = "Joe"
        Dim lastName As String = Nothing

        Dim cust As New Customer
        cust.AddNewCustomer(firstName, lastName)

    End Sub

End Module
```

In the preceding example, *firstName* is okay because it has a good name in it. However, notice that *lastName* is set to *null* (*Nothing* in VB). This would cause a *NullReferenceException* if *AddNewCustomer* tried to call a string operation on the parameter, the code that *AddNewCustomer* calls could potentially throw a *NullReferenceException,* or (assuming that *null* is considered invalid in this case) you could end up saving bad data. Since *AddNewCustomer* doesn't have an implementation, this is all speculation, but this outlines a few of the many problems that can occur if you allow your business objects to accept data that is bad for your program.

The macro demonstrated in this section will show how to check a string parameter for *null,* empty, or white space and throw an *ArgumentNullException.* This will prevent callers from passing bad data and give them a meaningful message. To create a macro, you will need to locate the position in the code where the macro starts (if applicable), start recording, perform VS actions, and stop recording. It's somewhat like using a video recorder where you have to find a TV show, start the recording, allow the show to play, and then stop recording. Perform the following steps to create the parameter validation macro:

1. Click the *firstName* parameter of the *AddNewCustomer* method so that the cursor is inside of the *firstName* parameter identifier. This is important because we need the parameter name in the code.

2. Start the macro recorder by selecting Tools | Macros | Record TemporaryMacro or press CTRL-SHIFT-R.

3. For C#, press CTRL-LEFT ARROW, CTRL-SHIFT-RIGHT ARROW, and CTRL-C. For VB, press CTRL-LEFT ARROW, CTRL-SHIFT-RIGHT ARROW, SHIFT-LEFT ARROW, and CTRL-C. This copies the parameter name.

4. For C#, press CTRL-F to bring up the Find And Replace window, type { into Find What, click Find Next, Close the Find And Replace window, press END, and press ENTER. For VB, press END and press ENTER. This positions the cursor to begin entering code.

5. Type **if** and press TAB twice (the *if* snippet), type **string.IsNullOrWhiteSpace(** into the condition, press CTRL-V to paste the parameter name as the argument, and type). For C#, press ENTER. For VB, press DOWN ARROW. The cursor moves to the body of the *if* statement (as you would expect with the *if* snippet). This sets up the validation check for the parameter, seeing if it is *null* (*Nothing* in VB), an empty string, or some white space character such as space or tab.

6. Type **throw new ArgumentNullException("**, press CTRL-V to paste the parameter name, type **", "**, press CTRL-V to paste the parameter name, type a space, and type **value is not valid.")**. For C#, add a semicolon, **;**, to the end of the line. This is the action to perform when the value is not valid, throwing an exception to let the caller know that the value is not good.

7. Press DOWN ARROW and press ENTER. This positions the cursor after the code, which might be convenient if you want to continue typing from this point.

8. Select Tools | Macros | Stop Recording TemporaryMacro or press CTRL-SHIFT-R to stop recording.

You've now recorded a macro. To check the preceding steps against what you've produced, here's a revised *AddNewCustomer* method, showing what the results should look like:

C#:

```csharp
using System;

class Customer
{
    public int AddNewCustomer(string firstName, string lastName)
    {
        if (string.IsNullOrWhiteSpace(firstName))
        {
            throw new ArgumentNullException(
                "firstName",
                "firstName value is not valid.");
        }

        int newCustID = 0;

        // Logic to add customer

        return newCustID;
    }
}
```

VB:

```vb
Public Class Customer

    Function AddNewCustomer(
        ByVal firstName As String,
        ByVal lastName As String) As Integer

        If String.IsNullOrWhiteSpace(firstName) Then
            Throw New ArgumentNullException(
                "firstName",
                "firstName value is not valid.")
        End If

        Dim newCustID As Integer = 0

        ' Logic to add customer

        Return newCustID

    End Function

End Class
```

In the preceding code, I've moved the *ArgumentNullException* arguments to separate lines to fit the book's line length, but this is what you should see. Next, you can test the macro by running it. Click the *lastName* parameter and select Tools | Macros | Run TemporaryMacro or press CTRL-SHIFT-P. That will produce the following code:

```
public int AddNewCustomer(string firstName, string lastName)
{
    if (string.IsNullOrWhiteSpace(lastName))
    {
        throw new ArgumentException("lastName", "lastName value is not
valid.");
    }

    if (string.IsNullOrWhiteSpace(firstName))
    {
        throw new ArgumentException("firstName", "firstName value is
not valid.");
    }

    int newCustID = 0;

    // Logic to add customer

    return newCustID;
}
```

Now, you can run this macro on any of the string parameters of methods in your class and quickly add validation support. The only problem at the present time is that the macro is overwritten as soon as you begin recording a new macro and the macro is gone if you close VS. The next section addresses this problem by showing you how to save the macro.

Saving a Macro

You can save macros to be reused in later sessions. To save the macro, select Tools | Macros | Save TemporaryMacro. VS will save TemporaryMacro and open the Macro Explorer window, shown in Figure 12-8.

VS uses TemporaryMacro as the name of whatever macro it will record. Therefore, you must rename the macro if you want to keep it because the next recording will overwrite this macro. Rename the file macro to **ValidateStringParameter** by right-clicking TemporaryMacro in Macro Explorer, showing the context menu, and selecting Rename.

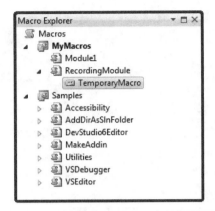

Figure 12-8 The Macro Explorer window

In the Macro Explorer, you can add new Macro Projects, which are containers for holding macro modules, by right-clicking Macros and selecting New Macro Project. If someone shares their Macro Project with you, right-click Macros and select Load Macro Project to find the project in the file system and load it. Macro modules hold macros, and you can right-click any macro project; such as MyMacros or Samples in Figure 12-8, and select New Module to add new macro modules. You can find all of these commands on the Tools | Macros menu too.

To run an existing macro, double-click the macro in Macro Explorer.

To change a macro, you can either re-record or edit an existing macro. The next section explains how to edit a macro.

Editing Macros

Macros are editable, allowing you to modify previously recorded macros or create a brand new macro. To edit a macro, right-click the macro in Macro Explorer and select Edit. You'll see the Macro editor, shown in Figure 12-9, which contains the code for the ValidateStringParameter macro created in the preceding section.

In Figure 12-9, you can see that the editor opens the macro in a code editing window. The language is VB, so if the language you normally program with is C#, you might want to review the VB portions of Chapters 2 through 4 as a refresher. The features of Macro editor are very similar to the normal VS IDE, except that now you must work with Macro Projects and Modules. Listing 12-3 shows the macro code from Figure 12-9. In Listing 12-3, both the C# and VB macros are written in VB. However, the C# code is for a macro that works on C# code and the VB code is for a macro that works on VB code.

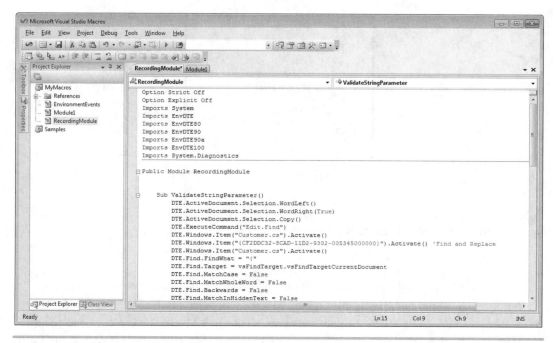

Figure 12-9 The Macro editor

Listing 12-3 Code for the ValidateStringParameter macro

C#:

```
Option Strict Off
Option Explicit Off
Imports System
Imports EnvDTE
Imports EnvDTE80
Imports EnvDTE90
Imports EnvDTE90a
Imports EnvDTE100
Imports System.Diagnostics

Public Module RecordingModule


    Sub ValidateStringParameter()
        DTE.ActiveDocument.Selection.WordLeft()
        DTE.ActiveDocument.Selection.WordRight(True)
        DTE.ActiveDocument.Selection.Copy()
        DTE.ExecuteCommand("Edit.Find")
```

```
        DTE.Windows.Item("Customer.cs").Activate()
        DTE.Windows.Item("{CF2DDC32-8CAD-11D2-9302-005345000000}")
.Activate() 'Find and Replace
        DTE.Windows.Item("Customer.cs").Activate()
        DTE.Find.FindWhat = "{"
        DTE.Find.Target =
vsFindTarget.vsFindTargetCurrentDocument
        DTE.Find.MatchCase = False
        DTE.Find.MatchWholeWord = False
        DTE.Find.Backwards = False
        DTE.Find.MatchInHiddenText = False
        DTE.Find.PatternSyntax = vsFindPatternSyntax
.vsFindPatternSyntaxLiteral
        DTE.Find.Action = vsFindAction.vsFindActionFind
        If (DTE.Find.Execute() =
vsFindResult.vsFindResultNotFound) Then
Throw New System.Exception("vsFindResultNotFound")
        End If
        DTE.Windows.Item(
"{CF2DDC32-8CAD-11D2-9302-005345000000}").Close()
        DTE.Windows.Item("Customer.cs").Activate()
        DTE.ActiveDocument.Selection.EndOfLine()
        DTE.ActiveDocument.Selection.NewLine()
        DTE.ActiveDocument.Selection.Text = "if"
        DTE.ExecuteCommand("Edit.InsertTab")
        DTE.ExecuteCommand("Edit.InsertTab")
        DTE.ActiveDocument.Selection.Text =
"string.IsNullOrWhiteSpace("
        DTE.ActiveDocument.Selection.Paste()
        DTE.ActiveDocument.Selection.Text = ")"
        DTE.ExecuteCommand("Edit.BreakLine")
        DTE.ActiveDocument.Selection.Text =
"throw new ArgumentNullException("""
        DTE.ActiveDocument.Selection.Paste()
        DTE.ActiveDocument.Selection.Text = """, """
        DTE.ActiveDocument.Selection.Paste()
        DTE.ActiveDocument.Selection.Text =
" value is not valid."");"
        DTE.ActiveDocument.Selection.LineDown()
        DTE.ActiveDocument.Selection.NewLine()
    End Sub
End Module
```

  VB:

```
Option Strict Off
Option Explicit Off
Imports System
Imports EnvDTE
```

```
Imports EnvDTE80
Imports EnvDTE90
Imports EnvDTE90a
Imports EnvDTE100
Imports System.Diagnostics

Public Module RecordingModule


    Sub ValidateStringParameter()
        DTE.ActiveDocument.Selection.WordLeft()
        DTE.ActiveDocument.Selection.WordRight(True)
        DTE.ActiveDocument.Selection.CharLeft(True)
        DTE.ActiveDocument.Selection.Copy()
        DTE.ActiveDocument.Selection.EndOfLine()
        DTE.ActiveDocument.Selection.NewLine()
        DTE.ActiveDocument.Selection.Text = "if"
        DTE.ExecuteCommand("Edit.InsertTab")
        DTE.ExecuteCommand("Edit.InsertTab")
        DTE.ActiveDocument.Selection.Text = "string.IsNullOrEmpty("
        DTE.ActiveDocument.Selection.Paste()
        DTE.ActiveDocument.Selection.Text = ")"
        DTE.ActiveDocument.Selection.LineDown()
        DTE.ActiveDocument.Selection.Text =
"throw new ArgumentNullException("""
        DTE.ActiveDocument.Selection.Paste()
        DTE.ActiveDocument.Selection.Text = """, """
        DTE.ActiveDocument.Selection.Paste()
        DTE.ActiveDocument.Selection.Text =
" value is not valid."")"
        DTE.ActiveDocument.Selection.LineDown()
        DTE.ActiveDocument.Selection.NewLine()
    End Sub
End Module
```

In Listing 12-3, all of the namespaces that begin with *EnvDTE* have code that allows you to manipulate the VS environment. The macro itself is a *Sub* within a *Module*.

Each of the statements corresponds to the steps used to create the macro in the preceding section. For example, the Find And Replace window has several options, which this macro populates, regardless of whether they contribute toward the purpose of the macro.

Opening a macro in the editor can be very useful if you want to make a quick change, without needing to re-record the entire macro. For example, what if you missed a keystroke or misspelled something? You can just edit the code, save the file, close the Macro editor, and then re-run the macro. In fact, there is a problem with the macro for C#; it will only work on the file you ran it in. This problem doesn't occur in the macro for VB. I'll show you how to fix this problem, but let's open the macro editor first.

You can open the Macro editor through VS by selecting Tools | Macros | Macros IDE, start a new project, add a module to the project, and add a *Sub* to the *Module* as a new macro. Then code the macro by typing **DTE.** and using Intellisense to find various parts of the IDE. The cryptic parameter to *Windows.Item, {CF2DDC32-8CAD-11D2-9302-005345000000},* for the Find And Replace window is called a Globally Unique Identifier (GUID). A GUID is often used as a special identifier for software components and is the method used in VS to uniquely identify tools. So, *DTE.Windows.Item("{CF2DDC32-8CAD-11D2-9302-005345000000}").Activate()* is a way to reference and open the Find And Replace window.

There is a problem with the macro for C# in Listing 12-3, because it will only work in the Customer.cs file in VS. The VB code below is provided for your convenience, but this problem only occurs with the macro written for C# code; the VB macro works fine on the VB code below. If you created a new class named Product in a file named Product.cs and added an AddNewProduct method like the following, the macro will try to open and write into the Customer.cs file, which is not the result you want:

C#:

```
using System;

namespace ConsoleApplication1
{
    class Product
    {
        public int AddNewProduct(string productName)
        {
            int newProdID = 0;

            // Logic to add product

            return newProdID;
        }
    }
}
```

VB (doesn't have problem that occurs in C# code):

```
Public Class Product

    Function AddNewProduct(ByVal productName As String) As Integer

        Dim newProdID As Integer = 0
```

```
    ' Logic to add product

    Return newProdID

  End Function

End Class
```

To fix the problem with the macro (for the C# code) opening the Customer.cs file, notice that the macro has three statements that activate the Customer.cs file. Comment out each of these statements as shown in the following excerpt:

...

    'DTE.Windows.Item("Customer.cs").Activate()

...

    'DTE.Windows.Item("Customer.cs").Activate()
    DTE.Find.FindWhat = "{"

...

    'DTE.Windows.Item("Customer.cs").Activate()

...

If you were to write your own macro via code, a quick way to figure out what code you have to write is to start the macro recorder in VS (CTRL-SHIFT-R), use the VS feature you want to code, stop recording (CTRL-SHIFT-R), and save the macro. Then inspect the code in the Macro editor and copy the parts you need. This technique is especially valuable to figure out how to open windows, such as the Find And Replace window discussed in the preceding paragraph. For even more help, there are several example macros under the Samples folder, shown in Figure 12-9, showing you different ways to write VS macros.

Summary

Now you know about various techniques for customizing VS. You learned how to customize projects and save your work as a custom project template. In a related task, you saw how you can create a new file and then save that file as a custom item template. This gives you the ability to use projects and project items in a way that you want. In addition to using snippets that ship with VS, you learned how to find the definition of existing snippets and either modify a snippet or create a brand new snippet from scratch. You also saw how to organize snippets with the Snippets Manager. Finally, you learned how to record and save repeatable actions with VS macros. You can also use the Macro editor to customize existing macros or create new ones on your own.

Macros are very powerful, but VS has even more capabilities for allowing you to extend the IDE. You'll learn how to extend VS by writing Add-Ins in the next chapter.

Chapter 13

Extending Visual Studio 2010

Key Skills & Concepts

- Create an Add-In with VS

- Learn What Types of Add-Ins to Create

- Deploy an Add-In

Previous chapters discussed many ways to use VS, and the preceding chapter showed you a few ways to create your own customizations. In particular, macros offer the ability to perform repeatable actions and give you access to much of what VS has to offer. Taking customization one step beyond macros, this chapter shows you how to extend VS functionality with a software component called an Add-In.

Essentially, an Add-In is a software component that allows you to add new capabilities to VS that haven't existed before. The Add-In plugs into VS, and you can run it as if it were part of VS. This chapter shows you how the process of creating an Add-In works. You'll see how to add functionality to make an Add-In perform any task you want. Besides creating an Add-In, this chapter points you in the right direction so that you can figure out how to access the different parts of VS. The specific example in this chapter is an Add-In that finds all of the shortcut keys in VS and prints them to the Output window. With knowledge of how to create an Add-In, you'll learn how to deploy the Add-In so that it can be loaded into VS. We'll begin with a walk-through of how VS helps you create an Add-In.

Creating a Visual Studio Add-In

As when creating other project types in VS, you can run a project wizard to create an Add-In for VS. The following discussion will show you how to start and run the Add-In Project Wizard and examine the results.

Running the Add-In Project Wizard

You would start the Add-In project the same way you would any other project. The difference is that an Add-In Project Wizard asks more questions than normal. The following steps take you through the process of the Add-In Project Wizard and explain the various screens and questions you'll need to answer.

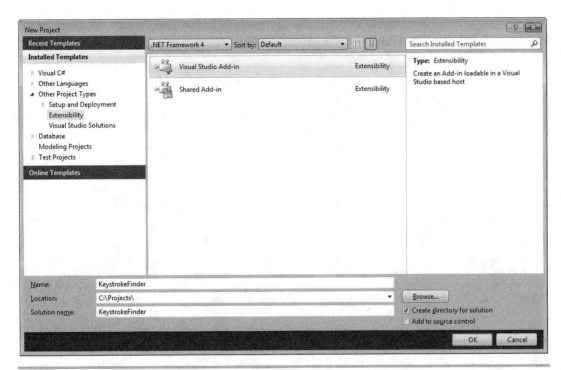

Figure 13-1   Selecting a Visual Studio Add-In in the New Project window

1. Open VS and press CTRL-SHIFT-N to open the New Project window. Select Other Project Types | Extensibility and observe that there are two types of Add-In project types: Visual Studio Add-In and Shared Add-In. The Shared Add-In is what you would use to create a Microsoft Office Add-In. The Visual Studio Add-In is appropriately named because it describes what we want to do. Figure 13-1 shows what the screen should look like.

2. Select Visual Studio Add-In. Name the project **KeystrokeFinder**, specify the location where you want the project to be, and click OK. Click Next to pass the Welcome screen and you'll see the Select A Programming Language screen, shown in Figure 13-2.

3. Pick the language you would like to use. This book doesn't discuss C++, but it would be safe to pick either C# or VB, which you can learn more about in Chapters 2 through 4. Click Next to reveal the Select An Application Host window, shown in Figure 13-3.

4. Your choices include Microsoft Visual Studio 2010 and Microsoft Visual Studio 2010 Macros. Checking Microsoft Visual Studio 2010 will allow the Add-In to work in the VS environment, which you've used for most of this book. Checking Microsoft Visual

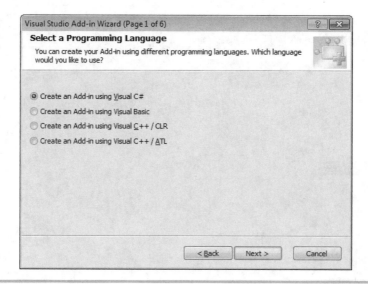

Figure 13-2 The Select A Programming Language window

Studio 2010 Macros will allow this Add-In to work with the Macro Editor, explained in the preceding chapter. We're only interested in VS for the current Add-In, so check only Microsoft Visual Studio 2010 (not the Macros option). Click Next to display the Enter A Name And Description window, shown in Figure 13-4.

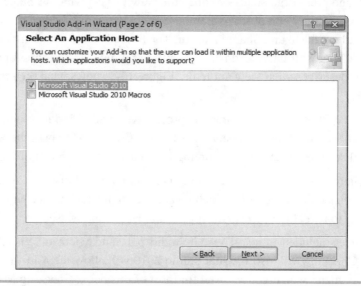

Figure 13-3 The Select An Application Host window

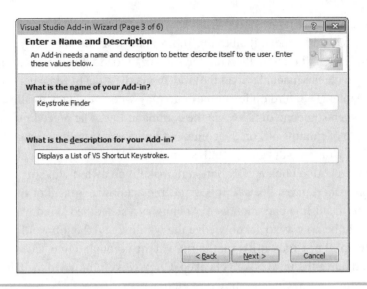

Figure 13-4   The Enter A Name And Description window

5. The Enter A Name And Description window starts by appending " – No Name provided." and " – No Description provided." to the name of the project in the name and description fields, respectively. Just delete the defaults and add the name and description you want the Add-In to have. The Add-In will be named after what you put here, and users will be able to read the description in the VS Add-In Manager, which I'll discuss later in this chapter. Click Next to display the Choose Add-In Options window, shown in Figure 13-5.

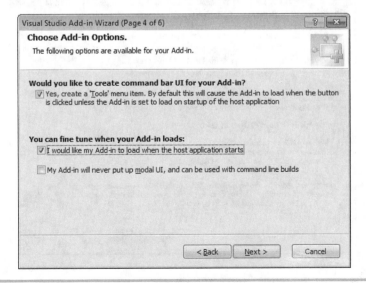

Figure 13-5   The Choose Add-In Options window

6. The first choice in Figure 13-5, "Would you like to create command bar UI for your Add-In?" will add a menu item to the Tools menu with the name of your Add-In. Check the second box too, allowing the Add-In to load when VS loads; the alternative being that you can manually load the Add-In via the Add-In Manager, discussed later in this chapter. The third option comes into play when you want to allow the Add-In to work when someone runs VS via the command line. The preceding chapter shows an example of running VS on the command line when installing the global project templates by running devenv /installvstemplates. Popping up a modal window (one that requires you to click an OK button to make it go away) will stop a command-line operation from running because it is expecting acknowledgment of the modal window. If that command-line operation were running as a scheduled Windows background job, there would be no way to acknowledge the window and the job would not work. So, check the third box only if it's safe to run via the command line. Check the first two boxes and leave the third box unchecked. Click Next to move to the Choosing 'Help About' Information window, shown in Figure 13-6.

7. You can optionally show an About window for your Add-In. Check the box and modify the text that you would like to show in the About box. Click Next and click Finish on the Summary window.

After a minute VS will create a new solution and project that contains items that help you create an Add-In. The next section discusses what those project items are.

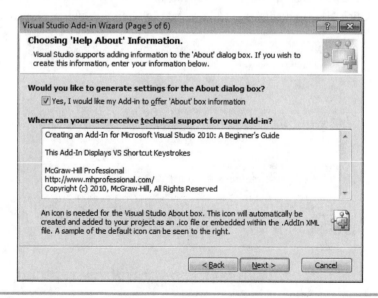

Figure 13-6 The Choosing 'Help About' window

Examining an Add-In Wizard Solution

After running the New Project Add-In Project Wizard, you'll have a solution with a project that has skeleton code forming the basis of the application. Not only will you need to know what files are available, but you'll also need to understand a couple of interfaces and how to implement the interface methods properly. If you're a little rusty on interfaces, now might be a good time to visit Chapter 4 for a review. What you mostly need to know about this project is that there are new references, a *Connect* class, and a couple of *.AddIn files. Refer to Figure 13-7 as we discuss each of these Add-In project items.

Looking at assembly references (under the References folder), you might wonder what all the assemblies are with *EnvDTE* names. Pulling the name apart, Env is short for environment and DTE means Development Tools Extensibility. So, *EnvDTE* is an assembly containing code that allows you to extend the VS development environment. Each assembly represents functionality for a particular version of VS: *EnvDTE* is for VS.NET (the first version of VS that supported .NET development) and VS 2003, *EnvDTE80* is for VS 2005, *EnvDTE90* is for VS 2008, and *EnvDTE100* is for VS 2010 (the subject of this book). The reason you need references to all of the *EnvDTE* versions is that each new version builds upon the previous with new functionality, rather than replacing the older version. Therefore, you'll sometimes encounter classes, interfaces, or

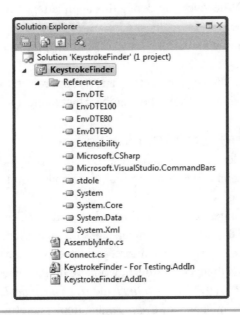

Figure 13-7   An Add-In project in Solution Explorer

methods that are numbered, such as the *IDTExtensibility* and *IDTExtensibility2,* where *IDTExtensibility2* is a more recent version with additional members. I'll explain what the *IDTExtensibility2* interface does later, but what you should get out of this example is how each version of the *EnvDTE* assemblies manages newer versions of code. This scheme promotes the addition of new functionality for each version of VS without sacrificing backward compatibility.

The *Connect* class contains the code that interacts with VS to make an Add-In work. Remember, this is a VS project, just like all of the other projects you can create. You're free to add classes containing your functionality and have code in *Connect* call your classes, organize code into folders, or add a class library to the solution and call code in the class library. The next section discusses internals of *Connect* in detail.

The other items of note in this project are the files with the *.AddIn extensions. These are the deployment files. There was a time when you were required to go into the Windows registry to configure an Add-In, but not anymore. The Add-In configuration is done in the *.AddIn files, which contains XML. In a later section of this chapter, you'll see the internals of the *.AddIn file and learn how to manipulate this file for deployment.

Additionally, one of the *.AddIn files has a shortcut arrow, which is a special shortcut to a file used for debugging. If you look at the properties for this shortcut file, you'll notice that it points at your Documents\Visual Studio 2010\Addins\folder, which is a deployment location. Whenever you debug this application, VS uses the debugging *.AddIn file to load the Add-In in a new copy of VS. You would manipulate the Add-In in the new copy of VS, and your current copy of VS, in debugging mode, can hit breakpoints and debug the Add-In.

Now that you know the key elements of an Add-In project, the next section drills down into the *Connect* class and describes the members that interact with VS to run an Add-In.

Drilling into the *Connect* Class

The *Connect* class implements two interfaces, *IDTExtensibility2* and *IDTCommandTarget,* and contains several members. Before examining the code, you'll learn about the interfaces, their members, and purpose.

The purpose of the interfaces (*IDTExtensibility2* and *IDTCommandTarget*) is to help manage the lifetime of the Add-In. VS understands these interfaces, but it doesn't know anything about the code you write. Therefore, you have to bridge the gap between your code and what VS needs to make an Add-In work. To do this, you use a class (*Connect*) that implements the interfaces (*IDTExtensibility2* and *IDTCommandTarget*). Then you place your code into methods, members of *Connect,* that implement (match) the interfaces. When VS communicates with the interfaces, your code (implementing the interface) executes.

Member	Purpose
OnAddInsUpdate	Add-In is either loaded or unloaded.
OnBeginShutdown	Add-In is running and VS shuts down.
OnConnection	Add-In is loaded.
OnDisconnection	Add-In is unloaded.
OnStartupComplete	VS has started up and then Add-In is loaded.

Table 13-1   The *IDTExtensibility2* Interface

It's like people from different countries trying to communicate, where they have a subject to discuss but need a common language to be able to understand each other; the common language would be the interface between the people.

The first interface to discuss is *IDTExtensibility2,* whose purpose is to let VS manage loading and unloading of the Add-In. Loading and unloading are important because VS loads Add-Ins when it starts and unloads Add-Ins when it shuts down. There are certain actions that you might want to take, depending on when the Add-In is loaded and what type of information you might need access to. For example, the very first time an Add-In is ever loaded, you might want to perform a special operation like configuration or asking the user if she would like to register your Add-In. Table 13-1 shows the members of *IDTExtensibility2* and describes their purpose.

The second interface that *Connect* implements is *IDTCommandTarget.* When building an Add-In, you need a way for the VS IDE to execute the Add-In. For example, you will create a named command that exposes the Add-In as a menu item in the Tools menu. Whenever a user selects the menu item, the named command will execute and run your Add-In code. *IDTCommandTarget* is the interface VS uses to execute your Add-In. Table 13-2 shows the members of *IDTCommandTarget* and describes their purpose.

Each of the methods of both the *IDTExtensibility2* and *IDCommandTarget* interfaces are implemented by the provided *Connect* class. Listing 13-1 shows each of these members with full documentation comments and skeleton code. The code in Listing 13-1 is in C#, but it is very informative to take the overview of the interfaces from the previous table and then

Member	Purpose
Exec	Called by VS to execute your Add-In.
QueryStatus	Called by VS to determine if the command should be enabled, invisible, or supported.

Table 13-2   The *IDTCommandTarget* Interface

take an even closer look at the comments in the code for a better understanding of what that code does. The code comments are exactly the same in VB. Some of the comments refer to the host application, where the host is either the VS IDE or the VS Macro Editor, as was selected while running the Add-In Project Wizard in the preceding section and shown in Figure 13-3. I've removed the contents of each method because subsequent sections of this chapter will explain important method implementations and how to make the Add-In perform useful operations.

Listing 13-1   Skeleton code for the *Connect* class

```
using System;
using Extensibility;
using EnvDTE;
using EnvDTE80;
using Microsoft.VisualStudio.CommandBars;
using System.Resources;
using System.Reflection;
using System.Globalization;

namespace KeystrokeFinder
{
    /// <summary>The object for implementing an Add-in.</summary>
    /// <seealso class='IDTExtensibility2' />
    public class Connect : IDTExtensibility2, IDTCommandTarget
    {
        /// <summary>
        /// Implements the constructor for the Add-in object.
        /// Place your initialization code within this method.
        /// </summary>
        public Connect()
        {
        }

        /// <summary>
        /// Implements the OnConnection method of the
        /// IDTExtensibility2 interface. Receives notification
        /// that the Add-in is being loaded.
        /// </summary>
        /// <param term='application'>
        /// Root object of the host application.
        /// </param>
        /// <param term='connectMode'>
        /// Describes how the Add-in is being loaded.
        /// </param>
```

```
/// <param term='addInInst'>
/// Object representing this Add-in.
/// </param>
/// <seealso class='IDTExtensibility2' />
public void OnConnection(
    object application, ext_ConnectMode connectMode,
    object addInInst, ref Array custom)
{
}


/// <summary>
/// Implements the OnDisconnection method of the
/// IDTExtensibility2 interface. Receives notification
/// that the Add-in is being unloaded.
/// </summary>
/// <param term='disconnectMode'>
/// Describes how the Add-in is being unloaded.
/// </param>
/// <param term='custom'>
/// Array of parameters that are host application specific.
/// </param>
/// <seealso class='IDTExtensibility2' />
public void OnDisconnection(
    ext_DisconnectMode disconnectMode, ref Array custom)
{
}


/// <summary>
/// Implements the OnAddInsUpdate method of the
/// IDTExtensibility2 interface. Receives notification
/// when the collection of Add-ins has changed.
/// </summary>
/// <param term='custom'>
/// Array of parameters that are host application specific.
/// </param>
/// <seealso class='IDTExtensibility2' />
public void OnAddInsUpdate(ref Array custom)
{
}


/// <summary>
/// Implements the OnStartupComplete method of the
/// IDTExtensibility2 interface. Receives notification
/// that the host application has completed loading.
/// </summary>
/// <param term='custom'>
```

```
/// Array of parameters that are host application specific.
/// </param>
/// <seealso class='IDTExtensibility2' />
public void OnStartupComplete(ref Array custom)
{
}


/// <summary>
/// Implements the OnBeginShutdown method of the
/// IDTExtensibility2 interface. Receives notification
/// that the host application is being unloaded.
/// </summary>
/// <param term='custom'>
/// Array of parameters that are host application specific.
/// </param>
/// <seealso class='IDTExtensibility2' />
public void OnBeginShutdown(ref Array custom)
{
}


/// <summary>
/// Implements the QueryStatus method of the
/// IDTCommandTarget interface. This is called
/// when the command's availability is updated
/// </summary>
/// <param term='commandName'>
/// The name of the command to determine state for.
/// </param>
/// <param term='neededText'>
/// Text that is needed for the command.
/// </param>
/// <param term='status'>
/// The state of the command in the user interface.
/// </param>
/// <param term='commandText'>
/// Text requested by the neededText parameter.
/// </param>
/// <seealso class='Exec' />
public void QueryStatus(
    string commandName,
    vsCommandStatusTextWanted neededText,
    ref vsCommandStatus status,
    ref object commandText)
{
}
```

```
/// <summary>
/// Implements the Exec method of the IDTCommandTarget
/// interface. This is called when the command is invoked.
/// </summary>
/// <param term='commandName'>
/// The name of the command to execute.
/// </param>
/// <param term='executeOption'>
/// Describes how the command should be run.
/// </param>
/// <param term='varIn'>
/// Parameters passed from the caller to the command handler.
/// </param>
/// <param term='varOut'>
/// Parameters passed from the command handler to the caller.
/// </param>
/// <param term='handled'>
/// Informs the caller if the command was handled or not.
/// </param>
/// <seealso class='Exec' />
public void Exec(
        string commandName, vsCommandExecOption executeOption,
        ref object varIn, ref object varOut, ref bool handled)
{
}
private DTE2 _applicationObject;
private AddIn _addInInstance;
    }
}
```

You've had an overview of what the *IDTExtensibility2* and *IDTCommandTarget* interfaces do and reviewed the comments in Listing 13-1. In the next section, you'll see how to add your own code to the interface methods to make the *KeystrokeFinder* Add-In perform some useful work.

Adding Functionality to an Add-In

When implementing the functionality of an Add-In, you'll be most concerned with capturing the call to *Exec,* which VS calls whenever the user selects the Tools menu item for your Add-In. This section will also cover a couple of other methods: *OnConnection,* which contains a lot of initialization code, and *QueryStatus,* which is handy for managing the state of the Add-In menu item. We'll look at *OnConnection* first so that you can see how the Add-In is initialized.

Reviewing the *OnConnection* Method

As you learned earlier, the *Connect* class implements various interface methods so that VS can call into those methods to run your Add-In. One of the primary methods is *OnConnection,* which is a member of the *IDTExtensibility2* interface. VS calls *OnConnection* when the Add-In loads. When calling *OnConnection,* VS passes four parameters that you can use to initialize the Add-In. The Add-In Project Wizard, covered in a previous section of this chapter, generates much skeleton code that uses parameter values in *OnConnection* to initialize the Add-In. While the example in this chapter doesn't modify the *OnConnection* method, understanding the code is helpful in learning how the Add-In initializes and how it does affect the code you will write later. We'll first take another look at *OnConnection* parameters and then examine the generated code.

Understanding *OnConnection* Parameters

The *OnConnection* method has four parameters. Each of the parameters are passed to the *OnConnection* method by VS; these parameters provide all of the information necessary for initializing the Add-In. Table 13-3 lists each parameter and its purpose.

Member	Type	Purpose
application	Compile-time type is *Object,* but the runtime type is defined by the version you're at. For example, on older versions of VS, the runtime type of Application was *DTE,* but the runtime type of Application in VS 2010 is *DTE2.*	Application is the parent object for the entire VS automation model. You use this to access all of the windows, commands, and other parts of the IDE.
connectMode	Enum of type *ext_ConnectMode*	Read this parameter to figure out when and how the Add-In was loaded. In a following section, you'll see how the *OnConnection* method reads this value to figure out when the Add-In loads for the first time.
addInInst	The compile-time type is *Object,* but runtime type is *AddIn.*	This refers to the Add-In itself, allowing you to inspect various properties of the Add-In.
custom	Array	These aren't used in the current example, but consider the fact that we're implementing an interface. Besides VS 2010, you could have another application (host) that supported Add-Ins that implement the *IDTExtensibility2* interface. Those hosts could use the custom array parameter to pass information specific to that application. Therefore, *custom* is another extensibility point to make the *IDTExtensibility2* interface more flexible.

Table 13-3 *OnConnection* Method Parameters

Reviewing *OnConnection* Generated Code

You know that the purpose of the *OnConnection* method is to help initialize the Add-In, and you've seen the parameters populated by VS and what each parameter means. Listing 13-2 shows the code generated by VS after the Add-In Project Wizard completes. It reflects the result of choosing to have a command bar UI, shown in Figure 13-5. Code comments were omitted to place more focus on the code itself.

Listing 13-2   The *OnConnection* method

C#:

```csharp
public void OnConnection(
    object application, ext_ConnectMode connectMode,
    object addInInst, ref Array custom)
{
    _applicationObject = (DTE2)application;
    _addInInstance = (AddIn)addInInst;
    if(connectMode == ext_ConnectMode.ext_cm_UISetup)
    {
        object []contextGUIDS = new object[] { };
        Commands2 commands =
          (Commands2)_applicationObject.Commands;
        string toolsMenuName = "Tools";

        Microsoft.VisualStudio.CommandBars.CommandBar
            menuBarCommandBar = ((
                Microsoft.VisualStudio.CommandBars.CommandBars)
                _applicationObject.CommandBars)["MenuBar"];
        CommandBarControl toolsControl =
            menuBarCommandBar.Controls[toolsMenuName];
        CommandBarPopup toolsPopup =
          (CommandBarPopup)toolsControl;

        try
        {
            Command command = commands.AddNamedCommand2(
                _addInInstance, "KeystrokeFinder",
                "KeystrokeFinder",
                "Executes the command for KeystrokeFinder",
                true, 59, ref contextGUIDS,
                (int)vsCommandStatus
                    .vsCommandStatusSupported+
                (int)vsCommandStatus.vsCommandStatusEnabled,
```

```
                        (int)vsCommandStyle
                            .vsCommandStylePictAndText,
                        vsCommandControlType
                            .vsCommandControlTypeButton);

                if((command != null) &&
                    (toolsPopup != null))
                {
                    command.AddControl(
                        toolsPopup.CommandBar, 1);
                }
            }
            catch(System.ArgumentException)
            {
            }
        }
    }
```

VB:

```
Public Sub OnConnection(
    ByVal application As Object,
    ByVal connectMode As ext_ConnectMode,
    ByVal addInInst As Object,
    ByRef custom As Array) Implements IDTExtensibility2.OnConnection
    _applicationObject = CType(application, DTE2)
    _addInInstance = CType(addInInst, AddIn)

    If connectMode = ext_ConnectMode.ext_cm_UISetup Then

        Dim commands As Commands2 =
            CType(_applicationObject.Commands, Commands2)
        Dim toolsMenuName As String = "Tools"

        Dim commandBars As CommandBars =
            CType(_applicationObject.CommandBars, CommandBars)
        Dim menuBarCommandBar As CommandBar =
            commandBars.Item("MenuBar")

        Dim toolsControl As CommandBarControl =
            menuBarCommandBar.Controls.Item(toolsMenuName)
        Dim toolsPopup As CommandBarPopup =
            CType(toolsControl, CommandBarPopup)

        Try
```

```
Dim command As Command =
    commands.AddNamedCommand2(
        _addInInstance, "KeystrokeFinderVB",
        "KeystrokeFinderVB",
        "Executes the command for KeystrokeFinderVB",
        True, 59, Nothing,
        CType(vsCommandStatus.vsCommandStatusSupported,
            Integer) +
        CType(vsCommandStatus.vsCommandStatusEnabled,
            Integer),
        vsCommandStyle.vsCommandStylePictAndText,
        vsCommandControlType.vsCommandControlTypeButton)

    command.AddControl(toolsPopup.CommandBar, 1)
Catch argumentException As System.ArgumentException
End Try

    End If
End Sub
```

Dissecting Listing 13-2 into its constituent parts demonstrates the role *OnConnection* has and how it affects subsequent code. The first part of the method obtains references to a couple of important objects: *application* and *addInInst.* The following excerpt shows how to obtain a reference to these objects and convert them to *DTE2* and *AddIn,* respectively. The references to *_applicationObject* and *_addInInstance* are fields of the *Connect* class, which is important because now other methods of the class will be able to access these objects.

C#:

```
_applicationObject = (DTE2)application;
_addInInstance = (AddIn)addInInst;
```

VB:

```
_applicationObject = CType(application, DTE2)
_addInInstance = CType(addInInst, AddIn)
```

The remaining code in *OnConnection* sets up the menu item under the Tools menu, as directed by choosing to build a command UI, shown in Figure 13-5. However, this only occurs one time—the first time the application runs. To make sure the menu item sets up one time, the code checks the *connectMode* parameter to see if it's set to *ext_ConnectMode.ext_cm_UISetup,* as shown in the following code. The remaining code in the *OnConnection* method will only execute if the following condition is true:

C#:

```
if(connectMode == ext_ConnectMode.ext_cm_UISetup)
```

VB:

```
If connectMode = ext_ConnectMode.ext_cm_UISetup Then
```

The first time the code runs, the code within the preceding *if* statement will execute, creating a menu item for the KeystrokeFinder Add-In in the Tools menu. Code examples that follow in this section are all contained within the preceding *if* statement; this is good information to know because it shows you how to navigate the VS object model to find something.

The following code uses *_applicationObject* to get a list of commands, which is a list of all the actions you can take with VS. As discussed earlier, *_applicationObject* is type *DTE2* and serves as the parent object for accessing all functionality in VS.

C#:

```
Commands2 commands =
    (Commands2)_applicationObject.Commands;
```

VB:

```
Dim commands As Commands2 =
    CType(_applicationObject.Commands, Commands2)
```

In the VS automation object model, a menu item is called a *CommandBar*. So, you get a reference to a *CommandBars* collection, again through *_applicationObject,* to reference the *MenuBar,* which is the main VS menu, assigned to *menuBarCommandBar*:

C#:

```
Microsoft.VisualStudio.CommandBars.CommandBar
    menuBarCommandBar = ((
        Microsoft.VisualStudio.CommandBars.CommandBars)
        _applicationObject.CommandBars)["MenuBar"];
```

VB:

```
Dim commandBars As CommandBars =
    CType(_applicationObject.CommandBars, CommandBars)
Dim menuBarCommandBar As CommandBar =
    commandBars.Item("MenuBar")
```

Within the *CommandBars* collection, *menuBarCommandBar,* you then look into the *Controls* collection, which is a list of menus on the main menu to find the Tools menu, assigned to *toolsControl* as follows:

C#:

```
string toolsMenuName = "Tools";
CommandBarControl toolsControl =
    menuBarCommandBar.Controls[toolsMenuName];
```

VB:

```
Dim toolsMenuName As String = "Tools"
Dim toolsControl As CommandBarControl =
    menuBarCommandBar.Controls.Item(toolsMenuName)
```

In the VS automation object model, an individual menu is a *CommandBarPopup,* assigned to *toolsPopup* as follows:

C#:

```
CommandBarPopup toolsPopup =
  (CommandBarPopup)toolsControl;
```

VB:

```
Dim toolsPopup As CommandBarPopup =
    CType(toolsControl, CommandBarPopup)
```

Now you have a reference to the menu where the menu item for the Add-In must be added. You are ready to add the command, using the *AddNamedCommand2* method of the commands collection. Remember that earlier code assigned these commands from the application object to the commands variable. A quick review of the arguments to *AddNamedCommand2* gives you the gist of what's happening: The code passes a reference to the Add-In; provides a menu item name and description; and indicates that the status of the command is supported and enabled, the menu item will have pictures and text, and the type of menu item is button (can be clicked). If you want all the details of this method call, now is a good time to refer to the documentation. While it's important to understand the major interfaces, such as *OnConnection* for *IDTExtensibility2,* memorizing every API call might not be the most productive use of your time when you're just starting out. The following code shows the call to *AddNamedCommand2*:

C#:

```
Command command = commands.AddNamedCommand2(
    _addInInstance, "KeystrokeFinder",
    "KeystrokeFinder",
    "Executes the command for KeystrokeFinder",
```

```
    true, 59, ref contextGUIDS,
    (int)vsCommandStatus
        .vsCommandStatusSupported+
    (int)vsCommandStatus.vsCommandStatusEnabled,
    (int)vsCommandStyle
        .vsCommandStylePictAndText,
    vsCommandControlType
        .vsCommandControlTypeButton);
```

VB:

```
Dim command As Command =
    commands.AddNamedCommand2(
        _addInInstance, "KeystrokeFinderVB",
        "KeystrokeFinderVB",
        "Executes the command for KeystrokeFinderVB",
        True, 59, Nothing,
        CType(vsCommandStatus.vsCommandStatusSupported,
            Integer) +
        CType(vsCommandStatus.vsCommandStatusEnabled,
            Integer),
        vsCommandStyle.vsCommandStylePictAndText,
        vsCommandControlType.vsCommandControlTypeButton)
```

AddNamedCommand2 returned a *Command* object, *command,* which must be placed into VS somewhere so that a user can click it to invoke the Add-In. The next statement accomplishes this task by adding *command* to the Tools menu. As you may recall from previous examples, the code searched for and obtained a reference to the Tools menu. After ensuring that both the *command* and *toolsPopup* refer to valid objects (a best practice), the following code places command into the first position (at the top) of the Tools menu:

C#:

```
if ((command != null) &&
    (toolsPopup != null))
{
    command.AddControl(
        toolsPopup.CommandBar, 1);
}
```

VB:

```
command.AddControl(toolsPopup.CommandBar, 1)
```

This completes the responsibilities of the *OnConnection* method. If you had your own code for initializing the Add-In, the *OnConnection* method would be a good place to put it. The preceding example was useful because now you know how to access VS menus and commands. The example also demonstrated the importance of the main application object and how it's used as the starting point for getting to other part of VS.

As you may recall, the *OnConnection* method assigned the main application object to *_applicationObject,* a field of the *Connect* class. This is important because now you have access to the main application object, and you'll see how it's used in the next section, which shows you how to execute your Add-In via the *Exec* method.

Implementing the *Exec* Method

Whenever a user starts your Add-In, VS calls the *Exec* method of the *IDTCommandTarget* interface. The *Exec* method is important because that's where you add your code to implement the behavior of your Add-In. The previous sections discussed code that is generated by VS, but Listing 13-3 contains code for the *Exec* method that you should enter yourself to make the KeystrokeFinder Add-In work. The purpose of the Add-In for this section is to list all VS commands and their associated shortcut keys. The list of commands and shortcuts will be displayed in the VS Output window. Listing 13-3 shows the *Exec* method for the KeystrokeFinder Add-In.

Listing 13-3   Implementing the Exec method

C#:

```csharp
public void Exec(
    string commandName, vsCommandExecOption executeOption,
    ref object varIn, ref object varOut, ref bool handled)
{
    handled = false;
    if(executeOption ==
        vsCommandExecOption.vsCommandExecOptionDoDefault)
    {
        if (commandName ==
            "KeystrokeFinder.Connect.KeystrokeFinder")
        {
            OutputWindow outWin =
                _applicationObject.ToolWindows.OutputWindow;
            OutputWindowPane outPane =
                outWin.OutputWindowPanes.Add(
                    "Keyboard Shortcuts");
            outPane.Activate();

            foreach (Command cmd in
                _applicationObject.Commands)
            {
                object[] cmdBindings =
                    cmd.Bindings as object[];
```

```
                    if (cmdBindings.Length > 0)
                    {
                        string bindingStr =
                            string.Join(", ", cmdBindings);
                        outPane.OutputString(
                            "Command: " + cmd.Name +
                            ", Shortcut: " + bindingStr +
                            "\n");
                    }
                }

                handled = true;
                return;
            }
        }
    }
```

VB:

```
Public Sub Exec(
    ByVal commandName As String,
    ByVal executeOption As vsCommandExecOption,
    ByRef varIn As Object, ByRef varOut As Object,
    ByRef handled As Boolean) Implements IDTCommandTarget.Exec
    handled = False
    If executeOption =
        vsCommandExecOption.vsCommandExecOptionDoDefault Then
        If commandName =
            "KeystrokeFinderVB.Connect.KeystrokeFinderVB" Then

            Dim outWin As OutputWindow =
                _applicationObject.ToolWindows.OutputWindow

            Dim outPane As OutputWindowPane =
                outWin.OutputWindowPanes.Add(
                    "Keyboard Shortcuts")

            outPane.Activate()

            For Each cmd As Command In _applicationObject.Commands

                Dim cmdBindings As Object() =
                    CType(cmd.Bindings, Object())

                If cmdBindings.Length > 0 Then

                    Dim bindingStr As String =
                        String.Join(", ", cmdBindings)
```

```
            outPane.OutputString(
                "Command: " & cmd.Name &
                ", Shortcut: " & bindingStr &
                Environment.NewLine)

          End If

      Next

      handled = True
      Exit Sub
    End If
  End If
End Sub
```

The *executeOption* parameter of *Exec* allows you to determine whether you want to prompt the user for input, perform the action, or show help, which are options of the *vsCommandExecOption*. All you need to do is check the option and perform the operation for the current value of *executeOption*. In the current Add-In, we only check for *vsCommandExec OptionDoDefault,* which means to just perform the operation:

C#:

```
if(executeOption ==
    vsCommandExecOption.vsCommandExecOptionDoDefault)
```

VB:

```
If executeOption =
    vsCommandExecOption.vsCommandExecOptionDoDefault Then
```

The example in this chapter only has one command, but you could potentially have multiple commands if you decided to add more commands in the *OnConnection* method. Add an *if* statement to ensure you're executing code for the proper command, such as the following code:

C#:

```
if (commandName ==
    "KeystrokeFinder.Connect.KeystrokeFinder")
```

VB:

```
If commandName =
    "KeystrokeFinderVB.Connect.KeystrokeFinderVB" Then
```

As you learned earlier, the application object is the starting point for accessing all VS objects. Since we need to write to the Output window, the code accesses the *ToolWindows* property of the application object, which provides access to multiple VS windows. The following code obtains a reference to the *OutputWindow,* adds a new pane, and activates the pane:

C#:

```
OutputWindow outWin =
    _applicationObject.ToolWindows.OutputWindow;
OutputWindowPane outPane =
    outWin.OutputWindowPanes.Add(
        "Keyboard Shortcuts");
outPane.Activate();
```

VB:

```
Dim outWin As OutputWindow =
    _applicationObject.ToolWindows.OutputWindow

Dim outPane As OutputWindowPane =
    outWin.OutputWindowPanes.Add(
        "Keyboard Shortcuts")

outPane.Activate()
```

Going back to the application object, we need to access the *Commands* collection, using a *foreach* loop to access each *Command* object. Each command name is in the *Name* property. The *Bindings* property is a collection of shortcut keys for the command. Some commands have no shortcut keys, as indicated by an empty *Bindings* collection (its *Length* property will be set to 0), so we skip them. The following code shows how to iterate through all VS commands and print each command name and associated shortcut keys to the Output window:

C#:

```
foreach (Command cmd in
    _applicationObject.Commands)
{
    object[] cmdBindings =
        cmd.Bindings as object[];

    if (cmdBindings.Length > 0)
    {
        string bindingStr =
            string.Join(", ", cmdBindings);
        outPane.OutputString(
            "Command: " + cmd.Name +
```

```
            ", Shortcut: " + bindingStr +
            "\n");
    }
}

handled = true;
```

   VB:

```
For Each cmd As Command In _applicationObject.Commands

    Dim cmdBindings As Object() =
        CType(cmd.Bindings, Object())

    If cmdBindings.Length > 0 Then

        Dim bindingStr As String =
            String.Join(", ", cmdBindings)

        outPane.OutputString(
            "Command: " & cmd.Name &
            ", Shortcut: " & bindingStr &
            Environment.NewLine)

    End If

Next

handled = True
```

Notice how we set *handled* to *true,* letting VS know that the code recognized and acted on the command. Besides letting users execute the Add-In, you want to ensure their experience with the Add-In is logical and the command displays its status properly, as you'll learn about in the next section.

Setting Status with *QueryStatus*

While VS is working with your Add-In, it will call the *QueryStatus* method of *IDTCommandTarget* to ensure it displays the command properly. Listing 13-4 shows the default implementation of *QueryStatus.*

Listing 13-4 The *QueryStatus* method

   C#:

```
public void QueryStatus(
    string commandName,
```

```csharp
    vsCommandStatusTextWanted neededText,
    ref vsCommandStatus status,
    ref object commandText)
{
    if(neededText ==
        vsCommandStatusTextWanted
            .vsCommandStatusTextWantedNone)
    {
        if(commandName ==
            "KeystrokeFinder.Connect.KeystrokeFinder")
        {
            status =
                (vsCommandStatus)
                vsCommandStatus.vsCommandStatusSupported|
                vsCommandStatus.vsCommandStatusEnabled;
            return;
        }
    }
}
```

VB:

```vbnet
Public Sub QueryStatus(
    ByVal commandName As String,
    ByVal neededText As vsCommandStatusTextWanted,
    ByRef status As vsCommandStatus,
    ByRef commandText As Object) Implements IDTCommandTarget.
QueryStatus

    If neededText =
        vsCommandStatusTextWanted.vsCommandStatusTextWantedNone Then

        If commandName =
            "KeystrokeFinderVB.Connect.KeystrokeFinderVB" Then

            status =
                CType(vsCommandStatus.vsCommandStatusEnabled +
                    vsCommandStatus.vsCommandStatusSupported,
                    vsCommandStatus)

        Else

            status = vsCommandStatus.vsCommandStatusUnsupported

        End If
    End If
End Sub
```

The *QueryStatus* method in Listing 13-4 checks the *commandName* to ensure it's working with the right Add-In. If so, it sets the status parameter to a combination of values from the *vsCommandStatus* enum. In Listing 13-4, the status is supported and enabled.

This demonstrated how to create an Add-In. Next, you'll learn how to deploy the Add-In.

Deploying an Add-In

There are two files involved in deploying your Add-In: a *.AddIn file and *.dll. The *.AddIn file contains registration information for your Add-In, and *.dll is the class library output assembly that contains your Add-In.

You can deploy the *.AddIn file by copying it into a folder that VS recognizes. There is a specified set of folders that VS recognizes, but you can add your own folder location. To see what the VS settings are, select Tools | Options | Environment | Add-in/Macros Security. You'll see a window similar to Figure 13-8. The Add-in/Macros Security window also has options that allow you to determine if macros can run, if any Add-Ins can load, or if Add-Ins are allowed to load over the Internet.

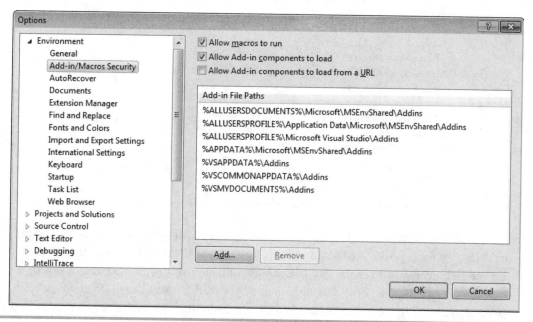

Figure 13-8   The Add-in/Macros Security window

In addition to the *.AddIn file, you'll need to determine where the Add-In class library file (*.dll) will reside. By default, the Add-In Project Wizard assumes that the *.dll file is deployed in the same location as the *.AddIn file. Listing 13-5 shows the contents of the *.AddIn file. The location of the *.dll file is specified in the *Assembly* element, which can be either a file system path or a URL.

Listing 13-5   Contents of the * .AddIn file

```xml
<?xml version="1.0" encoding="UTF-16" standalone="no"?>
<Extensibility xmlns=
"http://schemas.microsoft.com/AutomationExtensibility">
    <HostApplication>
        <Name>Microsoft Visual Studio</Name>
        <Version>10.0</Version>
    </HostApplication>
    <Addin>
        <FriendlyName>Keystroke Finder</FriendlyName>
        <Description>
Displays a List of VS Shortcut Keystrokes.
        </Description>
        <AboutBoxDetails>
Creating an Add-...
        </AboutBoxDetails>
        <AboutIconData>...</AboutIconData>
        <Assembly>KeystrokeFinder.dll</Assembly>
        <FullClassName>
KeystrokeFinder.Connect
        </FullClassName>
        <LoadBehavior>1</LoadBehavior>
        <CommandPreload>1</CommandPreload>
        <CommandLineSafe>0</CommandLineSafe>
    </Addin>
</Extensibility>
```

Another way to work with Add-Ins is via the Add-In Manager, which you can open by selecting Tools | Add-in Manager. Figure 13-9 shows the Add-In Manager with the KeystrokeFinder Add-In in the list. Checking Available Add-Ins immediately loads or unloads the Add-In, checking Startup indicates whether the Add-In will load when VS starts, and checking Command Line makes the Add-In load if a user runs VS (devenv.exe) via the command line.

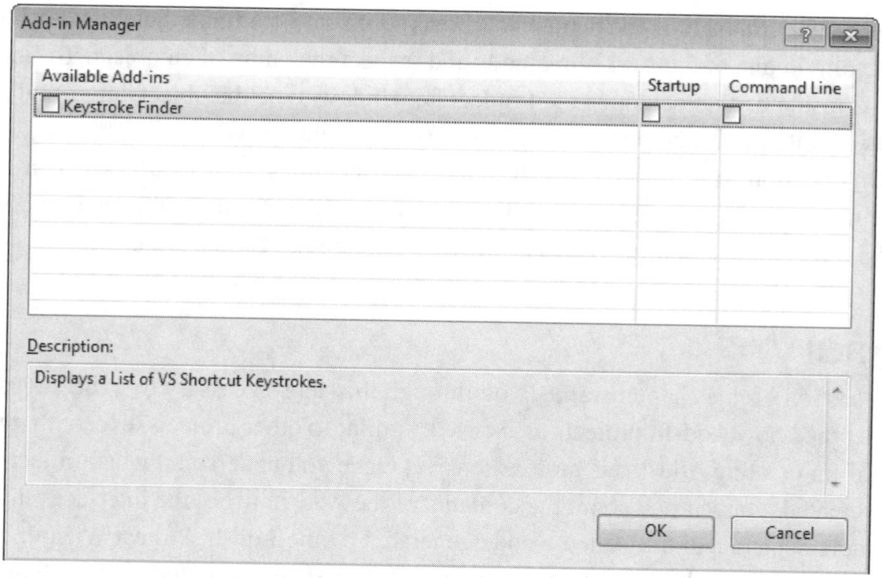

Figure 13-9   The Add-In Manager

Once the Add-In is deployed and loaded, a user can run the Add-In by selecting Tools | KeystrokeFinder. When the Add-In runs, the Output window will contain a listing of commands and shortcut keys. To see the results, you should open the Output window, CTRL-W-O, before running the Add-In.

Now you know how to create and deploy an Add-In, but you'll also need some guidance in moving forward to help you create your own Add-Ins. The next section provides that guidance.

Where to Go Next

As you've seen in previous sections, the application object is central to getting started with Add-In development. Whenever you need to find something, use the application object reference, press the DOT on your keyboard, and Intellisense will show you properties such as commands and windows.

As you view the application object properties, have the VS documentation open, telling you what each property means and providing example code of how it works.

Sometimes there aren't examples and the documentation isn't as clear as it could be. In those cases, you might have to perform some investigation. The tools to perform this investigation include the debugger's breakpoints and the Immediate window. Set a breakpoint in one of the Add-In methods and inspect the value of an object. To find out what is inside that object, open the Immediate window, type the object name, and press DOT to let Intellisense help you find properties you're interested in.

On occasion, you'll have properties that are collections. In that case, you can write code in the Add-In method you want the access the collection through, add a *foreach* (*For Each* in VB) loop, and print values of the collection to the Output window.

Summary

Each section of this chapter walked you through the steps necessary to write an Add-In. You learned how Add-In projects are started, similar to other projects, except that the wizard for creating Add-Ins is more extensive. Once you understood what project items were created, you learned about the contents of the Add-In itself, the interfaces that are implemented, and the skeleton code generated by the Add-In Project Wizard. This chapter showed you how to add code to the Add-In to make it perform a search of all VS commands and their related shortcut keys. This process demonstrated how you could access anything throughout VS via code. You learned how to deploy and manage an Add-In and then finished off with tips on moving forward to create your own Add-Ins.

This is the last chapter of this book, but only the beginning for your software development experience using Microsoft Visual Studio 2010. I sincerely appreciate your reading my book and hope that it propels you to greater skill and success.

—Joe Mayo

Part V

Appendixes

Appendix A

Introduction to XML

Extensible Markup Language (XML) is an open-standards cross-platform way of specifying documents. At its origins, XML was used to represent data, but it has grown in use to include user interface technologies and even executable logic. While there are many practical uses of XML, this book is mostly concerned with explaining how XML is used for ASP.NET, Silverlight, and Windows Presentation Foundation (WPF), all of which are discussed in chapters of this book. In each of these scenarios, some specialization of XML is being used to construct user interfaces. In ASP.NET, you use XML for HTML (XHTML). Both Silverlight and WPF use XML Application Markup Language (XAML), pronounced "Zamel." Before learning about XHTML or XAML, you might want an introduction or refresher on XML, which is the purpose of this appendix. While this introduction won't teach you everything about XML, it will give you the essentials that can help when seeing how XML is being used.

VS 2010 XML Editor

You can create your own XML documents in VS 2010 with the XML editor. There are a couple of ways to open a new XML document, within or without a project. Without a project, select File | New | File and select XML File, and click OK. You can rename the file (for instance, Customer.xml) when saving. Within a project, right-click the project, select Add | New Item, select the Data list, select XML File, give the document a name (for instance, Customer.xml), and click OK. What this gives you is an editor with Intellisense support that is better than Notepad. Listing A-1 shows an XML document that holds customer data.

Listing A-1   An XML document example

```
<?xml version="1.0" encoding="utf-8" ?>
<customer id="7">
  <name>Joe</name>
  <address>123 4th St</address>
</customer>
```

As you can see in Listing A-1, an XML document is readable text. It contains data, and the meaning of that data is specific to the applications that need to use it. The following sections will decipher Listing A-1 and explain what each part of the document means.

XML Prefixes

The top of the document in Listing A-1 contains an XML prefix, repeated here for convenience:

```
<?xml version="1.0" encoding="utf-8" ?>
```

The prefix is common for letting applications reading the document know that it is indeed an XML document. The version is self-describing. Encoding is important because it specifies the binary format of the text. If you have one application passing data to another application, it's important that both applications can read the document and are using the same encoding. The utf-8 encoding is the default and for the purpose of this book is the only encoding you will care about.

The angle brackets, < and >, define the markup in XML. For the file prefix, content is placed between <? and ?> character sequences, but as the following sections show, most other markup is different.

XML Elements

The XML elements in Listing A-1 are customer, name, and address. Each element is defined by matching pairs of markup, following this pattern:

```
<elementName>value</elementName>
```

In the previous example, *elementName* is the name of the element and value is the data associated with that element. Elements always have a begin tag and an end tag. You can identify the end tag because it always follows the begin tag eventually (there may be other element tags nested in between the pair) and contains a forward slash character before the element name.

The value in the previous example can sometimes be blank, meaning there is no value for that element. A value can also be one or more elements, such as customer, in Listing A-1, which contains name and address elements. In Listing A-1, the value of name is *Joe* and the value of address is *123 4th St.* In addition to elements, you can have attributes, discussed next.

Attributes

An attribute decorates an element with a single value, such as in the following example:

```
<elementName attributeName="attributeValue">
    elementValue
</elementName>
```

Notice that the attribute, *attributeName,* is inside of the start tag of the element. It contains an equal sign and a quoted value. You can have multiple attributes on a single element and they'll be separated by spaces. Remember that attributes can have only one value, but if you need to define more than one value, you must use elements.

Examples of attributes in Listing A-1 are version and encoding in the prefix and id on customer.

Namespaces

Another important part of XML that you'll need to understand is namespaces. In Chapter 2, you learned how namespaces in C# and VB help give a unique identity to code within a given namespace. The purpose of namespaces in XML is similar. In the case of Listing A-1, there is a customer element, but think about how many different programs work with customer data. A customer in one program will not be defined the same as a customer in another program, and you need a way to tell them apart, which is where namespaces come in. You would define your customer data in a namespace of your choosing, and some other developer would define a unique namespace for their customer. That way, your programs won't ever be confused if they try to read the wrong data. Listing A-2 shows how to use a namespace to make a customer unique.

TIP

You might have noticed that the namespaces in Listing A-2 look like Web addresses. However, this is just coincidence and is a common practice used to increase the chance that the namespace is unique. In reality, the namespace is just a string, which catches people new to namespaces off guard. For example, http://mcgraw-hill.com/vs2010bg is a different namespace than http://mcgraw-hill.com/vs2010bg/ because the extra forward slash on the end is a different string. So, if you made this mistake, then it's possible that a program won't recognize the data as being a valid format because the data is in a different namespace than what the program expects. Remember that a namespace is a unique string, not a Web address.

Listing A-2   XML namespace example

```
<?xml version="1.0" encoding="utf-8" ?>
<customer id="7"
  xmlns="http://mcgraw-hill.com/vs2010bg"
  xmlns:a="http://somedomain.com/addresses">
  <name>Joe</name>
  <a:address>123 4th St</a:address>
</customer>
```

Namespaces are specified by placing an *xmlns* attribute on an element, either with or without a prefix. The *xmlns* without a prefix specifies the default namespace for all of the elements where the namespace resides and child elements of the element where the namespace resides. This means that customer and name are in the *http://mcgraw-hill.com/vs2010bg* namespace.

Namespaces can also have prefixes to help you target where they are applied. In Listing A-2, there is an *xmlns:a,* where *a* is the prefix for the *http://somedomain.com/*

addresses namespace. The convenience of prefixes is that they help the XML be more readable. In Listing A-2, the address namespace is decorated with the *a:* prefix, as in *<a:address>* to indicate that address belongs to the *http://somedomain.com/addresses* namespace. Without the prefix, you would be forced to write the address element as follows, which is more difficult to read:

```
< http://somedomain.com/addresses:address>
    123 4th St
</ http://somedomain.com/addresses:address>
```

I added line breaks for readability, but in practice the only part of the data read is the value and not the white space, such as newlines, surrounding it.

The XML Menu

When you open an XML document in VS, you'll see an XML menu appear with options for running, debugging, and profiling XML Transformation (XSLT) documents and working with schemas. XSLT is used by a running program or utility to change an XML document from one form to another. An *XML schema* is an XML document that describes the allowable format of another XML document. An XML schema is to an XML document what a SQL table definition is to the data that the table holds. Both XSLT and schemas are outside the scope of this book, but now you know where the tools are in case you need to work with them.

Configuring XML Options

Selecting Tools | Options will open the VS Options window. From the Options window, you can select Text Editor XML and configure many options associated with writing XML documents, such as turning on line numbering or specifying tag formatting.

Summary

You should now understand the basics of working with XML in VS. You learned how to create an XML document and what prefixes, elements, attributes, and namespaces are. You also learned how to find the XML options to customize your XML document-editing experience. XML is the foundation upon which XAML and XHTML are based, which is covered in later appendices. This should give you familiarity with the XML that is presented in the chapters of this book.

Appendix B

Introduction to XAML

XML Application Markup Language (XAML), pronounced "Zamel," is an XML-based language for building user interfaces. You'll find XAML being used in both Windows Presentation Foundation (WPF) and Silverlight applications. WPF is for desktop application development, and Silverlight is for Web-based development. Both WPF and Silverlight have much in common through programming with XAML. Therefore, this Appendix provides an introduction to XAML and shows you how to perform layouts, which are common to both WPF and Silverlight. This Appendix can be useful before reading the WPF and Silverlight chapters so that you can get the most out of what is specific to each technology. For simplicity, I'll demonstrate concepts by using a WPF application, but what you learn will be applicable to both WPF and Silverlight. Before reading this Appendix, you might want to read or review Appendix A for an introduction to XML, which will provide you with familiarity of basic XML syntax.

Starting a WPF Project

As you are reading a book about VS, it's only natural that you would want to experience XAML from within the VS IDE. As stated earlier, we'll use a WPF Application project for describing XAML because it has fewer files and is simpler than a Silverlight application. To create the WPF Application project, select File | New | Project and select WPF Application in the New Project window. Name the application anything you like and click OK. What you'll see is a new project that has Window1.xaml file open in VS with contents similar to Listing B-1.

Listing B-1   A new XAML file

```
<Window x:Class="WpfApplication1.MainWindow"
        xmlns="http://schemas.microsoft.com/winfx/2006/xaml/presentation"
        xmlns:x="http://schemas.microsoft.com/winfx/2006/xaml"
        Title="MainWindow" Height="350" Width="525">
    <Grid>

    </Grid>
</Window>
```

In VS, the default layout for *Window1.xaml* is to have a visual designer on the top half of the work window and XAML in the lower half. You can view the full XAML document by grabbing the top edge of the XAML half and dragging it to the top of the screen so that you are only looking at the XAML editor. The first thing you should notice about Listing B-1 is that it is an XML document with elements, attributes, and namespaces. Each of the items you see has special meaning, as will be discussed in the following sections.

Elements as Classes

For XAML to be meaningful as code, elements must be associated with classes. The *Window* element in Listing B-1 is associated with a class named *WpfApplication1* *.MainWindow*, specified by the *x:Class* attribute. The *x* prefix aliases the *http://schemas* *.microsoft.com/winfx/2006/xaml* namespace, where the *Class* attribute is defined. By mapping the element to a class, you allow VS to compile the XAML into code that runs. Notice that the default namespace is *http://schemas.microsoft.com/winfx/2006/xaml/* *presentation*, which defines how each of the elements without prefixes will be compiled to code. The important fact to realize here is that when writing XAML, you are creating a document that will be translated into executable code for you at compile time.

Attributes as Properties

Title, *Height*, and *Width* are attributes of the Window element in Listing B-1. When VS compiles the XAML, each of the attributes of elements will be translated to properties of the class that the element is translated to. More specifically, the WpfApplication1. MainWindow class will have *Title*, *Height*, and *Width* properties. Each of the properties will be set with the value assigned to their corresponding attributes.

Executing the XAML Document

Remember that this is not a tutorial on WPF and that the focus needs to be on understanding how XAML works. Nevertheless, it's informative to see what happens when XAML is compiled and executed. Press F5 or click the Start Debugging button on the toolbar to run this program. What you'll see is a window similar to Figure B-1.

Figure B-1 shows how the *Window* element executed, creating an application window with normal title bar, minimize and close buttons, and borders. You can also see the results of applying the attributes of the *Window* element where *MainWindow* appears on the title bar and the dimensions are set by *Height* and *Width*.

This illustrates the power of XAML, where you can produce sophisticated results without writing a line of C# or VB code yourself. Of course, all of the XAML translates to code, but the declarative nature of XAML lets you say what you want without having to specify how it's done. XAML saves you from writing a lot of code to produce equivalent results. The code that actually runs is generated for you.

Figure B-1 Executing XAML

Property Elements

You've seen how attributes translate to properties. In addition to attributes, XAML has property elements, which are child elements where one or more other elements become assigned to a property. An example of a property element would be the Content property of a Button. A Button is a class in both WPF and Silverlight that a user can click to produce some action in your program. The Content property of the Button determines what the user sees. To describe the difference between a property attribute and a property element, I'll show you an example of both with the Content property of the Button class. Listing B-2 shows a Button with its Content set as an attribute.

Listing B-2   A Button with Content set as an attribute

```
<Window x:Class="WpfApplication1.MainWindow"
        xmlns="http://schemas.microsoft.com/winfx/2006/xaml/presentation"
        xmlns:x="http://schemas.microsoft.com/winfx/2006/xaml"
        Title="MainWindow" Height="350" Width="525">
    <Button Content="Click Me" />
</Window>
```

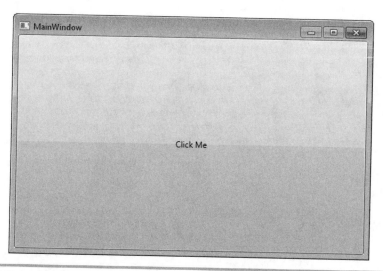

Figure B-2 A Button with its Content attribute set as Text

In Listing B-2, you can see that the *Window* has a contained *Button* element whose *Content* attribute contains text. Figure B-2 shows what this looks like when running.

A powerful feature of XAML is property elements that allow you to add sophisticated markup that will be assigned to a class property. In the case of the Button, we'll enhance the *Content* property as a property element in XAML to show how to add content other than text. The following markup is the Button from Listing B-2, enhanced to hold an image instead of text. For readability, I added a line break for the value of the *Source* attribute:

```
<Button>
    <Button.Content>
        <Image Source=
"C:\Users\Public\Pictures\Sample Pictures\Penguins.jpg" />
    </Button.Content>
</Button>
```

Instead of setting the *Content* attribute, the preceding example uses property element syntax, where the child element is named *<parentElementName.attributeName>*. The benefit of property element syntax shown in the preceding code is that the *Content* property will now be set to an image. With attribute syntax, you were limited to text, but with property element syntax, you can put anything in a button. Of course, instead of what I did with the image, you would want to use common sense and only add content that is meaningful for the application. Figure B-3 shows the new button with the image.

Figure B-3 Button with Content property element set to Image

TIP

VS provides XAML editor support by allowing you to place your cursor between begin and end tags, pressing ENTER, and indenting the start position of the cursor on the new line between the start and end tags. From that point, you can type < and begin working with Intellisense to select the element and attribute you need to implement with property element syntax.

Markup Extensions

Another extensibility point in XAML is markup extensions, which allow you to set an attribute to reference another value. Common uses of markup extensions include data binding and resource usage. Data binding is the practice of associating data with a user interface control. For example, if you needed to show a customer record on the screen, you would bind each property of the customer object to parts of the screen, such as binding a customer name to a TextBox on the screen. You'll see examples of data binding in the WPF and Silverlight chapters of this book, Chapters 8 and 10. Right now, it's important to concentrate on what a markup extension is, and you'll see an example that applies a resource to an element.

A *resource* is some type of object or value that can be used by multiple controls. For example, you can define a special color for buttons on your screen in one place and then use a markup extension to point all of these buttons to the same resource. That way, you can change the color resource in one place and all buttons referring to that color resource will change automatically. Listing B-3 defines a brush resource of a specific color and shows how to reference that brush from multiple buttons using a markup extension.

Listing B-3   Markup extension for using resources

```
<Window x:Class="WpfApplication1.MainWindow"
        xmlns="http://schemas.microsoft.com/winfx/2006/xaml/presentation"
        xmlns:x="http://schemas.microsoft.com/winfx/2006/xaml"
        Title="MainWindow" Height="350" Width="525">
    <Window.Resources>
        <SolidColorBrush x:Key="ButtonBrush" Color="Yellow" />
    </Window.Resources>
    <StackPanel>
        <Button Background="{StaticResource ResourceKey=ButtonBrush}"
            Content="Button One" />
        <Button Background="{StaticResource ResourceKey=ButtonBrush}"
            Content="Button Two" />
    </StackPanel>
</Window>
```

The *Window.Resources* element in Listing B-3 is a property element of *Window*. It contains a *SolidColorBrush* with *Color* set to *Yellow*. Everything in WPF and Silverlight is drawn with brushes, which define colors, gradients, images, media, or patterns. In this case, we'll keep it simple with a single color, which is what *SolidColorBrush* is good for. The point here is not what a brush is, but the fact that the brush is a resource that will help demonstrate how to use a markup extension to access that resource. It's important to assign a key to every resource because that key is what resource markup extensions use to identify the resource.

You can see the markup extension assigned to the *Background* attributes of the *Button* elements in Listing B-3. Markup extensions are surrounded by curly braces. Within the curly braces are the extension type and attributes associated with the extension. In Listing B-3, the extension type is *StaticResource,* which allows you to refer to a resource. The *ResourceKey* attribute of the *StaticResource* extension specifies the particular resource to use. The value, *ButtonBrush,* matches the key of the *SolidColorBrush* resource. So, the value of the *BackGround* attribute of the *Button* elements is a *StaticResource* for a *SolidColorBrush* that has its color set to *Yellow*. This effectively means that the *Buttons* will have *Yellow* backgrounds.

To see the value of using resources, consider the situation you would be in if you set the *BackGround* attribute of each button directly to *Yellow* instead of using the

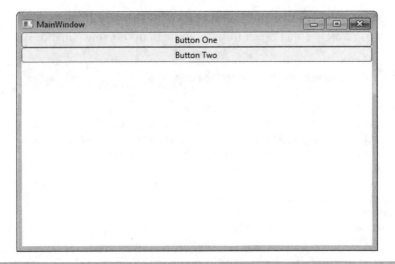

Figure B-4 Two Buttons using the same resource via a markup extension

StaticResource markup extension. Further, think about the amount of work you would need to do if you wanted to change the background color of all buttons, resulting in recoding each individual button. However, with the *StaticResource* markup extension, you can change the color in the *SolidColorBrush* resource, and the *BackGround* of all buttons will change without any additional work. Figure B-4 shows each of the buttons. Though you can't tell the background color in the gray scale of this book, I promise that they are yellow.

Summary

This appendix introduced you to XAML, which is the XML document type used to build user interfaces for WPF and Silverlight. You learned that elements map to classes and attributes map to class properties. You also learned how to specify property elements to gain more control than what you can get with attributes alone. Finally, you learned about the syntax of a markup extension and how the *StaticResource* markup extension allows you to reference resources. You're now ready to approach the WPF and Silverlight chapters in this book, which use XAML heavily to build their user interfaces.

Index

Symbols

< > (angle brackets), 405
{ } (braces), 40, 57, 160
? (question mark), 162
_ (underline), 55
/ integer, 62
& operator, 62
+ operator, 62

A

accessors, 84, 86
Add Reference window, 122–123
Add-In Project Wizard, 372–383, 398
add-ins, 371–400
    adding functionality to, 383–397
    creating, 372–383
    deploying, 397–399
    general information, 372, 399–400
Analyze menu, 15
angle brackets < >, 405
anonymous types, 198–199, 206
API (application programming interface), 5
application icons, 120
application programming interface (API), 5
applications
    artifacts, 116, 117, 136

building with ASP.NET MVC, 262–264
Click-Once, 120
COM, 121, 124, 134
compiling, 129–135
Console. *See* Console applications
including databases with, 253
Java, 300–301
Microsoft Office, 124
OOB, 294–297
output path, 134
Silverlight, 285–298
state of, 160–166
Web, 152–153
Windows Services, 33
WPF. *See* WPF
Architecture menu, 15
arguments, 75–78, 153
arrays, 62–63, 107–108
artifacts, 116, 117, 136
ASP.NET
    deploying Web services, 315, 317,
        325–326, 336
    described, 250
ASP.NET MVC, 249–284
    building applications, 264–284
    creating Controllers, 254–256, 268–269
    creating Models, 254
    displaying Views, 256–261
    managing routing, 262–264

ASP.NET MVC (*continued*)
  MVC objects, 250–254, 270–276
  overview, 250–251
  starting ASP.NET MVC project, 251–254
ASP.NET MVC Project Wizard, 261
ASP.NET projects, 33
assemblies, 114, 119, 122–129
Assembly Information option, 118, 121–122
assembly name, 118, 119
assembly references, 122–129
associations, 201
authentication, 184, 319, 322
automatic properties, 85–86
Autos window, 160–161, 162

B

backing field, 85, 86
binding, 234–247
bookmarks, 44–45
braces { }, 40, 57, 160
branching statements, 57–61
breakpoints, 155–158
  conditional, 172
  creating, 156–157
  customizing, 157–158
  managing, 158
  overview, 155
  using, 171–173
bugs, 167–179. *See also* debugging
build event macros, 134
build order, 131–132

C

C# compiler, 133, 135
C# language
  case sensitivity, 40, 53
  code editor options, 46–47
  considerations, 13
  included with Visual Studio, 36
  inheritance, 70
  Intellisense, 50–51
  popularity of, 36
  primitive types, 53
  vs. VB language, 13, 36, 115–116
C++ language, 31, 36, 154, 373
C# projects, 31, 33, 115–116, 150, 151. *See also* projects
Call Hierarchy feature, 148–150
call sites, 148–150, 163
Call Stack window, 163
Canvas layout, 225–226

capitalization issues, 40, 53
Cascading Style Sheets (CSS), 252, 344
case sensitivity, 40, 53
character sets, 174
child classes, 70, 71
child/parent relationship, 187–192, 206
Class Designer, 137–141
  code generation, 138–141
  using, 137–141
  visualizing code with, 137–138
class libraries, 33, 36–38, 125–129
Class Library projects, 119, 124, 125–129
class locators, 44
class snippet, 71–72
class type, 68
Class view, 136
classes
  child, 70, 71
  creating, 68–72
  creating for interfaces, 98–101
  custom definitions, 68–70
  debugging and, 148
  finding, 44
  inheritance, 70–72
  instantiating objects from, 69
  parent, 70
  Program, 41–42
  snippets, 71–72
  syntax, 68–70
  WCF, 308–314
cleaning solutions/projects, 130–131
click events, 228–234, 246
Click-Once applications, 120
CLR (Common Language Runtime), 154
code. *See also* programming languages; programs
  automatically generated, 4–5
  breakpoints in. *See* breakpoints
  Call Hierarchy feature, 148–150
  call sites, 148–150, 163
  in class libraries, 126–129
  debugging. *See* debugging
  generating with Class Designer, 138–141
  hierarchical model, 114–115
  IntelliTrace, 165–166
  for interfaces, 101–106
  managed, 154
  on McGraw-Hill Web site, 103
  Pin To Source feature, 164–165
  reusing, 149
  skeleton, 4–5, 39–43
  snippets. *See* snippets
  stepping through, 158–159
  unmanaged, 154
  unsafe, 133, 134
  using in class libraries, 126–129
  visualizing with Class Designer, 137–138

code editor. *See* VS Code editor
code libraries. *See* class libraries
code-behind file, 228–234
coding, 49–66. *See also specific languages*
    branching statements, 57–61
    classes. *See* classes
    debugging. *See* debugging
    enums, 55–57
    expressions. *See* expressions
    Intellisense. *See* Intellisense
    methods. *See* methods
    primitive types, 52–54
    running programs, 51–52
    snippets. *See* snippets
    tools for, 148–150
    VS features, 4–5
    Web service calls, 329–336
collections
    advantages of, 110
    generic, 107–110
    object, 194–197
    vs. arrays, 62–63
color schemes, 25
COM (Component Object Model) applications, 121, 124, 134
COM Interop, 133, 134
COM objects, 124
ComboBox control, 241–243
command-line arguments, 153
Common Language Runtime (CLR), 154
compiler constants, 150
compilers
    assembly references, 123
    C#, 133, 135
    considerations, 4, 86, 96
    errors/warnings, 123, 134, 204, 344
    optimizations, 150, 152
    settings, 133–135
    VB, 134–135
compiling applications, 129–135
Component Object Model. *See* COM
compression, 131
computation expressions, 54
conditional breakpoints, 172
Connect class, 378–383
Console applications
    creating, 37–39, 115–116
    debugging, 144–179
    described, 32, 36
    skeleton code, 39–43
context sensitivity, 16
Control Libraries, 33
controls. *See also specific controls*
    Silverlight, 290–293
    WPF, 226–234

.cs extension, 68
CSS (Cascading Style Sheets), 252, 344
custom types, 52
Customer class, 167
CustomerRepository class, 168–171

D

data, 181–214. *See also* databases
    adding to tables, 186–187
    binding, 234–247
    dirty, 173
    displaying in grid, 244–247
    handling with LINQ to SQL, 200–214
    querying with LINQ, 194–214
    reading/saving, 243–244
    working with in WPF, 234–247
data model, 200
data sources, 234–241, 244
database diagram, 190–192
database projects, 34
databases, 182–194. *See also* data
    authentication, 184
    connections to, 183–184
    creating, 183–184
    including with applications, 253
    Server Explorer, 182–193
    settings, 193–194
    stored procedures, 192–193
    tables. *See* tables
DataGrid option, 244–247
Debug class, 133–134
DEBUG compilation constant, 133–134, 150
Debug configurations, 150, 153
Debug mode
    configuring, 150–155
    running programs in, 156, 171
    starting programs in, 156, 171
Debug Output folder, 151, 152
debug properties, 152–155
debugging, 143–180
    application state, 160–166
    Call Hierarchy feature, 148–150
    Call Stack, 163
    configuring Debug mode, 150–155
    described, 51
    evaluating expressions, 151–152, 162
    finding bugs, 171–174
    fixing bugs, 174–175
    history, 166
    null reference exceptions, 175–179
    properties, 150–155
    on remote machines, 153–154
    running applications, 152–153

debugging (*continued*)
  running programs with debugging, 52
  running programs without debugging, 51
  sample program with bugs, 167–179
  starting programs in Debug mode, 156, 171
  stored procedures, 154
  VS Debugger, 166–179
  .vshost files, 151–152
  Web applications, 152–153
delegates, 90, 94–96. *See also* events
Delphi language, 5
dependencies, 131–133
development-time code tools, 148–150
diagnostic events, 165–166
directories
  Create Directory, 116
  name, 317
  physical, 328
  virtual, 315
dirty data, 173
.dll extension, 119, 124
do loops, 65–66
docking windows, 18–19
DockPanel layout, 223–224
documentation, 11
Dynamic Data projects, 33

E

Edit menu, 14
elements
  accessing, 110
  in arrays, 107–108
  as classes, 411
  in generic lists, 109–110
  property, 412–414
else snippets, 58–59
else statements, 58–59
Enable Managed Code option, 154
endless loops, 157
enums, 55–57
environment
  IDE, 4, 13
  macros, 134, 342, 360–370
  snippets. *See* snippets
  templates. *See* templates
environment settings
  considerations, 13
  default, 11, 12–13, 28–30, 31
  exporting, 23–24
  importing, 24–28
  modifying, 13, 22–30
  resetting, 28–30
errors. *See also* warnings
  compiler, 123, 134, 204, 344
  considerations, 134

controllers, 278
  null reference exceptions, 93, 175–179
  vs. warnings, 134
event handlers, 91, 95–96, 228–234
event keyword, 93
EventHandler class, 94–95
events, 91–93. *See also* delegates
  click, 228–234, 246
  code completion for, 95–96
  described, 90, 91
  diagnostic, 165–166
  example, 91–93
  handling, 228–234
  null, 93
  use of, 91–93, 95
.exe extension, 119
Exec method, 391–395
Export Template Wizard, 346
expressions
  branching, 57–59
  considerations, 49
  described, 54
  evaluating during debugging,
    151–152, 162
  performing computations, 54
  primitive types, 54
  viewing, 163–164
Extensible Markup Language. *See* XML

F

F# language, 31, 36
false/true conditions, 55, 57, 62
fields
  backing, 85, 86
  considerations, 81, 83
  declaring, 81–83
  described, 69, 81
  example of, 68, 69
  using, 81–83
  vs. properties, 83
file locks, 154
File menu, 14
File Properties window, 122
File Transfer Protocol (FTP), 315, 317, 319
files
  code-behind, 228–234
  compressing, 131
  .dll, 124
  hidden, 117–118
  log, 7, 166
  .pdb, 151
  project, 116–121
  .vshost, 151–152
  XML, 134
floating windows, 19–20

folders
    hierarchy of, 116–118
    projects, 116–118
    snippets, 358–359
    solutions, 116–118
for loops, 61–64
foreign keys, 187–192
FTP (File Transfer Protocol), 315, 317, 319

G

GAC (Global Assembly Cache), 122–123
generic collections, 107–110
generic lists, 109–110
get accessors, 84, 86
Global Assembly Cache (GAC), 122–123
Global.asax file, 253
Globally Unique Identifier (GUID), 121
graphical user interface (GUI), 95
Grid layout, 220–222
GUI (graphical user interface), 95
GUID (Globally Unique Identifier), 121

H

Help menu, 15
hidden files, 117–118
HTML (Hypertext Markup Language)
    considerations, 260
    helper methods, 272–273, 278
    viewing code, 256–261
    XHTML, 404

I

.ico extension, 120
Icon setting, 118, 120
icons, 16–17, 120, 236, 295
IDE (integrated development environment), 4, 13
if snippets, 58–59
if statements, 57–59
IIS (Internet Information Server), 314–326
immediate if operator, 55
Immediate window, 162
impedance mismatch, 201
Implements keyword, 101
Import and Export Settings Wizard, 22–32, 45
Imports directive, 129
indicator margin, 44
inheritance, 70–72
instance methods, 74–75
instances, 40–41, 129, 148
int type, 78, 80
Integer keyword, 54

integrated development environment (IDE), 4, 13
Intellisense
    C# options, 50–51
    Consume First mode, 47
    described, 5
    saving keystrokes with, 49–51
    snippet completion lists, 47, 49, 50
    Standard mode, 47
    switching between modes, 47
    using, 49–51
    writing expressions, 163
IntelliTrace window, 165–166
interface snippets, 106
interfaces, 96–106
    creating, 97
    creating classes for, 98–101
    modifying, 97
    overview, 96
    WCF, 302–308, 377–383, 389
    writing code for, 101–106
Internet Information Server (IIS), 314–326
item templates, 347–353
items. *See* project items

J

Java applications, 300–301
JavaScript, 253, 257, 272, 288
joins, 205–209

K

keyboard shortcuts, 15, 44, 47
keywords, 47

L

Language Integrated Query. *See* LINQ
languages
    C#. *See* C# language
    C++, 31, 36, 154, 373
    Delphi, 5
    F#, 31, 36
    HTML. *See* HTML
    included with VS 2010, 36
    Visual Basic. *See* VB
    WSDL, 301
    XAML. *See* XAML
    XML. *See* XML
libraries. *See* class libraries
library files. *See* assemblies
license key, 8
licensing terms, 7–8
LINQ (Language Integrated Query), 186, 194–214

LINQ projections, 198–199
LINQ to SQL, 200–214
    creating items, 305
    deleting data, 212–214
    inserting data, 210–211
    multiple tables, 205–210
    overview, 200
    querying, 203–210
    setting up, 200–201
    updating data, 211–212
    WPF applications, 246–247
LINQ to SQL Designer, 200–203
LINQ to SQL Wizard, 200, 205
ListBox control, 241–243
lists, generic, 109–110
local variables, 81
Locals window, 160–161, 162
log files, 7, 166
loops, 61–66
    endless, 157
    for, 61–64
    while, 64–65

M

Macro Editor, 365–370, 374, 380
Macro Explorer, 364–365
macros, 134, 342, 360–370
Main method, 40–41, 49, 120
manifest, 120–121
Manifest setting, 118, 120–121
markup extensions, 414–416
MasterPages, 257–260, 270, 273
mathematical operators, 54
McGraw-Hill Web site, 103
member locators, 44
Memory window, 173
menu bar, 14–15
method results, 78–80
methods, 72–80. *See also specific methods*
    adding parameters to, 75–78
    calling, 72–75
    declaring, 72–75
    delegates. *See* delegates
    events. *See* events
    instance, 74–75
    naming, 40–41, 231
    overview, 72
    private, 74
    public, 74
    returning values from, 78–80
    shared, 74
    snippets, 80
    static, 41, 74
    using, 72–75
Microsoft Developer Network (MSDN), 6, 326

Microsoft Office applications, 124
Microsoft Office projects, 34
Model View Controller. *See* ASP.NET MVC
MSDN (Microsoft Developer Network), 6, 326
MVC objects, 250–254, 270–276. *See also* ASP.NET MVC

N

namespace snippet, 47–48
namespaces
    assembly references and, 122
    default, 116, 119, 328, 406
    overview, 42–43
    Root, 119
    setting, 119
    VB, 43
    XML, 406–407
naming conventions, 40–43, 116, 231
.NET assembly references, 123–124
.NET CLR. *See* CLR
.NET Framework, 38, 90, 119, 124, 320
.NET Framework Class Library, 13
.NET types, 53–54
New Project window, 37, 115–116
New Project Wizard, 39, 253
null events, 93
null reference exceptions, 93, 175–179
null values, 176–179

O

object collections, 194–197
objects
    COM, 124
    creating, 139
    debugging and, 148
    instantiating from classes, 69
    MVC, 250–254, 270–276
Office applications, 124
Office project types, 124
Office projects, 34
OnConnection method, 384–391
OOB (Out-of-Browser) functionality, 294–297
operating systems. *See specific Windows systems*
operators
    immediate if, 55
    mathematical, 54
    ternary, 55, 57
optimization, 131
Options menu item, 15
Options window, 45, 46, 154–155
Other Windows menu item, 14
Out-of-Browser (OOB) functionality, 294–297
Output type, 119–120
Output Type setting, 118, 119–120

P

parameters, 75–78
parent classes, 70
parent/child relationship, 187–192, 206
.pdb files, 151
Pin To Source feature, 164–165
primary keys, 186–189, 191, 201
primitive types, 52–54
private modifier, 83
private variables, 85
product key, 8
Program class, 41–42, 44, 137
programming languages. *See also* languages
    C#. *See* C# language
    C++, 31, 36, 154, 373
    Delphi, 5
    F#, 31, 36
    included with VS 2010, 36
    Visual Basic. *See* VB
programs. *See also* code
    debugging, 52, 156, 171
    pausing execution of, 157
    running, 51–52
project items, 21, 86, 116
Project Properties window, 118–122
projections, 198–199
projects. *See also* solutions
    adding to solutions, 117–118
    artifacts, 116, 117, 136
    ASP.NET MVC. *See* ASP.NET MVC
    "bare bones," 36–39
    build order, 131–132
    building/rebuilding, 129–130
    C#, 31, 33, 115–116, 150, 151
    C# vs. VB, 115–116
    Class Designer visualization, 137–138
    Class Library, 119, 124, 125–129
    cleaning, 130–131
    compiler settings, 133–135
    Console. *See* Console applications
    creating, 36–39, 115–116
    database, 34
    deleting, 116
    dependencies, 131–133
    folders, 116–118
    hidden files, 117–118
    hierarchical relationships, 116–118
    location, 37
    Microsoft Office, 34
    modifying, 343–344
    naming/renaming, 37, 115–116, 119, 126
    navigating with Class view, 136
    new, 31–32
    optimizing, 131
    organizing principles, 114–115
    overview, 31–32

property settings, 118–122
recent, 116
referencing assemblies, 122–129
resetting references, 126
saving as templates, 344–346
searching for, 38
SharePoint, 34
Silverlight, 285–298
sorting, 38
templates for. *See* templates
types of, 30–34
viewing available, 30–32
viewing with Class Designer,
    137–141
WCF. *See* WCF
web, 33, 286
Windows Projects, 32–33
WPF. *See* WPF
properties
    accessors, 84
    automatic, 85–86
    debug, 150–155
    declaring, 81–86
    described, 81
    example of, 83–84
    projects, 118–122
    setting, 228
    using, 81–86
    vs. fields, 83
Properties folder, 117, 118
Properties window, 118–122, 139, 227–233
property elements, 412–414
property snippet, 86
public access modifier, 74

Q

queries. *See also* LINQ to SQL
    on multiple tables, 205–210
    object collections, 194–197
    stored procedures, 192
QueryStatus method, 395–397
question mark (?), 162
Quick Watch window, 163–164

R

refactorings, 5
Reference Paths, 125
references
    adding to COM objects, 124
    assembly, 122–129
    class libraries, 125–126
    external .dll files and, 124
    resetting, 126

Release configurations, 150, 153
releases, 6, 11, 12
remote debugging, 153–154
repository, 265–268, 282
resources, referencing, 414–416
Resources option, 121
Root namespace, 119
routing, 262–264

S

scope, 160–161
search features, 38, 158
select statement, 59–60
serialization assemblies, 133
Server Control projects, 33
Server Explorer, 182–193
service reference, 326–334
service releases, 6, 11, 12
set accessors, 84, 86
shared methods, 74
shared modules, 41
SharePoint projects, 34
shortcut keys, 15, 44, 47
Silverlight, 285–298, 326, 336. *See also* XAML
Silverlight applications, 285–298
skeleton code
    automatically generated, 4–5
    Console application, 39–43
.snippet extension, 354
snippets
    class, 71–72
    creating, 353–358
    do loops, 65–66
    else, 58–59
    examining, 354–356
    for each loops, 63–64
    for loops, 62
    if statements, 58–59
    interface, 106
    library of, 358–359
    method, 80
    namespace, 47–48
    overview, 47–48
    pick list, 47
    property, 86
    switch statement, 60–61
    using, 47–48
    while loops, 64–65
snippets folders, 358–359
Snippets Manager, 359
Solution Explorer, 116–118
    Console application creation, 38
    managing build order, 131–132
    managing dependencies, 131–133

opening/closing items, 21
overview, 16
working with controls, 227
solution folders, 116–118
solutions. *See also* projects
    adding projects to, 117–118
    artifacts, 116, 117, 136
    building/rebuilding, 129–130
    cleaning, 130–131
    contents, 38–39
    described, 38
    folders, 116–118
    hierarchical relationships,
      116–118
    naming, 115–116
    organizing principles, 114–115
    showing, 116–117
sorting/searching features, 38, 158
source code. *See* code
source control, 116
SQL. *See* LINQ to SQL
StackPanel layout, 222–223
Start page, 15
Startup object, 118, 120
statements
    branching, 57–61
    considerations, 49
    else, 58–59
    if, 57–59
    using Intellisense with, 49–51
static keyword, 40
static methods, 41, 74
Status bar, 16
Step Over operation, 159
stored procedures
    databases, 192–193
    debugging, 154
    in LINQ to SQL, 209–210
Sub Main method, 40
switch statement, 59–61
switch statement snippets, 60–61
system icons, 120
System namespace, 42, 43
system requirements, 6

T

tabbed windows, 20–21
tables
    adding data to, 186–187
    adding to databases, 185–187
    considerations, 201, 202
    foreign keys, 187–192
    multiple, 187–192, 205–210
    performing queries on, 205–210

target framework, 119
Target Framework setting, 118, 119
Team Foundation Server (TFS), 15
Team menu, 15
templates
    creating, 343–347
    exporting, 344–346
    implementing, 342–353
    item, 347–353
    options, 345–346, 352–353
    overview, 342–343
    saving projects as, 344–346
ternary operator, 55, 57
Test menu, 15
TFS (Team Foundation Server), 15
title bar icons, 16, 17
toolbar, 15
Toolbox
    Class Designer, 138–139
    general information, 16–20
    working with controls, 227–228
Tools menu, 15
Trace class, 133–134
TRACE compilation constant, 133–134, 150
true/false conditions, 55, 57, 62
types. *See also specific types*
    anonymous, 198–199, 206
    class, 68
    considerations, 41
    custom, 52
    described, 68
    .NET, 53–54
    Office projects, 124
    primitive, 52–54

U

UAC (User Account Control), 120
underline (_), 55
Until condition, 65
Until keyword, 65
User Account Control (UAC), 120
user interface, 226, 234, 251, 404
using directives, 43, 129

V

value keyword, 84
values
    null, 176–179
    returning from methods, 78–80
variables
    application state, 160–166
    described, 52

    local, 81
    primitive types, 52–54
    private, 85
    in scope, 160–161
    watching in Watch window, 161–162
    watching with Pin To Source, 164–165
VB (Visual Basic.NET)
    considerations, 13
    inheritance, 70
    popularity of, 36
    primitive types, 53
    vs. C# language, 13, 36, 115–116
VB compiler, 134–135
.vb extension, 68
VB namespaces, 43
VB projects. *See also* projects
    assembly references, 124
    naming, 116
    target framework, 119
    vs. C# projects, 115–116
VBA (Visual Basic for Applications), 34
View menu, 14
Views, 256–261
virtual directories, 315
Visual Basic for Applications. *See* VBA
Visual Basic.NET. *See* VB
Visual Designer, 191, 220, 227, 228
Visual Studio 2010. *See* VS 2010
Visual Studio Hosting Process, 154
Visual Studio projects, 30–34. *See also* projects
void keyword, 40, 74
VS (Visual Studio) 2010
    add-ins. *See* add-ins
    described, 4
    documentation, 11
    installing, 6–13
    interface, 13–16
    languages included with, 36
    license key, 8
    licensing terms, 7–8
    managing windows, 16–21
    modifying environment settings, 22–30
    navigating, 13–16
    privacy statement, 7
    product key, 8
    releases, 6, 11, 12
    restoring default settings, 28–30, 31
    starting, 13–14
    system requirements, 6
    versions, 6, 7
VS Code editor, 45–48
VS Debugger, 166–179
VS editor, 5
VS Recent Projects list, 116
VS2010ImageLibrary file, 120
.vshost files, 151–152

W

warnings, 23, 134, 189, 190. *See also* errors
Watch windows, 161–162
WCF (Windows Communication Foundation), 299–338.
  See also Web Services
    communicating with WCF services, 326–338
    hosting WCF services, 314–326
    overview, 300–301
    starting WCF projects, 301–314
WCF classes, 308–314
WCF contract, 302–308
WCF projects, 301–314
WCF services. *See* Web services
Web applications
    building controllers, 254–256
    creating, 251–254
    creating models, 254
    customer management, 264–284
    debugging, 152–153
    displaying views, 256–261
    managing routing, 262–264
    portal-style, 34
web projects, 33, 286
Web Service Description Language (WSDL), 301
Web services, 299–338. *See also* WCF
    adding to Web sites, 337–338
    communicating with, 326–338
    hosting on IIS, 314–326
    overview, 300–301
    proxies, 328–333
    used by clients, 336–337
Web Services projects, 33
Web sites
    adding Web services to, 337–338
    creating on IIS, 315, 317–321
    deploying Silverlight applications to, 297–298
    deploying Web services, 315, 317, 325–326, 336
web.config file, 253
while loop snippets, 64–65
while loops, 64–65
Win32 resources file, 121
windows, managing, 16–21
Windows 7 systems, 6, 34, 315–317
Windows 2003 systems, 6
Windows 2008 systems, 6, 34, 300, 321
Windows Application projects, 119, 120
Windows Communication Foundation. *See* WCF
Windows Forms, 32, 219
Windows menu, 15
Windows Presentation Framework. *See* WPF
Windows Projects, 32–33
Windows Services, 33
Windows versions, 6

Windows Vista systems, 6, 34
Windows XP systems, 6, 34
wizards
    Add-In Project Wizard, 372–383, 398
    ASP.NET MVC Project Wizard, 261
    Export Template Wizard, 346
    Import and Export Settings Wizard, 22–32, 45
    LINQ to SQL Wizard, 200, 205
    New Project Wizard, 39, 253
    options for, 5
work area, 15
working directory, 153
WPF (Windows Presentation Framework),
  217–247
    binding data, 234–247
    Click-Once applications, 120
    controls, 226–234
    layouts, 220–226
    output types, 120
    starting projects, 218–220, 410–411
    working with data in, 234–247
    XAML. *See* XAML
WrapPanel layout, 224–225
WSDL (Web Service Description Language), 301

X

XAML (XML Application Markup Language), 409–416
    attributes, 411
    considerations, 218
    controls, 227
    elements, 411
    markup extensions, 414–416
    overview, 410
    property elements, 412–414
    Silverlight projects, 286–290
    starting WPF projects, 218–220, 410–411
    WPF controls, 228
XAML documents, executing, 411–412
.xaml extension, 227
XHTML (XML for HTML), 404
XML (Extensible Markup Language)
    introduction to, 403–407
    WCF services, 300–301, 330
XML Application Markup Language. *See* XAML
XML documentation file, 134
XML Editor, 356, 404
XML files, 134
XML for HTML (XHTML), 404
XML menu, 407
XML serialization, 134
XML Transformation (XSLT), 407
XSLT (XML Transformation), 407